# Governing Sustainability

The crisis of unsustainability is, above all else, a crisis of governance. The transition to a more sustainable world will inevitably require radical changes in the actions of all governments, and it will call for significant changes to the lifestyles of individuals everywhere. Bringing together some of the world's most highly regarded experts on governance and sustainable development, this book examines these necessary processes and consequences across a range of sectors, regions, and other important areas of concern. It reveals that the governance of sustainable development is politically contested, and that it will continue to test existing governance systems to their absolute limits. As both a state-of-the-art review of current thinking and an assessment of existing policy practices, it will be of great interest to all those who are preparing themselves – or their organisations – for the sustainability transition.

W. NEIL ADGER is Professor of Environmental Economics at the University of East Anglia.

ANDREW JORDAN is Professor of Environmental Politics at the University of East Anglia.

# Governing Sustainability

Edited by

W. NEIL ADGER AND
ANDREW JORDAN

DAMAGED

CAMBRIDGE
UNIVERSITY PRESS

CAMBRIDGE UNIVERSITY PRESS
Cambridge, New York, Melbourne, Madrid, Cape Town, Singapore, São Paulo, Delhi

Cambridge University Press
The Edinburgh Building, Cambridge CB2 8RU, UK

Published in the United States of America by Cambridge University Press, New York

www.cambridge.org
Information on this title: www.cambridge.org/9780521518758

© Cambridge University Press 2009

First published 2009

Printed in the United Kingdom at the University Press, Cambridge

*A catalogue record for this publication is available from the British Library*

*Library of Congress Cataloguing in Publication data*
Governing sustainability / edited by W. Neil Adger and Andrew Jordan.
    p.    cm.
  Includes bibliographical references and index.
  ISBN 978-0-521-51875-8 (hardback) – ISBN 978-0-521-73243-7 (pbk.)
  1. Environmental policy.    2. Sustainable development.
  I. Adger, W. Neil.    II. Jordan, Andrew, 1968–    III. Title.
  GE170.G686 2009
  333.7–dc22        2008049117

ISBN 978-0-521-51875-8 hardback
ISBN 978-0-521-73243-7 paperback

*To Tim O'Riordan – a constant source of inspiration, guidance and bonhomie over the years.*

# Contents

# Figures

# Tables

# Contributors

**W. Neil Adger** is Professor in the School of Environmental Sciences and Programme Leader of the Tyndall Centre for Climate Change Research at the University of East Anglia, Norwich, UK.

**Katrina Brown** is Professor in the School of Development Studies and Deputy Director of the Tyndall Centre for Climate Change Research at the University of East Anglia, Norwich, UK.

**Jacquelin Burgess** is Professor of Human Geography and Head of the School of Environmental Sciences at the University of East Anglia, Norwich, UK.

**Judy Clark** is retired from a career of teaching and research in the Department of Geography, University College London, UK.

**Simon Dietz** is a Lecturer in Environmental Policy in the Department of Geography and Environment at the London School of Economics and Political Science, UK.

**Andy Dobson** is Professor of Politics in the School of Politics, International Relations and Philosophy, Keele University, UK.

**Jill Jäger** is a Senior Researcher at the Sustainable Europe Research Institute, Vienna, Austria.

**Andrew Jordan** is Professor of Environmental Politics in the School of Environmental Sciences at the University of East Anglia, Norwich, UK.

**Philip Lowe** is the Duke of Northumberland Professor of Rural Economy in the School of Agriculture, Food and Rural Development at the University of Newcastle upon Tyne, UK.

**Eric Neumayer** is Professor in Environment and Development, in the Department of Geography and Environment at the London School of Economics and Political Science, UK.

**John O'Neill** is the Hallsworth Professor of Political Economy in the School of Social Sciences at the University of Manchester, UK.

**Tim O'Riordan** is an Emeritus Professor in the School of Environmental Sciences, University of East Anglia, Norwich, UK, and a Member of the UK Sustainable Development Commission.

**Matthew Paterson** is Professor in the School of Political Studies, University of Ottawa, Canada.

**Ortwin Renn** is a Professor in the Interdisciplinary Research Unit on Risk and Sustainable Technology Development at the University of Stuttgart, Germany.

**Andy Stirling** is a Professorial Fellow in Science and Technology Policy Research, University of Sussex, Brighton, UK.

**Albert Weale** is a Professor in the Department of Government, University of Essex, Colchester, UK.

**Katy Wilkinson** is a doctoral student in the School of Agriculture, Food and Rural Development at the University of Newcastle upon Tyne, UK.

# Abbreviations

| | |
|---|---|
| AAAS | American Association for the Advancement of Science |
| ALARA | As Low As Reasonably Achievable |
| ALARP | As Low As Reasonably Practicable |
| BSE | Bovine Spongiform Encephalopathy ('mad cow disease') |
| CAN | Climate Action Network |
| CAP | Common Agricultural Policy |
| CDM | Clean Development Mechanism |
| CPRE | Campaign to Protect Rural England |
| CSERGE | Centre for Social and Economic Research on the Global Environment |
| DEFRA | Department for Environment, Food and Rural Affairs |
| ECFESD | European Consultative Forum on the Environment and Sustainable Development |
| EMA | Emissions Marketing Association |
| ESA | Environmentally Sensitive Area |
| FSC | Forest Stewardship Council |
| GATS | General Agreement on Trade in Services |
| GATT | General Agreement on Tariffs and Trade |
| GM | Genetically Modified/Genetic Modification |
| GNP | Gross National Product |
| IETA | International Emissions Trading Association |
| IHDP | International Human Dimensions Programme on Global Environmental Change |
| IIASA | International Institute of Applied Systems Analysis |
| IMF | International Monetary Fund |
| IPCC | Intergovernmental Panel on Climate Change |
| ISO | International Organization for Standardization |
| ISTS | Initiative on Science and Technology for Sustainability |

| JI | Joint Implementation |
| MA | Millennium Ecosystem Assessment |
| MAFF | Ministry of Agriculture, Fisheries and Food (UK) |
| MCM | Multi-Criteria Mapping |
| MDGs | Millennium Development Goals |
| MP | Member of Parliament (UK) |
| MTBE | Methyl Tertiary Butyl Ether (a fuel additive) |
| NFU | National Farmers' Union |
| NGO | Non-Governmental Organisation |
| OECD | Organisation for Economic Co-operation and Development |
| PBEL | Plastic Bag Environmental Levy |
| PCB | Polychlorinated Biphenyls |
| RAINS | Regional Air Pollution INformation and Simulation |
| RDR | Rural Development Regulation |
| SERI | Sustainable Europe Research Institute |
| TRIMS | Trade-Related Investment Measures |
| TRIPS | Trade-Related Intellectual Property Rights |
| TWAS | The Academy of Sciences for the Developing World |
| UNCTAD | United Nations Conference on Trade and Development |
| UNDP | United Nations Development Programme |
| UNECE | UN Economic Commission for Europe |
| UNEP | United Nations Environment Programme |
| UNFCCC | United Nations Framework Convention on Climate Change |
| WCED | World Commission on Environment and Development |
| WMO | World Meteorological Organization |
| WSSD | World Summit on Sustainable Development |
| WTO | World Trade Organization |
| WWF | World Wide Fund for Nature |

# Foreword

Very few people in mainstream politics today have begun to understand the nature of the impending sustainability crunch. They still see sustainability as an environmental issue, requiring measured and (hopefully) timely regulatory or market responses to keep the show on the road.

Only a handful of people, including the redoubtable and inspirational Tim O'Riordan, have resolutely kept on pointing out to them that sustainability is *of course* about the physical and biological systems on which we humans still utterly depend, is *of course* about the economic and social policies nations must deploy (however inadequately) to sustain those systems, but, first and foremost, it is about *governance*: who decides what on behalf of whom to secure which objectives over what period of time?

As Neil Adger and Andrew Jordan point out in their excellent overview, 'there is no mystery about sustainability'. One way or another, the human species will end up living sustainably on planet Earth: the laws of nature and the laws of thermodynamics always have and eventually always will take precedence over our ephemeral and hugely arrogant ambitions to live outside those laws. Anyone can live as an outlaw for a while, as an individual, but at the species level, it is not smart and it's definitely not sustainable.

That much is certain. How we embed that realisation in our political and economic systems, and how quickly we can achieve that, is an altogether less certain question. Mainstream political parties are having massive, currently intractable, problems trying to adapt the business-as-usual model of progress that would appear, in the minds of most people, to have served us so well over the last sixty years. Green parties around the world have little difficulty breaking free of those business-as-usual mindsets, but still find it extraordinarily difficult to bring more than a small percentage of people with them.

Hardly surprising, therefore, that there is a growing school of thought that the real innovation and dynamism in governance systems for a sustainable world lies anywhere other than in conventional political parties.

This collection offers some hugely stimulating insights into that particular conundrum – and, in the process, unashamedly puts the emphasis where it now needs to be: we now know, more or less, what we need to do to secure a sustainable world, but how the hell are we going to do it?

JONATHON PORRITT CBE
Founder Director of Forum for the Future, Chairman of the
UK Sustainable Development Commission and author of
*Capitalism as if the World Matters* (2007, Earthscan)

# *Preface*

The environment is in crisis. The climate is changing, rivers and lakes are polluted, fisheries are overexploited, and there is no corner of the world where human impact is not apparent. At the same time, millions of the world's poor continue to live in abject poverty, while the richer nations of the world are confronting an epidemic of chronic obesity. These crises of human development are very much of our own making. It is the relationship between humans and their environment and, ultimately, the relationship between us all that is at the root of the sustainability problematique endlessly discussed at, but not resolved by, meetings of the world's governments in Stockholm, Rio and Johannesburg in 1972, 1992 and 2002, respectively. Consequently, it is this relation-ship that has to be a full part of any solutions to the almighty mess that we as a human race now face.

This book starts from the belief that the crisis of unsustainability is, first and foremost, a crisis of *governance*. Governance, however, is a multidimensional and highly contested term within academia. If we zoom out and explore what is or is not being done actually to *govern* societies in ways that facilitate rather than undermine sustainability, it is abundantly clear that the governance of sustainable development is likely to be a hugely complicated and politically contested undertaking.

It is precisely for these reasons that we decided to bring together some of the world's foremost experts on governance and sustainable development and ask them to debate the future direction and governance of human society. This conference took place in Norwich in June 2005 as part of a series of events to mark the 'retirement' of Tim O'Riordan from the internationally renowned School of Environmental Sciences at the University of East Anglia, UK. We believed the subject matter demanded an interdisciplinary approach, so we invited contributors from a diverse range of disciplines ranging from political science, economics and geography, through to development studies, sociology, philosophy and environmental science. When we suggested that they should subsequently re-craft their papers into a series of interlinked book chapters on the theme of governance and sustainable development, they enthusiastically agreed.

We would like to thank all our contributors for their patience and dedication; all of them revised their contributions several times to implement our editorial guidance. We would particularly like to thank Matthew Paterson, Jacquelin Burgess and Judy Clark, who joined the writing team after the conference. Without the hard work of all the authors, this book would have never seen the light of day. Together, they show that in spite of the definitional and terminological confusion surrounding the term governance, what is needed to govern for sustainability is, as Jonathon Porritt argues in his Foreword, surprisingly clear; what we as a human race lack is the political and, ultimately, the *societal* will to establish the necessary governance mechanisms and procedures.

We would also like to thank the UK Economic and Social Research Council (ESRC) for funding the underlying research through the Programme on Environmental Decision (2001–7) at UEA and through funding for the conference as part of Social Sciences Week in 2005. Emily Sheldon and Dawn Turnbull provided excellent logistical support prior to and throughout the conference. Last, but certainly not least, we would like to thank Tim O'Riordan for concluding the conference and this book in his own uniquely incisive way. Tim's thinking – developed and refined over the last four decades – permeates every single chapter of this book. We hope that the conference and this book provide a sufficiently fitting tribute to the enormous contribution that he has made to our collective understanding of the governance of sustainability.

NEIL ADGER

ANDREW JORDAN

*Norwich, March 2008*

# PART I

# Overview and Context

# 1 Sustainability: exploring the processes and outcomes of governance

W. NEIL ADGER AND ANDREW JORDAN

## Process and outcome: an introduction

The concept of sustainable development commands wide, almost universal, support. The idea of sustaining human development resonates with strongly held convictions in every society about the present and the future. It does so, in large part, because as individuals we tend to be instinctively averse to losing anything. Indeed, social scientists tell us that most people are much more averse to losing than they are open to the possibility of gaining. Hence we do not wish, either collectively or individually, to lose what we already have in our environment and society. But ever since the principle of sustainable development was first articulated (for example in *Our Common Future* by the Brundtland Commission in 1987), promoting human wellbeing while simultaneously conserving the natural environment has proven to be highly elusive.

In fact, the more that society has sought to develop more sustainably, the more it has come to realise the immensity of the change it implies for human societies. Sustainable development – or sustainability (we regard the two as being synonymous) – challenges us to understand the nature of the natural resources on which we ultimately depend. But it also challenges us to articulate and act on the values that are inherent in our relationship with nature. We meet both these challenges through the institutions that allow collective action in governing the environment and our relationship to it. Both the processes and outcomes of these relationships are critical.

The very acute feeling, powerfully expressed in the *Report of the World Summit on Sustainable Development* (United Nations, 2002) and the *Millennium Ecosystem Assessment* (2005), that things have got worse – not better – in the two decades since the Brundtland Commission, has re-strengthened the demand for systems of governance that are capable of putting society on a more sustainable track.

Sometimes the demand is for more 'sustainable governance' (ECFESD, 2000); sometimes, it is for 'governance for sustainable development' (Ayre and Callway, 2005; Newig *et al.*, 2008). Others have called for 'reflexive governance for sustainable development' (Voss *et al.*, 2006). And still others have promoted grand ambitions such as 'earth system governance' (Biermann, 2007) or 'global environmental governance' (Speth and Haas, 2006). But the sentiment underlying all these usages remains the same: governance matters and will continue to matter enormously if there is to be any realistic prospect of an orderly transition to sustainability.

Sustainability is elusive because of the nature of global economic forces and the uneven distribution of political power. The world is in thrall to the carbon economy as never before, driving unprecedented environmental change through the consumption of resources and water and the degradation of land. The carbon economy and the location of the effectively dwindling stocks of oil also continue to drive geopolitical instability. The power of states and governments has been harnessed to promote capitalism through trade blocs and agreements and through capturing influence over oil and other resources. While Harvey argues that governments and capitalism often exercise their logic of power to different ends, it is clear that the 'new imperialism' (Harvey, 2003), focused on influence over resources such as oil, is antithetical to sustainability. Governing sustainability may be a distinct and radical opposing force to this imperialist logic. (But it is, however, easy to be despondent when sustainability often appears to be a sideshow.)

There is no mystery about sustainability. At its core, sustainability is a state whereby what is to be sustained – i.e. human development – is genuinely sustainable in the long term. Sustainability is therefore an outcome with universal appeal. The issue becomes more controversial when we ask: precisely what should be sustained? Environmental sustainability suggests sustaining aspects of the natural world, eco-systems, and natural and cultural heritage in a manner that means that they are sacrosanct or certainly that they take precedence over other material goals such as economic growth. It becomes even more controversial when we ask: how should these things be sustained? That is, how should the process of moving towards greater sustainability be governed?

In this book we refer to sustainability as a process of change in the way that society is organised. In particular, we are interested in how human societies have sought to alter the myriad ways in which they exploit the world around them in line with the ecological principle of sustainability. The simultaneous desire for economic growth and environmental protection and social harmony has always lain at the heart of environmental politics and policy making. Brundtland tried hard to address the tensions between them by 'sending out the intuitively appealing message' that sustainability is possible (although far from easy) (Carter, 2007: 207–8).

*Our Common Future* succeeded incredibly well in popularising this particular interpretation of sustainability, creating a 'veritable industry of deciphering and advocating' in relation to its meaning and implementation (Kates *et al.*, 2005: 11). These discussions have helped to bring about and inform governmental conferences, the first held in Rio in 1992 and another in Johannesburg in 2002, which powerfully re-affirmed sustainable development as an overarching objective of human development.

Despite widespread support, debates abound as to whether sustainability is a well-honed principle, a concept, a positive vision, a normative idea or a discursive construct (for example, Lele, 1991; Meadowcroft, 2000; Dryzek, 2005; Kates *et al.*, 2005). In this book, we do not aim to close this debate, were such a thing possible or desirable. Rather, we argue that sustainability has at least two important dimensions which are relevant to the way in which it is governed: the first is concerned with outcomes, the other with processes.

By *outcomes* we mean the overall quality or sustainability of human wellbeing and the ecosystems on which it ultimately depends. The way in which this line of thinking was developed in the Millennium Ecosystem Assessment – the four-year-long scientific appraisal of the condition of the world's ecosystems (Millennium Ecosystem Assessment, 2005) – is illuminating. In its all-encompassing framework, sustainability was seen to depend not only on the materials necessary for a good life, but also on good social relations and, implicitly, on the relationships between individuals and societies and their natural environment. Crucially, the way in which humans perceive, value, and experience environmental loss was seen to be just as important as the absolute scarcity of resources or the quality of human life.

This takes us directly to the second important dimension of sustainability: how the *process* through which we engage with our environment and the rest of society is shaped and directed – or governed – in ways that determine the future of both. A process-centred dimension is intimately bound up with the whole notion of *governing*, namely those activities which make a 'purposeful effort to guide, steer, control, or manage sectors or facets of societies' (Kooiman, 1993: 2). The basic claim that process – and hence governance – matters, has received growing support right across the social sciences, in relation to issues as diverse as equity, vulnerability, social exclusion, wellbeing and happiness (Frey, 2001; Satterfield *et al.*, 2004; Layard, 2005). Simply using the natural world wisely and within limits is not sufficient to ensure individual or collective sustainability. If we ignore social marginalisation, vulnerability and the uneven distribution of benefits from human development, then we risk sowing the seeds of future conflict and witnessing the breakdown of collective responsibility. In other words, the processes of decision making directly affect the sustainability of their outcomes.

However, the claim that 'process matters' is likely to be an anathema to those who analyse sustainability from a more natural science or economic perspective, where the focus tends to be much more firmly on the objective identification and measurement of outcomes. For example, in the natural sciences, the most fundamental limits to human development are essentially seen to be biological and physical in nature; beyond these, any further decline is predicted to be catastrophic and potentially irreversible (e.g. Lenton *et al.*, 2008). Economists have tried to capture this thinking in notions such as critical natural capital and safe minimum standards.

But Bromley suggests that by focusing exclusively on physical or biological system characteristics, economists and natural scientists risk heading into a conceptual *cul de sac*. They need to recognise that there are in fact 'two realms: human interaction with nature and human interaction with others with respect to their interaction with nature' (Bromley, 2005: 201). In other words, the separation of humans from nature, and even the domination of nature inherent in many world views (White, 1967), ignores the immediacy and pervasiveness of social and ecological interactions. These distinctions between how society acts and how nature responds are both arbitrary and unhelpful (Berkes and Folke, 1998).

Governance is therefore intimately connected to the notion of sustainability, which in turn is 'a political concept, replete with governance questions' (Farrell *et al.*, 2005: 143). But what sorts of questions might these be? Two in particular stand out. The first is deceptively simple but goes back to our distinction between process and outcome-centred approaches: what is sustainability? Brundtland was very careful to present it in only the most 'general terms' (WCED, 1987: 46), more as a set of guiding (and very often contradictory) sub-principles and values, than a fixed blueprint to be universally and uncritically applied in all contexts. Some have argued that this ambiguity represents the term's greatest weakness (e.g. Lele, 1991). But, for others, sustainability is not an 'objectively determinate quantity' (Stirling, 1999: 112): 'the creative tension between a few core principles and openness to re-interpretation and adaptation to different social and ecological contexts' provides it with the elasticity needed to remain enduringly relevant (Kates *et al.*, 2005: 20).

The second governance-related question is: how is sustainability put into effect? Sustainability will not just happen in a natural or pre-ordained manner. It needs to be carefully thought about, deliberated over, and eventually implemented. These processes of deliberation, argumentation and discussion are constitutive of governance. Brundtland was generally agnostic about whether sustainability should be pursued through hierarchical, market or more networked modes of governance; it considered this to be just the kind of question that particular communities and jurisdictions should work out for themselves.

But clearly the choice of which governing mode or instrument to apply will never be entirely open or value-free, given that existing governance systems are themselves deeply implicated in unsustainable patterns of development. Similarly, systems of governance are in a state of unprecedented flux, for all sorts of reasons associated with processes of economic globalisation, urbanisation and demographic change, mass communication and the challenges of new technologies (Young *et al.*, 2006). Any attempt, therefore, to select a particular instrument or mode for a particular sustainability-related task is fraught with difficulty.

The remainder of this chapter seeks to explore the role that governance plays in how society addresses these two questions. The next section explores the meaning of sustainability in a little more detail, identifies its most critical sub-principles and values, and discusses what they imply for their governance. The third section examines what is meant by governance, a term which has enjoyed

enormous attention right across the social sciences as well as in wider
society, but which is not always used consistently or in an empirically
informed way. To clarify this situation, we set out three different
interpretations – theoretical, empirical and normative – and explain
how they connect back to the distinction we have drawn between
sustainable development processes and outcomes. The fourth section
explores the relationship between governance and sustainable development, both empirically and conceptually, and the final section
draws together the main themes of our argument in the context of the
remainder of this book.

## What is sustainable development?

The Brundtland Commission popularised the term sustainable development, but did not coin it. It first rose to prominence in the 1980
*World Conservation Strategy* but its roots go much further back.
What Brundtland did was re-launch it in a way that substantially
broadened its appeal. It did so by demonstrating how sustainability is
a common challenge for both the countries of the industrialised North
and the less affluent South. The title – *Our Common Future* – was
deliberately chosen to emphasise that the world was suffering from
common and interlinked problems, namely chronic poverty in the
South and mounting social and environmental concerns in the North.
Instead of talking about trade-offs between the three pillars of sustainable development – society, the economy and the environment –
after Brundtland, the search intensified for synergies between them.

In 1987, Brundtland famously defined sustainable development as:
'development that meets the needs of the present without compromising
the ability of future generations to meet their own needs' (WCED,
1987: 43). But the definition also emphasised the centrality of two
further key concepts:

- the concept of needs, in particular the essential needs of the world's
  poor, to which overriding priority should be given; and
- the idea of limitations imposed by the state of the technology and
  social organization on the environment's ability to meet present and
  future needs (WCED, 1987: 43)

It is pointless searching for a precise definition of sustainability. To
do so would be counter-productive because, as Hajer (1995: 14) has

argued, the coalition for sustainability would quickly dissolve if it was ever defined more precisely than this. It is striking that none of the chapters in this book go that far beyond the baseline definition quoted above. In this book we explore how the term is used by actors operating in different contexts to realise their objectives (see also Dryzek, 2005: 146–7), this being the essence of Brundtland's own interpretation of sustainable development. For Kates *et al.* (2005), this malleability:

allows it to remain an open, dynamic and evolving idea that can be adapted to fit ... very different situations and contexts across space and time ... its openness to interpretation enables participants at multiple levels ... within and across activity sectors ... to redefine and re-interpret its meaning to fit their own situation.

This process of redefinition and interpretation is, as the chapters of this volume reveal, mostly concerned not with pinning down the exact meaning of sustainability *per se*, but with exploring the interplay between different *sub-principles* of sustainable development in different decision-making situations. These include the following: inter- and intra-generational equity; poverty alleviation; public participation in decision making; technological and environmental limits to growth; environmental policy integration, etc. This list was subsequently extended and further elaborated in a number of internationally endorsed documents, including the Rio Declaration and, of course, Agenda 21.

Of these, the notion of limits has always remained centre stage. The idea that, globally, we are living beyond our means was first popularised by the *Limits to Growth* report in 1972. Meadows *et al.* (1972) predicted that global ecological constraints in the form of resource availability and pollution loading would have a significant constraining effect on human development in the twenty-first century. The notion of carrying capacity has, of course, always had a central place in conservation biology, being a central feature of Hardin's (1968) treatise entitled 'The tragedy of the commons', in which he showed how open-access resources tend to be depleted beyond their carrying capacity.

There are, of course, those who dispute the very idea that there are immutable limits to human development. These criticisms focus both on the scientific credibility of any attempt to measure limits, and on the ability of human ingenuity to overcome them if some types of production and natural assets are substitutable for each other. But the technological route to sustainability is fraught with danger. In their update to *Limits*, Meadows *et al.* (2005) discuss the role of technological adaptations, suggesting that the more successfully society delays the constraining effect of limits through economic and social adaptations, the more likely it is to run into several at the same time.

The debate concerning limits has fundamentally changed in the period since the publication of *Our Common Future*. Concerns about resource scarcity have gradually given way to a greater understanding of the interdependencies between earth systems and the potential surprises and feedbacks caused by the tendency to use the environment as a sink. These have emerged as the focus of an emerging trans-discipline known as earth system science. The feedbacks and thresholds are manifest most clearly in relation to climate change at the global scale (Schellnhuber *et al.*, 2006), as well as in the emergence of new infectious diseases, land use and cover change, and a range of other unforeseen global changes leading to large-scale unsustainability and societal conflict. These types of disruption were also identified by Diamond (2004) in his much more social science account of the factors that triggered the collapse of ancient societies.

These sub-principles can, and often do, conflict sharply with one another, hence the need for systems of governance to arrive at co-ordinated policies. Indeed, systems of governance can and should be configured in ways that not only encourage and facilitate societal dialogue, but also transform attitudes and beliefs in ways that actively promote sustainability (Newig *et al.*, 2008; Voss *et al.*, 2006).

## What is governance?

Governance is a term in good currency, but it is often used very loosely to refer to a host of what can in practice be very different things. The combination of conceptual vagueness and loose application has certainly boosted the term's popularity, but it has also raised questions about its utility (Kohler-Koch and Rittberger, 2006: 26). There are, we believe, three key points to understand about governance. Firstly, and most importantly, governance is not the same as governing. In the first section we explained that governing refers to those social activities which seek to 'guide, steer, control, or manage' societies (Kooiman, 1993: 2). Governance, on the other hand, describes the patterns that emerge from the governing activities of diverse actors that can be observed in what is deemed acceptable norms of behaviour, and divergent institutional forms (Ostrom, 2005).

Second, governance is not the same as government: while government centres on the institutions and actions of the state, the term governance allows non-state actors such as businesses and non-governmental organisations (NGOs) to be brought into any analysis of societal steering (Lemos and Agrawal, 2006: 298). What encourages so many social scientists to use the term governance instead of government is its ability to 'cover the whole range of institutions and relationships involved in the process of governing' (Pierre and Peters, 2000: 1).

Third, governance is not tied to a particular period of time or geographical place: it is a concept that travels easily across these analytical categories. In fact, its lack of geographical specificity has allowed scholars to examine aspects of governance operating at totally different spatial scales – international, national and sub-national – or even across many scales (Bache and Flinders, 2004; Cash *et al.*, 2006).

It is fair to say that at first, the literature on governance was 'eclectic and relatively disjointed' (Stoker, 1998: 18). But by the 2000s it had consolidated around two core meanings (Pierre and Peters, 2000: 24) – the first theoretical and analytical and the other more empirical. The conflation of these two has proven to be a constant source of confusion, as the term has been used both to describe different empirical phenomena *and* to explain why they occur. This is not surprising: many of the theories and analytical frameworks have themselves emerged out of, and been informed by, empirical observations. Nonetheless, it is perhaps more accurate to speak of three major governance discourses.

## Discourse I: the empirical phenomenon of governance

Analysts have seized on the term governance to try and capture important phenomenological changes in the processes of governing. In particular, governance is now widely used as a shorthand phrase which encapsulates the changing form and function of the state in contemporary industrialised societies, specifically its diminishing size and its increasing tendency to deploy less coercive policy instruments.

The perception that we are living in a more polycentric society is often seen to be a function of macro processes such as globalisation and devolution, as well as specific reform efforts (such as new public management) which have sought to roll back the state and provide more services through markets (Pierre and Peters, 2000: 83–91).

By using the term governance instead of government, analysts are in effect drawing attention to the empirical fact that more policies are implemented by a much wider array of public, private and voluntary organisations than would have traditionally been included within a purely governmental framework (Flinders, 2002: 52). So if the extreme form of government was the strong state in the era of 'big government' (Pierre and Peters, 2000: 25), then the most extreme form of governance is an essentially self-organising and co-ordinating network of societal actors (Jordan and Schout, 2006).

One of the more obvious hallmarks of this trend towards greater governance is the appearance of more and more new modes of governance such as voluntary agreements and market-based instruments, as well as systems of self-regulation through which societal actors effectively steer themselves (Schout and Jordan, 2006; Treib et al., 2007). In the international sphere, scholars of international relations believe that governance is manifest in the increasing empirical prevalence of interstate agreements, multinational institutions and organisations, and new forms of public–private and private–private co-operation (Levy and Newell, 2004). They suggest that there is such a thing as global governance in a global system which has traditionally been viewed through the prism of sovereignty and statehood (Dingwerth and Pattberg, 2006: 189–93; Biermann, 2007).

Whether and to what extent these changes have had a long-term impact on the steering capacity of the state remains a very moot point. Marks et al. argue that there are essentially two positions that one can take on this issue. The society-centric view suggests that the state has been progressively hollowed out in the era of governance and its steering capacity denuded, as more and more policy competences have moved up to international bodies or out to non-state actors (Marks et al., 1996). Conversely, the state-centric view holds that, while the state may have weakened in the sense that it delivers fewer services than it did in the 1960s and 1970s, it remains the most dominant actor in society and a key site of accountability and legitimacy (Mann, 1997; Gamble, 2000).

## Discourse II: governance theory

For some, governance is, and will for ever remain, a 'descriptive label' (Richards and Smith, 2002: 3). However, other commentators have sought to use it to explain some of the empirical patterns described in the previous section. Flinders, for example, has sought to advance a governance theory which, he believes, raises important issues of control, co-ordination, accountability and political power (Flinders, 2002: 70). It should now be apparent that many discussions of governance theory are couched in terms of the three main modes of governing; namely markets, networks and hierarchies. The increasing empirical prevalence of networks as the preferred mode of governing in many states, as well as in the EU, has in turn encouraged scholars to elaborate and refine the theoretical precepts of these three concepts (Thompson, 2003), thereby emphasising the extent to which the development of new empirical and theoretical understandings of governance remain subtly interlinked. For example, the increasing empirical prevalence of network-based modes of governance in the EU has generated new typologies (Treib *et al.*, 2007) and attempts to measure their co-ordinating performance (Jordan and Schout, 2006) vis-à-vis hierarchical modes of governing.

That these empirical manifestations of governance have triggered much theoretical reflection is one thing, but to say that they add up to a coherent theory of governance is something altogether different. Sceptics have argued that there is not, and never will be, a grand theory of governance (Young, 2005). It is telling that even the most eager exponents of governance as theory are relatively modest in their claims. Both Flinders (2002: 52) and Pierre and Peters (2000: 7) concede that it only exists in a very embryonic form. Similar opinions have been expressed by those studying global governance (Dingwerth and Pattberg, 2006: 199–200; see also Hewson and Sinclair, 1999; Biermann, 2007) and global environmental governance (Young, 2005).

## Discourse III: governance as normative prescription

The third way in which governance is used is much more prescriptive, i.e. as something which should be adopted to achieve some preferred end point (Kohler-Koch and Rittberger, 2006: 29). One of the most

14 W. Neil Adger and Andrew Jordan

well-known examples is that of 'good governance' (e.g. World Bank, 2002). Good governance equates to an efficient public service, an independent judiciary, an accountable system for allocating funds, a respect for law and order, as well as human rights. The Organisation for Economic Co-operation and Development (OECD) seeks to propagate this interpretation of good governance by benchmarking best practices in relation to different policies and administrative capabilities, as well as sustainability (van Kersbergen and van Waarden, 2004: 144–5). Similarly, corporate governance relates to the various ways in which private companies are directed, administered or controlled, in order to be accountable to various different stakeholders. It has received considerable attention since the high-profile collapse of large firms such as Enron and Worldcom.

Normative applications of the term governance are also to be found in the international relations field, where they offer a 'vision of how societies should address the most pressing global problems' (Dingwerth and Pattberg, 2006: 193). Chief amongst these is globalisation, for which the creation of a global governance architecture is seen as one potentially important antidote (Biermann, 2007). Here, the EU is often held up as a role model. The Commission on Global Governance (1995) has provided one of the most detailed and comprehensive explanations of how this vision could be put into effect.

The problem is not really one of definitions but of different perspectives. The underlying causes of, and solutions to, unsustainability are, in reality, deeply contested. A managerial discourse suggests that the roots of unsustainability are poverty, a lack of property rights, unpriced ecological services, and protectionism and unsustainable resource use brought about by lack of government regulation (see Dobson, 1998). The remedy for this diagnosis is one of economic growth to reduce poverty, the delineation of individual property rights, and the creation of markets in ecosystem services. By contrast, an alternative discourse identifies disempowerment, gender inequality, resource exploitation, trade and consumerism as the main causes. The remedy to unsustainability within this discourse involves a redistribution of the world's wealth, more democratic decision-making structures and precautionary approaches to technology development. Hence different diagnoses of the causes of unsustainability lead to diametrically different governance remedies.

## Governance and sustainability

In this section we use these three interpretations to disentangle and make sense of the literature on governance and sustainable development. What follows is not intended to be a systematic review of the literature, but rather an attempt to identify and explore some of the main themes. The first point to make is that the literature has undoubtedly burgeoned in recent years; the second is that the vast majority is either empirical or normative, or some combination of the two (e.g. Biermann, 2007). Some authors have deliberately sought to emphasise the differences between the two by referring to 'governance and sustainable development' and 'governance for sustainable development' (e.g. Farrell *et al.*, 2005: 127). While the former is more interested in exploring how sustainable development has been variously interpreted and pursued in different governance systems, the latter seeks to identify and test what governance systems are needed to make sustainability a reality 'in a way that is true to the gravity and complexity of the task' (Farrell *et al.*, 2005: 130). In the remainder of this section, we review these two interpretations, and analyse how they are taken forward by the various contributors to this book.

### *Normative interpretations*

Sustainability is, at root, a 'fundamental normative idea' (Meadowcroft, 2000: 371) and a great deal of effort has been devoted to identifying what governance changes are needed to put it into effect. These attempts have been formally defined as 'sustainability governance', namely 'the deliberate adjustment of practices of governance in order to ensure that society eventually proceeds along a sustainable trajectory' (Meadowcroft *et al.*, 2005: 5; see also ECFESD, 2000: 6, 8). Because the outcome – sustainability – cannot be defined in advance for all places, governance for sustainable development should be, it has been claimed, an interactive and reflexive process of debate and dialogue, which is suitably equipped to deal with difficult choices, endless struggles and the risk of serious disappointments (Meadowcroft *et al.*, 2005: 6–8). Similar, normative, visions or 'projects' (Biermann, 2007: 4) have been identified at more global levels. For example, Biermann (2007: 10) argues that 'earth system governance' should be 'adaptive to changing circumstances, participatory through involving civil society at all levels, accountable and legitimate as part of new democratic governance beyond the nation state, and at the same time fair for all participants'.

Many of these normative prescriptions can be traced back to *Our Common Future*. Brundtland was, of course, painfully aware that sustainability is really just an idea; what matters is what people actually do with it. The final chapter of *Our Common Future* was therefore deliberately entitled 'Towards common action – proposal for institutional and legal change'. Later on, a whole annex (Annex 1) provided a proposed summary of legal principles supporting environmental protection and sustainable development. Had her committee been meeting today, the title of both would almost certainly have included the word 'governance'. The gist of Chapter 12 of *Our Common Future* is summarised in Box 1.1.

---

**Box 1.1.** Towards Common Action – Proposal made by the Brundtland Commission for Institutional and Legal Change

- Getting at the source: supporting development that is economically and ecologically sustainable;
- Integrating institutions: ensuring that environmental protection and sustainable development are integrated into the remit of all sectors and levels of government;
- Strengthening international frameworks: ensuring that national and international law keeps up with the scale of environmental and human development;
- Dealing with the effects: enforcing environmental protection measures and resource management; strengthening the UN Environment Programme;
- Assessing global risks: identifying, assessing and reporting of risks of irreversible damage to natural systems and threats to human wellbeing;
- Making informed choices: supporting the involvement of an informed public, NGOs and the scientific community; increasing co-operation with industry;
- Investing in the future: ensuring that multilateral financial institutions make a fundamental commitment to sustainable development; exploiting new and additional sources of revenue to support development in the South.

*Source:* summarised from WCED (1987: 308–47).

---

Since 1987, these prescriptions have been endlessly refined and reformulated into documents such as the 1992 Rio Declaration and Agenda 21. A decade later, world leaders adopted two follow-up documents at the 2002 World Summit on Sustainable Development: a short political declaration (the Johannesburg Declaration on Sustainable Development) and a sixty-seven-page Plan of Implement-ation, the very first page of which noted that: 'good governance within each country and at the international level is essential for sustainable development' (United Nations, 2002: para. 4).

In 2002, OECD produced a checklist for policy makers entitled 'Improving Policy Coherence and Integration for Sustainable Develop-ment' (OECD, 2002). The OECD is adamant that this is 'not a compilation of quick fix solutions or recipes' (OECD, 2002: 1), but nonetheless claims that it draws 'attention to the main obstacles to be overcome at the national level' and is therefore 'intended to contribute to the building of longer-term governance *for* sustainable develop-ment' (OECD, 2002: 1, our emphasis). This checklist is summarised in Box 1.2. Most of these items are addressed in various ways by the contributors to this book, although not always in such normative terms.

## Empirical descriptions and assessments

Those who have adopted a more empirical perspective are interested less in how the two terms should be interpreted, and more in under-standing how they are interpreted by social actors in a variety of settings. Many of those working in this vein would probably share Lafferty and Meadowcroft's view that, until recently, the literature on sustainability amounted to 'a great deal of discursive smoke' – but little in the way of empirical 'fire' (Lafferty and Meadowcroft, 2000: 2). Some of the most comprehensive assessments produced in an empirical frame of reference are those by Lafferty, O'Riordan and their various co-workers (O'Riordan and Voisey, 1997; Lafferty and Eckerberg, 1998; O'Riordan, 1998; Lafferty, 2001, 2004).

Much of this work has adopted a fairly critical tone. Some of the very earliest work focused on the implementation of Agenda 21 both nationally and at more local levels. These analyses found pockets of good practice, but also plentiful examples of business-as-usual. More recent reviews of national sustainable development strategies (Steurer,

**Box 1.2.** The OECD checklist for improving governance for sustainable development

**A common understanding of sustainable development:**

- Is the concept of sustainable development sufficiently clear and understood by the public?
- Is it well understood by public organisations and across levels of government?

**Clear commitment and leadership:**

- Is there clear commitment at the highest level to the formulation and implementation of sustainable development objectives and strategies?
- Is this commitment effectively communicated across sectors of government?

**Specific institutional mechanisms to steer integration:**

- Is there an institutional 'catalyst' in charge of enforcing sustainable development strategies?
- Are there specific reviews of laws and regulations to check whether they conflict with sustainable development?
- Is sustainable development integrated into budgeting, appraisal and evaluation activities?

**Effective stakeholder involvement:**

- Do mechanisms exist with government or independent organisations to ensure that consumers are informed about the consequences of their consumption decisions?
- Are there guidelines on when, with whom, and how consultations should be carried out?
- Are transparency mechanisms being reinforced at different levels of government?

**Efficient knowledge management:**

- Are there transparent mechanisms in place for managing conflictual knowledge?
- Is the flow of information between the scientific community and decision makers efficient and effective?

*Source:* summarised from OECD (2002).

2007) have found that the vast majority of countries are still elaborating their first strategies over a decade after Rio. Most of these gravitated 'towards the cosmetic rather than the ideal' (Meadowcroft, 2007: 161), several steps removed from where the most strategically important decisions are made in the state. In relation to the principle of environmental policy integration, analysts have identified pockets of innovation and solid implementation, but also many examples of weak and even non-existent integration (Jordan and Schout, 2006; Jordan and Lenschow, 2008). Much the same has been said about various examples of more integrated 'sustainability appraisal' (Scrase and Sheate, 2002; Turnpenny *et al.*, 2008). Meanwhile, the adoption of new environmental policy instruments has grown massively since Rio, but too little is known about their outcomes to make any definitive judgements about their effectiveness. But what is clear is that new market instruments have tended to supplement rather than supplant regulation. Government, in other words, remains alive and well in the era of governance (Jordan *et al.*, 2005).

Finally, there has been a lively debate about the empirical manifestations of sustainability in the international system, focusing on the existence of international agreements, multilateral organisations and private organisations such as multinational corporations, as well as the various parts of the UN system (Levy and Newell, 2004; Glasbergen *et al.*, 2007). If we broaden out a little more to look at work on global environmental governance with a sustainability dimension, the scale of the changes appears even greater (Jasanoff and Martello, 2004; Lemos and Agrawal, 2006; Speth and Haas, 2006). But whether they represent a long-term decline in state steering capacity remains a very moot point. From a critical or political economy perspective, many of them are transitory and epiphenomenal; they certainly do little to change the underlying dynamic of the capitalist economic system.

## Where next?

Evidently, the relationship between governance and sustainability can be approached from a number of different disciplinary perspectives, as well as for quite different purposes – namely describing what has happened and prescribing what should happen. However, the existing literature tends to be either normative or empirical. Given the perceived need to base policy making on the firmest evidence base, it is surprising that the dialogue between these two has, at least in terms of learning and applying lessons, been rather limited.

Where should the literature on governance and sustainability head in the future? First, there is certainly a need to move beyond grand theorising and typologies of governance, and undertake more detailed empirical testing to assess the extent to which the world is indeed witnessing a shift from government to governance (Kooiman, 2003: 4–5; van Kersbergen and van Waarden, 2004: 165).

Second, the emerging literature on the governance of sustainability could do more to engage with the mainstream literature on governance and global governance. This could be mutually beneficial, because the former has tended to be over-dominated by theories, typologies and analytical frameworks, whereas the latter has – at least until now – been much more empirically driven.

Third, there is a need for more work which sees the governance of sustainability in terms of both processes and outcomes. There is a real danger that governance becomes a static phenomenon, expressed, for example, in the presence or absence of particular modes or instruments of governing. Process is just as important, as is the causal relationship between those instruments and outcomes. In short, we need to analyse them all in a more dynamic and interactive manner (Pierre and Peters, 2000: 22). If, to paraphrase Rhodes (1997: 53), 'the mix between the modes is what really matters', then we need to know what forms of governing lead to what sorts of outcomes, bearing in mind the importance of political legitimacy and public accountability.

Finally, there is a danger that governance research becomes a rather dry and technocratic exercise of counting and cataloguing different governing instruments or (in a more normative vein) trying to identify the right governing tool for the job, without reflecting on the fact that agreement on the nature of the job often remains highly elusive. It is noticeable that a great deal of the existing literature operates within what might be described as a fairly pluralistic tradition, in the sense that it underplays the importance of the more structural sources of power (van Kersbergen and van Waarden, 2004: 166) or fails to investigate the outcomes of governance (i.e. governance for whom?).

## Governing sustainability: a plan of this book

Our aim is to elaborate whether individual and collective action could move the world towards a more sustainable future. The underlying values and priorities, world views of nature, and the relationship to risk and equity determine the set of institutional outcomes and governance processes that will take us toward (or away) from this goal. Much of the evidence across the natural sciences suggests that efforts to date have been inadequate and that technology and science are as much part of the problem as the solution.

In Chapter 2, Katrina Brown gives a striking illustration of this very point when she reviews what has actually been achieved since global change and interdependence were recognised and became part of public discourse. She argues that the world has in fact become *less* sustainable in the past two decades; far too many environmental and development trends are heading in the wrong direction to claim otherwise. Empirical examples of governance are multiplying as governments struggle to retain control in an increasingly globalised world, riven by inequalities and increasingly dominated by private corporations. But when she closely examines the performance of one governance-friendly solution – policy integration – she finds that its putative advantages are far from secure. Brown identifies a number of other important dimensions of integration which appear in many accounts of governance, namely those between different scales of governance, different types of knowledge, and different academic disciplines.

Drawing on a review of the Millennium Ecosystem Assessment, she finds that these forms of integration are simply not occurring to the extent necessary. Although she admits that the empirical bases for some of her claims are still rather thin, she strongly suspects that integration (broadly understood) cannot easily be imposed on societies by states or supranational bodies, but also will not autonomously appear, as in society-centric accounts of governance. This raises a very fundamental dilemma for those seeking to govern. Finally, she argues that experience suggests that the win–win–win solutions sought by Brundtland are very much the exception, not the rule – a deeply discomforting finding for those who assume that governance for sustainable development is likely to be a consensual rather than a conflictual affair.

*Part II: Governance and Government*

The remainder of the chapters in this book are grouped into four broad parts, which address the same core issues raised in this chapter but from different theoretical and empirical perspectives. Part II is broadly concerned with examining the relationship between society and the state. The state is a good place to start, because it provides a benchmark against which continuity and change in governance can be understood (Pierre and Peters, 2000: 25).

In Chapter 3, Albert Weale builds on Brown's discussion of integration, but from a much more state-centric perspective. This, he argues, is warranted by the state's virtual monopoly over one of the key means of societal steering, namely taxation, and the central part it plays in developing and implementing international conceptions of sustainability, as well its role in ensuring that formal policy-making activities remain accountable and legitimate. His argument proceeds by way of a number of propositions about the relationship between government and governance. Thus he too finds that, while governance warrants academic attention, some of the claims made about its prevalence, as well as the steering capacity of traditional forms of government, tend to be greatly overblown.

Weale argues that there is unlikely ever to be a single, standard model of governance for sustainable development; different countries tend to adopt their own national styles and approaches, a fact which should demand an explanation rather than moral condemnation. Finally, he sounds a note of caution with respect to some of the demands for integration noted in Brown's chapter. Thus he argues that in the messy world of everyday politics it sometimes makes more sense to pursue environmental policy integration by strengthening the administrative size and power of environment ministries than by issuing an ambitious but unenforceable proclamation that all parts of the state should integrate the environment into their work.

In Chapter 4, Philip Lowe and Katy Wilkinson provide a more political take on the challenge of integrating the environment for sustainability. They do so by examining the attempts made by environmental pressure groups to green the agricultural sector in the UK – a context which has traditionally privileged producer groups, namely farming interests, over those pushing for environmental sustainability. By drawing on a very detailed empirical analysis of one environmental group, they reveal that in the era of governance, the state is not – as noted above – in a totally dominant position; like the pressure groups themselves, it has had to adapt quickly to rapidly changing political, legal and economic circumstances.

Despite its relatively small size, Lowe and Wilkinson reveal that this group successfully applied multiple strategies – direct action, lobbying and promoting fresh ideological perspectives on agriculture – to out-manoeuvre more established groups. Interestingly, it managed to secure an entirely new form of governance – the Environmentally Sensitive Areas scheme – through which the EU now pays farmers to preserve natural landscapes. One of the most powerful points to emerge out of their analysis is that governance is not simply a tech-nocratic exercise of finding 'the right tool for the job'. On the con-trary, governance for sustainable development is an intensely political process of argumentation and interest group intermediation.

In Chapter 5, Matthew Paterson extends this political perspective on governance by examining the political economy of sustainability. He begins by noting the extraordinary growth in the number of international environmental regimes since the 1970s, a phenomenon which some have interpreted as a symptom of global governance. Paterson, however, maintains that they have to be seen as but one part of the broader system of global capitalism. So rather than seeing the sovereign state as an internally coherent actor, with clear prefer-ences and enjoying an unrivalled degree of agency, his political economy approach argues that it will always remain embedded in a set of complex and contradictory social relationships which structure its actions in ways that support the interests of capital. Crucially, global governance is part of the problem of unsustainability, not a politically neutral set of tools for engendering sustainable development. Although he stops well short of writing off sustainability as an ideological smokescreen, he does encourage us to ask who or what is served by the attempts made to embed sustainability frameworks in policy, society and the economy.

## Part III: Governance and Civil Society

Moving out still further from the formal apparatus of the state, Part III examines a number of key issues which are raised by the perceived need to govern sustainability, namely the role of individuals through notions of citizenship. In Chapter 6, Andy Dobson identifies citizenship as a tool for changing societal attitudes and behaviour. It is very much consistent with the society-centric view of governance noted above, rather than the more state-centric ones. He investigates the scope for employing citizenship – or what he terms ecological citizenship – by comparing it with currently the most popular alternative form of governance – the market-based instrument. He argues that fiscal incentives such as road pricing in the UK and taxes on disposable plastic bags in Ireland have produced very rapid alterations in behaviour. At a time when governments are searching hard for ways to achieve behaviour change, these achievements appear highly attractive.

But, for Dobson, changing behaviour and changing attitudes are not the same: attitudes work at a much deeper level than behaviour. So while behaviour can be changed quite quickly, the alterations may not endure. Attitudes, by contrast, are harder to shift, but once altered are likely to remain so. He then considers the scope for changing both by deploying the 'tool' of ecological citizenship. While acknowledging the need for more empirical research in this area, his findings – that citizenship is more likely to produce lasting change than fiscal incentives, but will take time to take root – are highly suggestive and very worthy of more research. Crucially, he argues that citizenship is unlikely to emerge spontaneously in a 'self-governed' manner; on the contrary, it requires new educational systems and democratic spaces in which it can thrive. So while he approaches governance from a society-centric perspective, he in effect concludes by making a case for greater governmental action.

In Chapter 7, Jill Jäger examines the role of science in the transition to sustainable development. She argues that sustainability requires fundamental changes in the way that science is produced and translated into policy. This raises hugely important questions about the governance of knowledge production and dissemination. In her chapter, she explores the interaction between science and society in ways that are significantly more normative than the chapters in Part I. Science-as-usual, she contends, simply will not do; governance for sustainability requires a new kind of science which is more problem-oriented, more reflexive and participatory. Crucially, the aim of sustainability science (Kates *et al.*, 2001) should not simply be to identify and explicate problems; it should also actively explore solutions to them – something, clearly, which goes well beyond what most mainstream scientists are used to providing. In the remainder of her chapter, she discusses the various challenges – for the conduct and structure of science, for society, and of course for the state more broadly – which flow from these aspirations.

In Chapter 8, Jacquelin Burgess and Judy Clark continue to focus on the public's role in the governance of sustainability. The enhancement of public participation is, as noted above, widely portrayed as one of the defining features of governance and also a key sub-principle of sustainability. Burgess and Clark argue that, while public and stake-holder participation is, rhetorically at least, part of the working culture of many organisations, surprisingly little is known about its effectiveness in public policy making. Drawing on an analysis of the views of different practitioners involved in environmental regulation, they show that participatory exercises generate a number of important benefits, but (echoing a point made by Katrina Brown in Chapter 2) take time to set up and can be very costly to maintain. With the drive to move participation in policy making 'upstream', the tension between the desire for accountable, open and responsive governance has, they argue, become more acute.

## Part IV: Governance and Decision Making

Part IV addresses the much more practical problem of how to make decisions in relation to sustainability when public attitudes and values are in conflict, and the underlying science is uncertain. In Chapter 9, Andy Stirling focuses on the tense relationship between two of the most commonly cited sub-principles of sustainable development, namely widening public participation and applying precaution. He thoroughly unpacks them both and explores some of their mutual interdependencies, which he shows are, in turn, related to a number of different ways in which the term sustainability is employed.

Thus Stirling shows that the precautionary principle tends to be defined and applied by scientists and bureaucrats working in committees of experts as though it were a straightforward and relatively technical decision rule. Such an approach, he argues, produces quick decisions but, lacking the input of the public, they may quickly unravel as circumstances change. It would be far better, he claims, to abandon the search for objectivity and 'quick fixes' and instead find ways to involve the public at the very start of the process (see also Chapter 8). This, he claims, requires not only governance, but more reflexive systems of governance (Voss *et al*., 2006): a tall order, given the status quo.

In Chapter 10, Ortwin Renn also examines the difficulties which commonly emerge when attempts are made to apply the precautionary principle. Dismissing the classical approach to understanding risk, he advances a more deliberative approach to decision making, with an enhanced input from a wider array of stakeholders. He concludes that such an approach not only helps to implement the precautionary principle, but sustainable development as well. In fact, it can help to make sustainability more concrete and utilisable in specific decision-making situations. However, while this approach has gained wide acceptance amongst academic risk analysts, it has not yet been applied in prevailing governance systems. Although Renn identifies isolated examples where communities have successfully participated in risk decisions, an obvious challenge is to understand better why deliberative approaches are so rare and how their utility can be increased, bearing in mind some of the costs associated with involving the public in scientifically complex issues.

In Chapter 11, Simon Dietz and Eric Neumayer offer an economic perspective on the relationship between governance and sustainable development. Given that the market is probably the most dominant mode of governance in the world today and that economics is centrally concerned with understanding how humans behave in market situations, economists should (in theory at least) have a lot to add to the debate about governing sustainability. In their analysis, Dietz and Neumayer identify two relevant paradigms that have emerged in economics over the last forty years: an environmental and resource economics paradigm and an ecological economics one. They review the relative strengths and weaknesses of both. They conclude that both have made significant analytical contributions which have informed the design of different tools and methods of governing, such as market-based instruments, green accounting and cost–benefit analysis.

Drawing on the example of the *Copenhagen Consensus* orchestrated by Bjorn Lomborg, they argue that attempts to identify a single, optimal path of human development are doomed to fail. Their conclusion – that economists need to pull back from the theoretical ideal of maximising global utility, and debate the merits and demerits of specific tools and methods of governance as part of an interdisciplinary endeavour – resonates powerfully with the points made by Stirling and Renn.

The final chapter in Part IV is by John O'Neill. He examines the themes of human welfare and the substitutability of different types of capital (highlighted by Dietz and Neumayer) from first principles. The substitutability of capital is something that has generated a huge amount of academic commentary and debate in the sustainability literature. O'Neill finds that, as with many great debates in academia, it has been marked by both concealed agreement and exaggerated conflict. He argues that environmental goods are not substitutable by other goods because they answer to quite distinct dimensions of human wellbeing. Thus, certain critical habitats matter because they have a certain history (comprising what we have described as distinct *processes* of creation), not simply because of their physical attributes (i.e. *outcomes*).

O'Neill argues that the failure of the metaphor of natural capital used by economists is symptomatic of a failure to capture the many different ways in which humans relate to their environment. Building on themes developed in Chapters 8, 9 and 10, as well as our distinction between processes and outcomes, he claims that sustainable development raises all sorts of political and ethical issues that cannot easily be captured in standard economic terms or technical decision-making procedures.

Finally, in Part V, Tim O'Riordan shows why sustainability is such a slippery concept for governance. The irony, he claims, is that sustainability is supposed to be transformational, yet its efforts at transforming governance have tended to build in reforms that actively resist, not promote, any meaningful transition to effective sustainability. In short, empirical governance is too dependent on non-sustainable models of human values and developmental goals to be suitable for sustainability. In the remainder of his chapter, he draws together and reflects on these different perspectives, and looks forward to the next phase of research on governing sustainability.

## References

Ayre, G. and Callway, R. (eds.) 2005. *Governance for Sustainable Development*. London: Earthscan.

Bache, I. and Flinders, M. (eds.) 2004. *Multi-level Governance*. Oxford University Press.

Berkes, F. and Folke, C. 1998. 'Linking social and ecological systems for resilience and sustainability', in Berkes, F. and Folke, C. (eds.) *Linking Social and Ecological Systems*. Cambridge University Press, pp. 1–25.

Biermann, F. 2007. 'Earth system governance as a cross cutting theme of global change research', *Global Environmental Change* 17: 326–37.

Bromley, D. W. 2005. 'The poverty of sustainability: rescuing economics from platitudes', *Agricultural Economics* 32: 201–10.

Carter, N. 2007. *The Politics of the Environment*. Second edition. Cambridge University Press.

Cash, D. W., Adger, W. N., Berkes, F., Garden, P., Lebel, L., Olsson, P., Pritchard, L. and Young, O. 2006. 'Scale and cross-scale dynamics: governance and information in a multi-level world', *Ecology and Society* 11(2): 8. URL: www.ecologyandsociety.org/vol11/iss2/art8/.

Commission on Global Governance 1995. *Our Global Neighbourhood*. Oxford University Press.

Diamond, J. 2004. *Collapse: How Societies Choose to Fail or to Succeed*. New York: Viking.

Dingwerth, K. and Pattberg, P. 2006. 'Global governance as a perspective on world politics', *Global Governance* 12: 185–203.

Dobson, A. 1998. *Justice and the Environment*. Oxford University Press.

Dryzek, J. 2005. *The Politics of the Earth*. Second edition. Oxford University Press.

European Consultative Forum on the Environment and Sustainable Development (ECFESD) 2000. *Sustainable Governance*. Brussels: European Commission.

Farrell, K. N., Kemp, R., Hinterberger, F., Rammel, C. and Ziegler, R. 2005. 'From "for" to governance for sustainable development in Europe', *International Journal of Sustainable Development* 8: 127–50.

Flinders, M. 2002. 'Governance in Whitehall', *Public Administration* 80: 51–76.

Frey, B. 2001. *Inspiring Economics: Human Motivation in Political Economy*. Cheltenham: Elgar.

Gamble, A. 2000. *Politics and Fate*. Cambridge: Polity.

Glasbergen, P., Biermann, F. and Mol, A. P. J. (eds.) 2007. *Partnerships, Governance and Sustainable Development: Reflections on Theory and Practice*. Cheltenham, UK: Elgar.

Hajer, M. 1995. *The Politics of Environmental Discourse*. Oxford University Press.

Hardin, G. 1968. 'The tragedy of the commons', *Science* 162: 1243–8.

Harvey, D. 2003. *The New Imperialism*. Oxford University Press.

Hewson, M. and Sinclair, T. (eds.) 1999. *Approaches to Global Govern-ance Theory*. State University of New York Press.

Jasanoff, S. and Martello, M. (eds.) 2004. *Earth Politics: Local and Global in Environmental Governance*. Cambridge, MA: MIT Press.

Jordan, A. J. and Lenschow, A. (eds.) 2008. *Innovation in Environmental Policy? Integrating the Environment for Sustainability*. Cheltenham, UK: Edward Elgar.

Jordan, A. J. and Schout, A. 2006. *The Coordination of the European Union*. Oxford: Oxford University Press.

Jordan, A. J., Wurzel, R. and Zito, A. 2005. 'The rise of new policy instruments in comparative perspective', *Political Studies* 53: 477–96.

Kates, R. W., Clark, W. C., Corell, R., Hall, J. M., Jaeger, C. C., Lowe, I., McCarthy, J. J., Schellnhuber, H. J., Bolin, B., Dickson, N. M., Faucheux, S., Gallopin, G. C., Grubler, A., Huntley, B., Jäger, J., Jodha, N. S., Kasperson, R. E., Mabogunje, A., Matson, P., Mooney, H., Moore, B., O'Riordan, T. and Svedin, U. 2001. 'Sustainability science', *Science* 292: 641–2.

Kates, R. W., Parris, T. M. and Leiserowitz, A. 2005. 'What is sustainable development?' *Environment* 47(3): 8–21.

Kohler-Koch, B. and Rittberger, B. 2006. 'The governance turn in EU studies', *Journal of Common Market Studies* 44 (Annual Review): 27–49.

Kooiman, J. (ed.) 1993. *Modern Governance*. London: Sage.

Kooiman, J. 2003. *Governing as Governance*. London: Sage.

Lafferty, W. (ed.) 2001. *Sustainable Communities in Europe*. London: Earthscan.

Lafferty, W. (ed.) 2004. *Governance for Sustainable Development*. Chel-tenham, UK: Elgar.

Lafferty, W. and Eckerberg, K. (eds.) 1998. *From the Earth Summit to Local Agenda 21*. London: Earthscan.

Lafferty, W. and Meadowcroft, J. (eds.) 2000. *Implementing Sustainable Development*. Oxford: Oxford University Press.

Layard, R. 2005. *Happiness: Lessons from a New Science*. London: Penguin.

Lele, S. M. 1991. 'Sustainable development: a critical review', *World Development* 19: 607–21.

Lemos, M. C. and Agrawal, A. 2006. 'Environmental governance', *Annual Review of Environmental Resources* 31: 297–325.

Lenton, T. M., Held, H., Kriegler, E., Hall, J. W., Lucht, W., Rahmstorf, S. and Schellnhuber, H. J. 2008. 'Tipping elements in the Earth's climate system', *Proceedings of the National Academy of Sciences* 105: 1786–93.

Levy, D. and Newell, P. (eds.) 2004. *The Business of Global Environmental Governance*. Cambridge, MA: MIT Press.

Mann, M. 1997. 'Has globalization ended the rise and rise of the nation state?', *Review of International Political Economy* 4: 472–96.

Marks, G., Hooghe, L. and Blank, K. 1996. 'European integration from the 1980s: state centric versus multi-level governance', *Journal of Common Market Studies* 34: 341–78.

Meadowcroft, J. 2000. 'Sustainable development: a new(ish) idea for a new century', *Political Studies* 48: 370–87.

Meadowcroft, J. 2007. 'National sustainable development strategies: features, challenges and reflexivity', *European Environment* 17: 152–63.

Meadowcroft, J., Farrell, K. N. and Spangenberg, J. 2005. 'Developing a framework for sustainability governance in the EU', *International Journal of Sustainable Development* 8: 3–30.

Meadows, D. H., Meadows, D. L., Randers, J. and Behrens, W. W. 1972. *The Limits to Growth*. New York: Universe Books.

Meadows, D. H., Randers, J. and Meadows, D. L. 2005. *Limits to Growth: the Thirty Year Update*. London: Earthscan.

Millennium Ecosystem Assessment (MA) 2005. *Ecosystems and Human Well-Being: Synthesis*. Washington DC: Island Press.

Newig, J., Voss, J.-P. and Monstadt, J. (eds.) 2008. *Governance for Sustainable Development: Steering in Contexts of Ambivalence, Uncertainty and Power*. London: Routledge.

OECD 2002. *Improving Policy Coherence and Integration for Sustainable Development: A Checklist*. Paris: OECD.

O'Riordan, T. (ed.) 1998. *Transition to Sustainability: The Politics of Agenda 21 in Europe*. London: Earthscan.

O'Riordan, T. and Voisey, H. (eds.) 1997. *Sustainable Development in Western Europe: Coming to Terms with Agenda 21*. London: Frank Cass.

Ostrom, E. 2005. *Understanding Institutional Diversity*. Princeton University Press.

Pierre, J. and Peters, B. G. 2000. *Governance, Politics and the State*. Basingstoke, UK: Macmillan.

Rhodes, R. A. W. 1997. *Understanding Governance*. Milton Keynes, UK: Open University Press.

Richards, D. and Smith, M. 2002. *Governance and Public Policy*. Oxford: Oxford University Press.

Satterfield, T. A., Mertz, C. K. and Slovic, P. 2004. 'Discrimination, vulnerability, and justice in the face of risk', *Risk Analysis* 24: 115–29.

Schellnhuber, H. J., Cramer, W., Nakicenovic, N., Wigley, T. and Yohe, G. (eds.) 2006. *Avoiding Dangerous Climate Change*. Cambridge, UK: Cambridge University Press.

Scrase, J. and Sheate, W. R. 2002. 'Integration and integrated approaches to assessment: what do they mean for the environment?' *Journal of Environmental Policy and Planning* 4: 275–94.

Speth, J. and Haas, P. 2006. *Global Environmental Governance*. Washington DC: Island Press.

Steurer, R. 2007. 'From government strategies to strategic public management', *European Environment* 17: 201–14.

Stirling, A. 1999. 'The appraisal of sustainability', *Local Environment* 4: 111–35.

Stoker, G. 1998. 'Governance as theory', *International Social Science Journal* 155: 17–28.

Thompson, G. F. 2003. *Between Hierarchies and Markets: The Logic and Limits of Network Forms of Organisation*. Oxford University Press.

Treib, O., Bähr, H. and Falkner, G. 2007. 'Modes of governance: towards a conceptual clarification', *Journal of European Public Policy* 14: 1–20.

Turnpenny, J., Nilsson, M., Russel, D., Jordan, A., Hertin, J. and Nykvist, B. 2008. 'Why is integrating policy assessment so hard?' *Journal of Environmental Planning and Management*, **51**.

United Nations 2002. *Report of the World Summit, on Sustainable Development*. A/CONF.199/20 and A/CONF.199/20/corr.1. New York: United Nations.

van Kersbergen, K. and van Waarden, F. 2004. 'Governance as a bridge between disciplines', *European Journal of Political Research* 43: 143–71.

Voss, J.-P., Bauknecht, D. and Kemp, R. (eds.) 2006. *Reflexive Governance for Sustainable Development*. Cheltenham, UK: Edward Elgar.

White, L. 1967. 'The historical roots of our ecological crisis', *Science* 155: 1203–7.

World Bank 2002. *Governance and Development*. Washington DC: World Bank.

World Commission on Environment and Development (WCED ) 1987. *Our Common Future*. Oxford: Oxford University Press.

Young, O. R. 2005. 'Why is there no unified theory of environmental governance?' in Dauvergne, P. (ed.) *Handbook of Global Environmental Politics*. Cheltenham, UK: Edward Elgar.

Young, O. R., Berkhout, F., Gallopin, G. C., Janssen, M. A., Ostrom, E. and van der Leeuw, S. 2006. 'The globalization of socio-ecological systems: an agenda for scientific research', *Global Environmental Change* 16: 304–16.

# 2 | Human development and environmental governance: a reality check

KATRINA BROWN

## Introduction

In the post-Johannesburg, post-Rio and post-development era, it appears that the global problems of both widespread poverty and environmental degradation just get worse, not better (see Steffen *et al.*, 2004). The impacts of the global political economy of oil and the entrenchment of underdevelopment in Africa and parts of Asia are endangering planetary resilience and making many people's livelihoods and wellbeing more precarious. In some respects, the world has moved further away from sustainable development, not towards it.

Since Brundtland's 1987 vision of interdependence gained currency (WCED, 1987; see also Chapter 1), the synergy between the goals of international development and environmental conservation have often been taken for granted. To date, however, systems of national and international governance have found this synergy very difficult to achieve. Many attempts have been made by governments and global systems of governance to integrate the objectives of international development and environmental sustainability. These have been undertaken through bilateral and multilateral environmental agreements, at one scale, through to the promotion of decentralised integrated conservation and development projects at more local scales. This integration element of environmental governance is often held up as one of the panaceas for sustainable governance.

This chapter presents an analysis of the experience and types of integration, and outlines a set of fundamental challenges which remain if real progress is to be made. These include: finding a meaningful and realistic approach to the inclusion of key actors to ensure legitimate decision making; utilising and recognising diverse knowledges and values; and re-modelling systems of governance to support sustainability at different spatial scales.

## Integrating development and environmental concerns

The integration of concerns about development – particularly the welfare of the poor in poor countries – and environment has, as noted in the previous chapter, been fundamental to the conceptualisation, interrogation and operationalisation of sustainable development since Brundtland. Sustainable development is founded on the belief that there is synergy to be found between the objectives of development and environmental conservation. Synergy in this context means mutual and positive reinforcement. Based on this notion of synergy, much of the sustainable development rhetoric and policy of the 1990s (fuelled by neoliberal ideology and belief in the market) sought so-called 'win–win' solutions to problems of environment and development (Pearce and Warford, 1993). Twentieth-century environmentalism coalesced around the notion that mutual dependence, interdependence and integration between these goals is both attainable and desirable. However, relatively little analysis has focused on the nature of the linkages and the systems of governance that are needed to secure them.

One recent attempt at conceptualising and assessing the integration between development and environmental governance has been the Millennium Ecosystem Assessment (or MA). The MA was a global, multi-scale assessment, involving some 1,360 scientists from 95 countries. It was reviewed by an 80-person board of review editors and 850 reviewers (www.maweb.org; Millennium Ecosystem Assessment, 2005). It was governed by and through a partnership of UN agencies, businesses and non-governmental organisations (NGOs). It was linked to the major global conventions on biodiversity, desertification, climate change and wetland conservation. From the outset, the MA sought to assess the integration of development and environment by specifically addressing the links between ecosystem services and the benefits they provide for human wellbeing, and how these are changing. The MA's conceptual framework analysed ecosystem services and the impacts of change on multiple dimensions of human wellbeing (Millennium Ecosystem Assessment, 2003). It showed how provisioning, regulating, supporting and cultural services lead to security, basic materials for a good life, health, and good social relations. The framework drew on the work of Amartya Sen (e.g. Sen, 1999) in defining human wellbeing as a set of opportunities and capabilities, rather than simply assets and income. Hence, the MA defined the constituents of wellbeing as underpinning freedoms and choice (Millennium Ecosystem Assessment, 2003: 5).

The MA's conceptualisation of these linkages provides a detailed and analytically useful set of representations of how development and environmental governance can be integrated. The view is clearly very much influenced by: 1) a systems approach; and 2) a dynamic appreciation of conceptions such as resilience and vulnerability, and puts a strong emphasis on the provision of ecosystem functions and services, rather than species and habitats.

The findings of the MA are summarised in Box 2.1. They provide a sobering picture of the relationship between human wellbeing and the health of ecosystems at the start of the twenty-first century. They also powerfully confirm many of our worse fears and expectations. They

---

**Box 2.1** Key findings of the Millennium Ecosystem Assessment

- Over the past 50 years, humans have changed ecosystems more rapidly and extensively than in any comparable period of time in human history, largely to meet rapidly growing demands for food, fresh water, timber and fuel;
- The changes that have been made to ecosystems have contributed to substantial net gains in human wellbeing and economic development, but these gains have been achieved at growing costs in the form of the degradation of many ecosystem services, increased risks of nonlinear changes, and the exacerbation of poverty for some groups of people; the costs and benefits are increasingly skewed;
- The degradation of ecosystem services could grow significantly worse during the first half of this century and is a barrier to achieving each of the Millennium Development Goals;
- The challenge of reversing the degradation of ecosystems while meeting increasing demands for their services can be partially met under some of the future scenarios considered by the MA, but these involve significant changes in policies, institutions and practices that are not currently under way.

*Source*: Millennium Ecosystem Assessment (2005).

imply that we are in fact moving further from the goals of sustainable development rather than closer to them. This is particularly true if we examine the situation in many developing countries of the world, and consider the possible implications for attainment of the Millennium Development Goals (MDGs), the internationally agreed targets for human development. There are eight MDGs, each with specific targets (eighteen in all) and measurable indicators, covering key aspects of development including poverty and hunger, education, child mortality, maternal health, women's empowerment and environmental sustainability (see www.developmentgoals.org). Many countries in sub-Saharan Africa, Central Asia, parts of South and Southeast Asia, and some regions of Latin America are currently off-track with respect to meeting these goals. Although their attainment may be intricately linked to ecosystem health (Chopra *et al.*, 2005: chapter 19), the goals have been criticised for separating development and environmental goals (e.g. Roe, 2003). Does this mean then that the integration of development and environmental governance is a more elusive and problematic strategy for the implementation of sustainable development than Brundtland's assumptions about the potential for synergy originally led us to believe?

## Integration analysed

Within the MA's framework, integrated responses are defined as those which intentionally, actively and simultaneously address ecosystem services and human wellbeing (Chopra *et al.*, 2005). This conceptualisation starts from the premise that previous attempts to address the impacts of human activities on ecosystems have traditionally been based on sector-by-sector approaches, which ultimately have resulted in fragmented actions and governance solutions. Coastal management in the UK would be the classic example of this, with different agencies involved in different aspects of planning and managing on and off-shore resources (Brown *et al.*, 2005a; Few *et al.*, 2007). So too would the EU's failed attempts to integrate an environmental dimension into all its policy sectors (Jordan and Lenschow, 2008). Integration has recently become an important concern in thinking about and putting into place sustainable solutions that support human development. However, integration is used by many different authors and advocated in many different areas of environmental governance and development policy, to the extent that it is taken almost universally as 'a good thing' and rarely qualified, defined or evaluated.

The term integration is understood and promoted in three different ways. First, the term is conceptualised in terms of how the linkages between social and ecological systems are understood and different kinds of knowledge brought together. Second, integration has governance dimensions, such as the way in which concerns for ecosystem services and human wellbeing are addressed in the formulation of legal frameworks, property rights and the organisation of government, civil society and the private sector, and how different actors are brought into governance processes. Third, integration is defined in terms of implementation, referring to how policies, decisions and management interventions and instruments are employed at different scales.

## *Integration as linking social and ecological systems*

Concerns about integration have grown since sustainability became an overarching, prominent paradigm to guide policy. It is widely accepted and argued that sustainable development necessarily requires the integration of social, economic and environmental goals. Indeed, that is its defining characteristic. However, debates surrounding sustainability have also motivated more fundamental changes in world views, which call for an integrated perspective on social and ecological systems. Human societies affect ecosystems and environmental conditions and, likewise, environmental conditions and ecosystems both impose constraints on, and provide opportunities for, societal development. Societies co-evolve with nature through dynamic and reflexive processes occurring at a variety of scales, from local to global. An emerging body of theory, for example in the Resilience Alliance (www.resalliance.org), defines such co-evolving systems as linked social-ecological systems (see Berkes and Folke, 1998; Folke *et al.*, 2002; Folke, 2006). Integration, therefore, begins with the recognition that environment and society are closely linked.

There is an emerging consensus about the need for a fundamentally different scientific approach to meet sustainability challenges, one which is capable of bridging the divide between disciplines that analyse the dynamics of ecosystems and those that analyse economics and social interactions. A concern has begun to emerge within many disciplines regarding the importance of integration across cognate disciplines. These concerns are being reflected in new interdisciplinary and multidisciplinary research initiatives and institutions such as sustainability science, as discussed by Jäger in Chapter 7 (see also Kasemir *et al.*, 2003; Cash *et al.*, 2006). Thus, it would appear that designing strategies to achieve sustainable environment–society interactions requires integration, in this case between different scientific disciplines. There is also a call for integration of different kinds of knowledge. Interventions to address the decline of ecosystems have drawn mostly on western scientific knowledge and world views. This has resulted in the exclusion of other equally valuable and valid types of knowledge; integration in this sense can be about the combination of different disciplines and knowledge systems. However, the development of integrative or 'sustainability' science is still in its infancy and faces resistance within institutions, and academia more broadly.

## Integration of different actors, stakeholders and institutions

Integration is also about the process of involving a broader range of actors in environmental governance. A growing body of evidence suggests that addressing environmental problems or managing natural resources often requires sustained collaboration between different actors. For example, many local communities which are dependent on natural resources for their livelihoods are deeply knowledgeable about their environment. They can demonstrate the capacity to define common rules and sanctions, all of which contributes to making them potentially effective resource managers (Berkes, 1999). However, on their own, these actors are unlikely to be able to deal with multiple pressures and constraints, such as trends in economic globalisation and neoliberalism (O'Brien and Leichenko, 2000; Liverman and Vilas, 2006). Berkes *et al.*, for example, show how the globalisation of fisheries has decreased the resilience of marine ecosystems. Exploitation of sea urchins and herbivorous reef fish species in the past three decades, in particular, has been shown to make reefs more vulnerable to recurrent disturbances such as hurricanes and to coral bleaching and mortality due to increased sea surface temperatures that constitute climate change (Berkes *et al.*, 2006). Hence, many fisheries globally face a double exposure, in the words of O'Brien and Leichenko (2000), to globalisation and to global environmental change. No local fishery, no matter how sustainably managed, can cope with the technologies of global fisheries exploitation.

Other actors have the capability to address such constraints; examples being governments, NGOs, businesses and donors. Underpinning stakeholder involvement is the notion of participation, which has become a central ingredient in improving the effectiveness, legitimacy and equity of environmental governance (Adger *et al.*, 2003). Participation and stakeholder inclusion can be seen as a form of integration between different actors concerned with environmental management. However, as further discussed below, although integration of different actors is a widespread stated goal of environmental governance, the results have been mixed and the form of involvement very often passive rather than active, and seen as a means to a pre-defined end.

## *Horizontal and vertical policy integration*

Integration is also about the way in which policy is developed and implemented and the use of different instruments to deliver policy objectives. In this context, integration is referred to as either horizontal or vertical (Lafferty and Hovden, 2003). Horizontal integration implies achieving greater coherence and integration within and among sectors and institutions. A horizontally integrated response is one that links actors, stakeholders and institutions at the same level or scale. Vertical integration implies linking discrete levels of governance, from local to international, and institutions across different levels. Vertical integration is important in contexts where hierarchical forms of management dominate, which, in the absence of collaboration and co-ordination, tends to lead to fragmented responses which are unable to deal with complex problems. A whole stream of research has developed in recent years examining multi-level environmental governance, as, for example, in the Centre for Social and Economic Research into the Global Environment (CSERGE)'s Programme on Environmental Decision Making (Adger *et al.*, 2003; Jordan and Schout, 2006; Jordan and Lenschow, 2008). Sustainable development can be seen as an inherently multi-level issue, with global and international scale initiatives, national sustainable development strategies, institutions and plans, and a range of local initiatives, such as Local Agenda 21s (see Brown *et al.*, 2005b). Furthermore, vertical integration is also crucial when promoting collaboration between actors at different scales. Policies and responses can also be integrated across different sectors and scales, working across different issues and multiple scales simultaneously. This area of cross-scale institutions has recently been the focus of research in the Resilience Alliance (see, for example, papers by Adger *et al.*, 2005; Cash *et al.*, 2006; Young, 2006, in a special issue of *Ecology and Society* (see www. ecologyandsociety.org)).

## The limits to integration

The review undertaken as part of the MA (see Brown *et al.*, 2005b) examined a wide range of responses and initiatives at different scales, ranging from international agreements and conventions, Agenda 21, national sustainable development strategies, different configurations of policy integration, and specific inter-sectoral and participatory approaches, such as sustainable forest management, integrated coastal zone management, integrated river basin and watershed management, and integrated conservation and development projects. This review suggests that a number of key factors determine when and where integrated responses are most appropriate and most likely to be successful. These are outlined in Box 2.2.

---

**Box 2.2** Key factors in effective integration of environment and development objectives in governance structures

Integration is only likely to be successful when:

- The full costs are taken into account
- Capacity exists in government and civil society institutions
- A feasible timescale to achieve objectives is possible
- There is compatibility and no obvious conflict between object-ives
- The legal and institutional frameworks supporting the response are already in place
- Relevant and timely information is at hand and extensive new data and research is not necessary.

*Source:* Brown *et al.* (2005b).

---

What emerges very strongly from this analysis is that integration cannot be imposed by external agencies, and will be more likely to be successful when key stakeholders – in government, private sector and civil society – possess a sense of ownership. In other words, integration cannot be driven from outside; objectives must reflect stakeholder priorities. The external imposition of integration is especially prevalent in developing countries, where funding frameworks and donor demands steered or forced integration, but where the structural constraints, especially within government, have undermined integration at different scales.

The MA's review of integration across different regions of the world and different spheres and scales reveals rather mixed results. Calls for integration – in terms of conceptualising environment–society relations, bringing different stakeholders to the table, and of implementing policy – are almost universal. But it is surprisingly difficult to identify many clear 'success stories' where an integrated approach has demonstrably yielded greater benefits than a non-integrated one. There are some generic lessons and higher order issues which need to be considered before integration can really make a difference. These are discussed in the following sections.

## Future challenges

There are fundamental challenges to integrating concerns for ecological sustainability with human development. Quite radical changes are necessary in the landscape of environmental governance to support greater integration. I argue that three fundamental shifts are required for successful integration of conservation of resources and enhanced human welfare or development. First, deliberative and inclusionary mechanisms are necessary. Second, plural knowledges and values must be acknowledged and integrated. And, third, institutions and interactions across scale must be accounted for.

But there are also important cultural, political and structural factors that hinder these changes from happening in many situations, as observed in empirical research in Amazonia, the Caribbean and elsewhere (for example, Brown and Rosendo, 2000; Brown *et al.*, 2002; Tompkins *et al.*, 2002). Many studies have similarly noted the importance of these external factors, but the study of them has not yet really been brought into the resilience field, and critical political-economic analysis is generally lacking.

## Deliberation, inclusion, participation and human development

Inclusion and participation has been a major focus of environmental governance discussions in the past two decades (see Chapter 1). There have been two interesting, but quite separate, debates in the literature about developed and developing countries. The issues have been framed in quite different ways, because of a number of factors which are more fully discussed in Brown (1999). The first concerns the role of the state. In developing countries, a distinct culture of self-help (for example, *harambee* in East Africa) and NGO and civil society has emerged. This is partly to do with indigenous institutions, but often is because of the near absence of an effective state apparatus at a local scale. Second, the nature of the issues and the links between extreme poverty and dependence on natural resources for livelihoods has been stressed in developing countries, where a more instrumentalist approach to inclusion has often been the norm. Third, participation has been a central focus of development agencies and has very often been about implementing discrete, externally led 'projects' rather than facilitating genuine, long-term societal change.

As a result, a critical literature has emerged, often highlighting how these participatory approaches have failed to take account of local contexts; further marginalised those who are already excluded from the benefits of mainstream economic development (such as women) and reinforced social, economic and political inequities; and generally made naive and simplistic assumptions about the nature of communities (see Brosius *et al.*, 1998; Cooke and Kothari, 2001; Ribot, 2006; Ribot *et al.*, 2006). Much new research demonstrates how the modes of participation employed in various projects have been passive, reflecting the values and interests of outsiders. They have generally not empowered local people, nor enabled them to have an effective say in decisions. Only very recently have the developed and developing country participatory discussions adopted a similar language of democracy and decentralisation. Ribot (2002) has highlighted the need for strong democratic and accountable government institutions for successful participation in developing countries. When governments are threatened by the outcomes of popular participation, they often move to re-appropriate resources and power in decision making (see the discussion in Ribot *et al.*, 2006).

Clearly, there is a need to move beyond 'participation' as practised conventionally in these attempts to integrate human and environmental dimensions of development – what Kasperson (2006) has dubbed the 'stakeholder express'. A wide range of mechanisms exist to facilitate this. We have done extensive research, for example, on inclusive decision making in relation to coastal management. In the case of a marine protected area in Tobago in the eastern Caribbean, a range of techniques were employed to facilitate conflict resolution and instigate more consensus-based decision making and management (Brown *et al.*, 2002). A number of different methods were used, including stakeholder analysis, focus groups, surveys, workshops and multi-criteria analysis, in order to include all the relevant stakeholder groups and enable debate and transparent decision making.

The key lessons that emerged from the process of stakeholder engagement are threefold. First, inclusion of all relevant actors necessitates a very thorough and rigorous analysis of stakeholders; different techniques are required to encourage people to participate and to articulate their views. Before intervention, the dynamics and politics of local society need to be understood. Second, building trust in the process and between different stakeholders takes time but is vital for the success of both process and outcome. Third, inclusionary approaches involve an ongoing and adaptive learning process. Consensus is not an end point or necessarily desirable. The process must evolve and be shaped by the actors themselves.

## Fostering fusion knowledge

In addition to the inclusion of all relevant stakeholders and transparent and open decision making, successful integrative approaches involve the flow of information and knowledge between stakeholders, and the integration of knowledge and experience into management. Knowledge concerns the way people interpret, understand and apply meaning to the world and to their experiences. Conventional scientific knowledge is usually contrasted with local or traditional knowledge. Local or traditional knowledge is seen as both an obstacle and an opportunity for environmental conservation. But knowledge – whether

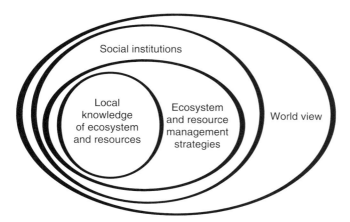

**Figure 2.1** Traditional ecological knowledge as a practice belief system: local knowledge is embedded within rules and norms and the world view of a particular culture
*Source:* Adapted from Berkes (1999).

local, traditional or scientific – cannot be viewed as a static resource. Different forms of knowledge are seen to bring valuable perspectives and they are integrated and utilised, and combined in a co-learning process. Ecological knowledge is a key link between social and eco-logical systems and can be used to interpret and respond to signals of ecosystem change, as evidenced, for example, by work done by Olssen and Folke (2001) in Lake Racken, Sweden.

Fikret Berkes' definition of 'traditional ecological knowledge' shows knowledge to be both cumulative and dynamic, building on experience and adapting to change and how it relates to institutions (Berkes, 1999). It requires that we take account of how knowledge is embedded within the management strategies, social institutions and, ultimately, the world views of different actors. It also views knowledge and practice and institutions as evolving and adapting to changes in contexts and circumstances. Berkes identifies four interrelated levels of ecological knowledge, depicted in Figure 2.1. The first, which is based on empirical observations, consists of local knowledge of animals, plants, soils and landscapes.

According to Berkes (1999), local knowledge in itself is not enough to ensure sustainable use of resources, although it might be sufficient to fulfil short-term survival objectives. At the second level, local knowledge is associated with a set of practices, tools and techniques, which requires an understanding of ecological processes. A third level involves developing social institutions and social organisations between different resource users to enforce systems of management. Fourthly, a world view, or paradigmatic knowledge, gives meaning to individual perceptions of the environment, and in turn shapes observations and social institutions. Local or traditional ecological knowledge is an integral part of the social learning processes necessary for integrated environmental governance. Social learning is how people learn to behave and use knowledge in social environments through interaction and deliberation. It thus helps to build the trust necessary for successful collaboration. The interplay between different forms of knowledge has been termed hybrid knowledge, knowledge-in-action, or fusion knowledge.

Our research with coastal communities in the Caribbean demonstrates very well how traditional ecological knowledge provides systematic and detailed knowledge of resources, change and processes. We were able to use this knowledge very positively in inclusionary decision making in order to validate and build trust about the impacts of different resource management, and to open discussions about sustainability. There were shared world views or visions of what a desirable future would look like, despite very severe conflicts over short-term decisions and resource use (Brown *et al.*, 2002). In contrast, in a frontier region of Amazonia, Maraba in eastern Para state of Brazil, research with colonist farmers revealed quite different aspects and patterns of local knowledge (Muchagata and Brown, 2000). Even very recent migrants to the region had detailed taxonomic knowledge of both forest flora and fauna species and their uses, and of soil types, more specific than the mapping and classification types developed by soil scientists. However, knowledge of processes (for example, of soil fertility management) amongst farmers was diverse and often contradictory. Furthermore, the nascent social institutions of the frontier – farmers' unions, the Landless Movement and agro-extractivist groups – each have very different world views and ideas about frontier development.

Building a shared understanding of what sustainability is, and what form of land use and environmental governance could work in this context, is likely to take considerably more time. The social learning and co-evolution of social institutions and local environmental management requires careful nurturing.

## New institutions – overcoming misfits

The empirical analysis of different attempts at integrating biodiversity conservation and development highlights the problem of institutional misfit. This term has been defined and research specifically developed under the International Human Dimensions Programme on Global Environmental Change (IHDP) (see, for example, Folke *et al.*, 1998). This misfit occurs both between the ecosystems and the institutions which seek to manage them, and between the different institutions involved in governance. For example, research in the grasslands of Nepalese Terai demonstrates how a highly dynamic, complex ecosystem, with a range of valuable species but important scientific uncertainties and welfare trade-offs, cannot be managed as a conventional, exclusively protected area. Ecosystem conservation was justified by the need to protect a few rare and emblematic species (in this case, the Bengal tiger and the Asian one-horned rhino), but the management approach sought to control the use of valuable grassland resources by local people and suppress the very disturbance which created the complex mosaic of different habitats in the first place. Short-term management was geared to meet externally defined ecological objectives at the expense of local livelihoods in one of the poorest countries in the world.

The nature of the ecosystem itself militates against a rigid, long-term management strategy. But the number and diversity of institutions involved in integrated projects also causes problems of fit (Brown, 2003). Our analysis of extractive reserves in Rondonia in Brazilian Amazonia demonstrates how integrating the objectives of conservation and development brings together a range of different institutions who might have very different world views and goals, scales of operation, and resources and capacities (Brown and Rosendo, 2000). These issues of fit become even more significant when working across scales. In the case of the extractive reserves, for example, the institutions range from local associations of rubber tappers, national unions, government ministries at municipality and state level, and international organisations such as the World Bank and WWF International.

Multi-stakeholder and co-management approaches are increasingly advocating these kinds of partnerships, but in a very unproblematised way. In the ideal situation, co-management of resources and shared responsibility between institutions of the state and of local resource users leads to reduced enforcement costs, the sharing of knowledge and information on the resource, and systematic learning between all parties. But governance partnerships are rarely this simple and they rarely involve just the community and the state. There is great heterogeneity within and between communities, and the networks they utilise. A meta-analysis needs to be undertaken among the successful examples of co-management on the patterns of interaction and other factors that explain their persistence (see Agrawal, 2001; Ostrom, 2005). Even if the local interactions, inclusion and integration of stakeholders and their interests can be established, working across scales introduces all kinds of new difficulties and complications. Research in the Caribbean suggests that the prerequisites for sustained interaction include: enabling constitutional order and legislation; giving organisations the ability to monitor and adapt their co-management experiments; and the presence of leaders and agents for change (Tompkins *et al.*, 2002).

## Conclusions: acknowledging and handling trade-offs

Integrating development and environmental concerns poses some critical challenges for the governance of sustainability. There are many indications that the world is moving further from, rather than closer to, global sustainability, and that the problems of ecosystem degradation and entrenched poverty are persistent. Governance-based institutions and policies to promote sustainability must, I argue, further seek to find new ways which allow marginalised voices and priorities to be heard and included: frame and utilise diverse knowledge; and handle problems that are seemingly intractable because of their multi-scalar characteristics. Fundamental changes in the institutions of environmental governance are necessary if there is to be any hope of successfully improving human welfare and environmental conservation to bring about meaningful change at a global scale. Much of the current policy prescriptions in conservation, for example, retreat from ideas about integrating biodiversity conservation with human development through integrated conservation development projects, because experience of more than two decades of investments have yielded few tangible benefits. They recognise that legal systems, incentives and markets, land use and taxation policies, and the underlying drivers of poverty and wealth and resource exploitation within society are what need to change (Naughton-Treves *et al.*, 2005).

It is clearly time to move away from an assumption of synergy to one where trade-offs are viewed as the norm rather than the exception (Barrett *et al.*, 2005). This is a central finding of the Millennium Ecosystem Assessment. It has also been forcefully argued by Sanderson (2005), who highlights the need for a new analytical framework for sustainability. These trade-offs are manifest in many forms (Brown, 2004). Trade-offs are common between different interests and priorities, particularly between economic development, social welfare and environmental goals. In effect there are frequent trade-offs between different stakeholders or users (winners and losers), and between different geographical and social scales (see Wells, 1992, for example). Indeed, a large body of evidence details the trade-offs between different sections of society and biodiversity conservation, often demonstrating that rich people benefit from conservation whilst the poor bear the brunt of the costs, with resultant negative impacts on social justice (e.g. Ghimire and Pimbert, 1997). Trade-offs also exist between long-term and short-term time horizons, where typically environmental conservation, as a long-term objective, is traded off against short-term economic benefits. So trade-offs themselves have social, temporal and spatial dimensions.

Because of the assumptions about synergy and the search for win–win solutions to problems of the global environment, we have failed to recognise and develop ways of dealing with trade-offs. The belief in win–win and the lack of attention to losers has undermined human welfare, and ultimately the losers have been the poor, the vulnerable and the powerless (O'Brien and Leichenko, 2003). A new realism is necessary in policy theory and practice to navigate the trade-offs, make difficult choices, and ensure that environmental governance does indeed integrate concerns for human development. How society can evaluate, negotiate and manage these trade-offs is at the core of current dilemmas in governance for sustainable development.

48 Katrina Brown

# References

Adger, W. N., Brown, K., Fairbrass, J., Jordan, A., Paavola, J., Rosendo, S. and Seyfang, G. 2003. 'Governance for sustainability: towards a "thick" analysis of environmental decision making', *Environment and Planning A* 35: 1095–110.

Adger, W. N., Brown, K. and Tompkins, E. L., 2005. 'The political economy of cross-scale networks in resource co-management', *Ecology and Society* 10(2): 9. URL: www.ecologyandsociety.org/vol10/iss2/art9/.

Agrawal, A. 2001. 'Common resources and institutional sustainability', in Ostrom, E., Dietz, T., Dolšak, N., Stern, P. C., Stonich, S. and Weber, E. U. (eds.) *The Drama of the Commons*. Washington DC: National Academy Press, pp. 41–85.

Barrett, C. B., Lee, D. R. and McPeak, J. G. 2005. 'Institutional arrangements for rural poverty reduction and resource conservation', *World Development* 33: 193–7.

Berkes, F. 1999. *Sacred Ecology: Traditional Ecological Knowledge and Resource Management*. Philadelphia: Taylor and Francis.

Berkes, F. and Folke, C. 1998. 'Linking social and ecological systems for resilience and sustainability', in Berkes F. and Folke C. (eds.) *Linking Social and Ecological Systems: Management Practices and Social Mechanisms for Building Resilience*. Cambridge University Press, pp. 1–25.

Berkes, F., Hughes, T., Steneck, R. S., Wilson, J. A., Bellwood, D. R., Crona, B., Folke, C., Gunderson, L., Leslie, H. M., Norberg, J., Nyström, M., Olsson, P., Österblom, H., Scheffer, M. and Worm, B. 2006. 'Globalization, roving bandits, and marine resources', *Science* 311: 1557–8

Brosius, J. P., Tsing, A. L. and Zerner, C. 1998. 'Representing communities: histories and politics of community-based natural resource management', *Society and Natural Resources* 11: 157–68.

Brown, K. 1999. 'Deliberative and inclusionary processes: learning from the South', in O'Riordan, T., Burgess, J. and Szerszynski, B. (eds.) *Deliberative and Inclusionary Processes: A Report from Two Seminars*. Working Paper PA-1999–06, Centre for Social and Economic Research on the Global Environment, University of East Anglia, Norwich. URL: www.uea.ac.uk/env/cserge.

Brown, K. 2003. 'Integrating conservation and development: a case of institutional misfit', *Frontiers in Ecology and the Environment* 1: 479–87.

Brown, K. 2004. 'Trade-off analysis for integrated conservation and development', in McShane, T. and Wells, M. (eds.) *Getting

*Biodiversity Projects to Work: Towards More Effective Conservation and Development.* New York: Columbia University Press, pp. 289–316.

Brown, K. and Rosendo, S. 2000. 'The institutional architecture of extractive reserves in Brazil', *Geographical Journal* 166: 35–48.

Brown, K., Tompkins, E. and Adger, W. N. 2002. *Making Waves: Integrating Coastal Conservation and Development.* London: Earthscan.

Brown, K., Few, R., Tompkins, E. L., Tsimplis, M. and Sortti, M. 2005a. *Responding to Climate Change: Inclusive and Integrated Coastal Analysis.* Technical Report 24, Tyndall Centre for Climate Change Research, University of East Anglia, Norwich. URL: www.tyndall.ac.uk.

Brown, K., Mackensen, J. and Rosendo, S. 2005b. 'Integrated responses', in Chopra, K., Leemans, R., Kumar, P. and Simons, H. (eds.) *Ecosystems and Human Well-being: Policy Responses*, Vol. 3. Washington DC: Millennium Assessment and Island Press, pp. 425–65.

Cash, D. W., Adger, W. N., Berkes, F., Garden, P., Lebel, L., Olsson, P., Pritchard, L. and Young, O. 2006. 'Scale and cross-scale dynamics: governance and information in a multi-level world', *Ecology and Society* 11(2): 8. URL: www.ecologyandsociety.org/vol11/iss2/art8/.

Chopra, K., Leemans, R., Kumar, P. and Simons, H. (eds.) 2005. *Ecosystems and Human Well-being: Policy Responses*, Volume 3. Washington DC: Millennium Assessment and Island Press.

Cooke, B. and Kothari, U. 2001. *Participation: the New Tyranny?* London: Zed Books.

Few, R., Brown, K. and Tompkins, E. 2007. 'Climate change and coastal management decisions: insights from Christchurch Bay, UK', *Coastal Management* 35: 255–70.

Folke, C. 2006. 'Resilience: the emergence of a perspective for social-ecological systems analyses', *Global Environmental Change* 16: 253–67.

Folke, C., Pritchard, L. Jr, Berkes, F., Colding, J. and Svedin, U. 1998. *The Problem of Fit between Ecosystems and Institutions.* IHDP Working Paper 2, Bonn: International Human Dimensions Programme on Global Environmental Change. URL: www.ihdp.uni-bonn.de/html/publications/workingpaper/wp02m.htm.

Folke, C., Carpenter, S., Elmqvist, T., Gunderson, L., Holling, C., Walker, B., Bengtsson, J., Berkes, F., Colding, J., Danell, K., Falkenmark, M., Gordon, L., Kasperson, R., Kautsky, N., Kinzig, A., Levin, S., Mäler, K.-G., Moberg, F., Ohlsson, L., Olsson, P., Ostrom, E., Reid, W., Rockström, J., Savenije, H. and Svedin, U. 2002. *Resilience and Sustainable Development: Building Adaptive Capacity in a World of Transformations.* Scientific Background Paper on Resilience for the process of The World Summit on Sustainable Development on behalf of The Environmental Advisory Council to the Swedish Government, April 16 2002. URL: www.sou.gov.se/mvb/pdf/resiliens.pdf.

Ghimire, K. B. and Pimbert M. P. (eds.) 1997. *Social Change and Conservation: Environmental Politics and Impacts of National Parks and Protected Areas.* London: Earthscan.

Jordan, A. J. and Lenschow, A. (eds.) 2008. *Innovation in Environmental Policy? Integrating the Environment for Sustainability.* Cheltenham, UK: Elgar.

Jordan, A. J. and Schout, A. 2006. *The Coordination of the European Union.* Oxford University Press.

Kasemir, B., Jäger, J., Jaeger, C. C. and Gardner, M. T. (eds.) 2003. *Participation in Sustainability Science: A Handbook.* Cambridge University Press.

Kasperson, R. E. 2006. 'Rerouting the stakeholder express', *Global Environmental Change* 16: 320–2.

Lafferty, W. and Hovden, E. 2003. 'Environmental policy integration: towards an analytical framework', *Environmental Politics* 12(3): 1–22.

Liverman, D. M. and Vilas, S. 2006. 'Neoliberalism and the environment in Latin America', *Annual Review of Environment and Resources* 31: 327–63.

Millennium Ecosystem Assessment 2003. *Ecosystems and Human Wellbeing: A Framework for Assessment.* Washington DC: Island Press.

Millennium Ecosystem Assessment 2005. *Ecosystems and Human Wellbeing: Synthesis.* Washington DC: Island Press.

Muchagata, M. and Brown, K. 2000. 'Colonist farmers' perceptions of fertility and the frontier environment in eastern Amazonia', *Agriculture and Human Values* 17: 371–84.

Naughton-Treves, L., Holland, M. B. and Brandon, K. 2005. 'The role of protected areas in conserving biodiversity and sustaining local livelihoods', *Annual Review of Environment and Resources* 30: 219–52.

O'Brien, K. L. and Leichenko, R. M. 2000. 'Double exposure: assessing the impacts of climate change within the context of economic globalisation', *Global Environmental Change* 10: 221–32.

O'Brien, K. L. and Leichenko, R. M. 2003. 'Winners and losers in the context of global change', *Annals of the Association of American Geographers* 93, 89–103.

Olssen, P. and Folke, C. 2001. 'Local ecological knowledge and institutional dynamics for ecosystem management: a study of Lake Racken watershed, Sweden', *Ecosystems* 4: 85–104.

Ostrom, E. 2005. *Understanding Institutional Diversity.* Princeton University Press.

Pearce, D. and Warford, J. 1993. *World Without End*. Oxford University Press.

Ribot, J. C. 2002. *Democratic Decentralization of Natural Resources: Institutionalizing Popular Participation*. Washington DC: World Resources Institute.

Ribot, J. C. 2006. 'Choose democracy: environmentalists' socio-political responsibility', *Global Environmental Change* 16: 115–19.

Ribot, J. C., Agrawal, A. and Larson, A. M. 2006. 'Recentralizing while decentralizing: how national governments re-appropriate forest resources', Special issue on Rescaling Governance and the Impacts of Political and Environmental Decentralization, *World Development* 34: 1864–86.

Roe, D. 2003. *The Millennium Development Goals: Hitting the Target or Missing the Point?* London: International Institute for Environment and Development.

Sanderson, S. 2005. 'Poverty and conservation: the new century's Peasant Question?' *World Development* 33: 323–32.

Sen, A. 1999. *Development as Freedom*. Oxford University Press.

Steffen, W., Sanderson, A., Tyson, P. D., Jäger, J., Matson, P. A., Moore III, B., Oldfield, F., Richardson, K., Schellnhuber, H. J., Turner II, B. L. and Wasson, R. J. (eds.) 2004. *Global Change and the Earth System: A Planet under Pressure*. Berlin: Springer.

Tompkins, E., Adger, W. N. and Brown, K. 2002. 'Institutional networks for inclusive coastal zone management in Trinidad and Tobago', *Environment and Planning A* 34: 1095–111.

Wells, M. 1992. 'Biodiversity conservation, affluence and poverty: mismatched costs and benefits and efforts to remedy them', *Ambio* 12: 237–43.

World Commission on Environment and Development (WCED) 1987. *Our Common Future*. Oxford University Press.

Young, O. 2006. 'Vertical interplay among scale-dependent environmental and resource regimes', *Ecology and Society* 11(1): 27. URL: www.ecologyandsociety.org/vol11/iss1/art27/.

# PART II

# Governance and Government

# 3 | Governance, government and the pursuit of sustainability

ALBERT WEALE

## Introduction

The sustainability agenda is large and radical. It covers inter-generational justice, resource use, pollution, urban and rural planning, participation, poverty and social inclusion. Faced with such a broad agenda, the political scientist is likely to despair and say that there have to be some boundaries around the concept, otherwise it becomes unworkable. This is too hasty a reaction. Sustainable development is open-textured as a concept but, in some contexts, this is an advantage rather than a handicap. It reminds us that there may be structural flaws of social and political organisation that need to be remedied rather than treating problems as anomalies to be rectified or discrete issues to be addressed. On the other hand, we cannot say something about everything at once. So I shall take the privilege of focusing on one component of sustainable development, namely that concerned with environmental protection, and in particular on the problems of institutional design in environmental governance. Although environmental protection is a necessary, and not a sufficient, condition of moving towards sustainability, we learn something by focusing upon a central case.

How might lessons from political science relate to the theme of sustainability? If any message comes out of the ethics of sustainability, it is that human beings live well when they learn to live within limits. Indeed, it is an error to think that scarcity and limits, in and of themselves, are a form of evil or misfortune. Tennis would be a much less interesting game without the net, even though some of us consistently fail to get our first serves in. Learning the limits of political reform does not stop us re-crafting governance systems for the purposes of sustainability. On the contrary, if our understanding is correct, it enables that crafting to take place more intelligently.

In this chapter, I shall discuss a number of propositions that emerge from the work of political scientists who have studied political processes and the policy institutions related to environmental protection. The type of work referred to here uses the empirical method, seeking to abstract from the specifics of any one detailed policy process to generalise about some features of environmental policy making in general. Usually this method is cross-national comparative in scope, and even national case studies are located implicitly in a theoretical framework that is comparative.

On the principle that something interesting is more likely to arise from bold error rather than safe qualification, I set out my propositions as follows:

1. Governance matters, but so does government.
2. Representation, not participation, is the key problem of environmental policy making.
3. Path-dependence matters, but is not an absolute barrier to policy transfer and innovation.
4. There is more to be said for institutional concentration in the design of environmental ministries than one might think.
5. It is not obvious (to say the least) that environmental policy integration is the right way to secure greater sustainability.

Like other contributors to this book, I have not only been an assiduous reader and admirer of Tim O'Riordan's work, but also on some occasions a co-author. Our collaboration started in the mid 1980s after I arrived at the University of East Anglia as Professor of Politics. Talking one day in 1986, we started to speculate on the importance of two recent administrative reorganisations of pollution control, one in the UK with the creation of Her Majesty's Inspectorate of Pollution, and the other in Germany with the creation of the Environment Ministry. We thought that these two reorganisations were likely to reflect similar pressures towards integrated pollution control, and we decided to apply to the Anglo-German Foundation for a grant to study the processes in more detail. This research led to a number of joint publications (e.g. O'Riordan and Weale, 1989; O'Riordan and Weale, 1990; Weale, O'Riordan and Kramme, 1991). That research showed that our original conjecture was wrong: the reorganisations reflected not only the short-term differences of political context in the two systems but, more importantly, longer-standing differences of policy paradigm and operating style.

Although our collaboration and conversations have lasted over a long time, and although I have always learnt much from what Tim has to say, there is a difference of perspective between our two approaches. I look at the study of environmental politics and policy as a political scientist, interested in finding out how political activity and institutions operate within the field of environmental decision making. In this vein, I am interested in the similarities and differences between environmental policy making and policy making in other domains of public policy. I am also interested in the conditions that make for policy change and development. Tim, by contrast, is interested in the challenge that promoting sustainable development poses to conventional institutions. For him, this challenge means that policy making can no longer be conducted on a business-as-usual basis, whether we are talking about political parties, structures of government or the role of scientific advice. Instead, sustainable development calls for new forms of governance and governing. Asked to sum up this difference of approach, I would adapt the words of Bernard Shaw's St Joan: I look at things as they are and ask 'why?'; Tim looks at things as they might be and asks 'why not?'

The comfortable thing to say about this difference is that these are complementary perspectives. Often this is so. However, there is a sense in which political science has as much claim to be called a dismal science as economics, perhaps even more so. In drawing attention to the way that decision making works and the limits of the feasible, political scientists risk appearing to be wet blankets. Nature is interrelated and complex, say the environmentalists; institutions work best when they have specific and well-defined tasks, say the political scientists. Emerging problems call for new ways of thinking and working, say the environmentalists; patterns of political decision making and behaviour depend on the historical paths that led to current arrangements, say the political scientists. Sustainable development need not be a zero-sum competition between wellbeing and environmental protection, say the environmentalists; never forget that politics is about the choice among competing values, say the political scientists.

These differences of perspective are real and cannot easily be eliminated, but it is possible to go some way towards bridging the divide that Shaw's St Joan identified. The propositions with which I shall be concerned are phrased as lessons of policy advice, principles that policy makers should bear in mind when thinking about institutional reform and design. The propositions are middle-range empirical generalisations about the ways in which institutions work. It would be wrong to take them as law-like generalisations. They are much more in the mode of the old 'advices to princes' literature of which Machiavelli's *The Prince* is the most famous example. In short, I seek to show how the programme for change that emerges from the sustainable development literature can be tempered by some lessons from our understanding of institutions in environmental governance.

## Governance matters but so does government

'Governance' is – as noted in Chapter 1 – one of those words that people feel free to use to cover a wide variety of concerns, and there appear to be as many senses of the term as there are people who use it. Despite this protean usage, there is some value in the term (see Kjær, 2004: 189–91). It points to changes that have taken place in policy making over the last thirty years that alter the character of political relations. In particular, these changes have led to a de-concentration of authority and an increasing complexity in the process of making and enforcing decisions. As part of these broad changes, three features may be picked out.

First, the policy-making process in all industrialised countries has seen an increase in the range of interested parties (now termed 'stakeholders') thought to have legitimate standing in the making of policy decisions, the setting of environmental standards, and the responsibility for taking action. In the UK, these changes are marked by a contrast between a standard-setting system that relied upon the great and the good, as well as the social values embodied in pollution control inspectorates (Ashby and Anderson, 1981: 136), to one lauded by the Royal Commission on Environmental Pollution in its twenty-first report (RCEP, 1998), in which standard setting was expected to be explicit, transparent and based upon an open engagement with public values. In other European countries, the changes are reflected in departures from the old corporatist systems of decision making, whether these new patterns are reflected in the practice of negotiation with target groups, as in the Netherlands (compare Liefferink,

1996; Weale, 1992: chapter 5), the use of innovative consultative mechanisms, as in Denmark, or the use of referendums in decision making, as in Sweden and Switzerland. Though varied in form and effect, the historic assumption was that concentrated patterns of authority produced adequate solutions to the policy problems that political systems faced. To say that there has been a transition from government to governance is a way of saying that this assumption can no longer be made.

Environmental politics is both a cause and a consequence of these changing patterns. It is a cause in so far as the rise of new social movements embodying post-materialist values could not be accommodated in the corporatist and quasi-corporatist patterns of policy making that predominated in Western Europe, the Commonwealth and – in a more complex form – the USA between 1945 and 1975. Politics is, in Schattschneider's (1960) famous phrase, the mobilisation of bias, and if the political struggle is primarily between capital and labour, as was widely assumed during the *trente glorieuses*, then a productivist bias will be built into political decision making to the detriment of the environment. Groups and actors representing other values will, as noted in Chapter 4, need to disrupt this policy structure in order to have their voices heard and their concerns registered, whether these relate to farming, land-use planning, transport or pollution control. In practice, their capacity and need to do so depend specifically upon the institutional details of the ways in which policy was made, as Kitschelt's (1986) contrast between the anti-nuclear movements in Germany and Sweden showed. Yet, whatever the precise details, the development of environmental voice was bound to change the character of the venues within which that voice was articulated.

The second feature of policy making that leads people to speak of governance is the growth of international regimes and the importance of international rule making (see also Chapter 5). Though clearly more than a regime, if less than a federation, the EU exemplifies more than any other body what is involved here. Across its range of operations, the EU exists as a system of authoritative rule making, without its having a government. Instead, the content of EU environmental measures is decided through a vertically and horizontally complex process of decision making, in which a wide variety of actors are involved (see Weale *et al.*, 2000; Zito, 2000; Wurzel, 2002). By contrast with the situation of an elected government, accountability and responsibility in such a multi-level system of governance is diffused rather than locatable in a governing team.

Thirdly, according to a governance perspective, policy making, and even more particularly policy implementation, is a matter of negotiation rather than authoritative imposition. If firms can negotiate the voluntary adoption of pollution control for the imposition of mandated standards, if the internalisation of environmental responsibility takes place in organisations, and tradable permit systems operate to enable individual enterprises to determine their own optimal mix of cost and pollution control, then we are in a world that is more complex than that in which governments are the sole guardians of the public interest.

It is largely an empirical question as to how far these changes mark radical differences in policy making. My own view, for what it is worth, is that enthusiastic proponents of the governance thesis have overemphasised the extent to which governments could rely upon the conventional formal instruments of authority and power during the period that preceded the presumed era of governance. As evidence for this evaluation, one could cite the Robens Committee's report on health and safety at work, published in 1972, which argued that, because of asymmetries of information between regulators and the regulated, it would always be necessary to negotiate compliance and rely upon the internal processes of firms (Committee on Health and Safety at Work, 1972). In other words, the features of policy process that many take to be signs of governance may simply reflect the particular characteristics of the issues being dealt with, not any change in the way in which citizens and corporate actors are governed. Be that as it may, there has been a change in political processes, such that those features associated with governance have become more important. Even with this concession, however, it does not follow that understanding governments, and their role, is any less important. And this is so for a number of reasons.

First, states have the monopoly of the legitimate use of the instrument of taxation. The exceptions, most notably the powers the EU enjoys in respect of its own revenue, qualify but do not overturn this general truth. Although public expenditure may be relatively unimportant in environmental policy, with administrative regulation playing a more important role than in policy sectors like health and social security, taxation is still central in so far as economic instruments are to play a role in environmental policy, as urged by Tim O'Riordan, among others (O'Riordan, 1997). For example, until the last few years, only Singapore used congestion charging effectively as a means of traffic control. In the last few years, the habit has been spreading to places like London and Stockholm. Although the greening of tax systems has a long way to go, the fact that taxation is a potentially important instrument of pollution control and environmental protection means that the institutions that control taxation remain important. Indeed, in a world in which economic policy has come increasingly to rest upon the primacy given to controlling inflation through independent monetary authorities, the control of fiscal policy becomes more important, since it is through fiscal policy that the effects on the real economy of monetary discipline are mediated.

Second, although the rise of international rule making is often said to contribute to the rise of governance and the decline of governments, there are good reasons for concluding the opposite. International agreements often follow the logic of an assurance game, in which the parties are willing to commit themselves to action provided that they can be assured that other states are also willing to commit themselves to action. In that sort of context, participants in any negotiation require that all the parties can credibly commit to an agreed course of action. Pollution control and resource protection agreements are almost paradigm cases of this assurance logic. It makes sense to limit your emissions under the condition that others will also limit their emissions, in a world in which the standard form of agreement is often one of reductions from some baseline figure.

Governments are the parties to these agreements, and they require of other governments some evidence that the measures will be binding upon their populations. If we are looking for an example of how important this feature of international negotiations is, we have only to consider the implications of the failure of the US government to commit itself to the Kyoto targets on climate change and to the institutions and policies relating to climate change. In the absence of a credible commitment by the US government, even those governments most concerned about climate change find it more difficult to take action that threatens the economy – whatever the long-term relationship between economy and environment.

To say that governments are still important in the context of environmental protection is not, then, to deny that processes of government have changed in a way that can be conveniently, if rather too simply, summarised by the idea of the rise of governance. It is certainly not to conceive of the legitimate monopoly of coercive force in a given territorial area as now the most important distinguishing characteristic of the state. It is to say, however, that sometimes the unique and distinctive authority of the state is a vital condition in the achievement of environmental protection.

## Representation, not participation, is the key issue in policy making

Consider a stylised account of the character of policy making before the rise of governance. Suppose we say, with Schumpeter (1954), that a democracy is not a political system in which the people rule, but rather a political system in which the people choose who is to rule them. In these circumstances, governments are formed as a result of processes of party competition, either directly as in first-past-the-post electoral systems or indirectly as in coalition systems. Governments make decisions, balance competing objectives and determine policy initiatives. At the end of their period of office, the electorate judges how good a job they have done and whether some alternative team of office-seekers is likely to do a better job. There are variations one can play on this story, for example relating to how well or badly electoral competition mediates between government and people and the extent of party identification and loyalty among the mass electorate. Nevertheless, as an account of democratic authority, the story is relatively clear.

Implicit in this account of party competition for office through elections is an account of political representation. The notion of representation can be given various senses (Pitkin, 1967) but, cutting a long story short, the Schumpeterian account of democracy conceives of governing parties as authorised (one sense of representation) to act in the substantive interests (another sense of representation) usually in a way that is responsive to the preferences or opinions (a third sense of representation) of their electorate. It is important in this story that parties, unlike interest or cause groups, have a programme, that is to say a set of policy commitments across the whole range of public policy. To be a potential government is to be willing to confront not just the issues on which you have something distinctive to say, but any issue that may come up for decision or evaluation.

The Schumpeterian account of democracy has been contested in normative terms for many years, on the grounds that it gives an impoverished sense to the notion of citizenship. Judged by the standards of the (highly idealised) Athenian *polis*, which is often taken to be the benchmark in normative democratic theory, a Schumpeterian account of democracy seems to set low standards of performance and aspiration for citizens. But as a description, rather than a prescription, it seems to work relatively well – but for one thing. Schumpeter notoriously argued that in a well-functioning democracy, there should be 'no back-seat driving'. On this account, the articulation of interests and viewpoints between elections, activities that are the core tasks of interest and cause groups, are a pathology of democracy rather than an essential element of its functioning.

This view has only to be stated for it to be seen to be inadequate for developed democracies, both descriptively and normatively. All such democracies contain procedures for governments to consult on matters of public policy and proposed initiatives. This is not to say that these mechanisms work well. Tim O'Riordan's own study of the Sizewell B Inquiry (O'Riordan *et al.*, 1988) highlighted some of the problems associated with trust, agenda setting and control of information. But, whatever the defects, it is impossible to give an account of the legitimacy of modern democracy without acknowledging the central place of regular processes of public consultation and procedures for members of the public to influence governments between elections.

What has happened in the last thirty years, partly as a result of the criticisms that Tim O'Riordan (2004) and others have mounted, as well as such experiences as the Brent Spar episode, is an attempt to invigorate and innovate in the sphere of public consultation and involvement. The disillusionment with conventional forms of public consultation has coincided with an enormous amount of innovation in the techniques of public consultation, including planning forums, citizens' juries, deliberative polls, consensus conferences and the like. The effect of this thinking and innovation has been especially marked in the UK, where in recent years a great deal of experimental activity has taken place designed to improve methods of consultation and communication. The 1998 report of the Royal Commission on Environmental Pollution can be taken as a *paean* of praise to these initiatives and an encouragement to develop them even further.

This is not the place to raise questions of general evaluation over new forms of public consultation, but there is one issue to which I wish to draw attention, and that is the question of representation. Methods of public consultation are often described in terms of their being modes of citizen participation, and in a literal sense this is true, since they typically afford an opportunity for any member of the public to contribute towards policy deliberation. However, the proportion of the population that is, or could be, feasibly involved even on major issues is vanishingly small. Except where referendums are used, as in Switzerland on genetic modification or Sweden on nuclear power, it is simply wrong to treat consultation primarily as a mode of general participation. Rather, what happens is that professionally organised interest and cause groups use the means of public involvement to advance their own policy proposals and solutions.

There is, of course, nothing wrong with organised groups using consultation processes to advance their aims. Indeed, they would not be doing their job if they did anything else. However, the practice does raise important questions about representation. These questions are most acutely raised in EU environmental decision making, since an important part of the organised environmental constituency, in the form of the European Environment Bureau, is paid for or supported by the Commission. This being so, it can hardly be the case that the institutions of governance are in dialogue with representatives of civil society, since there is no connection or process of authorisation that empowers those groups to speak on behalf of the wider society (see Greenwood, 2007). Since the EU cannot be characterised as a system of party government, the decision-making system seems more of an echo chamber than an instantiation of dialogue or democratic deliberation.

One problem here, I conjecture, is the nature of environmental protection as an issue. One striking feature of environmental politics is the contrast between the public salience of environmental protection in general terms (these issues move people to action or to the streets) and the technical nature of much detailed policy making. Moreover, for political parties the environment is a valence, rather than positional, issue. That is to say, all parties tend to adopt the rhetoric of being in favour of environmental protection, so that it is difficult to institutionalise political debate about the relative merits of different political positions, by comparison, for example, with discussions about the relative merits of low taxation and the standards of public services. In short, it is difficult politically to represent competing views about environmental protection through the conventional methods of party competition. Neither the process of party representation nor the processes of functional representation appear to work very well.

## Path-dependence matters, but is not an absolute barrier to policy transfer and innovation

In recent years, policy analysts have shown a great deal of interest in the phenomenon of path-dependence in institutional design. Path-dependence exists when an institutional arrangement at one point of time makes it more likely that a similar or related institutional arrangement will exist at a later point in time, even when there is no functional need for the similarity. Institutions are stickier than they are functionally required to be.

A simple example will illustrate the point. Consider a legislature elected by a system of first-past-the-post. Such a rule of election makes it less likely that the electoral system will be changed in the direction of proportional representation, even when there are good reasons for doing so, since elected representatives acquire an interest in the rule remaining in place. The original selection of the first-past-the-post system will have had an arbitrary element to it, but once the institution is established, positive feedback mechanisms exist that reinforce its stability. These feedback processes are the reason why Pierson (2000) links path-dependence to the idea of increasing returns to scale. Just as once a firm has established an initial advantage it may not be vulnerable to competition because it can consolidate its position as it grows, so political institutions may not be amenable to change because of the political incentives they contain.

Empirical instances along these lines are familiar in the study of environmental policy from the 'national policy styles' literature (e.g. Richardson, 1982; Vogel, 1986). In that literature, national policy systems were seen to be characterised by distinctive institutional styles, reflecting features of their characteristic modes of operation. For example, the UK's style of policy making was seen to be informal, closed to public participation, placing a heavy emphasis upon scientific advice and committed to flexibility. The style of the USA or Germany, by contrast, was seen to be formal, rigid, dominated by legal processes and modes of reasoning, and more willing to mandate technologically feasible solutions, even when they were expensive in cost–benefit terms.

One reason why path-dependence in this sense might exist follows from the logic of comparative advantage. Comparative advantage refers to the idea that where two countries make similar products it is rational for each to concentrate its production in that line in which it has a comparative advantage. Total output is maximised by each country producing more of the commodity in which its production costs are lower. The cost of wine production in France is lower than that in Finland. It may also be that the cost of producing mobile phones is lower in France than in Finland. But if the relative advantage of France in the wine sector is greater (as I suppose it to be), it will still pay France to concentrate more resources in wine production, purchasing mobile phones from Finland. When countries follow the logic of comparative advantage in this way, the composition of output will differ from nation to nation depending on the relative costs of production.

There are analogues to this idea of comparative advantage in environmental policy. Consider a situation in which policy makers in one country can rely upon a higher level of voluntary compliance with an environmental policy strategy than they could do in another country. Since voluntary activity is cost-free, it follows that societies with higher levels of environmental awareness among citizens can dispense with administrative and political control more readily. Some might find it a paradox in this connection that it is in those societies with the highest levels of public consciousness about environmental problems, for example in Scandinavia, that we also find the most elaborate legislative and administrative arrangements. However, the sense of paradox is weakened once we realise that even those who are most ready to comply voluntarily with measures of environmental protection will need the assurance that their efforts will not be exploited by others less scrupulous than themselves.

Path-dependence may also arise from the logic of policy information as a transnational public good. If the US Environmental Protection

Agency is willing to go to the trouble of producing published toxicity estimates for chemical compounds, then there is no need for other countries to undertake the same effort. Consequently, we would expect to find some politico-institutional technology in the US that we would not find elsewhere. Here we have an example of an Olsonian process (Olson, 1965), in which a 'large' actor finds it advantageous to produce a public good for a group, even when the other members of that group do not bear any share of the costs of production of that good, a phenomenon that Olson labelled as the exploitation of the large by the small. (It is, of course, still consistent with this phenomenon for there to be an under-supply of the relevant public good, a situation borne out by the paucity of toxicity information for many chemicals.)

Although these pressures towards persistent national differences undoubtedly exist, they should not be taken to imply that there are rigid constraints on the extent to which policy approaches can be innovative or adapted from other systems. One reason for this is that functional effectiveness – or rather the lack thereof – will often lead policy makers to understand that some policy instruments work well for some problems but not for others. For example, the control of pollution through administrative regulation is likely to be more effective when dealing with stationary sources than when dealing with dispersed sources. Thus, the administrative regulation of a factory discharging waste to water or to air is likely to be more effective than it would be to use the same instrument to control the behaviour of domestic gardeners using pesticides or fertilisers (to the extent to which it is not possible to impose on manufacturers an absolute ban on the use of certain substances). These generalisations hold in a variety of circumstances. Thus, when societies face a range of common problems, we should not expect effective governance arrangements to vary, and when they do they will come under pressure from those who are concerned with issues of effectiveness.

In any case, the claim that there are distinctive national styles of regulation needs considerable qualification. There are significant differences of style among different regulatory sectors within national systems. Secondly, styles can change. The transformation of policy systems towards new modes of governance, including such matters as innovation in public participation, illustrates features where historical traditions and the incentives they create can lose their grip. (Indeed, even in the field of electoral rules there have been significant changes in a number of countries in recent years.) Thirdly, the spread of particular policy technologies in the environmental sector – most notably environmental impact assessment (Taylor, 1984) – shows how ideas from one national system can be taken up and adapted by others.

From this analysis, there is both bad and good news. The bad news is that policy transfer and adaptation may well be quite difficult, even when institutions are ostensibly trying to do the same thing. Consider the question of whether it is possible somehow to merge high German environmental standards and British pragmatism in the making of EU environmental policy. The actress Isadora Duncan once proposed to Bernard Shaw that they had a child together on the grounds that, with his brains and her looks, it would be a wonderful specimen. Shaw declined the offer with the words, 'Ah, madam, but suppose it had my looks and your brains.' Similarly, many people might like to see a mixture of German standards and British pragmatism in EU environmental policy. But suppose we ended up with British standards and German pragmatism?

The good news is that, despite these variations, we can derive some lessons of a general kind from comparative analysis, provided that we focus on issues of functional effectiveness and ask how well institutions are adapted to perform the tasks that we need them to perform. In the next section, I look at one issue under this general heading.

## There is more to be said for institutional concentration than many analysts have said

I have already noted that Tim and I started our joint work by considering an issue of organisational form and structure. How best, in terms of the tasks that they had to pursue, should environmental policy institutions be organised? Note that even thinking this an important question reinforces the importance of government, rather than just governance, since it is governmental administrative institutions that are of concern.

If we compare institutional arrangements across Europe, there is great diversity at the level of national governments in the way that environmental protection functions are brigaded, so that the concentration of environmental policy functions differs considerably (Weale *et al.*, 2000: chapter 6). By a function, I mean an activity carried out to achieve particular purposes. Examples of functions in this sense include: controlling polluting discharges to water, air or soil; regulating the marine environment; developing policy on environmental impact assessments; formulating policies on alternative policy instruments; conducting or commissioning research on environmental problems; or controlling radioactive emissions. Although there is a tendency over time towards the concentration of environmental functions, the degree of concentration so far obtained owes as much to the political circumstances of national governments as it does to the inherent logic of environmental policy integration.

Although there is no one right pattern, there is a strong case for the concentration of environmental functions in a single ministry. This helps build and strengthen the existing administrative capacity of environmental ministries and agencies. This is important in Mediterranean Europe, where existing ministries are often new, as in Spain, or have relatively low political status. In the past, the Directorate General for the Environment in the European Commission took steps to build administrative capacity by promoting exchanges of administrators, but this process can clearly go further. But the problem is not simply one for the South. There have been rumours at different times of a break-up of the Dutch environment ministry, and in the UK the merging of the transport and environment ministries into one 'super-ministry' in 1997 encountered the problem of diluting the environmental orientation of the whole (Jordan, 2002).

In proposing a concentration of functions I am not advocating that it would be sensible for environment ministries to engage in long and costly turf disputes with other ministries (disputes which they might not win) in order to wrest more formal powers for themselves. But there is a public interest in ensuring that certain functions are carried out competently within an organisation centrally committed to the task of environmental protection. Among these functions, I would rank the following as the most important: standard setting in the light of an informed understanding of the relevant science; compliance monitoring; and policy evaluation and analysis. Although the first of these is normally well developed, the second and third are often less central.

Paradoxically, the desire to concentrate environmental functions in a ministry may lead to a lowering of its status. This effect arises because lack of concentration can arise in one of two ways: some environmental functions are not in the environment ministry; and some non-environmental functions are in the environment ministry. So, creating a genuinely concentrated environment ministry may lower its status. In the case of the German reorganisation that Tim and I studied, for example, it was sometimes argued that moving environmental functions out of the Interior Ministry weakened the environmental cause because the new ministry was of relatively low status. Despite these consequences, my own judgement would be that in the longer term it is worth concentrating functions.

The strongest argument I know against the attempt to concentrate environmental functions in one ministry is based on the observation that environmental questions are subject to the issue attention cycle, an observation on which Edda Müller (1986) has built in her study of environmental administration in Germany. Summarising a very complex study, Müller argues that the concentration of environmental functions in an environment ministry will strengthen the hand of environmental policy makers when the issue attention cycle is high, but weaken it when it is low. Despite the wealth of empirical detail with which Müller illustrates this position, its basic logic is quite simple: on its own, an environment ministry is quite weak when there is little public pressure, since its political status is not high; but when there is public pressure, environmental concerns will be compromised with the demands of a large ministry if functions are located in a non-specialist ministry.

The logic of Müller's argument certainly persuades me, but its implications for principles of institutional design are not clear. Certainly it is not possible to assemble and disassemble environmental functions in a ministry depending on the stages of the issue attention cycle. The organisation of environmental functions is the sort of question that is settled only once in a while, and a decision has to be made, bearing in mind that public attention will wax and wane. This conclusion also runs counter to the view that I have often heard expressed by well-intentioned environmental policy makers, namely that they will know that they are doing their job when there is no more need for an environment ministry. This thought brings us on to the issue of environmental policy integration.

## Policy integration is not the right way to secure environmental improvements

It is a truism that environmental damage is a by-product of otherwise legitimate activities, such as industry, agriculture and transport. There is a tendency to infer from this fact that the best way to think about environmental policy is as an integrated component of all other public policies. Yet, we at least ought to consider the extent to which success in environmental policy depends upon policy makers being able to focus on achieving a specific policy outcome.

It is usually very difficult for policy analysts to detect the outputs of policy measures, since so many variables intervene between action and consequence that attributing causality is difficult. However, the German Large Combustion Plant Ordinance of 1983 is an exception to this rule. Within a few years of its implementation there was a sharp decline in sulphur dioxide emissions per head. For a policy analyst finding it difficult to identify policy outputs, let alone policy outcomes, the German policy is very striking. To be sure, simply focusing upon this success ignores complicated side-effects. For example, the installation of flue-gas desulphurisation equipment in German power stations led to a problem of how to dispose of the gypsum sludge that was a by-product of some of the processes (see Weale *et al.*, 1991). This is not simply an economic problem; it is also an environmental problem. However, it is here that we are likely to come up against the limitations on attention spans that standard operating procedures impose on policy makers, not to mention the fact that the wider the range of consequences you include in your policy calculus, the more ammunition you give to potential opponents of the policy. The environmental implications of flue-gas desulphurisation were among the reasons that opponents of clean air policy in the UK gave for not adopting stringent controls on acid emissions.

A second example is that of Dutch water pollution charges. As Mikael Skou Andersen (1994) has shown in his comparative study, the Dutch approach has led to significant reductions in polluting emissions, and this seems largely to have been accomplished by a combination of the deterrent effect of the charges and the positive effect of recycling the revenues into clean technologies. An important feature of this example, therefore, is getting away from the complications of designing charges that strike some optimal balance between economic cost and pollution control but instead going for improvements that are technically feasible through the incentive provided by charges.

My third example is taken from the USA and is based on Ronald B. Outen's (1987) contrast between two pieces of US legislation: the 1972 Clean Water Act and the Toxic Substances Control Act. These two pieces of legislation operate on the basis of different decision criteria. The first requires the removal of pollutants from waste streams into water just when it is technically and economically feasible to do so. The second requires an elaborate balancing of risks and benefits to the environment from any particular decision. Outen, at least, is convinced that, whereas the first has been relatively successful, the second has not really succeeded in removing pollutants from the environment.

From these examples, what can we infer about the general conditions for the success of environmental policies? Inference is, of course, always difficult, and these are only three examples. But they are taken from widely differing administrative and political contexts, so if there is anything to learn it is likely to reflect some general underlying features of administrative behaviour. In my view, what these examples share is that they involved concentrated attention upon a limited range of problems in cases where technical solutions were known to exist or could reasonably be anticipated in future years. The narrowing of attention span means that the target becomes tangible and the technical possibilities mean that all it is necessary to do is assemble the resources – and normally also the political will – to put money into the relevant technical investments.

Critics of this approach will say that it is too narrowly focused. Precisely because environmental problems arise as the by-product of otherwise legitimate activities, it is necessary to think of environmental policy as a dimension of the full span of public policy. The difficulty here, however, is fundamental, and it can be brought out by considering the obvious analogy, namely financial control of public expenditure. Why was the UK Treasury a traditionally powerful department, even before Gordon Brown's long tenure in office? The answer is that it is the department with the responsibility for imposing financial discipline on the spending of all other departments. In other words, it can impose its mandate across the full range of government departments. The technology of control is in principle quite simple (though obviously complex in practice): the allocation of a cash budget. Under the rule that departments cannot spend what they have not been authorised to spend, the Treasury can go on to assert influence over the content of a whole range of policies.

In principle, why could not the same happen with a more powerful environment department asserting control over the extent to which departments consumed or imposed stress upon natural resources? The answer is that such a department would lack the essential instrument of control, namely something equivalent to the simple measuring rod of money. The situation for our hypothetical powerful environment ministry would be akin to that of the Treasury up to the mid 1970s when it sought to supplement its financial control with control over real resources in terms of volume planning (the number of beds per patient, the number of teachers per pupil and so on). The system collapsed because it was not possible to assert control over such a diverse list of items. Cash limits, though crude, are good at controlling cash but, like Oscar Wilde's cynic, those who operate them may know the price of everything but the value of nothing. With natural resources, it is precisely their value that is important.

## Conclusions

If I have been successful in my argument, I can be brief in my conclusions. Government matters. The traditional concern of democratic government with representation matters. Institutions of governments are products of the past, but are not trapped in the legacy of the past. The organisation of government matters. The chosen form of policy matters.

I do not anticipate that Tim O'Riordan will necessarily disagree with any of these claims. I think he will want to say, however, that a broader range of things also matter – including empowering the weak and disadvantaged, securing a more holistic public culture, and reorientating the vision of the scientific community. I agree. But it is not that I think that politics is only the art of the possible, since sometimes politics is about making things possible that are not thought to be so. Yet is there not also a case for saying that if we understand institutions and their limits, we shall reform them more successfully, even if the reforms seem less radical?

# References

Andersen, M. S. 1994. *Governance by Green Taxes*. Manchester, UK: Manchester University Press.

Ashby, E. and Anderson, M. 1981. *The Politics of Clean Air*. Oxford, UK: Clarendon.

Committee on Health and Safety at Work 1972. *Report*. London: HMSO.

Greenwood, J. 2007. 'Organized civil society and democratic legitimacy in the European Union', *British Journal of Political Science* 37: 333–57.

Jordan, A. J. 2002. *The Europeanization of British Environmental Policy*. Basingstoke, UK: Palgrave.

Kitschelt, H. 1986. 'Political opportunity structures and political protest: anti-nuclear movements in four democracies', *British Journal of Political Science* 16: 57–85.

Kjær, A. M. 2004. *Governance*. Cambridge, UK: Polity Press.

Liefferink, D. 1996. *Environment and the Nation State: The Netherlands, the European Union and Acid Rain*. Manchester, UK: Manchester University Press.

Müller, E. 1986. *Innenwelt der Umwelpolitik*. Opladen, Germany: Westdeutscher.

O'Riordan, T. (ed.) 1997. *Ecotaxation*. London, UK: Earthscan.

O'Riordan, T. 2004. 'Environmental science, sustainability and politics', *Transactions of the Institute of British Geography* 29: 234–47.

O'Riordan, T. and Weale, A. 1989. 'Administrative reorganisation and policy change', *Public Administration* 67: 277–94.

O'Riordan, T. and Weale, A. 1990. *Greening the Machinery of Government*. London, UK: Friends of the Earth.

O'Riordan, T., Kemp, R. and Purdue, M. 1988. *Sizewell B: The Anatomy of a Decision*. Basingstoke, UK: Macmillan.

Olson, M. 1965. *The Logic of Collective Action*. Cambridge, MA: Harvard University Press.

Outen, R. B. 1987. 'Environmental pollution laws and the architecture of tobacco road', in Committee on Multimedia Approaches to Pollution Control, *Multimedia Approaches to Pollution Control: A Symposium Proceedings*. Washington DC: National Academy Press, pp. 139–43.

Pierson, Paul 2000. 'Increasing returns, path dependence, and the study of politics', *American Political Science Review* 94: 251–67.

Pitkin, H. 1967. *The Concept of Representation*. Berkeley, CA: University of California Press.

RCEP (Royal Commission on Environmental Pollution) 1998. *Setting Environmental Standards: Twenty-first Report*. London, UK: HMSO.

Richardson, J. J. (ed.) 1982. *Policy Styles in Western Europe*. London, UK: George Allen and Unwin.

Schattschneider, E. E. 1960. *The Semi-Sovereign People: A Realistic View of Democracy in America*. New York: Holt, Rinehart and Winston.

Schumpeter, J. A. 1954. *Capitalism, Socialism and Democracy* (First edition 1943). London, UK: Allen and Unwin.

Taylor, S. 1984. *Making Bureaucracies Think*. Palo Alto, CA: Stanford University Press.

Vogel, D. 1986. *National Styles of Regulation*. Ithaca, NY: Cornell University Press.

Weale, A. 1992. *The New Politics of Pollution*. Manchester, UK: Manchester University Press.

Weale, A., O'Riordan, T. and Kramme, L. 1991. *Controlling Pollution in the Round*. London, UK: Anglo-German Foundation.

Weale, A., Pridham, G., Cini, M., Konstadakopulos, D., Porter, M. and Flynn, B. 2000. *Environmental Governance in Europe*. Oxford, UK: Oxford University Press.

Wurzel, R. K. W. 2002. *Environmental Policy-Making in Britain, Germany and the European Union: The Europeanisation of Air and Water Pollution Control*. Manchester, UK: Manchester University Press.

Zito, A. 2000. *Creating Environmental Policy in the European Union*. New York: Palgrave.

# 4 How do environmental actors make governance systems more sustainable? The role of politics and ideas in policy change

PHILIP LOWE AND KATY WILKINSON

## Introduction

Opening up fields of economic management to forms of environmental planning that are publicly accountable is a critical aspect of the transition of society towards sustainable development. But this is not an easy or straightforward task for those seeking to govern society. Indeed it has been at the core of environmental politics since the 1970s. As Carter (2001: 162, 191) remarks, 'the structural power of producer interests in capitalist society' means that 'more often than not, the interests of producer groups trump those of environmental groups, and economic growth takes priority over environmental protection'. In this chapter, we address the question of what viable options are available to environmental groups to fundamentally alter the unequal terms of these encounters in governing systems, and thus make sustainable governance a more realistic possibility.

We do so by examining the repeated efforts of one group – the Campaign to Protect Rural England or CPRE – to penetrate the inner workings of the agriculture policy sector – or community – in the UK. What is unusual about the CPRE is that, as a reasonably well-resourced and well-established environmental group, it has persistently sought to defeat the agriculture policy community since the 1970s. In its own self-estimation, it was 'one of the first environmental organisations to challenge the assumption that farming was a natural conservator of a beautiful countryside' (CPRE Policy Committee 23 July 1992 Appendix A, para. 5). Its experience therefore allows us a unique opportunity to reconsider not only the intransigence of such policy communities in governance systems but also theories about the way in which pressure groups adjust their strategies and tactics in relation to the structural challenges they face. Both these issues are absolutely central to any discussion of governance for sustainable development.

Using press releases, qualitative interviews and the CPRE's own archival documents, we present a longitudinal analysis of the interaction between the CPRE, government and producer interests over the past eighty years. The agricultural sector is an excellent arena in which to explore the interlinked themes of governance and sustainable development. Carter (2001: 176) suggests that 'the agriculture sector provides the classic illustration of how policy communities have hampered the development of sustainable environmental policies'. The agriculture policy community, comprising producer and state interests, is a closed one which, it is suggested, has persistently ignored, marginalised, deflected or neutralised environmental concerns. A number of studies have examined the ability of the agriculture policy community to rebuff the efforts of environmental and consumer groups to get new issues on to the agricultural agenda (Cox *et al.*, 1986; Smith, 1990; Glasbergen, 1992; Lowe *et al.*, 1997). As crises (most notably disease outbreaks) in the agriculture sector have attracted public attention to the narrow range of interests represented in the policy process, governments over the past twenty years or so have attempted to broaden the scope of interest group and stakeholder consultations. Many more opportunities now exist for groups such as the CPRE to engage with policy makers and routinely participate in policy formation. Not only do non-state actors bring legitimacy to policy making by ensuring the representation of different viewpoints, but their incorporation into the policy process may help to ensure broad support for particular policies. Decision makers now recognise that 'environmental groups both represent and help form public opinion on environmental issues and their views should therefore be taken into account' (Rawcliffe, 1998: 6). Throughout the past decade, such groups have taken on an additional role in policy delivery and implementation, in the movement towards participative governance (see Chapter 1). An additional aim of this chapter is to explore the ability of the CPRE to exploit these emerging opportunities in order to promote sustainable governance.

## The context dependency of pressure group strategies

How do pressure groups respond to and shape the context in which they operate? Grant's account of the relationship between pressure group status and tactics was the first to gain wide currency in the literature. Dividing pressure groups into 'insider' and 'outsider' categories according to their perceived influence over policy outcomes, he suggested that those characterised as 'outsiders' could be further distinguished: between those that wished to gain insider status; and those that were 'ideological outsiders' unwilling to be drawn into the policy community (Grant, 1989: 15–16). Implicit is the assumption that groups can gain access to policy makers through a change of tactic; that by abandoning confrontational stances, and assuming a degree of responsibility, they may 'earn' a place in the circle of influence over policy.

This assumption was subsequently criticised by Marsh and Rhodes (1992), who suggested that it actually confused status and tactics. Groups might assume 'insider' tactics in the hope of gaining access, but this was no guarantee of success, as policy networks refined their own mechanisms for exclusion and management of dissenting groups: 'policy networks do not necessarily seek to frustrate any and all change but to contain, constrain, redirect and ride-out such change, thereby materially affecting its speed and direction' (Rhodes and Marsh, 1992: 195–6). Groups therefore seldom achieved access in a simple and direct process of negotiation and switch of tactics. The ability of policy networks to manage external pressures depended on their internal cohesiveness, argued Marsh and Rhodes, and they adopted the terms 'policy community' and 'issue network' to distinguish between closed, stable associations of pressure groups and looser, more volatile networks of interests (Marsh and Rhodes, 1992: 251).

The evident flaw in Marsh and Rhodes's typology was the difficulty in objectively determining whether any given policy network is either a policy community or an issue network. This is exacerbated by the increasing use of consultation lists which give the appearance of involving a large array of groups in the policy formation process, while in reality very few may be heeded (Maloney *et al.*, 1994). Nevertheless, their assertion that groups cannot simply gain access to policy makers by deliberate tactical measures is one which has been taken up and elaborated. It is argued that the farming unions consciously brought about the effective exclusion of potentially opposing groups through the depoliticisation of agricultural issues and the creation of a monopoly of technical expertise (Smith, 1992, 1993).

Even if it is accepted that pressure groups cannot simply adopt a particular strategy in order to gain access to policy networks, it is still necessary to account for changes in pressure group behaviour over time, including forms of strategy change, as well as the phenomenon of previously excluded groups gaining footholds in closed policy communities. Marsh and Smith proposed a resolution that characterised the relationship between groups and networks as dialectical, defined as 'an interactive relationship ... in which each affects the other in a continuing iterative process' (Marsh and Smith, 2000: 5). They see three key relationships: between the structure of the policy network and the agents within it; between the network and the context in which it operates; and between the network and the policy outcome. Agents in a policy network bring strategic knowledge to the structured context, which shapes the actions of other agents in the network. However, the process is one of almost constant iteration, as these actions in turn affect both the agents' strategic knowledge and the structured context (Marsh and Smith, 2000: 5). The novel aspect of Marsh and Smith's argument is that they favour neither structure nor agency as the dominant determinant of the policy network composition or the policy outcomes that it produces. Each dialectical relationship is potentially of equal importance.

Richardson (2000) takes an alternative approach, highlighting the determinant effect of the policy network context on the strategy and behaviour of the agents within it. Pressure group behaviour is modified by changes to the policy network in which it is attempting to operate. These changes may be structural factors affecting the operation of governmental 'machinery' and the avenues of communication and decision making. Alternatively, they may involve the climate of receptivity among public or governmental audiences to the ideas and objectives of the policy network. Richardson differs from both Grant and Marsh and Smith in de-emphasising the scope for actors to directly affect the policy network context, suggesting that they are instead obliged to react to the opportunities arising from institutional or paradigmatic change, modifying their objectives in order to achieve wider acceptance of their policy priorities.

Richardson identifies three major causes of change in the 'climate' for pressure group action, and four forms that pressure group responses may take. The main causes are advances in knowledge, changes in party leadership, and movements in public opinion. As a result of these, the government may seek to frame policy problems in new ways – a process complicated by the tendency towards inter-linking policy sectors which typically results in:

a degree of 'overcrowding' of each, hitherto autonomous, policy sector as stakeholders from other policy communities demand and get entry. Policy communities and networks may become linked in a rather messy and unpredictable chain of actors, who do not know each other well and who do not speak the same 'language' (Richardson, 2000: 1008).

The dynamics of the network change as previously favoured groups lose their influence, and those who were previously 'outsiders' are able to provide newly required expertise or may simply have found more favourable ground for their ideas. The emergence of new groups and the linking of policy sectors produce new perspectives on policy debates which may sweep through different policy sectors. One example of what Richardson refers to as a 'policy virus' was the spread of Thatcherite ideas of public management in the 1980s.

The four responses that the groups within the network can adopt are as follows. The first is to accept their own demise and leave the network (Richardson, 2000: 1019). A less drastic step, secondly, is to seek alternative venues: whether they be institutional ones, such as other government departments, the law courts or, increasingly, the European Union (EU); or venues of expression, such as the use of direct action or media appeals by groups seeking to garner attention for their ideas that formal channels no longer offer. For groups wishing to remain in the policy network in the face of a policy virus, the critical consideration is:

the degree to which new ideas and knowledge can be accommodated in existing and agreed policy frames … or whether completely new frames emerge, backed by new adversarial coalitions (Richardson, 2000: 1018).

Thus, thirdly, pressure groups may adapt their goals to fit the virus, effectively making concessions to the new direction of the policy network in the hope of incremental progress that will benefit their own objectives in the long term. Fourthly, they may seek to adapt the virus to suit their own policy goals, though Richardson acknowledges that this is a more difficult task (Richardson, 2000: 1019).

## The greening of agriculture: a case study of the CPRE

### *The origins of the CPRE and its early attitude towards agriculture*

The CPRE was established in 1926 as the Council for the Preservation of Rural England, a London-based group comprising a small number of intellectuals, members of the artistic establishment, and the landed aristocracy (Lowe *et al.*, 1986: 12). It sought to draw in a range of organisations concerned over the future of the countryside including, for example, the National Farmers' Union (NFU) and the Country Landowners' Association (CLA). Throughout the inter-war period, the group campaigned against ribbon development, roadside advertisements, and uncontrolled urban expansion, though remaining largely a 'propaganda' group (Allison, 1975: 117). County-based groups were set up and became affiliated, giving the parent CPRE coverage of most of rural England.

The most influential piece of legislation for the CPRE was the 1947 Town and Country Planning Act, which established a framework for local authorities to plan and regulate the use and development of land and buildings. The definition of 'development' specifically excluded 'the use of any land for the purposes of agriculture or forestry (including afforestation), and the use for any of those purposes of any building occupied together with the land so used'. These exemptions for agriculture occasioned no dispute at the time they were formulated, reflecting the romantic view of farming held by the rural preservationists and the overriding commitment of the government to the expansion of domestic food production.

Agriculture had been in a chronic state of depression since the 1880s, and farming practices seemed to pose no threat to other rural interests and pursuits. On the contrary, it was felt that the debilitated condition of farming exacerbated many other threats to the countryside, such as urban encroachment, the decline of rural communities and the flight from the land. Not only was the countryside under attack from the towns, but rural life was disintegrating from within. A secure and revitalised farming industry was seen as the essential guardian of both the social life and the natural beauty of the countryside. As a later director of the CPRE reflected, there was 'an apparent consensus founded on the belief that those who farm and own and afforest rural

Britain are also its best conservationists' (Hall, 1981: 10). This
sentiment was shared by policy makers, the NFU and the CPRE alike,
and hence a key function of the 1947 Act was to protect the countryside
from urban development.

Few people anticipated the rapid transformation in agricultural
practices which was to occur in the post-war period. Agricultural
intensification, fostered as a national economic priority by post-war
governments and realised through the adoption of new chemical and
breeding technologies, the spread of mechanisation and the consoli-
dation of holdings, began to transform the rural environment. As the
scale of this revolution in agriculture gradually became apparent,
there was an enlargement of the CPRE's focus from urban and
industrial pressures as the main threat to landscape and wildlife to a
preoccupation with the destructive effects of changing farming and
forestry practices and technologies. One of their first successes came as
a response to the introduction of factory production methods, particularly broiler houses, from the mid 1950s onwards, which drew
attention to the anomaly whereby industrial-type buildings – often
badly sited and of poor design – could be erected without any form of
consultation if intended for agricultural use. Agricultural intensification
also pressed more and more upon marginal land, as new technology
and grants from the Ministry of Agriculture encouraged the improvement of land which had previously been relatively unproductive
through, say, fertilisation or drainage. The CPRE also began to press
for powers to control agricultural land-use change in protected areas –
for example, it sought unsuccessfully to amend the Countryside Act
1968 during its passage through Parliament, to give national park
authorities power to control moorland conversion.

## The 1970s: modern environmentalism

It was not until the 1970s that the concept of agricultural change
having a transforming effect upon the rural landscape was fully
grasped. Prior to this time, the CPRE had responded to the gathering
environmental problems of modern agriculture in an *ad hoc* manner.
In other words, it sought to bring successive problems (industrial-type
farm buildings, big silos, moorland reclamation, etc.) into a policy
domain – land-use planning – where it and its values were entrenched.
Nevertheless, the successes of new and more radical environmental

groups such as Greenpeace and Friends of the Earth introduced the possibility of alternative courses of action, including direct action and a more confrontational stance that questioned the premises of policy. The then director of the CPRE, Chris Hall, remarked that the success of such 'deep green' organisations meant that the CPRE was able and 'ready to challenge the growth assumptions' underlying government programmes 'in a way that would have been unthinkable four of five years ago' (Hall, 1976: 175).

However, the CPRE faced its own image problem: the new style of environmental politics, more popular and more radical, made the CPRE's respectability and behind-the-scenes lobbying appear 'staid and aloof' (Lowe and Pye-Smith, 1980: 3). In reaction, the group increasingly emphasised its own green credentials. Its policies became more bold, none more so than with respect to agriculture. The CPRE put forward a proposal for a comprehensive notification system whereby farmers would have to give notice to the local planning authority of any intention to alter the landscape substantially.

The group was encouraged to formulate a more direct challenge to the policy imperatives driving agricultural intensification. When the Ministry of Agriculture held an unprecedented public inquiry in 1978 into a controversial project to drain grazing marshes at Amberley Wild Brooks in West Sussex, the CPRE fielded an economist who forcefully and successfully challenged the economic rationale of the grant-aided scheme as well as its environmental repercussions. The CPRE's triumph led it to question 'the impact upon the countryside of contemporary farming methods and the economic imperatives from which they spring' (CPRE Annual Report 1978: 3). However, to pursue an economic critique of farming subsidies required a significant shift in the CPRE's lobbying strategy, away from its heartland – the operation of the town and country planning system, where it was an insider – to the unfamiliar realm of agriculture policy.

## The 1980s: penetrating agriculture policy and responding to Thatcherism

The importance of gaining access to the agriculture policy community was great, as 'failure to be closely involved with policy formation in the crucial initial stages within the central departments of government often means that conservation groups are later faced with an uphill campaign against a course of action to which officials, ministers and major interests have become committed' (Lowe *et al.*, 1986: 125). However, agriculture policy at this time was subject to neo-corporatist political management in which the main producer organisations were entrenched in state structures. Such arrangements were typically closed and highly resistant to the involvement of external political actors. These intrinsic difficulties were compounded by the change in government in 1979. The climate of opinion under the new Thatcher government was unsympathetic to conservationist and environmental concerns.

The CPRE had little alternative but to adopt a much more campaigning stance, making use of the media and parliamentary pressure, publicising threats to the countryside arising from the government's deregulatory drive, and fighting key public inquiries. The parliamentary passage of the new government's major environmental legislation – the Wildlife and Countryside Act of 1981 – proved a major battleground. The CPRE campaigned hard for the regulation of agricultural changes that could potentially damage protected areas. In the face of mounting evidence of the widespread destruction of areas and features of conservation value through agricultural intensification, ministers were obliged to introduce a system whereby farmers in protected areas would have to give notice of their intention to undertake potentially damaging changes. To appease the farming lobby, however, the government also amended the legislation to require that official conservation bodies, if they were to pursue their objections to what was proposed, would have to buy the farmers off. This requirement was potentially very self-limiting. The conservation authorities were starved of cash and it was feared that this would severely constrain them in exercising their new-found power to object to destructive agricultural change. It also seemed iniquitous to the CPRE that conservation funds should be used, in effect, to counter the damaging consequences of agricultural subsidies.

In this way, the CPRE was drawn into criticisms of the Common Agricultural Policy (CAP). It was increasingly apparent that British farming's embrace of the CAP following entry to the EU had unleashed a new wave of farm investment and intensification. Just as the CPRE came to see the CAP as the motor of destruction of the rural environment, so the policy began to attract political and popular opprobrium over the rising costs of storing and disposing of mounting agricultural surpluses – portrayed in the press as 'food mountains'. As a general disposition towards rationalisation and accountability emerged in government, economic criticisms of the CAP found favourable ground (see, for example, Bowers and Cheshire, 1983), and proved decisive when farm subsidies were directly linked to environmental damage, prompting the UK government to withdraw a range of capital grants for farmers.

As it looked to have environmentally damaging subsidies withdrawn, as well as general farm supports reoriented to be environmentally benign, the CPRE's criticisms of agriculture policy expanded to include the whole system of protected and subsidised prices for farmers under the CAP (Sinclair, 1985). Having warned ministers that 'if [the agricultural ministry's] policies did not change the issue would become a major source of political embarrassment to the Government' (CPRE press release, 6 July 1984), the CPRE set out to pursue these criticisms through various avenues, namely: supporting local protests against the destruction of traditional landscapes; mounting press campaigns publicising the scale of countryside losses from agricultural intensification; supporting parliamentary questions and early day motions to marshal back-bench opinion; and making representations to the European Commission and European Parliament.

The CPRE used the EU dimension of their policy involvement as a means to coerce the government; not as a parallel venue to their usual domestic realm of influence over policy, but as a venue with the potential to act in direct opposition. The CPRE had been involved in the establishment of the European Environmental Bureau, formed to assist national environmental groups to lobby the EU, and this proved an effective avenue for the group in monitoring and seeking to influence the trickle of environmental legislation emerging from the Community. However, it afforded no access to the Community's distinctly neo-corporatist structures of agricultural policy making. So the CPRE used its connections to lobby European ministers of the environment to prepare an analysis of the environmental implications of the CAP, as part of its efforts to get the UK Department of the Environment to challenge the Ministry of Agriculture, Fisheries and Food (MAFF). Likewise, when the UK government claimed that it was not allowed under EU law to make agricultural payments to farmers for environmental purposes, the CPRE obtained its own independent legal opinion suggesting that this was acceptable, seriously undermining the legitimacy of MAFF. The government climbed down but sought a new heading in the relevant European regulation explicitly allowing it to pay farmers in so-called environmentally sensitive areas (ESAs) to maintain traditional farming systems and activities. Once the principle of ESAs had been established, the CPRE looked to expand this component of what came to be known as 'agri-environment policy'.

The group also stepped up its efforts to penetrate MAFF. Although only agricultural interests were consulted in MAFF's annual price review, through which the UK government formulated its negotiating positions for the setting of tariffs and subsidies in Brussels, from 1985 onwards the CPRE began to submit its own unsolicited evidence. The then Director of the CPRE declared that 'CPRE are now no longer content to leave agriculture policy to be determined in cabal by the Ministry ... the National Farmers Union and the Country Landowners' Association' (CPRE press release, 3 January 1985). In 1989, frustrated at the unresponsiveness of the agriculture policy community, the CPRE collated these submissions and issued them as a publication entitled *Paradise Protection*, detailing the threat that subsidised farm prices posed to valued countryside. The bad publicity that this attracted finally forced MAFF's hand to admit the CPRE into its annual consultations on price fixing – the first environmental organisation to be included.

While the CPRE continued to pursue its challenge to agriculture policy, the group's main preoccupation through the mid 1980s was to direct growing unease about the impact of Conservative economic policies on the environment back onto its traditionally favoured ground: domestic land-use planning. Two circulars – *Green Belts* and *Land for Housing* were watered down after more than sixty MPs – orchestrated by the CPRE – registered their opposition and came out in support of stricter land-use controls (Flynn and Lowe, 1992). By 1988, Thatcher had declared a commitment to protecting the environment in a speech to the Royal Society later regarded as a watershed moment for the sustainable development movement (Jordan, 2002: 39).

## The 1990s: Europeanisation and sustainable development

The CPRE's oppositional politics linking conservation arguments to the case for the economic rationalisation of agricultural policy had gained some notable successes by the late 1980s, including the ending of capital grants that encouraged environmentally damaging farm intensification and the introduction of a completely new type of conservation-oriented payment for farmers. However, there were considerable risks in associating the environmental cause with pressure for the market-oriented reform of agriculture policy. The argument of many economists and right-wing politicians at this time was that price subsidies should be removed altogether and a free market in farm products introduced. It was claimed that this would undoubtedly benefit the rural environment, as it would eliminate artificial incentives to intensify production.

However, the CPRE wanted a planned and managed countryside not a free-market countryside. It feared the neglect of the landscape as much as an over-intensive agriculture. With the fall in farm incomes in the late 1980s, 'the dangers of dereliction and problems with farm diversification [became] of equal significance to the dangers of intensification', as the environmental problems associated with farming in decline were perceived by the CPRE to be just as great as those of farming in the ascendancy (interview with Andy Wilson, then responsible for agriculture and landscape policy, 12 March 1991). It also became alarmed at the prospect favoured by Conservative ministers of linking together cuts in farm prices with a relaxation of planning controls in the countryside, to encourage farmers to redevelop their land and buildings and diversify out of agriculture. This radical, free-market approach was seen by the CPRE as simply substituting one set of threats to the countryside with another. It therefore consciously distanced itself from the free-market critique of the CAP and developed a policy position of promoting a reorientation of agricultural supports towards environmental management objectives.

This line of thinking brought the CPRE closer to the position that the NFU leadership was beginning to adopt as it sought to take on board the environmentalist critique of modern agriculture. They too were wary of the free-market approach as threatening farm incomes, but had come to accept the inevitability of the reform of the CAP and saw prospects for renewing the legitimacy of agricultural supports through emphasising farmers' positive contribution to environmental management. In 1991, at the initiative of the NFU, a joint statement of intent was issued with the CPRE on the need for CAP reform. It argued that the 'means of securing the continuation of farming across the bulk of our countryside must be put forward alongside any proposal for budgetary controls'. To achieve this, 'farmers should receive direct payments for the countryside and environmental management they undertake' (letter dated 7 February 1991). The two were brought together partly through their joint opposition to the European Commission's original proposal for CAP reform, which suggested a switch away from providing support to farmers through high subsidised prices, towards direct income payments weighted towards those who most needed them (i.e. social payments for small European farmers). But the collaboration also came about because, in the view of the CPRE, 'the context of the debate [had] changed': the NFU had come to realise the need for reform of agricultural supports with environmental management as a central objective (interview with Andy Wilson, 12 March 1991).

The CPRE and NFU also found themselves united against other opponents, particularly the radical green groups that had provided the impetus for the change in tactics of the 1980s but which had an ideological preference for small farmers and organic farming practices. In the words of Andy Wilson, the CPRE were now 'having more to say to the NFU and arguing against the fundamentalist, cockeyed, and politically ill-thought-out views of the deep greens' (interview with Andy Wilson, 12 March 1991).

Thus, by the early 1990s, the CPRE had achieved more of a semi-insider status over agriculture policy. And at this stage it drew up its own detailed reform proposal for the CAP – employing an agricultural economist to help with the technical argument and the costings. The principles behind the CPRE's alternative support system were that:

food production should be rewarded by market mechanisms alone ... Public support, as far as payments to farmers are concerned, should be focused instead on the environmental benefits which the market does not adequately provide (Jenkins, 1990: 6).

Specific proposals were set out for shifting the basis of financial support to an environmental one, within a framework of tighter environmental regulation of farming practices.

The CPRE pressed this set of principles through two phases of CAP reform, first in the early 1990s (1990–2) and second in the late 1990s (1997–9). It was a minor player at the European level although its stance concurred with that adopted by other reformist environmental groups. Named after the European Agricultural Commissioner, the eventual MacSharry reform of 1992, as well as cutting back on farm support prices, particularly for cereals, broadened the scope of agri-environment supports and absorbed them into the mainstream of the CAP.

The CPRE approved of the overall direction of change but was critical of the pace. It faced a considerable dilemma in how to adjust its tactics to the new context, recognising that lobbying work would 'inevitably become more detailed as the CAP becomes less of a policy to ridicule and more one to refine and improve' (CPRE Policy Committee 23 July 1992, Appendix A, para. 11). Member States were given considerable discretion in how to implement agri-environment policy, and the CPRE found itself welcomed onto the national and regional consultative bodies set up in 1996 to steer the implementation of agri-environment policy in the UK. Despite its disappointment that only about 2 per cent of the CAP was initially allocated for agri-environment measures, it still saw this as 'an important "toe-hold" on which to push for bigger and better schemes' (CPRE Policy Committee, 6 May 1993, Appendix B, para. 23).

In seeking to influence agriculture policy beyond agri-environment measures, the group found itself stretched in gaining appropriate access. Contacts with MAFF were largely sporadic, especially with the important agricultural commodity and EC divisions. In any case, the UK government's line on CAP reform was 'welcome insofar as it contains a clear commitment to price cuts, but problematic in that the UK has failed to articulate a positive alternative which genuinely integrates environmental aspects' (CPRE Policy Committee, 29 April 1992, Appendix A).

As the UK government (now under John Major) began to prepare for the next phase of CAP reform, it sought to achieve a domestic consensus on the approach it should take. MAFF set up a CAP Review Group (1995) comprising outside experts and interests and, as a sign of the opening up of the agricultural community, the group included the CPRE's then director, Fiona Reynolds. However, the Review Group's final report backed a market-oriented reform, leading Reynolds formally to dissent from it. Subsequently she complained that '[e]nvironmental and social concerns, while present, are clearly subsidiary in the Government's view to a market-driven, free-trade perspective' (Reynolds, 1998). The CPRE had already decided that 'we cannot therefore be optimistic about achieving much at UK level, and should redouble our efforts to influence policy making in the EC' (CPRE Policy Committee, 29 April 1992, Appendix A, para. 20). However, in the EU, the group lacked the resources to develop any systematic contacts with the agricultural division of the European Commission (CPRE Policy Committee, 23 July 1992, Appendix A, para. 9).

These developments were, of course, part of an ongoing trend towards professionalisation in the CPRE, in line with many other environmental groups (Rawcliffe, 1998; Lowe *et al.*, 2001: 92). Professionalisation was facilitated by the growth in resources and staff of the group. It also related to a more technical phase in the development of environmental policy making as government accepted, at least nominally, a broad commitment to sustainable development. Much of this policy development related to an extensive and profound Europeanisation of UK environmental policy (Jordan, 2002).

## New Labour and the emergence of rural policy

While Europeanisation opened up new opportunities for political access that stretched the ability of the CPRE to make use of them, the election of the New Labour government in 1997 greatly perturbed its domestic political context. The CPRE's grassroots base was the shire counties – not Labour's natural territory. Labour's policy pre-occupations with the economy and public services did not accord high priority to the environment. Nor did its ideology of modernisation seem receptive to the cause of countryside protection. Blair's presidential style of government and the rise of the 'core executive' (that is the Cabinet, the Prime Minister's offices and the Cabinet Office) as a key governing body, marginalised the CPRE's established channels within government departments, quangos and local authorities. Thus the group struggled to make its concerns relevant to the new political agenda. In the event, a vigorous newspaper and TV-oriented campaign against housing development through urban expansion onto Green Belt land proved decisive in re-establishing the standing of the group with the government, at least in relation to the group's core policy domain of land-use planning (Murdoch and Lowe, 2003).

However, the CPRE remained 'less certain' about where they stood, and what the government was trying to achieve, in terms of agriculture and rural policy, and the CPRE were relegated to 'outsiders' in the policy network (interview with Tony Burton, 20 June 2000). The government's move to formulate a rural policy as a counterpart to its urban policy – initiated in 1998 and culminating in the 2000 Rural White Paper – thus presented the group with a significant opportunity. In response the CPRE was at pains to express its role as a countryside group, covering more bases than other environmental organisations, and to '[explain] to Labour the progressive, modern view of the countryside that is not warm beer and cricket' (interview with Tony Burton, 20 June 2000). While the group attempted in this way to reinvent its message, the changing political structure, which saw the rise of the No.10 Policy Unit, the Performance and Innovation Unit and individual political advisors, gave the CPRE new opportunities for access and influence over policy.

The Labour government also had to develop its stance on the pending wave of CAP reform. The European Commission published its initial Agenda 2000 proposals for the CAP in July 1997. These set a path for a potentially radical change in which farm production subsidies would be pared back and a new 'second pillar' to the CAP would be established to support rural development and environmental enhancement. The 'second pillar' was embodied in the Rural Development Regulation (RDR) of 1999, which marked a significant step towards transforming the CAP from a sectoral policy for farm commodity support into an integrated rural and environmental policy. Alistair Rutherford, CPRE Rural Policy Officer, noted:

The architecture of CAP is changing for the better. Although damaging subsidies remain, it is moving from a highly centralised policy focused on agricultural prices to a much broader rural and locally adaptable policy which can help to meet environmental and social needs in the countryside. (CPRE press release, 1998 CAP Reforms – 4 *Steps in the Right Direction*, 18 March 1998).

Even though the CPRE was a minor player in the formation of the Regulation at the European level, the strong degree of discretion allotted to Member States by the Regulation offered greater scope for the CPRE to lobby the UK government. This allowed it not only to influence the implementation of the Regulation to maximise its value for rural conservation, but also, crucially, to shape the new structures of implementation in ways that would favour its own access in the future to the policy field that the 'second pillar' opened up. The group proved particularly effective in this regard precisely because it was able to link together the different venues of decision making – the EU, national and local levels – that potentially came into play in devising the domestic structures and procedures for preparing the Rural Development Plans that Member States had to put in place to bring the RDR into effect.

An equally important consideration for UK environmental groups was the amount of resources available under the RDR. EU agricultural ministers had provided for 10 per cent of CAP funds to be devoted to the 'second pillar' in the period 2000–6. But the percentage allocated to the UK was much lower, largely because it was based on the take-up of previous discretionary schemes under the CAP, which past UK governments had tended to ignore. However, under Agenda 2000, Member States were allowed to modulate, that is to use their discretion to move more resources from the first to the second pillar of the new CAP (basically creaming off part of their allotted farm production subsidies to enlarge the pot of agri-environmental grants available nationally). For environmental groups to make anything of the potential of the RDR it was essential that they persuade the UK government to modulate. However, their approach had to be chosen carefully. The NFU was strongly opposed to modulation, and with farm incomes severely depressed it was the natural position for MAFF to adopt also. However, as modulation was a political decision that had to be taken at Cabinet level (the RDR was subject to domestic co-financing, meaning that modulated money would have to be matched pound for pound by the UK Treasury), the CPRE and other environmental organisations mounted a strong campaign to win the Minister and government over. They utilised a variety of approaches, playing particularly on the government's vulnerability to charges of a shortage of funding for popular agri-environment schemes, a shortage that would be perpetuated by Agenda 2000 unless there was some re-juggling of CAP funds within the UK. Ministers were also won round by the argument that modulation would allow them financial scope to pursue a new direction for agriculture policy within the UK and would put them in the vanguard of CAP reform amongst EU Member States (Cabinet Office, 1999). In December 1999, the Agriculture Minister announced his intention to make use of the scope for modulation to greatly expand the funding for the implementation of the RDR. The RDR, he said, 'represents the long term future of public supports for farm businesses and the rural economy [and] a significant opportunity for improvement of the rural environment and the countryside' (House of Commons Hansard, 7 December 1999, col. 703).

In tandem with these efforts to expand the funding of the RDR, the CPRE led a campaign to ensure that MAFF took an expansive view of the procedural possibilities opened up by the RDR. This was much more subject to the judgement of civil servants. Each Member State was required to draw up territorially based seven-year Rural Development Plans 'at the most appropriate geographical level'. The plans were intended to deliver a range of environmental, agricultural and rural development grant schemes part-funded by the EU, in an integrated way that was responsive to the diverse needs and circumstances in individual countries and regions. In drawing up the plans, Member States were required to consider economic, environmental and social impacts and to consult with interested parties. It was left to the discretion of Member States whether and how decentralised these plans should be. With the establishment by Labour of devolved structures of administration in the UK, it was accepted that there should be separate programming of the RDR for Scotland, Wales and Northern Ireland and, therefore, for England too. However, there was little specific impetus for civil servants to go further and set up new systems of decentralised planning, consultation and administration for the RDR below the England level. The CPRE, however, was keen to open the new rural development planning process further, particularly to make it potentially accessible to its county and regional groups. It was therefore necessary to encourage the relevant officials to take a very forward-looking view in putting the RDR into effect and to convince them that a decentralised approach would be supported by rural and conservation organisations. MAFF officials, in general, were anxious to work out how they might fit in with New Labour's enthusiasm for regional government but had no experience at operating at that level. Here, the CPRE was able to combine, to decisive effect, its detailed understanding of the policy context, its insider access to MAFF, and its extensive sub-national links to rural professional and voluntary networks. By setting up a seminar with a select group of professionals, interest group representatives and the MAFF official charged with preparing the England Rural Development Plan, the CPRE was able to promote its proposals. According to the official, the CPRE 'had a pretty good input into determining the structure of implementation of the plan' (interview with Lindsay Cornish, 31 March 2000), which included having separate regional chapters subject to their own local consultation processes. The CPRE thus helped effect a convergence between the decentralising structures of CAP second pillar programming and the increasingly regionalised structures of decision making in land-use planning.

The future success of the CPRE is by no means assured. The group is, however, established as a key member of the policy network, a position which will only be strengthened by the implementation of the latest (post-2006) round of agri-environment-centred CAP reforms.

## Making governance systems more sustainable: a discussion

This case study offers us not only an insight into the workings of a single pressure group, but also allows us to gauge the potential for such 'outsiders' – often dismissed as resource poor and forced to rely on direct action – to succeed in promoting their aims. The CPRE has, despite its relatively small size and the purported exclusionary tactics of the agriculture policy community, succeeded in establishing sustainable development on the political agenda and encouraging governments to reorientate the wider systems of governance towards sustainable development. Nevertheless, the group's status within the policy network is by no means assured and at times of political upheaval it has been forced, like many others, to pursue a firefighting strategy in order to avoid exclusion. The CPRE's success is a consequence of tenacity rather than impact, of incremental gains over high profile achievements.

The CPRE had exploited its expertise in the land-use planning realm throughout the 1960s and 70s and gained a reputation as a reliable and respectable group even though with a small resource base. The incoming Conservative government in 1979 almost entirely closed down this avenue of influence. Environmental concerns suffered generally throughout the early years of the Thatcher administration, as her radical economic policies created a slowdown in both pollution control and environmental improvement measures (Flynn and Lowe, 1992; Jordan, 2002: 32–4). Business interests, with strong objections to the 'limits to growth' debate, dominated policy networks while alternative points of access for pressure groups were simultaneously swept away during a period of 'quangocide'. Regulation of business in any form was avoided, and deregulation of land-use planning was explicitly pursued as a political priority.

The CPRE was unable to adapt this policy virus – part of the pervasive 'new public management' ethos – and instead targeted the emerging 'deep green' movement spearheaded by large membership groups such as Greenpeace and Friends of the Earth. The populist style of campaigning pursued by these groups brought environmentalism into ascendance as a social movement, but the CPRE was limited in its participation by its more conservative membership base and its desire to remain close to government. Unlike other Western European countries, Britain did not experience the dramatic rise of a green party and without support from the mainstream political parties, the radical ecology groups eventually began to flounder. However, the raised profile of environmental concerns coincided with 'New Right' criticisms of agricultural supports and growing external pressure from other countries for more liberalised systems of international trade. Rather than seek to 'freeload' on alternative policy viruses, the CPRE now attempted direct engagement with the new form of critique. By engaging environmental economists (though this title was not claimed by them at the time), the group was able to challenge government in its own language. It was helped in this regard by several key public inquiries which 'assumed even greater significance not only for expressing opposition to controversial developments but also for the opportunity provided to challenge the policies on which they were based' (Flynn and Lowe, 1992).

Throughout this period, the CPRE could claim no decisive victories or policy strongholds to rival those of groups like the NFU. The neoliberal approach to agriculture was tempered by the existence of a supranational policy framework which was (and largely remains) welfarist, Keynesian and interventionist, meaning that little headway could be made without wider EU support. It has been posited, however, that 'established insider groups, well entrenched in long-standing policy communities which have delivered high returns for their investment in insider status, can eventually lose out to other groups who choose to operate in different venues and who manage to construct a new image of existing policy problems' (Richardson, 2000: 1011). Through the pursuit of multiple strategies – direct action, engaging with New Right perspectives on agriculture, and promoting planning controls as a tool of sustainable rural governance – the CPRE has been able to outmanoeuvre more established groups. The introduction of the Environmentally Sensitive Areas scheme, which effectively paid farmers to preserve traditional landscapes, marked the beginning of an ongoing environmental turn in agriculture policy which producer groups have been unable to resist.

Since 1997, New Labour have consolidated the move away from productivist agriculture. The CPRE has again been able to commandeer several of the government's new policy priorities. Their planning expertise complemented Labour's interest in housing, while recognition of the changing electoral composition of the countryside – no longer dominated by farmers and landowners but by a potentially Labour-voting service class – gave the CPRE political capital as a representative of the new rural voice. Blair's most trumpeted innovation in rural policy, the creation of the Department for Environment, Food and Rural Affairs (DEFRA) in 2001 has had an uncertain impact upon the CPRE's success to date. Although, at the outset, the NFU expressed dismay at the omission of 'farming' from the new department's title, a significant shift in policy towards supporting sustainable rural development has failed to materialise (Donaldson *et al.*, 2006). In addition, the merging of MAFF and the Department of Environment in 2001 closed off an alternative venue which the CPRE had in the past used to gain leverage against the farming lobby. The latest round of CAP reforms, however, has helped to entrench the environmental agenda in agriculture, and a reversal of the current trend away from production supports seems improbable. The same supranational structure which in the 1980s hindered the domestic pursuit of these post-productivist goals now acts as a guarantee that they will be implemented despite the efforts of the farming lobby.

As our empirical example shows, the ability of one relatively small interest group to defeat a set of entrenched interests and exert a major influence over the policy process should not be overstated. However, as the political agenda shifts to incorporate a broader range of interests in agricultural policy, and the decision-making process is opened up to previously excluded groups, many new opportunities arise for active participation and promotion of the CPRE's objectives. The CPRE has been innovative in exploiting these opportunities, adapting both its strategy and, occasionally, its goals in order to sustain its pressure on government and the producer-oriented policy community with its productivist agenda. As such, the CPRE has made incremental steps towards establishing sustainable development as a priority for the future of agri-environmental policy and, in so doing, has gained a position as a highly regarded and trustworthy partner in the (re)design of governance systems.

## References

Allison, L. 1975. *Environmental Planning*. London: Allen and Unwin.

Bowers, J. and Cheshire, P. 1983. *Agriculture, the Countryside and Land Use: An Economic Critique*. London, UK: Methuen.

Cabinet Office 1999. *Rural Economies*. London, UK: Performance and Innovation Unit, Cabinet Office.

Carter, N. 2001. *The Politics of the Environment*. Cambridge, UK: Cambridge University Press.

Cox, G., Lowe, P. and Winter, M. 1986. 'Agriculture and conservation in Britain: a policy community under siege', in Cox, G., Lowe, P. and Winter, M. (eds.) *Agriculture, People and Policies*. London, UK: Allen and Unwin, pp. 181–215.

Donaldson, A., Lee, R., Ward, N. and Wilkinson, K. 2006. *Foot and Mouth – Five Years On: The Legacy of the 2001 Foot and Mouth Disease Crisis for Farming and the British Countryside*. Centre for Rural Economy, University of Newcastle upon Tyne.

Flynn, A. and Lowe, P. 1992. 'The greening of the Tories: the Conservative Party and the environment', in Rudig, W. (ed.) *Green Politics Two*. Edinburgh, UK: Edinburgh University Press, pp. 9–36.

Glasbergen, P. 1992. 'Agri-environmental policy: trapped in an iron law? A comparative analysis of agricultural pollution controls in the Netherlands, the United Kingdom and France', *Sociologia Ruralis* 32: 30–4.

Grant, W. 1989. *Pressure Groups, Politics and Democracy in Britain*. Hemel Hempstead, UK: Philip Allan.

Hall, C. 1976. 'The amenity movement', in Gill, C. (ed.) *The Countryman's Britain*. London, UK: David and Charles, pp. 162–75.

Hall, C. 1981. 'They plough the fields and shatter: the defence of the landscape', *Ecos* 2(1): 10–13.

Jenkins, T. 1990. *Future Harvests: The Economics of Farming and the Environment*. London, UK: Campaign to Protect Rural England and World Wide Fund for Nature.

Jordan, A. J. 2002. *The Europeanisation of British Environmental Policy: A Departmental Perspective*. Basingstoke, UK: Palgrave.

Lowe, P. and Pye-Smith, C. 1980. 'No nukes in Ambridge? An interview with Chris Hall', *Ecos* 1(4): 3–6.

Lowe, P., Cox, G., MacEwen, M., O'Riordan, T. and Winter, M. 1986. *Countryside Conflicts: The Politics of Farming, Forestry and Conservation*. Aldershot, UK: Gower.

Lowe, P., Clark, J., Seymour, S. and Ward, N. 1997. *Moralizing the Environment: Countryside Change, Farming and Pollution*. London, UK: Routledge.

Lowe, P., Murdoch, J. and Norton. A. 2001. *Professionals and Volunteers in the Environmental Process*. Centre for Rural Economy, University of Newcastle upon Tyne.

Maloney, W., Jordan, G. and McLaughlin, A. 1994. 'Interest groups and public policy: the insider/outsider model revisited', *Journal of Public Policy* 14: 17–38.

Marsh, D. and Rhodes, R. (eds.) 1992. *Policy Networks in British Government*. Oxford, UK: Clarendon.

Marsh, D. and Smith, M. 2000. 'Understanding policy networks: towards a dialectical approach', *Political Studies* 48: 4–21.

Murdoch, J. and Lowe, P. 2003. 'The preservationist paradox: modernism, environmentalism and the politics of spatial divisions', *Transactions of the Institute of British Geographers* 28: 310–32.

Rawcliffe, P. 1998. *Environmental Pressure Groups in Transition*. Manchester, UK: Manchester University Press.

Reynolds, F. 1998. 'Environmental planning: land-use and landscape policy', in Lowe, P. and Ward, S. (eds.) *British Environmental Policy and Europe*. London, UK: Routledge, pp. 232–43.

Rhodes, R. and Marsh, D. 1992. 'New directions in the study of policy networks', *European Journal of Political Research* 21: 181–205.

Richardson, J. 2000. 'Government, interest groups and policy change', *Political Studies* 48: 1006–25.

Sinclair, G. 1985. *How to Help Farmers and Keep England Beautiful*. London, UK: Campaign to Protect Rural England and Council for National Parks.

Smith, M. 1990. *The Politics of Agricultural Support in Britain: The Development of the Agriculture Policy Community*. Aldershot, UK: Dartmouth.

Smith, M. 1992. 'The agriculture policy community: maintaining a closed relationship', in Marsh, D. and Rhodes, R. (eds.), *Policy Networks in British Government*. Oxford, UK: Clarendon, pp. 27–50.

Smith, M. 1993. *Pressure, Power and Policy: State Autonomy and Policy Networks in Britain and the United States*. New York: Harvester Wheatsheaf.

# 5 | Global governance for sustainable capitalism? The political economy of global environmental governance

MATTHEW PATERSON

## Introduction

This chapter explores the dynamics of environmental governance specifically related to the global sphere – the patterns of environmental rule making and authority which transcend state boundaries. It argues that while such governance is commonly seen in terms of a tragedy of the commons arising out of the anarchy of the interstate system, it is more fruitful to analyse these dynamics in relation to a conception of global capitalism. While efforts to govern global environmental problems started out as attempts to regulate the side-effects of existing forms of capitalist development, they have increasingly been organised to channel capitalism in novel directions. This chapter begins by arguing for this way of understanding global environmental governance in general and charts the shifts in the way that governance regarding the environment has related to trends within the organisation of global capitalism. It then outlines the ways in which contemporary governance can be understood to be pursuing sustainable capitalism. It explores this latter theme focusing primarily on climate politics, both as the most prominent element in contemporary global environmental governance, but also as a key test of the extent to which 'governing for sustainable development' can be regarded as being on a successful path. It argues that the key mechanisms that have emerged to promote this sustainable capitalism are those directly working to create new sites of market activity (specifically emissions trading regimes), those seeking to expand market access across the globe (such as the Clean Development Mechanism), and those seeking to shape investment behaviour by large institutional investors (such as the Carbon Disclosure Project). The pursuit of sustainable capitalism lies in the potential synergistic effects of these elements, which I explore in the Conclusions.

## Global environmental governance: international anarchy or global capitalism?

From its inception in the late 1960s, the modern environmental crisis was widely regarded to have intrinsically global dimensions. While some are sceptical about this global character (Sachs, 1993; Chatterjee and Finger, 1994), seeing in this the effect of the strategies of globalising firms, or in Vandana Shiva's phrase 'the greening of the global reach' (Shiva, 1993), or as a means by which states can externalise and avoid their responsibilities through strategies of blaming others (Hay, 1994), for most, environmental problems have distinct characteristics that require global forms of governance.

These characteristics include the particular characteristics of many environmental problems themselves. Some are transboundary problems, where pollution generated in one jurisdiction flows across borders and damages others, such as with acid rain, while others, such as fisheries, are referred to as common pool resources, where different countries draw upon resources which move across borders. Some environmental problems, such as climate change, are, in effect, pure public goods, where no single state can solve the problem or insulate itself from ill effects. These phenomena are held to generate pressures for transnational, or even global, governance. However, the particular type of governance to be pursued differs, given the different problem types.

Another pressure for global environmental governance comes from the globalisation of the economy, which means that states meet obstacles to addressing the environmental problems they face because of the way that such problems are embedded in production and consumption processes not totally within their control, or where if they acted unilaterally, their economies would be harmed in competitive global markets. This generates pressures for collective action to avoid these economic spillover problems.

It is thus not surprising to have seen considerable pressures for governance at the global level. This governance has taken many different forms, and forms which are increasingly diverse. At the core, however, are still interstate treaties, which have seen extraordinary growth since the early 1970s. Ron Mitchell's exhaustive analysis of the growth of these agreements shows an average of sixteen signed a year between the Stockholm UN Conference on the Human

Environment in 1972 and the Rio de Janeiro Conference on Environment and Development in 1992, but an average of nineteen signed a year from 1992 to 2003 (Mitchell, 2003). These are usually understood through the lens of 'international regimes' (Young, 1989; Haas *et al.*, 1993; Vogler, 1995). That is, sets of 'principles, norms, rules and decision-making procedures around which actors' expectations converge' (Krasner, 1983: 2). Thus, international environmental regimes consist of the development of a series of norms principally about how states should behave in relation to environmental problems, which are then articulated in more concrete contexts as rules guiding the limitation of specific emissions, the transfer of new technologies, the protection of particular species or ecosystems, and so on.

The logic underpinning the focus on, and analysis of, international regimes is that the principal dynamic of world politics is constituted by its specifically anarchic character; that international politics is defined by the lack of an overarching government capable of enforcing rules in ways that states are usually assumed to be able to do within their own territories. This assumption is shared across a range of perspectives from so-called realist (Waltz, 1979), to liberal institutionalist (Keohane, 1989), and constructivist (Wendt, 1999). In debates in international environmental politics, the vast majority of the literature (see Bernstein, 2001, for an important constructivist exception) adopts an institutionalist approach, using the notion of international regime to account for the emergence of what can legitimately be called a network of global environmental governance (e.g. Young, 1997; see also Chapter 1).

The academic debates in international relations respond implicitly, and occasionally explicitly, to a prevalent debate in the late 1960s and since about the implications of international anarchy for the resolution of environmental problems. A classic argument in environmental debates has focused on the apparent contradiction between the global character of environmental problems and the organisation of international politics into a world of separate, sovereign, self-regarding states. The metaphor invoked is Garrett Hardin's misnamed tragedy of the commons (Hardin, 1968),[1] where the pursuit of individual interests in a context where access to resources is unrestricted means both that those resources are inevitably overused, and that actors are unable to agree to limit their exploitation without externally imposed rules. The metaphor was more loosely present during environmental debates in the 1970s through the notion encapsulated in the title of Barbara Ward and René Dubos' book *Only One Earth* (Ward and Dubos, 1972), and later adopted in the Brundtland Report's rhetoric of 'the earth is one but the world is not' (WCED, 1987: 27). This logic is extended in its most forthright form in William Ophuls' *Ecology and the Politics of Scarcity* (Ophuls, 1977), where this contradiction between state sovereignty and global ecology is taken to imply the necessity of abandoning the former and the development of a global Leviathan capable of enforcing rules in the pursuit of global sustainability.

The essence of the liberal institutionalist argument about international regimes is to suggest that while international anarchy is still the defining feature of international politics, it is not the case that states are completely unable to co-operate to achieve mutually beneficial outcomes. Institutionalists frequently draw on the game-theoretic logic that when you iterate a game such as the Prisoner's Dilemma, which approximates Hardin's tragedy, co-operation is much more possible than in a one-shot game. They argue that there are a number of strategies by which individual states can procure co-operation, and a number of roles which can be played by international actors, such as secretariats and expert advisors, to further such co-operation. As a consequence of such co-operation and institutionalisation, global environmental *governance* (the dense set of rules and norms which are for the most part accepted by states as regulating their behaviour) can occur in the absence of a global *government* (a single source of such rules which has the coercive power to enforce them) (see Rosenau, 1992, and Chapter 1).

Institutionalists are thus able to account for the extraordinary growth of international environmental regimes in terms of the ability of states to pursue mutual interests even in the face of conflicts. While much debate about the strength and effectiveness of this governance has taken place (see Young, 1999; Miles *et al.*, 2002), less attention has been focused on what drives the specific *character* of global environmental governance. Why do the norms and rules agreed take the specific form they do? As Bernstein persuasively shows, the limits of the liberal institutionalist approach are that, while it can frequently explain why co-operation succeeds or fails in particular instances, and why and how international institutions affect the pattern of specific bargains struck, it fails to explain (or even to try to explain) the

content of the regimes themselves. Specifically, Bernstein demonstrates a broad shift in the norms underpinning regimes since the early
1970s, which can best be characterised as a shift from limits to growth
(Meadows *et al.*, 1972), to sustainable development (à la Brundtland
Report), to liberal (or free-market) environmentalism (Bernstein,
2001).

Bernstein couches his argument in constructivist terms; that is, in
terms of how actors interpreted the implications of the environmental
crisis and how those interpretations have been embedded in, and
constrained by, broader norms prevalent in international politics.
Thus he interprets the norm of limits to growth as having failed
because the broader norm of growth was too strong to allow its
acceptance, especially in a North–South context, with Southern
countries insisting on the right to development. While sustainable
development adapted environmental discourse to a broader norm
favouring growth both in North and South, it remained too interventionist in relation to the free-market norms that became hegemonic
during the 1980s and 1990s.

But there is, in my view, something deeply lacking in an analysis
which stops here, and does not explore why it is that these norms
prevailed and were the ones particularly important in shaping
environmental regimes. Why is it that broad *economic* norms shape
environmental ones, rather than, say, broad *human rights* norms?
To explain this, we need to turn to political-economy accounts of
global politics rather than the constructivism adopted by Bernstein.
Bernstein, following the logic of mainstream constructivism in US
international relations (in particular in the work of Alex Wendt),
starts with the proposition that the world is socially constructed,
but that this world is nevertheless a world of states operating in an
anarchic environment. This starting point limits his capacity to
respond properly to his own, very important, question, namely: what
drives the changes in norms which provide the content of global
environmental governance? From the political-economy point of view
I elaborate below, global environmental governance is fundamentally
about projects to pursue the possibility of greening capitalism.

Perhaps the fundamental question regarding how we understand
global environmental governance, then, is how we understand the
state. For all of the above approaches, the state is understood as an
actor, and individualistic at that. Realists and institutionalists both

explicitly adopt rational choice models. But even with constructivist approaches, where states' preferences, for example, are treated as inter-subjective, created through their interaction with one another rather than exogenously given, the state is nevertheless a single thing, abstracted from any social context. My premise is that this is central to understanding the dynamics of global environmental governance. Rather, we need specifically to understand the state as embedded in a set of complex and contradictory social relationships which structure how it acts; relationships which are conflictual and which change historically. Specifically, we need to understand the state as part of a *capitalist* social order.

This order is highly dynamic but at the same time unstable, and generates constant pressures on states to secure the conditions for economic growth, to redistribute wealth, to resolve the social conflicts arising within capitalist society, and to respond to periodic crises generated by capitalism. These crises include environmental challenges resulting from spillovers from particular elements of economic activity and growth. I turn now to the emerging phenomenon of global environmental governance to try to sustain this claim.

## From restraining development to promoting 'green' capitalism

If we look at the content of global environmental governance, it is striking that it can be readily understood as: (a) mirroring shifts in the way that globalising capitalism has been governed more generally; and (b) increasingly reflecting a shift towards efforts to design governance to reorganise capitalism according to the imperatives of sustainability. I will now explore these two claims in more detail.

The first claim can be readily shown through an analysis of Bernstein's (2001) argument in *The Compromise of Liberal Environmentalism*. The norms underpinning global environmental governance have manifestly shifted since the 1970s. At the Stockholm conference in 1972, the two dominant frames were those provided by the *Limits to Growth* report and the highlighting of the huge and widening global economic inequalities between North and South. The concrete treaties developed over the following decade or so focus on limiting particular types of economic activity, the production of specific pollutants, the exploitation and trade in a variety of species regarded as endangered, or on setting certain ecosystems as off-limits to economic development. Examples of these include the regimes to limit emissions of $SO_2$ and $NO_x$, the one banning production of substances causing stratospheric ozone depletion, and those on commercial whaling and the wise use of wetlands.

This form of environmental governance clearly corresponds to an era where capitalism was itself organised and governed through extensive planning, from tripartite corporatist management in most Western countries, to the nationalisation of many industries, and extensive multilateral management through the Bretton Woods system. In this era, the orthodox ideology amongst political and economic elites suggested that restricting certain forms of economic activity was seen to threaten the viability or legitimacy of capitalism as a whole, in the same way that the Bretton Woods agreements heavily limited capital movements for the same reason.[2]

By the 1980s, the problematic character of adopting limits to growth from the point of view of capitalism in general had become obvious. The emergence of sustainable development as an ideology during that decade can best be understood as an attempt to overcome the two basic political problems of the previous set of norms underpinning global environmental governance. The more obvious of these, given its diplomatic prominence and its explicit treatment by the Brundtland Commission, is the North–South conflict (Thomas, 1992; Chatterjee and Finger, 1994). A major component of *Our Common Future* was precisely a proposal for a North–South bargain on environmental problems, with significant transfers of technology and wealth envisaged in order to enable the South to grow out of poverty, while avoiding the environmental consequences that had occurred in the wake of Northern growth. This is underpinned in the way that sustainable development is defined in the report, as 'development which meets the needs of present generations without compromising the ability of future generations to meet their own needs' (WCED, 1987: 43). 'Present generations' in this phrase is usually taken to imply all those currently living. Thus, wherever present needs are not being met, action needs to be taken to ensure that they are. This responds to the clear sense amongst Northern policy makers, researchers, environmentalists and business leaders that talking about limits to growth clearly appeared, in the South, as a threat to pull up the ladder behind them.[3]

But the shift to sustainable development is more than just a political accommodation to overcome North–South conflicts. What the focus on Southern resistance to the idea of limits to growth tends to obscure was that, in the North, resistance from business groups and politicians to the idea of limiting growth was also developing in this period. This resistance can be seen most manifestly in rising resistance by firms to the costs associated with environmental regulation designed to limit pollutants and resource use, and so on. But at a more general ideological level, sustainable development, in its Brundtlandian form at least, was presented as the solution to the problem of dealing with the environmental crisis without limiting growth.

Thus, at one level, the emergence of sustainable development is an accommodation of the norms underpinning environmental governance with the basic growth imperative of capitalism. But it is still largely couched in the form of capitalism prevalent in the mid twentieth century. Rather than emphasising, as does limits to growth, its regulatory dimensions, it seeks to organise it within what can be seen as a green Keynesian bargain; that is, organising growth in a managed way, including redistributing wealth to stimulate consumption and growth. Bernstein rightly suggests that this sustainable development discourse is better understood as 'managed sustainable growth' (Bernstein, 2001: 69). Nevertheless, in the Brundtland Report, but more strongly outside it, one can see developing during the 1980s an increasing interest in the use of markets as mechanisms of governance. For the most part, the focus in *Our Common Future* is on large-scale, government-led policies to invest in renewable energy, agricultural improvements, and so on. Striking is the absence of what rapidly became the norm over the next few years – there is virtually no advocacy of market mechanisms (at least as we now understand them) in the Brundtland Report.

During the 1980s, and continuing into the 1990s, this 'managed sustainable growth' became increasingly out of step with the guiding philosophy underpinning economic governance globally and nationally. Economies have become managed according to what is usually known as neoliberalism. This started with the UK and the USA, and was promoted by crude pressure on developing countries through the International Monetary Fund (IMF) and World Bank Structural Adjustment Programmes, and through more subtle processes of 'harmonisation' across Western countries (the so-called Washington Consensus – see Williamson, 1990). Governments deregulated markets, privatised nationalised industries, deregulated financial flows, reduced taxes on corporations in particular, reduced rights for trade unions, and attempted, often unsuccessfully, to reduce the size of the welfare state. At the global level, this corresponded to the transformation of the General Agreement on Tariffs and Trade (GATT) into the World Trade Organization (WTO), the emergence of agreements such as the TRIPS (Trade-Related Intellectual Property Rights), TRIMS (Trade-Related Investment Measures) and GATS (General Agreement on Trade in Services), the failed attempt at the Multilateral Agreement on Investment, and so on.

Such a shift in economic management is frequently interpreted as reflecting and reinforcing shifts in the power within different blocs of business interests, from the Fordist bloc of heavy manufacturing, oil and chemicals, which underpinned the economic governance regime from the 1930s to the 1970s, towards a finance-led bloc which had risen from the ashes through the emergence of Eurodollar markets in the 1960s, the collapse of the fixed exchange rate regime in 1971, and the competitive deregulation of financial markets during the early 1980s in particular (on fractions of capital and the rise of global finance, see Cox, 1987; Helleiner, 1994; van der Pijl, 1998). The interests of finance in both deregulated solutions to problems like environmental ones, and the fetishisation of markets as solutions to all sorts of problems which is associated with the rise of finance, produced the ideological context within which environmental governance has developed since the late 1980s.

As Bernstein (2001) suggests, global environmental governance has since then become increasingly guided by an imperative less to *organise* and directly *manage* capitalist growth to pursue sustainability, than to enable private actors to pursue their economic interests in ways which simultaneously promote sustainability (see also Brown in Chapter 2). Ideologically, this started with the mantra about the advantages of market mechanisms over command and control policies (e.g. Pearce *et al.*, 1989; Helm, 1991). Regulations, as part of command and control, were said to impose very high costs on industries and consumers in the pursuit of reduced environmental impacts, reducing competitiveness and standards of living, and additionally blocking technical innovation, since regulations locked firms into stipulated technologies with no incentives to go beyond the required objectives.

Market mechanisms, by contrast, simply confined themselves to structuring the incentives facing economic actors, enabling them to meet goals in the manner most efficient for them.

Market mechanisms for environmental policy tend to operate in one of two ways. They may shape economic incentives directly through taxes and subsidies, thus creating incentives to behave in specific ways, and promoting the internalisation of external costs such as pollution. Alternatively, governments may create markets for environmental goods, such as through emissions trading, setting overall objectives, allocation of pollution rights, and allowing economic actors to decide how to respond through buying or selling additional permits. The market thus directly regulates behaviour. While market mechanisms are less widely used than their rhetoric suggests (Jordan *et al.*, 2003), they have nevertheless become the policy orthodoxy in relation to environmental governance, within and between states.

## Global governance for sustainable capitalism

The second claim made above was that, increasingly, environmental governance is directed towards shaping capitalism itself in a sustainable direction. There is clearly a question about what is meant by sustainable, which I address in the Conclusions. In this section, I seek to establish the claim that global environmental governance now largely operates to facilitate a particular type of capitalist development, rather than in either restricting capitalist development or heavily managing it. It is therefore, at the same time, designed to further the specific interests of certain businesses, create business opportunities for them, and stabilise a political coalition to legitimise the regime. The climate change and biodiversity regimes, in particular, can be seen as paradigms of this in terms of interstate governance, but what this also entails is the increasingly private character of global environmental governance. I will say a little about these two latter developments, and then focus on the climate regime to elaborate this character of global environmental governance more closely.

The biodiversity regime, articulated in the Convention on Biological Diversity (1992) and the Cartagena Protocol on Biosafety (2000), is striking in the evolution of the issue in the period up to the signing of the Convention in 1992. It moved from being ostensibly about the decline in *species* diversity and fears of the associated collapse of complex ecosystems on which all life on the planet depends to: (a) an issue of how to preserve *genetic* diversity because of the services rendered to humanity through its use in pharmaceuticals and in agriculture; and (b) a question of protecting the rights of those who controlled and, more precisely, manipulated such genetic diversity in order to produce medical or agricultural benefits. From the start of negotiations, biotechnology firms lobbied hard to have *ex situ* conservation of genes in gene banks treated as equal to *in situ* conservation in existing ecosystems.

It is also worth understanding that, at the same time as the UN Biodiversity Convention was being negotiated, the TRIPS agreement was being negotiated in the Uruguay Round of the GATT. The Uruguay Round also created the World Trade Organization. The biotechnology sector, along with the entertainment industry, pushed for the globalisation of very high standards of intellectual property protection, such as patents, copyright and trademarks. For biotechnology firms, the combination of increased patent protection and its legitimisation through the Convention on Biological Diversity of gene banks and genetic modification as forms of conservation has been crucial in enabling the expansion of the sector and the realisation of investment in genetic modification since the late 1970s. The biodiversity regime is thus principally organised around enabling large transnational firms to secure monopoly profits for their investments in genetic modification (see Newell, 2003).[4]

We have also witnessed an increasing privatisation of global environmental governance (Clapp, 1998). On the one hand this entails firms directly developing standards, certification and labelling schemes, production process rules, investment norms, and so on, with regard to environmental questions. This is, in effect, governance that bypasses interstate processes. Classic examples here are the International Organization for Standardization's ISO14000 series of environmental management standards (Clapp, 1998), the Forest Stewardship Council (FSC) and other forest certification schemes (Cashore *et al.*, 2004), insurance companies and climate politics (Paterson, 2001; Carlsson and Stripple, 2003; Jagers *et al.*, 2005).

Part of the dynamic of these forms of governance is to prevent state regulation, but they are nevertheless shaping business practice, potentially significantly. Should the variety of schemes to shape investment practice with regard to $CO_2$ emissions – the Carbon Disclosure

Project, the Global Reporting Initiative, UNEP's Financial Industries Initiative, and so on – succeed in generating a norm which treats $CO_2$-intensive firms as financial liabilities, then substantial change in investment in renewable energy can be expected (see UNEP FI, 2006). But, on the other hand, privatisation not only entails firms attempting to self-regulate to organise and legitimise their growth, but environmental NGOs attempting to fill the void left by declining regulation by states, through developing schemes to put pressure on firms to change practices (Newell, 2000).

The climate regime, as incarnated specifically in the Kyoto Protocol on Climate Change (1997) is perhaps the apogee of what I shall term global governance for sustainable capitalism. Key to Kyoto are three highly innovative mechanisms – emissions trading, Joint Implementation (JI) and the Clean Development Mechanism (CDM). Collectively, these are now being referred to as the carbon market.

The trading of emissions rights is the purest market mechanism. It involves the direct creation of a market itself which then acts directly as a regulatory mechanism, determining who engages in how much emissions abatement. Emissions trading schemes allocate allowances to emit pollutants within an overall ceiling or cap. Participants in the system are then allowed to trade the allowances amongst themselves. Therefore participants who can more easily reduce their emissions below their allocated allowances sell their surplus allowances to those who find it relatively harder to do so. The participants in the system could be states or firms, or some sort of hybrid, depending on the emissions trading system. It is argued that the economic benefit of emissions trading is that emissions reductions take place where it is cheapest to do so, thus reducing the overall costs of emissions reductions.[5]

Emissions trading has been an important element in arguments about how to organise emissions reductions internationally since the inception of climate change politics in the 1980s. Michael Grubb (1989) originally argued that emissions trading would provide a more politically feasible, economically efficient and internationally equitable solution than traditional means of organising emissions reductions. Some took up this idea over the next few years, notably UNCTAD (1992), but it was in the US statement at the UN Framework Convention on Climate Change (UNFCCC) Conference of the Parties (COP2) in Geneva in July 1996 that momentum started to build up for including emissions trading in what eventually became the Kyoto Protocol. There they shifted their position towards an acceptance of a binding emissions target, conditional upon the acceptance by other countries that such targets be pursued through 'flexible and cost-effective market-based solutions' (as quoted in Oberthür and Ott, 1999: 188). Such market mechanisms were then proposed by the USA in December 1996 and in a formal submission in January 1997, and throughout the run-up to Kyoto, the USA was the driving force for the inclusion of emissions trading and the other 'flexibility mechanisms'. While there were objections from continental European countries, from developing countries, and from environmental NGOs, after some bargaining emissions trading was included in Kyoto (see Oberthür and Ott, 1999: 188–91). Despite the initial resistance from a number of parties, the concept of emissions trading has gone on to be developed at national levels in the UK and Denmark. The European Union has also developed the first supranational greenhouse gas emissions trading system, and many other states are now in the process of developing such schemes. Some firms, such as BP, have developed their own internal trading schemes (Pulver, 2007).

The interesting question is how and why emissions trading took off so quickly from 1996 onwards. The response from economists and from most policy makers is that it provided for greater economic efficiency. Trading lowered the costs of emissions reductions, enabling states to commit themselves to such reductions and helping to overcome domestic opposition. Emissions trading as an instrument thus helped to overcome distributional conflicts between states with different costs of emissions reduction.

But this explanation does not explain the rapid growth in the popularity of emissions trading markets. Alongside the development of proposals for emissions trading schemes at global and national levels was a positive explosion of activity by financial market actors. During this period, a number of firms dedicated to trading carbon emerged, such as Ecosecurities or CO2e.com, as well as carbon market arms of many existing financial firms such as Barclays. A number of markets were organised as sites of trading such as the Chicago Climate Exchange, and two major market associations were formed – the International Emissions Trading Association (IETA) and the Emissions Marketing Association (EMA). Regular carbon finance conferences started to be organised (normally in London) where all these actors would meet, and Point Carbon emerged as an information service for the carbon markets, reporting on prices, policy changes, and so on. What explains this explosion of activity is that, while emissions trading can be understood in terms of economic efficiency, it very definitely operates through the creation of new markets in which firms can develop economic strategies and secondary markets. In fact, the futures market in this instance existed significantly before the real markets. In other words, the principal political-economic benefit of emissions trading is as a site of commodification of carbon in its role as a pollutant. Emissions trading as a project has been, and continues to be, propelled by the realisation by powerful financial actors that here was a new commodity to be sold, new profits to be made.

Joint Implementation (JI) and the Clean Development Mechanism (CDM) have significantly different features from emissions trading, but similarly operate to create and expand existing markets (see Halsnaes, 2002; Schwarze, 2002; Streck, 2004). They are similarly portrayed as measures that create flexibilities by allowing countries and firms to reduce emissions in the most cost-effective manner. The CDM, in particular, promotes emissions limitations beyond the countries that have formal obligations, to include the implementation of emissions reductions projects in developing countries.

These mechanisms should principally be understood in terms of the legitimisation of market access for firms from the EU, North America or Japan to countries in the South and in former Soviet Bloc states, the so-called economies in transition. JI creates a set of incentives under Kyoto for Western states and economies in transition, both Annex I countries to the UNFCCC. Western states have an incentive to promote their companies' overseas operations in economies in transition, and the economies in transition have a converse incentive to engage in projects with Western firms in order to gain both access to particular technologies and to reduce their emissions further. Similarly, the linkage between Kyoto emissions targets and the traditional state regulation of emissions works to create incentives for firms to look for investment opportunities abroad. Within the European Union emissions trading system, for example, firms can claim Emission Reduction Units by developing CDM or JI projects under Kyoto, but these also create Emission Reduction Units (or Removal Units in the case of a sinks project investing in, say, reforestation) for the state from which the investing firm comes.

JI has a complicated history. Like emissions trading, JI started life as a proposal during the negotiations of the UNFCCC, initially by the Norwegian climate change NGO, CICERO (Hanisch, 1991; Paterson, 1996: 110). The rationale was the same as for emissions trading: enabling cross-border investments in emissions reductions would facilitate cheaper reductions in emissions overall. This became embedded in the infamous articles 4.2(a) and (b) of the UNFCCC. The former suggested that 'these Parties (Annex 1, or industrialised countries) may implement such policies (to mitigate greenhouse gas emissions) jointly with other Parties', while the latter suggested that the reporting of policies and measures (the reporting, not the measures themselves) might help countries to reduce their emissions 'individually or jointly' (United Nations, 1992: Articles 4.2(a) and (b)).

Initially, developing countries were highly suspicious, arguing that such a measure was both a sneaky way of promoting emissions limitations commitments which they adamantly opposed, and a way for industrialised countries to avoid their own emissions reductions obligations. Environmental NGOs also emphasised the latter argument, in particular the need to limit the scope for such flexibility (e.g. CAN, 2000). But this conflictual pattern was broken, at least as regards the developing countries, by the Brazilian proposal shortly before Rio, quickly endorsed by the USA, for a Clean Development Mechanism, which would provide for industrialised countries to invest in emissions abatement in developing countries and claim it against their emissions reductions targets under Kyoto. The CDM was regarded as Kyoto's surprise (Werksman, 1998), since it seemed to represent a turnaround of developing country approaches to JI. Since then, if anything, developing countries have been progressively more enthusiastic about the CDM, arguing for its expansion both in terms of numbers of projects but, more importantly, in scope – for example with arguments to turn it from a project-oriented to a sector or programme-oriented body.[6]

There are plenty of questions about whether these measures actually contribute effectively to emissions reduction, and so on. Critically, JI and the CDM have increasingly been driven by the interests of private actors seeking investment and market-creation opportunities, and by state managers seeking to promote such opportunities for firms. This is perhaps less obvious than for emissions trading, but the interest is driven by a capacity to get into markets not previously occupied, to create market opportunities. As Streck suggests: 'what makes the CDM so appealing is that participation in the mechanism is driven by *pecuniary self-interest*' (Streck, 2004: 320, emphasis added). Schwarze's review (2002) of 'activities implemented jointly' projects shows that patterns of investment strongly reflect existing regional investment patterns by investor countries, with Japan and Australia investing exclusively in East Asia, the USA investing predominantly in Latin America, and Europe investing largely in economies in transition countries. The patterns of investment also reflect differences between Europe and the USA. Europe's projects are predominantly focused on energy technology, while the US approach is much more skewed towards forestry, reflecting a desire to offset emissions growth in the USA. More recently, it has become clear that well over half of the projects in the CDM process are going to four countries – China, India, Brazil and South Africa.

Policy makers and advisors repeatedly emphasise the need to overcome obstacles to the take-up of JI or CDM projects (e.g. Fankhauser and Lavric, 2003; Fichtner *et al.*, 2003). Some parts of the international organisational arrangements (notably UNEP's CD4CDM project, see http://cd4cdm.org/) are devoted to capacity building in developing countries, building up both institutions and awareness of the CDM in the South to enable projects to be developed. NGOs have also attempted to sell the CDM to private sector concerns by advocating it precisely in terms of its potential to create business opportunities. The World Resources Institute, for example, has argued that the CDM not only creates the possibility of offsetting company emissions of greenhouse gases and thus reducing risks of carbon exposure, but also that it can create commercial opportunities for investment in developing countries (Baumert, 2000). Shifts in the emphasis of the publication *Joint Implementation Quarterly* (www.jiqweb.org/dl.htm), which comments on the development of JI and CDM projects, are marked since its inception in 1995. Its initial coverage was couched primarily in terms of the environmental benefits of JI projects, while it presently focuses much more on JI and CDM projects as business opportunities. And international organisations such as UNCTAD have consistently promoted the 'emerging carbon market' (comprising emissions trading, JI and the CDM) in terms of how 'resource productivity makes protecting the climate a sound business proposition', and how the CDM makes it possible for developing countries to 'leap-frog technology streams' (Pronove, 2002). Significantly, UNCTAD also promotes the CDM as a means to develop 'international public–private partnerships under the Kyoto Protocol' (Stewart, 2000). More generally, such partnerships have become key to the broad patterns of neoliberal governance.

## Conclusions

In this chapter I have focused on climate change governance as an example of the most prominent part of global environmental governance and argued that it provides a useful guide to dominant trends. The first main trend is away from governance through regulatory mechanisms designed to restrict certain forms of economic activity and towards the promotion of a particular path of growth (in the case of the climate change regime to enabling renewable energy technologies, energy efficiency technologies and the like to be developed and diffused across the globe). The second trend is the construction of a political coalition which can legitimise the further development of global climate governance. In the climate change arena, this coalition involves not only renewable energy firms and the like, who are still relatively weak in most countries compared with fossil-fuel and automobile interests, but also financial sector interests. By creating potential markets for financial companies, it transforms the interests of those firms in relation to climate change. Given the dominance of finance within neoliberal globalisation, this situation would 'structurally select' (cf. Jessop, 1990) governance practices consistent with the interests of finance.

What of sustainability? The term sustainable is bandied about routinely but its meaning is unclear. My discussion in this chapter could suggest that sustainability is nothing but greenwash, an ideological smokescreen designed to mask the unsustainability of global capitalism. Many critics of emissions trading, the CDM, public–private partnerships, and so on, couch their criticisms precisely in these terms (see, for example, Bachram, 2004; Lohmann, 2005). But I would argue that the jury is still out on this question. What I have argued is not that dissimilar to standard ecological modernisation arguments (Weale, 1992; Hajer, 1995; Mol, 2001), except that the processes driving ecological modernisation are neoliberal and finance-led rather than social-democratic and corporatist.

The process of ecological modernisation, in effect, describes a process of economic transformation, driven by novel forms of economic governance, which enable economic growth and concurrent reductions of environmental impact. It strikes me, therefore, that it is possible that the sorts of 'governance through markets' could in the same way significantly change investment, production and consumption patterns. It is perfectly possible, for example, that the two elements identified above could combine to produce the decarbonisation of the economy, which is, of course, central to the achievement of sustainability. Specifically, the success of attempts made by investors to get firms to disclose $CO_2$-intensity depends to a large extent on the price signals given by carbon markets.

We are currently in a situation where decisions by states to ratchet up the commitments on the caps to be imposed on such markets would drive the carbon price up, so that investors would have powerful signals to move swiftly away from fossil fuels and towards renewable energy technologies, enhanced energy efficiency, and so on.[7] This may also be stimulated by increased fears of liability of firms and investors for climate damages (on this final point, see Allen and Lord, 2004). And it would seem unrealistic that such a shift to low-carbon technologies would mean that either growth is harmed or there is no 'real' environmental gain. It is quite possible that this process could be evaluated through a more robust account of sustainability (such as that elaborated by Katrina Brown in Chapter 2), specifically, one which insists on the radical reduction in consumption of non-renewable resources in the global economy.

This is not to say, of course, that the transformation is necessarily possible, and certainly not to say that it is without its contradictions. From the political-economy perspective adopted here, any form of capitalist development will be contradictory. Governance to promote a form of sustainable capitalism will be no exception. And this political-economy argument is a long way from being a purely technocentric one; the shifts in investment, production and consumption at the same time entail broad social and cultural changes. Transport is the clearest example of the need for social and cultural change;

whether sustainable transport is to be pursued through greening the car or overcoming automobile dependence, it most certainly entails dramatic changes in cultures of consumption and mobility (see Paterson, 2007). Indeed, Andy Dobson in Chapter 6 argues that measures which simply attempt to shape behaviour may fail decisively to change identities and attitudes.

But I suggest, in this chapter, that given the capitalist character of the world in which we live, the principal challenge in governing for sustainable development is to articulate an overall growth regime which can both sustain growth and achieve a reduction in the throughputs of non-renewable resources and pollution. Neoliberalism is starting to produce one such growth regime. There are, of course, critics who fundamentally and coherently oppose capitalism *per se*. But I cannot foresee the collapse of capitalism within the time-frames necessary to deal with challenges such as climate change. A challenge for critics who find capitalism either incoherent or politically objectionable is to articulate an alternative which is nevertheless a regime *for growth*.

## Notes

1 The tragedy is misnamed, as Hardin (1968) mistakes the character of property rights in traditional English commons, on which he bases his argument, since this tenure system incorporates the idea of land being held in common. His model, in fact, applies to what are now usually called open access resources, to which his logic of overexploitation (because of the lack of fit between individual and collective interests) is still frequently thought to apply.

2 The 'limits to growth' idea is now routinely read, rather persuasively I believe, in neoliberal ideology as an eco-socialist threat to capitalism, conveniently forgetting the irony that the idea and initial research to establish such limits was funded by the Club of Rome, one of the leading organisations of the transnational capitalist class of the era (van der Pijl, 1998).

3 Indeed, some in the West were explicit that the West should do this, as in Garrett Hardin's 'Living on a lifeboat' (Hardin, 1974).

4 I leave aside the highly politicised account of this process as encapsulated in the notion of biopiracy (Shiva, 1997). Whatever side one takes in this normative debate, it remains the case that the biodiversity regime is one designed to expand and legitimise the profit-making activities of a fairly small number of innovative and rapidly growing firms.

5 A prominent early argument, outlined clearly by Grubb (1989), was that emissions trading would also facilitate large-scale North–South transfers of finance and technology. These were needed, he argued, to allow developing countries to 'tunnel through' to low-carbon futures without the large international bureaucracy or transfer of authority that an international carbon tax would entail. This justice-oriented argument stimulated UNCTAD's (1992) early interest in emissions trading, but has, however, fallen by the wayside in justifying emissions trading over the years.

6 See, for example, the Indian proposals made at the COP12/MOP2 in Nairobi, November 2006, in the context of the dialogue on long-term co-operative action to address climate change by enhancing implementation of the Convention (Sethi, 2006).

7 One exception seems to be carbon capture and storage. At present, this seems expensive to do on a large scale, stimulated directly by any plausible price per ton of carbon. But we should remember that most of the other technologies, of which wind is paradigmatic, have experienced radical price reductions in short periods of time, in part because of these dynamic effects of investment, expansion of supply and technological innovation.

# References

Allen, M. R. and Lord, R. 2004. 'The blame game', *Nature* 432: 551–2.

Bachram, H. 2004. 'Climate fraud and carbon colonialism: the new trade in greenhouse gases', *Capitalism, Nature, Socialism* 15(4): 5–20.

Baumert, K. 2000. *The Clean Development Mechanism*. Presentation to the Safe Climate Sound Business Workshop, 18th September, World Resources Institute, Washington DC. URL: www.wri.org/wri/meb/wrisummit/pdfs/baumert.pdf.

Bernstein, S. 2001. *The Compromise of Liberal Environmentalism*. New York: Columbia University Press.

CAN (Climate Action Network) 2000. *COP6 CAN Position on the Clean Development Mechanism: Sustainable Development and Emissions Reductions*. The Hague: Climate Action Network. URL: www.climatenetwork.org/pages/publications.html.

Carlsson, S. and Stripple, J. 2003. 'Climate governance beyond the state', *Global Governance* 9: 385–9.

Cashore, B., Auld, G. and Newsom, D. 2004. *Governing Through Markets: Forest Certification and the Emergence of Non-State Authority*. New Haven, CT: Yale University Press.

Chatterjee, P. and Finger, M. 1994. *The Earth Brokers: Power, Politics and World Development*. London, UK: Routledge.

Clapp, J. 1998. 'The privatization of global environmental governance: ISO 14000 and the developing world', *Global Governance* 4: 295–316.

Cox, R. W. 1987. *Production, Power and World Order*. New York: Columbia University Press.

Fankhauser, S. and Lavric, L. 2003. 'The investment climate for climate investment: Joint Implementation in transition countries', *Climate Policy* 3: 417–34.

Fichtner, W., Graehl, S. and Rentz, O. 2003. 'The impact of private investors' transaction costs on the cost effectiveness of project-based Kyoto mechanisms', *Climate Policy* 3: 249–59.

Grubb, M. 1989. *The Greenhouse Effect: Negotiating Targets*. London, UK: Royal Institute of International Affairs.

Haas, P. M., Keohane, R. O. and Levy, M. A. 1993. *Institutions for the Earth: Sources of Effective Environmental Protection*. Cambridge, MA: MIT Press.

Hajer, M. 1995. *The Politics of Environmental Discourse: Ecological Modernisation and the Policy Process*. Oxford, UK: Clarendon.

Halsnaes, K. 2002. 'A review of the literature on climate change and sustainable development', in Markandya, A. and Halsnaes, K. (eds.) *Climate Change and Sustainable Development: Prospects for Developing Countries*. London, UK: Earthscan, pp. 61–7.

Hanisch, T. (ed.) 1991. *A Comprehensive Approach to Climate Change: Additional Elements from an Inter-disciplinary Perspective*, Report of a Workshop, Oslo July 1–3 1991. CICERO, University of Oslo.

Hardin, G. 1968. 'The tragedy of the commons', *Science* 162: 1243–8.

Hardin, G. 1974. 'Living on a lifeboat', *BioScience* 24: 561–8.

Hay, C. 1994. 'Environmental security and state legitimacy', in O'Connor, M. (ed.) *Is Capitalism Sustainable? Political Economy and the Politics of Ecology*. New York: Guilford Press.

Helleiner, E. 1994. *States and the Reemergence of Global Finance: From Bretton Woods to the 1990s*. Ithaca, NY: Cornell University Press.

Helm, D. (ed.) 1991. *Economic Policy Towards the Environment*. Oxford, UK: Blackwell.

Jagers, S., Paterson, M. and Stripple, J. 2005. 'Privatising governance, practicing triage: securitization of insurance risks and the politics of global warming', in Levy, D. and Newell, P. (eds.) *The Business of Global Environmental Governance*. Cambridge, MA: MIT Press, pp. 149–74.

Jessop, B. 1990. *State Theory*. Cambridge, UK: Polity Press.

Jordan, A. J., Wurzel, R. and Zito, A. (eds.) 2003. *New Instruments of Environmental Governance?* London, UK: Frank Cass.

Keohane, R. O. 1989. *International Institutions and State Power: Essays in International Relations Theory*. Boulder, CO: Westview.

Krasner, S. D. 1983. 'Structural causes and regime consequences: regimes as intervening variables', in Krasner, S. D. (ed.) *International Regimes*. Ithaca, NY: Cornell University Press.

Lohmann, L. 2005. 'Marketing and making carbon dumps: commodification, calculation and counterfactuals in climate change mitigation', *Science as Culture* 14: 203–35.

Meadows, D. H., Meadows, D. L., Randers, R. and Behrens, W. 1972. *The Limits to Growth*. London, UK: Pan.

Miles, E. L., Underdal, A., Andresen, S., Wettestad, J., Skjaerseth, J. B. and Carlin, E. M. 2002. *Environmental Regime Effectiveness: Confronting Theory with Evidence*. Cambridge, MA: MIT Press.

Mitchell, R. 2003. 'International environmental agreements: a survey of their features, formation and effects', *Annual Review of Energy and the Environment* 28: 429–61.

Mol, A. 2001. *Globalization and Environmental Reform: The Ecological Modernisation of the Global Economy*. Cambridge, MA: MIT Press.

Newell, P. 2000. 'Environmental NGOs and globalisation: the governance of TNCs', in Cohen, R. and Rai, S. (eds.) *Global Social Movements*. London, UK: Athlone, pp. 117–34.

Newell, P. 2003. 'Globalisation and the governance of biotechnology', *Global Environmental Politics* 3(2): 56–72.

Oberthür, S. and Ott, H. 1999. *The Kyoto Protocol: International Climate Policy for the 21st Century*. Berlin, Germany: Springer.

Ophuls, W. 1977. *Ecology and the Politics of Scarcity*. San Francisco, CA: Freeman.

Paterson, M. 1996. *Global Warming and Global Politics*. London, UK: Routledge.

Paterson, M. 2001. 'Risky business: insurance companies in global warming politics', *Global Environmental Politics* 1(4): 18–42.

Paterson, M. 2007. *Automobile Politics: Ecology and Cultural Political Economy*. Cambridge, UK: Cambridge University Press.

Pearce, D., Markandya A. and Barbier, E. 1989. *Blueprint for a Green Economy*. London, UK: Earthscan.

Pronove, G. 2002. *The Kyoto Protocol and the Emerging Carbon Market*. Unpublished paper, UNCTAD, Geneva. URL: http://r0.unctad.org/ghg/sitecurrent/download_c/publications.html.

Pulver, S. 2007. 'Making sense of corporate environmentalism: an environmental contestation approach to analyzing the causes and consequences of the climate change policy split in the oil industry', *Organization and Environment* 20: 1–40.

Rosenau, J. N. 1992. 'Governance, order, and change in world politics', in Rosenau, J. N. and Czempiel, E.-O. (eds.) *Governance without Government: Order and Change in World Politics*. Cambridge, UK: Cambridge University Press.

Sachs, W. (ed.) 1993. *Global Ecology*. London, UK: Zed Books.

Schwarze, R. 2002. Activities implemented jointly', in Schneider, S., Rosencranz, A. and Niles, J. (eds.) *Climate Change Policy: A Survey*. Washington DC: Island Press, pp. 293–304.

Sethi, S. 2006. *Dialogue on Cooperative Action*. Presentation to the 'Dialogue on long-term cooperative action to address climate change by enhancing implementation of the Convention: Second workshop, 15–16 November 2006'. Nairobi, Kenya. URL: http://unfccc.int/meetings/dialogue/items/3759.php.

Shiva, V. 1993. 'The greening of the global reach', in Sachs, W. (ed.) *Global Ecology*, London, UK: Zed Books, pp. 53–60.

Shiva, V. 1997. *Biopiracy: The Plunder of Nature and Knowledge*. Boston, MA: South End Press.

Stewart, R. 2000. *The Clean Development Mechanism: Building International Public–Private Partnerships under the Kyoto Protocol: Technical, Financial and Institutional Issues*. Geneva: UNCTAD.

Streck, C. 2004. 'New partnerships in global environmental policy: the Clean Development Mechanism', *Journal of Environment and Development* 13: 295–322.

Thomas, C. 1992. *The Environment in International Relations*. London, UK: Royal Institute of International Affairs.

UNCTAD (United Nations Conference on Trade and Development) 1992. *Tradeable Entitlements for Carbon Emissions Abatement*. INT/91 A29. Geneva: United Nations Conference on Trade and Development.

UNEP FI (United Nations Environment Programme, Financial Industry Initiative) 2006. *Using the Global Framework for Climate Risk Disclosure*. Geneva: United Nations Environment Programme, Financial Industry Initiative.

United Nations 1992. *Framework Convention on Climate Change*. New York: United Nations.

van der Pijl, K. 1998. *Transnational Classes and International Relations*. London, UK: Routledge.

Vogler, J. 1995. *The Global Commons: A Regime Analysis*. Chichester, UK: Wiley.

Waltz, K. 1979. *Theory of International Politics*. Reading, MA: Addison-Wesley.

Ward, B. and Dubos, R. 1972. *Only One Earth: The Care and Maintenance of a Small Planet*. New York: Norton.

WCED (World Commission on Environment and Development) 1987. *Our Common Future: Report of the World Commission on Environment and Development*. Oxford University Press.

Weale, A. 1992. *The New Politics of Pollution*. Manchester University Press.

Wendt, A. 1999. *Social Theory of International Politics*. Cambridge University Press.

Werksman, J. 1998. 'The clean development mechanism: unwrapping the Kyoto surprise', *Review of European Community and International Environmental Law* 7(2): 147–58.

Williamson, J. 1990. 'What Washington means by policy reform', in Williamson, J. (ed.) *Latin American Adjustment: How Much Has Happened?* Washington, DC: Institute for International Economics.

Young, O.R. 1989. *International Cooperation: Building Regimes for Natural Resources and the Environment*. Ithaca, NY: Cornell University Press.

Young, O.R. (ed.) 1997. *Global Governance: Drawing Insights from the Environmental Experience*. Ithaca, NY: Cornell University Press.

Young, O.R. (ed.) 1999. *The Effectiveness of International Environmental Regimes: Causal Connections and Behavioral Mechanisms*. Cambridge, MA: MIT Press.

# PART III

# Governance and Civil Society

# 6 Citizens, citizenship and governance for sustainability

ANDY DOBSON

## Introduction

This chapter contributes to the current debate regarding environmental attitudes and behaviour, and how to change them by employing systems of governance. It is also, I believe, a contribution to citizenship theory and practice, in that my enquiry into environmental attitudes and behaviour leads me to develop a notion of ecological citizenship which I take to differ in significant ways from the citizenship traditions which history has bequeathed us. Finally, to the extent that citizenship can be sensibly talked of as a potential governance tool for achieving sustainability, my argument bears directly on the two main themes of this book: governance and sustainability. Any move to enlist citizenship for the policy toolbox looks like a move towards governance rather than government – i.e. society self-steering rather than being steered by some hierarchically superior body – and I shall come back to this toward the end of the chapter.

As far as changing environmental attitudes and behaviour using different policy instruments is concerned, in the UK, at least, there is a very obvious front-runner: fiscal incentives. This is not a new idea, of course, and any primer on environmental economics will contain a description and assessment of them (e.g. Turner *et al.*, 1994). The idea, as we know, is that people are encouraged into environmentally beneficial behaviour through offering them financial advantages and penalties, to which they respond appropriately. The idea of fiscal incentives is a useful foil for the subsequent discussion here of environmental citizenship. Therefore in the next section I shall describe two examples from the British and Irish context before identifying two difficulties with this approach to changing attitudes and behaviour. This will lead, finally, to a discussion of environmental citizenship.

## Fiscal incentives: a tool of sustainable governance?

The first example of a fiscal incentive that I shall investigate is that of road pricing. It comes from the ancient city of Durham, in the north of England. Durham has a very beautiful and old city centre, which was beginning to suffer from the effects of too much traffic. City planners were therefore confronted with the challenge of dissuading people from driving their cars into the square. After much discussion, they decided to adopt a road pricing scheme. Where once it was free to drive your car into the square, it now costs £2.00 or so to take it there. The planners had no real idea whether this would work, but they hoped that traffic would be cut by 50 per cent within a year. In fact it was cut by 85 per cent in just a few months, with a 10 per cent increase in pedestrian activity, and increased use of the local bus service (CFIT, 2005). This was success beyond the planners' wildest dreams, and it seems to suggest that the fiscal route to changing people's environmental behaviour actually works.

The second example comes from the Republic of Ireland. On 4 March 2002, a Plastic Bag Environmental Levy (PBEL) was introduced as a charge on plastic shopping bags throughout Ireland (DELG, 2002). From that date, non-exempt bags have cost shoppers 20 pence (€0.15) each or so. As a result, the use of plastic bags has been cut by more than 90 per cent – removing over one billion plastic bags from circulation each year (BBC, 2002). Once again, the news seems completely good. Fiscal measures work and behaviour is changed, almost overnight.

There seems little doubt that fiscal incentives of this sort have a place in the policy toolbox of sustainable development. Governments would be foolish indeed to ignore these sources of motivation and the political possibilities they produce. But I also want to argue that if governments focus exclusively on these methods of changing our behaviour, they are likely to fall short of their objectives. Let me point out two difficulties with the 'fiscal self-interest' approach to the governance of sustainable development.

The first is that it is based on a 'self-interested rational actor' model of human motivation, according to which people do things either for some gain or to avoid some harm to themselves. This makes it seem realistic and hard-headed, but it has a soft underbelly. Once again an example will serve to make the point. Household waste in Britain is currently thought to be growing at 3 per cent per year, and the government is considering ways of getting people to throw less waste away. One suggestion is to impose a 'rubbish tax', so that people who throw away over-quota rubbish will be asked to pay a small tax – say £3.00 per bag (DEFRA, 2003). From one point of view the logic is impeccable: people will want to avoid paying the rubbish tax and so will reduce the amount of waste they throw away. But critics of the proposed scheme immediately pointed out that this model contains the seeds of its own demise. People uncommitted to the idea behind the scheme will take the line of least resistance in a way entirely consistent with the model of behaviour on which the scheme depends – but entirely at odds with its desired outcomes. As a newspaper editorial pointed out, 'Rather than pay up, the public are likely to vote with their cars and take their rubbish and dump it on the pavement, in the countryside or in someone else's backyard' (*The Guardian*, 12 July 2002).

So that is the first potential problem: financial penalties invite attempts to get around them. In another, but related, context, a whole industry has built up around means of making number plates illegible to cameras as cars enter the Congestion Zone in the centre of London, for example, so as to avoid paying the congestion charge. It is helpful to bear in mind the distinction between superficial signals and underlying rationales. Drivers in this case react to superficial signals given off by the financial disincentive without caring about, understanding or being committed to the underlying rationale for the incentives to which they respond.

Bearing this in mind, we could try a thought experiment. What would happen if a future Irish government took away the plastic bag tax? Would people revert to using a new plastic bag for each couple of items of shopping, or would the levy have had the effect of changing people's attitudes to the point that more sustainable behaviour was cemented in place? What would happen, say, if Durham City Council abandoned the road pricing scheme? Would people keep out of the city square? Or would they go back to their original and unsustainable behaviour?

It is possible to argue that the success of the Durham scheme has been bought at the cost of the failure to make anything other than a superficial impression on people's habits and practices. The change in behaviour lasts only as long as the incentives or disincentives are in place – and these are inevitably subject to the vagaries of fashion, experiment, and the direction of the political wind that happens to be blowing at the time.

The short-lived nature of the impact of taxes points to the second problem with the fiscal self-interest approach to environmental policy. We can illustrate the issue by returning to the Irish plastic bag example. According to the Irish government, the two stated aims of the scheme were 'to encourage the use of reusable bags and to change people's attitudes to litter and pollution in Ireland'. As far as the first aim is concerned, as we saw, the evidence is that the scheme has been a success. The use of plastic bags has been cut by 90 per cent, and a billion bags a year have been removed from circulation. So *behaviour* has changed. But have *attitudes* changed? Have people's attitudes to litter and pollution decisively changed in Ireland?

## Understanding the link between social attitudes and social behaviour

As far as I know, no follow-up research has been done on the specific question of whether attitudes to pollution in Ireland have altered. But the formula does raise the key distinction between changing *behaviour* and changing *attitudes*. The plastic bag levy is designed to do both, and the levy's aims are expressed in such a way as to make us think that there is an uncomplicated reciprocal relationship between the two: changes in behaviour will lead to changes in attitude, and changes in attitude will lead to changes in behaviour.

But a moment's reflection might lead us to think that the latter is more likely than the former – that changes in attitude will lead to changes in behaviour. On the face of it, it makes sense to think that if our underlying attitudes to waste and pollution change, changes to our behaviour will follow. The reverse effect – that a change in behaviour will lead to a change in underlying attitudes – seems less likely. We can change our behaviour in respect of the consumption of plastic bags without that change of behaviour 'overflowing' into a more general change of attitude as far as waste and pollution is concerned.

There is one rider to this apparently common-sense view, though: we should recognise the possibility that behaviour can be habituated over time. There could come a point at which the disincentives could be kicked away without making a difference to behaviour – so long as the behaviour had become habitual. From this point of view, any difference there might be between attitudes and behaviour is immaterial: if the point is to secure long-term changes in behaviour, then policies aimed at behaviour change only, without regard to underlying attitudes, can also work – as long as the behaviour is changed for long enough for it to become habitual.

Two responses might be made to this rider, in turn. First, in the context of the apparent need for widespread changes in behaviour, this bit-by-bit or sector-by-sector approach to change might be too limited. Second, and connected, it has often been pointed out that environmental problems are linked, and are caused by systemic problems which are only partially susceptible to a piecemeal approach (see, for example, Chapter 5). So part of the point of the attitudes approach is precisely that it involves actors in making connections between apparently discrete environmental issues. The danger with the behavioural approach is that it fails to encourage this type of social learning, and may even work actively to undermine it.

There seems good reason, then, to work a little longer with the distinction between underlying attitudes and superficial behaviour. We have seen some of the problems associated with focusing too much on the latter – yet this seems to be exactly what governments are doing. The UK government, for example, carried out a major review of its sustainable development strategy in 2004, and citizens were asked to comment on a document called *Taking it On* (DEFRA, 2004). The part of the document that deals with bringing about sustainable development is called, significantly, 'Changing behaviour' (DEFRA, 2004: 26–7), and much of the focus is on 'the market', 'economic instruments' and so on.

It is my view that governments committed to sustainable development – i.e. practically every government on the planet, formally at least – need to give some thought to changing attitudes as well as altering behaviour, since both are key to achieving the objective of sustainability. The stakes are high. I explain below how potentially disastrous it can be to get this wrong.

## Changing attitudes: what role for ecological citizenship?

Changing attitudes is easier said than done. Just where do we start? It would certainly help to begin with a broader picture of human motivation. The policies I have talked about thus far are all based on theories that have individuals acting out of self-interest. But we all know that some of us, some of the time, do things because we think they are the right thing to do, even if they conflict with our perceived self-interest.

At no point in the debate initiated by the UK government was this alternative approach canvassed, admirably captured in the following from Ludwig Beckman:

> the fact that the sustainability of the consumerist and individualist lifestyle is put in question undoubtedly raises a whole range of questions about how to reconstruct our society. What new economic and political institutions are needed? What regulations and set of incentives are necessary in order to redirect patterns of behaviour in sustainable directions? However, the question of sustainable behaviour cannot be reduced to a discussion about balancing carrots and sticks. The citizen that sorts her garbage or that prefers ecological goods will often do this because she feels committed to ecological values and ends. The citizen may not, that is, act in sustainable ways solely out of economic or practical incentives: people sometimes choose to do good for other reasons than fear (of punishment or loss) or desire (for economic rewards or social status). People sometimes do good because they want to be virtuous (Beckman, 2001: 179).

Beckman is gesturing here towards one aspect of a conception of environmental or ecological citizenship, and this is what I shall focus on in most of the rest of this chapter. I discuss the specific issue of environmental or ecological citizenship in greater detail in my book *Citizenship and the Environment* (Dobson, 2003). Below I summarise the citizenship arguments presented there as a counterpoint to the fiscal approach to environmental policy, and as a prelude to discussing their relative merits at the end of this chapter. We can begin by thinking about environmental citizenship in relation to the two principal traditions which 2,000 years of citizenship theory and practice have bequeathed us: liberal and civic republican citizenship. I am going to suggest that environmental citizenship bears a family relationship to these venerable traditions, but that it is a somewhat unruly child.

## *The liberal model of citizenship*

Let me take the liberal tradition first. One of the key tropes of liberal citizenship is, of course, the language of rights. Some would argue, indeed, that the rights of the citizen in relation to the state, and the entitlements that follow them, define liberal citizenship. So to the degree that environmental politics can be expressed in the language of rights, it can also be incorporated into the canon of liberal citizenship. There are three ways in which this might be done.

First, the list of human and, by extension, citizenship rights might be extended to include the right to a liveable and sustainable environment. This kind of right is increasingly a part of written constitutions – and especially newly minted ones.

A related, but more profound, point is that this right to a sustainable environment might be regarded as the precondition for the enjoyment of other political, civic and social rights. Socialists have traditionally argued that the right to free association means little without the material preconditions that make this right a real and daily possibility. Similarly, political ecologists suggest that without a liveable environment other formal rights cannot be substantively enjoyed.

Finally there is the possibility of rights *of* the environment. Most of the debate in liberal citizenship has been about *what* the entitlements of citizens should be – right to free speech, to free association, to rights of security of various types. Little attention has been given to *who* or *what* should have these rights, whatever they may be. This is the ecological challenge to liberal notions of environmental citizenship: to offer an immanent critique of the (liberal) conditions and characteristics that admit beings to the citizenship game. If some of those characteristics are possessed by beings other than human beings, should not these other beings be admitted to the charmed citizenship circle?

If any group of animals has a claim to be similar to humans in relevant respects it is the great apes. This thought has given rise to the Great Ape Project (GAP) (www.greatapeproject.org/); for the purposes of the project the great apes comprise 'human beings, chimpanzees, bonobos, gorillas and orang-utans'. The project's supporters ask for 'the removal of the non-human great apes from the category of property, and for the immediate inclusion within the category of persons'. The political aim is, 'to include the non-human great apes within the community of equals by granting them the basic moral and legal protection that only human beings currently enjoy' (www.greatapeproject.org/index.html). If and when the non-human great apes are categorised as 'persons' it will be hard to deny them some of the rights that liberal conceptions of citizenship bestow.

Some of these rights might be hard to ascribe to non-human animals (e.g. the right to vote), but non-human great ape versions of civil rights (e.g. the right to associate freely) and social rights (e.g. the right to social security) are by no means impossible to conceive.

## The civic republican model of citizenship

So liberal citizenship is amenable, yet peculiarly vulnerable, to the challenge of political ecology. We can now turn to the other great tradition which we have been bequeathed: the civic republican model. This seems to be a more straightforwardly robust ally for environmental conceptions of citizenship. Four features of civic republicanism resonate loudly with the impulses of political ecology: the focus on the common good, and the related notion of citizen obligation, the stress on political virtue, and the idea of the active citizen.

First, then, 'the environment' is a public good on which we all depend for the production and reproduction of daily life. It is indeed surely a fantasy to think that sustainability can always be a 'win–win' policy objective, in which each gain for the common good will also be a gain for each and every individual member of society. The environmental citizen's behaviour will be influenced by an attitude that is – in part, at least – informed by the knowledge that what is good for me as an individual is not necessarily good for me as a member of a social collective. Market-based instruments do not raise this possibility in any systematic way, and so are incomplete as prompts for social learning.

What of obligation, another key theme in civic republican citizenship? Again, we know that the civic republican's obligation is to work towards the common good – and it is not hard to see how this might provide a powerful resource for political ecologists. The stress on the quotidian, personal, nature of green politics is one of the strongest currents in political ecology. We are constantly enjoined to link the facts of the form of our daily behaviour with the state of the environment we find around us. Green politics urges us to connect the way we live our lives with the impact we make upon the natural world. We are made to feel responsible for the state of the environment, and simultaneously encouraged to see that we can do something about it.

This links to the third element of common cause between civic republicans and political ecologists: the importance of the exercise of virtue. For civic republicans, virtues are connected with improving the condition of the republic, while for political ecologists they are a means to the end of environmental sustainability. These differing objectives colour the virtues themselves. Civic republicanism is replete with tales of courage, sacrifice and manliness; while developing theories of ecological citizenship speak of justice, and of care, concern and compassion. A little later on I shall draw a distinction between virtues such as care and compassion, and the virtue of justice. Care and compassion have been rather instinctively – and unthinkingly – enlisted into service as the appropriate virtues for environmental citizenship. I believe there are principled reasons for resisting this ideological knee-jerk, and for claiming that justice is the first virtue of environmental citizenship. I shall explain why, shortly.

Finally, tying all this together is the vision of the citizen as an active political animal. The idea is that the aims of neither civic republicanism nor political ecology will be achievable without citizen participation. This is where the claims that the citizenship approach to sustainability takes us away from government and towards governance seem perhaps at their most persuasive. The argument is that sustainability requires a framework of rules and regulations, of course, and that it is the job of government to generate that framework. In the most effective cases, those subject to them will regard these rules and regulations as legitimate and will hopefully have participated in some form in their development and approbation.

But the political-ecological point goes further than this minimalist account of participatory activity. Sustainability, it is said, also requires daily vigilance by citizens themselves in regard to their impact on the environment. The form of citizens' daily lives – their 'participation' in the widest sense – is what shapes the contours of sustainability itself.

## The nature of ecological citizenship

So both the liberal and civic republican traditions of citizenship provide us with resources to think about the nature of environmental or ecological citizenship. Rights, obligation, the common good, virtue, participation, will all be present in the lexicon of environmental citizenship. But, as I said earlier, environmental citizenship is an unruly child of these traditions. Environmental citizenship makes two challenges to the liberal and republican traditions, and to mount them it draws on feminism and cosmopolitanism. Building on feminism, it takes seriously the idea that citizenship can properly be linked to the private realm. Along with cosmopolitanism, it asks whether the nation state – and its homologues – are an exhaustive expression of the political space of citizenship.

Let me take these points in turn, with the private realm first. Ecological politics is a quotidian politics – a politics that embraces and entails the everyday metabolistic relationship between individuals and the non-human natural world, as well as that relationship mediated by our presence and participation in 'public' bodies. We cannot, and do not, turn that relationship on and off when we cross some putative public–private divide. In a term borrowed from postmodernism, we are 'always already' consumers of environmental services and producers of waste, from the moment we are born to the moment we die, in public and in private, in sickness and in health. From this point of view it is perverse to regard campaigning for a recycling centre as an act of citizenship, and deny the accolade to the act of separating biodegradable and other materials just because you do it in the privacy of your own home. The ecological challenge is to regard both of these as acts of citizenship.

It might be objected at this point – or at a number of others – that citizenship, *by definition*, is about the public rather than the private realm, and so if we insist on politicising the private we cannot do so by enlisting the language of citizenship. But this forgets that political concepts are historical: their meaning changes with the times. It forgets that they are internally malleable: there is intellectual wriggle room in their conceptual structure. Above all, perhaps, it forgets that political concepts are *political*. This is to say that definitions cannot stand outside the relationships of political power they are intended to describe. They stand in a complex relationship to this power: neither simply reflecting it nor uncomplicatedly calling it into question. To this degree, citizenship is a site of political struggle, and feminist, cosmopolitan and ecological challenges to it amount to the challenge to incorporate these new politics in it.

So, if the personal is political, can citizenship really turn its back on private space? In a globalising world, has citizenship really got nothing to say about transnational obligation? Must citizenship remain silent about environmental sustainability in its infra- and extra-state contexts just because status-citizenship begins and ends with nation states and their homologues? It would seem strange for the definitional hold on citizenship as a concept to be so strong that it could not engage with 'private' political acts, nor have a view of the ties that might bind people in different parts of the world.

In this last context, the idea of the 'ecological footprint' comes into its own. This perhaps is where that young adolescent, the new kid on the citizenship block – environmental citizenship – is at its most recalcitrant. The ecological footprint is an expression of environmental impact – in this case, the environmental impact of individual citizens (Wackernagel and Rees, 1996). The impact we have on our environment is related to the 'quantity' of nature that we use or 'appropriate' to sustain our consumption patterns. In the globalising world in which we live, this impact extends in time and in space.

All theories of citizenship have a conception of political space – the space in which citizens move, and which constitutes the arena in which citizens' rights and obligations are exercised. All theories of citizenship also have an account of the obligations of citizenship, and the space and obligations of citizenship are usually related, if only in the sense that the obligations of citizenship are exhaustively exercised in the relevant citizenship space – the nation state, for example. The relevance of the ecological footprint to us is that it contains the key spatial and obligation-generating relationships that give rise to the exercise of specifically citizenly virtues in the environmental context.

The *nature* of the obligation is to reduce the occupation of ecological space, where appropriate, and the *source* of this obligation lies in remedying the potential and actual injustice of appropriating an unjust share of such space. It is especially important to see that this is a matter of justice, not of charity. I mentioned earlier that it was a mistake to jump too hastily to the conclusion that environmental citizenship is primarily informed by 'soft' virtues such as care and compassion. These are important virtues, for sure, but I argue that they are secondary and supplementary in relation to the first virtue of ecological citizenship, which is justice (Dobson, 2003: 129–35).

Thus the responsibilities of the environmental citizen are not the same as those that follow from the devastating 2004 tsunami in the Indian Ocean, for example. The key difference between my relationship to climate change and to the tsunami, is that I am partially responsible for the first and not at all responsible for the second. This prompts very different types of moral response. In general, in the case of suffering for which I am not responsible, compassion and charity are appropriate responses. Again, in general, in the case of suffering for which I am responsible, justice is the appropriate response.

This distinction is important, since the obligation structures of justice and of charity are very different. Charity is a notoriously weak basis for obligation: it is easily withdrawn ('terribly sorry, no spare change in my pocket this morning'). Crucially, the structure of giving contained within it reproduces the vulnerability of the recipient. Contrast this with justice. One can 'not do' justice, of course – just as one can 'not do' charity. But the obligation to do justice remains, even while it is not being done. Second, relations of justice are relations between putative equals. The element of paternalism that is present in charitable relations is absent in relations of justice.

There is perhaps something of an irony here, in that the response to the Indonesian tsunami and the more recent earthquake in Kashmir indicates that people do charity better than they do justice. It is a lot easier to do charity, of course. Charity can be switched on and off, while justice requires constant vigilance and political commitment.

In sum, those individuals, agencies, corporations and departments who (or which) occupy too much ecological space have a duty to reduce their impact for the sake of those who occupy too little. This is the principal duty of environmental citizenship.

The ecological footprint idea also explains and reflects the asymmetrical and non-reciprocal nature of ecological citizenship obligations. Obligations are owed by those in ecological space debt (those who occupy more than their fair share), and these obligations are the corollary of a putative environmental right to an equal share of ecological space for everyone. This is a demanding prospectus, especially under conditions in which, in so-called advanced industrial societies, individual room for ecological space manoeuvre is limited by living in a society which operates at a high level of systemic ecological space occupancy. It is difficult for individuals to make a difference, and the lesson we learn from modelling reductions of ecological footprint size in societies like the UK is that environmental citizenship cannot only be a matter of individuals trying to reduce their own ecological space occupancy, where appropriate, but also involves those same individuals working in the traditional spaces of the public sphere to move society as a whole in a different direction. All this puts the issue of liberal harm-avoidance principles in a different kind of perspective. Such principles are often accused of being far too tame and of not requiring enough of those who subscribe to them. But in the context of a phenomenon such as global warming it is clear that harm avoidance can involve perpetrators of harm in quite significant commitments – up to and including wholesale changes in lifestyle.

## Attitudes and behaviour: a reprise

Overall, then, the duty of the environmental citizen is to live sustainably so that others may live well. And this takes us back to the earlier part of this chapter. There I drew a distinction between attitudes and behaviour. I argued that attitudes work at a deeper level than behaviour, but that behaviour change is what most environmental policy is aimed at. The most common form of this type of policy is the 'fiscal incentive' policy. Environmental citizenship gets at things at a different level. It works at a deeper level by asking people to reflect on the attitudes that inform their behaviour. More specifically, it asks people to consider their behaviour in the context of justice and injustice.

In most cases, this may well give us the same answer as the 'fiscal incentive' route, but for different reasons. And the reasons are important. This can be illustrated through the Durham city centre car example:

- under a fiscal incentive policy, people stop driving into the city centre because of fear of a fine;
- from an environmental citizenship point of view, people drive less in general because they know that car driving contributes to global warming, that global warming affects poor people more than rich ones, and that too much car-driving leaves too big an ecological footprint.

In other words, the environmental citizen's behaviour is informed by a systemic understanding of the problems that lead to the perpetration of injustice in the form of the occupancy of unjust amounts of ecological space. Once this understanding is in place, a reversion to previous patterns of behaviour seems less likely than in the case of behaviour that reacts to fiscal incentives and disincentives. My suggestion, then, is that behaviour driven by environmental citizenship considerations is more likely to last – i.e. be sustainable – than

Table 6.1 *Prospects for behavioural and attitude change through building citizenship or promotion of fiscal incentives*

|                                   | Environmental citizenship | Fiscal incentives and disincentives |
| --------------------------------- | ------------------------- | ----------------------------------- |
| Change attitudes (long term)      | good                      | less good                           |
| Change behaviour (short term)     | less good                 | good                                |

behaviour driven by financial incentives. But there is a corresponding disadvantage. We should admit that environmental citizenship is much harder to 'get going' than fiscally driven behaviour. Fiscal incentives can change behaviour almost overnight, while environmental citizenship initiatives could take much longer. The dilemma can be illustrated with the grid in Table 6.1 that simply shows how the prospects for action may be distributed.

At this stage it is tempting to say that we do not have to choose between fiscal incentives and environmental citizenship. Given their respective and apparently complementary merits, cannot governments simply pursue them both at the same time? But research being carried out on the motivations that lie behind household sustainability in Sweden calls this into question.

Christer Berglund and Simon Matti (2006) point to recent research into people's negative responses to the introduction of economic incentives by analysing their intrinsic and extrinsic motivation to act sustainably. This research points to the importance of rethinking the interaction between different types of motivation: taking them in isolation appears to be a mistake, yet this is just what the 'both ... and' approach to citizenship and fiscal incentives does. Critically for us, it has been observed that monetary incentives can 'crowd out' other, intrinsic, sorts of motivation.

One example of this phenomenon at work is a case study of a 'token economy', where old people living in asylums were exposed to different economic incentives such as making their beds in exchange for vouchers. After some time, these people were no longer prepared to do anything if they were not paid for it, i.e. they were 'demoralised' (or perhaps 'de-moralised') by the incentive structure presented to them (Frey, 1999). Furthermore it seems that, once crowded out, the intrinsic motivation is not guaranteed to return when the monetary incentive is removed. All this calls into question the assumption that both kinds of policy can be pursued simultaneously without either one affecting the other.

Berglund and Matti provide us with a striking picture of government and people at odds with one another over the wellsprings of good environmental habits and practices. On the one hand there is the government, pursuing the consumer-orientated path. Lenart Lundqvist (2004: 166–7) has carried out a content analysis of official reports containing contemporary Swedish environmental policy, and he concludes that references to individuals as citizens are made only a total of sixteen times. By contrast, the words customer, consumer or individual are used about 470 times across, in total, 900 pages of text. Lundqvist draws the conclusion that the Swedish government cleaves to the idea of individuals as consumers passively reacting to market incentives, operating according to an economic rationality, rather than as citizens ready to take an active part in deliberating on the moral foundations of the policy itself. In interesting contrast, however, Berglund and Matti's own survey of 4,000 Swedish householders strongly suggests that respondents ascribe a far greater importance to the motivational values associated with altruism than the opposing values of self-enhancement (egoism), in explaining their behaviour.

This clash, or tension, between what the government thinks motivates people to behave in environmentally benign ways, and what actually motivates them, is serious. It would not matter so much, perhaps, if the government's approach simply did not work, in isolation and in its own terms. But the crowding-out thesis suggests that the government's approach will actually undermine already existing good behaviour. Berglund and Matti interpret their findings as suggesting that using the wrong incentives for producing behavioural change might both render these efforts ineffective *and* undermine already existing moral motivations.

## Conclusions: ecological citizenship – governance or government?

All of this calls into question the government's determination to focus wholly on fiscal incentives at the expense of environmental citizen-ship. Effectively, a whole vocabulary of action, built up over centuries, is going to waste. Plenty of research has recently been carried out into environmental citizenship (Dobson and Valencia, 2005; Dobson and Bell, 2006), and of all the findings to emerge from this work, perhaps the most consistent is that while governments need engaged citizens if sustainable development is to be a reality, these engaged citizens do not emerge fully formed from the social womb. 'Citizenship' requires government action, in the sense of policies to create the conditions for citizenship and the spaces in which it can be exercised.

In the terms that animate this book, this suggests that the citizenship approach to sustainability steers a course between governance and government. In truth, and as Jordan *et al.* (2005) point out, the distinction between the two is sometimes hard to maintain, and attempts to do so may divert us both from a proper understanding of what is going on, and from designing effective policy. Environmental citizenship is not a 'command and control' technique – it does not 'rest on recourse to the authority and sanctions of government' (Stoker, in Jordan *et al.*, 2005: 481). It might appear closer to governance, if this is taken to be about voluntary codes of conduct, but this misses the importance of the relationship between government and governance. There is little point, for example, in exhorting individual citizens to recycle their waste if the government, at whatever level, fails to provide the infrastructure to do so effectively. If governments want citizens to do their bit, then governments must do theirs.

## References

BBC (British Broadcasting Corporation) 2002. 'Irish bag tax hailed success'. URL: http://news.bbc.co.uk/1/hi/world/europe/2205419.stm.

Beckman, L. 2001. 'Virtue, sustainability and liberal values', in Barry, J. and Wissenburg, W. (eds.) *Sustaining Liberal Democracy: Ecological Challenges and Opportunities*. Houndmills, UK: Palgrave.

Berglund, C. and Matti, S. 2006. 'Citizen and consumer: the dual role of individuals in environmental policy', *Environmental Politics* 15: 550–71.

CFIT (Commission for Integrated Transport) 2005. 'Congestion charging in the UK'. URL: www.cfit.gov.uk/congestioncharging/factsheets/uk/#durham.

DEFRA (Department for Environment, Food and Rural Affairs) 2003. 'Beckett to take forward Strategy Unit's waste report'. URL: www.defra.gov.uk/news/2003/030506b.htm.

DEFRA (Department for Environment, Food and Rural Affairs) 2004. *Taking it On*. London, UK: DEFRA.

DELG (Department for Environment and Local Government, Ireland) 2002. 'Plastic bag environmental levy in Ireland'. URL: www.mindfully.org/Plastic/Laws/Plastic-Bag-Levy-Ireland4mar02.htm.

Dobson, A. 2003. *Citizenship and the Environment*. Oxford, UK: Oxford University Press.

Dobson, A. and Bell, D. (eds.) 2006. *Environmental Citizenship*. Cambridge, MA: MIT Press.

Dobson, A. and Valencia, A. (eds.) 2005. *Citizenship, Environment, Economy*. London, UK: Routledge.

Frey, B. S. 1999. 'Morality and rationality in environmental policy', *Journal of Consumer Policy* 22: 395–417.

Jordan, A., Wurzel, R. and Zito, A. 2005. 'The rise of new policy instruments in comparative perspective: has governance eclipsed government?' *Political Studies* 53: 477–96.

Lundqvist, L. 2004. *Sweden and Ecological Governance: Straddling the Fence*. Manchester, UK: Manchester University Press.

Turner, R. K., Pearce, D. and Bateman, I. 1994. *Environmental Economics: An Elementary Introduction*. London, UK: Harvester Wheatsheaf.

Wackernagel, M. and Rees, W. 1996. *Our Ecological Footprint: Reducing Human Impact on the Earth*. Gabriola, BC, Canada: New Society Publishers.

# 7 | The governance of science for sustainability

JILL JÄGER

## Introduction

Knowledge, and hence science more generally, should play a key role in shaping human future development and thus the prospects for sustainable development. It should also play a key role in the framing of agendas for economic, social and political innovation. The governance of knowledge and, by implication, of science more generally, is thus an important part of governance for sustainable development. The governance of knowledge for sustainable development chiefly addresses the ways in which science is organised in society so as to achieve a transition to sustainable development. Exploring a new social contract for the practice and focus of science is the key focus of this chapter.

The questions of when, why and how knowledge influences action have been addressed in a wide range of studies with increasing attention in recent years to the environmental arena (Clark *et al.*, 2006). The so-called 'rational actor' model assumes that policy makers undertake a careful analysis of the costs and benefits of available alternatives and always turn to scientists for an objective basis for their decisions (e.g. Lindblom, 1980). Other models see that decision makers are constrained with respect to their time, resources, knowledge and cognitive abilities and thus do not necessarily always turn to scientists for input (e.g. Kahneman *et al.*, 1982). Kingdon (1984) argued that rather than knowledge informing decision making, policy choices are made when 'windows of opportunity' open and streams of problems and solutions that are usually independent come together.

Other scholars have been openly sceptical about the influence of scientific information on decision making (e.g. Susskind, 1994; Haas, 2002). In the environment arena, there is considerable evidence, however, of iterative processes of interaction between policy makers, scientists and stakeholders that provide the linkages between knowledge and action (Jäger *et al.*, 2001). This chapter explores the challenge of linking knowledge and action to address the complex and persistent challenges of unsustainable development.

There is, as noted in Chapter 1, a plethora of definitions of the term 'governance' (Rhodes, 1997; Kooiman, 2003). In this chapter, governance is generally taken to denote the complex ways in which order and orientation are maintained in contemporary socio-political systems. Whereas 'governmental' systems of governance conjure up an image of formal structures ruling over people from the top down, the notion of governance highlights the increasingly important role that formal and informal institutions play in society (see Chapter 1).

A governance perspective looks at how order and orientation are achieved in a world of interdependencies and different interests, and underlines the role of actors outside of government. But whereas governance may have many objectives, sustainable development is concerned with 'quality of life' in a broad sense. It refers not just to our immediate concerns, but also to the needs of people far removed from us in space and time; it applies not just to material consumption and 'lifestyle' issues, but to human flourishing in the broadest sense, including our relationships with the non-human natural world, as well as the relationships between the developed and developing world with respect to environmental, social, institutional and economic development (Farrell *et al.*, 2005). Governance *for* sustainable development thus implies the deliberate adjustment of practices of governance in order to ensure that human development proceeds along a more sustainable trajectory. Governance for sustainable development is the effort to link the systems of governance with the objective of sustainable development.

Having identified these core themes, the rest of this chapter unfolds as follows. The next section identifies the genesis and main elements of what is now known as sustainability science, and outlines the sorts of challenges and questions it must address. Sustainability science, in turn, requires a 'new contract' between science and society, under which the science and technology community devotes increasing attention to the socially determined goals of sustainable development. In return, society undertakes to invest adequately to enable that contribution to take place. The different challenges – for science, for society, and for institutions – which flow from these are discussed in the third section. The following section explores what types of knowledge system are needed to underpin sustainability science. The most successful ones are likely to be those that are credible, salient and legitimate, bearing in mind that these three attributes are likely to remain in creative tension with one another. The fifth section analyses some of the challenges which emerge from these, including the need for what is referred to as effective boundary management. Finally, the concluding section argues that sustainability science is a particular case of what Stokes (1997) has characterised as 'use-inspired basic research' – that is, a quest for fundamental understanding motivated by concern about specific practical problems. It requires changes in the way that science itself is performed. In particular, problem-oriented research, participatory approaches and stakeholder involvement need to become a normal part of doing science for sustainability.

## Sustainability science

At a meeting held at Friibergh Manor, Sweden, in October 2000, a small group of international scientists discussed the emergence of 'sustainability science', which seeks to understand the fundamental character of interactions between nature and society (Kates *et al.*, 2001) and to harness science and technology in the quest to achieve transitions to sustainable development. They agreed that sustainability science approaches must: encompass the interaction of global processes with the ecological and social characteristics of particular places and sectors; integrate the effects of key processes across the full range of scales from local to global; and achieve fundamental advances in our ability to address such issues as the behaviour of complex, self-organising systems, as well as the responses of the nature–society system of governing to multiple and interacting stresses.

An initial set of core questions for sustainability science was proposed in order to focus research attention on these issues. These core questions (Kates *et al.*, 2001) were as follows:

• How can the dynamic interactions between nature and society – including lags and inertia – be better incorporated into emerging models and conceptualisations that integrate the Earth system, human development, and sustainability?
• How are long-term trends in environment and development, including consumption and population, reshaping nature–society interactions in ways relevant to sustainability?

- What determines the vulnerability or resilience of the nature–society system in particular kinds of places and for particular types of ecosystems and human livelihoods?
- Can scientifically meaningful 'limits' or boundaries be defined that provide effective warning of conditions beyond which the nature–society systems incur a significantly increased risk of serious degradation?
- What systems of governance – including markets, rules, norms and scientific information – can most effectively improve social capacity to guide interactions between nature and society toward more sustainable trajectories?
- How can today's operational systems for monitoring and reporting on environmental and social conditions be integrated or extended to provide more useful guidance for efforts to navigate a transition toward sustainability?
- How can today's relatively independent activities of research planning, monitoring, assessment and decision support be better integrated into systems for adaptive management and societal learning?

Clearly, the science that is necessary to address these questions differs to a considerable degree in structure, methods and content from traditional disciplinary science applied to issues of environmental sustainability. Progress in increasing the efficacy of science will require fostering a more problem-driven and interdisciplinary research, the building of capacity for this type of research, more coherent systems of research planning, operational monitoring, assessment and application. I argue, therefore, that progress will depend on changing the governance of knowledge.

In order to validate these core questions, it was necessary to organise a wide discussion within the scientific community – North and South – regarding key questions, appropriate methodologies, and institutional needs. Furthermore, it was important to provide a connection between science and the political agenda for sustainable development in national policy making and in international co-operation and treaty making. Hence the sustainability science consultations focused in particular on the World Summit on Sustainable Development (WSSD) in 2002. At the same time, work began on creating a research focus on the character of nature–society interactions, on our ability to guide those interactions along sustainable trajectories, and on ways of promoting the social learning that will be necessary to navigate the transition to sustainability.

Further discussions on sustainability science (ICSU, 2002) emphasised that research and development (R&D) priorities should be set and implemented so that science and technology contribute to solutions of the most urgent sustainability problems as defined by society, not just by scientists. While science has been very good at providing increasingly long lists of problems, there is an increasingly large demand for solutions. The substantive focus of much of the required R&D will have to be on the complex, dynamic interactions between nature and society (social–ecological systems). Since some of the most important interactions will occur in particular places, or particular enterprises and times, science and technology for sustainable development needs to be 'place-based' or 'enterprise-based,' embedded in the particular characteristics of distinct locations or contexts. The challenge is to help promote the relatively 'local' (place- or enterprise-based) dialogues from which meaningful priorities can emerge, and to put in place the local support systems that will allow those priorities to be implemented. In addition, regional consultations emphasised that sustainability science must develop a much firmer empirical foundation for its efforts.

A determined effort to move from case studies and pilot projects toward a body of comparative, critically evaluated knowledge is urgently needed. In addition, progress toward sustainability will require constant feedback from observations (including socio-economic indicators, world views and society–biosphere interactions); a point that was emphasised in one of the regional consultations, in particular. Such observations are necessary to provide reference points for theoretical debates and models on strategies for vulnerability reduction, and metrics for measuring practical progress. An observation system for sustainability science will need to be based on a large sample of comparative regional studies, emphasising meaningful, relevant and practical indicators.

## A new social contract for science?

Jane Lubchenco, as President of the American Association for the Advancement of Science (AAAS), argued that increasingly rapid rates of global change required 'a new Social Contract for science ... that would more adequately address the problems of the coming century than does our current scientific enterprise' (Lubchenco, 1998). The new contract, Lubchenco proposed, should involve a 'commitment on the part of all scientists to devote their energies and talents to the most pressing problems of the day, in proportion to their importance, in exchange for public funding'. This can be seen as a call for a change in the governance of science in the face of sustainable development challenges.

It has become clear, especially through the series of world conferences addressing human–environment interactions (namely, the Stockholm Conference in 1972, the Rio Conference in 1992 and the Johannesburg Conference in 2002) (see also Chapter 1), that while the relevance of science and technology to sustainable development is generally acknowledged, a large gap persists between what the science and technology community thinks it has to offer, and what society has demanded and supported. It is this gap that has led to calls for such a new contract, under which the science and technology community would devote an increasing fraction of its overall efforts to research agendas reflecting socially determined goals of sustainable development. In return, society would undertake to invest adequately to enable that contribution from science and technology, from which it would benefit through the improvement of social, economic and environmental conditions.

I argue that such a re-orientation for science and for its funding requires a number of specific steps that the scientific community will have to take for the 'contract' idea to move from inspiring rhetoric toward practical reality:

- *Increasing the demand for and supply of science and technology*: Making the 'new contract' a reality will require changes in both the 'demand' and the 'supply' sides of science and technology for sustainable development. In order to increase the demand for science and technology, it will be necessary to increase public and political awareness of the nature and magnitude of the challenges posed by transitions to sustainability. It will also mean convincing society that it can look to the science and technology community for contributions to solutions and increasing the supply of contributions. This will require building the capacity needed to scale up those contributions adequately to address the magnitude of the sustainability challenges. Partnerships with all major stakeholders will be necessary, including the private sector, the public health sector and civil society.

- *Moving beyond business-as-usual*: To become an attractive partner for society in the proposed 'new contract', the science and technology community needs to complement its traditional approaches with several new orientations. Again, this amounts to a change in the governance of science. In particular, research priorities should be set and implemented so that science and technology contribute to solutions of the most urgent sustainability problems as defined by society, not just by scientists. Furthermore, science and technology for sustainable development needs to become an enterprise committed to empowering all members of society to make informed choices, rather than providing its services only to states or other powerful groups. Finally, given the inevitably unpredictable and contentious course of social transitions towards sustainability, science and technology needs to see its role as one of contributing information, options and analysis that facilitate a process of social learning rather than providing definitive answers.

- *Focusing on socio-ecological systems in particular places*: The substantive focus of much of the research and development needed to promote sustainable development will have to be on the complex, dynamic interactions between nature and society, rather than on either the social or environmental sides of this interaction. Moreover, some of the most important interactions will occur in particular places, or particular enterprises and times. Science and technology for sustainable development therefore needs to be 'place-based', embedded in the particular characteristics of distinct locations or contexts. This means that science and technology will have to broaden where it looks for knowledge, reaching beyond the essential bodies of specialised scholarship to include endogenously generated knowledge, innovations and practices. Devising approaches for evaluating which lessons can usefully be transferred from one setting to another is a major governance challenge.

- *Enhancing credibility*: For knowledge to be effective in advancing sustainable development goals, it must be accountable to more than peer review. In particular, it must be sufficiently reliable (or credible) to justify people risking action upon it, sufficiently relevant (or salient) to decision makers' needs, and sufficiently democratic and respectful in its choice of issues to address, expertise to consider and participants to engage (i.e. socially and politically legitimate). Evidence presented in the regional consultations suggested that these three properties are tightly interdependent, and that efforts to enhance one may often undermine the others.

The new contract also poses institutional challenges. The existing institutions that support science and technology in the current governance structure for knowledge will have to be adapted in order to fulfil the new contract. In particular, there is a need for an improved dialogue between the science and technology community and problem solvers or practitioners pursuing sustainability goals. This is addressed in the next two sections of this chapter. In particular, it is necessary to understand which kinds of institutions can support the necessary dialogue and science–practice partnerships to contribute to solutions of sustainability problems. A particular institutional challenge is posed by the need to build partnerships with the business and industry sectors. Furthermore, interdisciplinary and transdisciplinary approaches will require institutional changes that enhance capacity building, which is also needed urgently in some parts of the world simply to strengthen the science and technology community. Finally, the new kind of science implied by all of the above steps will require changes in the funding of science and technology in order to secure steady, long-term financial support for problem-solving and solution-oriented research and development systems.

## Knowledge systems for sustainable development

While there is increasing interest in the question of how to harness science and technology for sustainable development, there is relatively little systematic scholarly understanding of what kinds of institutions are well suited for linking research, observation, assessment, traditional knowledge and technology innovation and development to sustainable development activities from global to local levels. Cash *et al.* (2003) suggest that an inquiry into the institutional dimensions of sustainability science could focus on several different classes of questions: mechanisms to empower decision makers in the science and technology agenda-setting process; institutional mechanisms to foster integration across disciplines, functions, levels and sources of knowledge; knowledge systems that are flexible and adaptive to evolving problems yet durable and committed to problems that require cumulative research efforts and long-term learning; facilitation of appropriate and timely participation; and resources and capacity for sustainable development activities. (See also http://sustsci.harvard.edu/questions/inst.htm.)

The first attempts to grapple with these questions were provided by Cash *et al.* (2003). A series of case studies suggests that efforts to mobilise science and technology for sustainability are more likely to be effective when they manage boundaries between knowledge and action in ways that simultaneously enhance the salience, credibility and legitimacy of the information that they produce. In a study of regional and global assessment processes, which are examples of efforts that manage the boundary between knowledge and action, these attributes of salience, credibility and legitimacy have been explored in detail (Farrell and Jäger, 2005).

Credibility refers to scientific and technical believability. The potential user of the information exchanged at the interface between knowledge and action has to be convinced that the facts and causal beliefs underlying that information are well founded, that they are consistent with well-established facts and causal beliefs, and that they were produced in a scientifically rigorous process. Furthermore, information is deemed to be credible, based on the credentials of those who produce it.

Salience reflects the ability of the information exchanges at the interface between knowledge and action to address the particular concerns of the user. For example, in the case of assessment processes, assessments that remain 'on the shelf' and do not lead to action are those that ask questions in which users are generally not interested. Achieving saliency requires the inclusion of potential users in all stages of the process, to ensure that their interests are taken into account.

Legitimacy is a measure of the political acceptability or perceived fairness to a user of an assessment process or interface between knowledge and action. In particular, users want to see that their interests have been fairly taken into account. This is affected very much by participation in the process of assessing knowledge. For example, legitimacy has been questioned when there was not enough participation from developing countries in global assessment processes. Likewise, for sustainable development, participation from

the scientific community together with representatives from government, business, industry and civil society contributes to a legitimate
assessment process.

As shown by Farrell and Jäger (2005), however, there is often a
constant but creative tension between the three attributes of credibility,
salience and legitimacy; in fact, the easiest ways of enhancing any single
attribute almost invariably cause declines in another. For example,
credibility can be enhanced by addressing only questions for which
scientific certainty is high or by allowing only the most renowned scientists to participate, regardless of the nation or sector they represent.
In the former case, salience could be reduced, because questions that
have priority with decision makers could be left out. In the second case,
legitimacy could be lost by failing to take the interests of potential users
into account. Balancing the three attributes is not easy, but is essential
for an effective interface between knowledge and action.

These tensions were seen, for example, in the work of the Intergovernmental Panel on Climate Change (IPCC), which was established by the United Nations Environment Programme (UNEP) and
the World Meteorological Organization (WMO) in 1988 with the
mandate to assess the issue of climate change. Many developing
countries opted not to send delegates to the initial IPCC meeting in
Geneva. Thus low numbers of developing country authors participated in the writing of the first IPCC report. The IPCC realised that
this posed a problem for the global legitimacy of its results and took
action to increase developing country participation (Miller, 2005).
However, developing country participants had fewer peer-reviewed
publications in English-language journals and the IPCC rules had to
be relaxed in order to allow citation of working papers, which were
originally seen as less scientifically credible for the intergovernmental
process.

Cash *et al.* (2003) looked at programmes linking knowledge with
action for sustainable development to see how their provisions for
boundary work at the interface between science and policy balanced the
trade-offs among the saliency, credibility and legitimacy of the information that they produced. They found three functions that contribute
to effective boundary management: communication, translation and
mediation. Active, iterative and inclusive communication between
experts and decision makers is one important way to make sure that
knowledge is seen as credible, salient and legitimate in the user

community. However, it is not enough to have good communication. Linking knowledge to action also requires that the experts and decision makers understand each other. This understanding is blocked by jargon, language, experiences and even presumptions about what constitutes persuasive argument. In the case of sustainable development, however, where there are multiple and contested definitions, even translation is not enough, and successful boundary organisations perform the function of mediation.

European management of acid rain provides another clear example of the value of communication, translation and mediation (Cash *et al.*, 2003). During the early 1980s, countries used their own experts to bolster their negotiating position and, not infrequently, to question the expertise of others. No widely accepted scientific assessment of the problem existed and no political agreement on action could be reached. Over the next decade, however, the International Institute of Applied Systems Analysis (IIASA) worked with relevant experts and policy makers to construct and apply the Regional Air Pollution Information and Simulation (RAINS) model. The modelling effort linked researchers from various disciplines (producing a more credible model of acid deposition and impacts) with the multinational delegates negotiating emission reduction protocols (producing information more salient to the policy debate). The RAINS model was used in the negotiations for protocols to the UN Convention on Long-Range Transboundary Air Pollution and thus facilitated discussion among parties with multiple interests regarding differences in perspective, methodology, preferences, values and desired outcomes. In this way, communication was enhanced and through the continual interaction of the negotiators and scientists the RAINS model was a tool for both translation and mediation. The iterated process of its construction, revision and application facilitated communication between model producers and model users that ensured that its information outputs were salient to negotiators, credible to scientists of all nations, and legitimate in not favouring the interests of any particular country.

Individual efforts in research, innovation, monitoring and assessment can clearly contribute to sustainability. But the full utility of such contributions depends on developing integrated knowledge systems, a lesson already learned in the agriculture, defence and health sectors. Cash *et al.* (2003) conclude that how knowledge systems for sustainability can best be structured still remains a question for scholarly research, practical experimentation and comparative learning. In the absence of a well-tested model, however, progress has been made on identifying several likely characteristics of such systems. In particular, the research on boundary organisations provides examples of knowledge systems able to deal with the trade-offs associated with perceptions of saliency, credibility and legitimacy within the expert and decision-making communities.

## Sustainability science: from knowledge into action

As shown above (and documented by the Forum on Science and Technology for Sustainability (http://sustainabilityscience.org)), considerable progress has been made in recent years in understanding and strengthening the role of science in supporting the transition to sustainability. However, much remains to be done, particularly in linking knowledge to action in the area of sustainable development. The World Summit on Sustainable Development in 2002 called for the creation of novel partnerships and dialogues to link sectors and regions in action-oriented, regionally focused initiatives to promote sustainability. While many partnerships were established around the time of the World Summit, none emerged as a global model for linking knowledge to action.

At the start of this millennium, the world's governments signed a Declaration with targets for the year 2015 – the Millennium Development Goals (MDGs) – including halving extreme poverty, cutting child mortality, rolling back infectious diseases, and providing safe drinking water (see also Chapter 1). Most of the MDGs, which were also endorsed at the World Summit on Sustainable Development, can benefit from the input of knowledge. In 2005, however, the United Nations Development Programme noted in its annual *Human Development Report* that 'there is little cause for celebration' (UNDP, 2005: 1). Most countries are off-track for most of the MDGs and 'the promise to the world's poor is being broken' (UNDP, 2005: 2). Evidently, more knowledge about environmental sustainability and reducing vulnerability to multiple stresses is not leading to action.

As a follow-up to the work on sustainability science described above, ISTS (Initiative on Science and Technology for Sustainability) and TWAS (the Academy of Sciences for the Developing World) identified two initiative areas in which both the need and potential for strengthening the linkage between scientific research and effective action programmes are particularly acute: integrated management of production/consumption systems; and enhancing resilience and reducing vulnerability of coupled human–environment systems. For these areas science-based, action-oriented partnerships for sustainability are being developed. That is, sustainability science is being put into practice through partnership teams with balanced membership from the science and technology, development, and environmental protection communities. Each partnership team is working to articulate the key science needed to facilitate solutions to sustainability problems in its respective area, illustrate the potential for creation and application of that science through focused case studies, and prepare implementation guidelines to facilitate action by WSSD-like partnerships around the world.

Parallel to setting up partnership teams, ISTS and TWAS began planning an 'International Dialogue on Science and Practice in Sustainable Development'. The aim was to increase radically the quantity and effectiveness of collaborations on sustainable development being pursued around the world between scientists and practitioners, and to enhance the world's capacity to establish and implement such activities. Interestingly, however, this process led to the conclusion that, in contrast to expectations, there was no general demand on the part of senior practitioners for broad-purpose, international 'dialogues' with scholars on matters relating to sustainability. Instead, there was a modest interest among some practitioners in focused dialogues on specific topics of immediate interest to them in the contexts in which they work. Similarly, there was not a general interest among scholars of sustainability in 'dialogues' in general. Rather, there was an interest by some scholars in better connecting their own research with relevant decision makers in their countries and regions. This experience has implications for 'sustainability science', since it shows where the linkages between science and practice can be made more easily.

A particular challenge, directly related to the governance of knowledge, is the lack of opportunities for young scientists to engage in and learn from work that directly links knowledge with action in the area of sustainable development. This was discussed, for example, in a panel at the 2005 AAAS annual meeting. It was organised by AAAS under the auspices of ISTS, TWAS and Leadership for Environment and Development International (LEAD). As Clark (2005) reports, the heart of the discussion was a panel of half a dozen young environmental scholars and development activists from China, India and Brazil. Their discussions raised issues that had been central to the call for a 'new contract between science and society' and emphasised the need for more recognition by the scientific community of the value of problem-driven work and more support by society in helping them to get on with the job. One very interesting proposal that came up through this dialogue, and which implies changes in the 'governance of science', is the recognition and support of volunteer efforts by scientists to work 'in the trenches' on pressing problems. In other professions, this kind of volunteer work has long been supported (e.g. in the legal and medical professions).

As Clark (2005) points out, setting up a successful programme of scientist volunteers for sustainability would require, above all else, 'that the scientific community and its gatekeepers formally acknowledge the importance of such volunteer work in professional careers'. The programme would also need a dedicated infrastructure. This example shows the value of dialogues between the science and practice communities for surfacing new ideas. In this case, the new idea contributes to a revitalised debate on the contract between science and society through its call for a dedicated effort to create recognition and support for volunteer work addressing sustainable development.

## Conclusions

The term governance denotes in a broad sense the complex ways in which order is maintained in contemporary socio-political systems. Governance *for* sustainable development implies the deliberate adjustment of practices of governance in order to ensure that human development proceeds along a more sustainable trajectory. This includes the practices surrounding the acquisition and deployment of knowledge. Dealing with complex human–environment systems at multiple scale levels is a major scientific challenge, which will also require changes in the way that science itself is performed. In particular, more problem-oriented research, participatory approaches and stakeholder involvement are required. An important challenge for governance for sustainable development lies in making open processes and continuous learning possible with bottom-up developments informing top-down policies and strategies – replacing the more common focus on determinate outcomes. All of this, of course, poses important governance challenges regarding the way in which we organise and manage the processes of interaction and decision making through which these objectives are achieved.

Efforts to harness science and technology for problem-solving in support of sustainable development raise a number of fundamental questions about the nature of complex, interactive socio-ecological systems. While pragmatic research and development can help contribute to solutions even when such fundamental questions remain unresolved, a parallel programme of research on underlying conceptual and methodological issues raised by problem-solving efforts must be part of a programme to harness science for sustainable development. As described at the beginning of this chapter, a first set of 'core questions' for sustainability science was compiled by Kates *et al.* (2001). Considerable progress has been made in carrying out relevant research since these questions were formulated.

Sustainability science is a particular case of what Stokes (1997) characterised as 'use-inspired basic research' – a quest for fundamental understanding motivated by concern about specific practical problems (Clark, 2007). Stokes argued that research of this kind has historically played a key and dynamic role in linking the semi-autonomous agendas of curiosity-driven fundamental science and solution-driven research. This general proposition suggests that sustainability science could be characterised as use-inspired basic research on the dynamics of complex human–environment systems, interacting with fundamental science on the Earth system (e.g. Steffen *et al.*, 2004) and the increasing body of field scale experience in applying knowledge and know-how to support of the goals of sustainable development (as exemplified, for example, by the work of TWAS).

Clearly the sciences of sustainability draw upon a wide range of academic disciplines, although the engagement has been stronger in some (e.g. ecology and geography) than in others (e.g. chemistry, engineering and health sciences). The challenges of sustainability will continue to require major contributions from discipline-based science. At the same time, however, it is necessary to develop an inter-disciplinary and transdisciplinary, action-oriented agenda to deal with the core questions of sustainability. The practices of science and of linking knowledge to action are, in places, already being adjusted to meet the demands of sustainability science, but major challenges, in particular those related to institutions that link knowledge to action, remain.

## Acknowledgements

I acknowledge with gratitude the many discussions with colleagues in the Initiative on Science and Technology for Sustainability and the joint publications on which I have drawn in writing this chapter.

## References

Cash, D. W., Clark, W. C., Alcock, F., Dickson, N. M., Eckley, N., Guston, D. H., Jäger, J. and Mitchell, R. B. 2003. 'Knowledge systems for sustainable development', *Proceedings of the National Academy of Sciences of the USA* 100: 8086–91.

Clark, W. C. 2005. 'A new social contract for science?' *Environment* 47(3): 1.

Clark, W. C. 2007. 'Sustainability science: a room of its own', *Proceedings of the National Academy of Sciences* 104: 1737.

Clark, W. C., Mitchell, R. B. and Cash, D. W. 2006. 'Evaluating the influence of global environmental assessments', in Mitchell, R. B., Clark, W. C., Cash, D. W. and Dickson, N. M. (eds.) *Global Environmental Assessments: Information and Influence*. Cambridge, MA: MIT Press.

Farrell, A. E. and Jäger, J. (eds.) 2005. *Assessments of Regional and Global Environmental Risks: Designing Processes for the Effective Use of Science in Decision-Making*. Washington DC: Resources for the Future.

Farrell, K. N., Kemp, R., Hinterberger, F., Rammel, C. and Ziegler, R. 2005. 'From 'for' to governance for sustainable development in Europe: what is at stake for further research?' *International Journal of Sustainable Development* 8: 127–50.

Haas, P. M. 2002. 'Science policy for multilateral environmental governance', paper presented at the International Workshop on 'The Multilateral Environmental Governance Regime: Structural Integration and the Possibility of a World Environment Organization'. United Nations Headquarters, New York, March 26–27, 2002.

ICSU (International Council for Science) 2002. *Science and Technology for Sustainable Development*. International Council for Science, Initiative on Science and Technology for Sustainability, and Third World Academy of Sciences. ICSU Series on Science for Sustainable Development, No. 9. International Council for Science: Paris. URL: www.icsu.org/Gestion/img/ICSU_DOC_DOWNLOAD/70_DD_FILE_Vol9.pdf.

Jäger, J., van Eijndhoven, J. and Clark, W. C. 2001. 'Knowledge and action: an analysis of linkages among management functions for global environmental risks', in Social Learning Group (eds.) *Learning to Manage Global Environmental Risks, Volume 2: A Functional Analysis of Social Responses to Climate Change, Ozone Depletion, and Acid Rain*. Cambridge, MA: MIT Press.

Kahneman, D., Slovic, P. and Tversky, A. 1982. *Judgment under Uncertainty: Heuristics and Biases*. Cambridge, UK: Cambridge University Press.

Kates, R. W., Clark, W. C., Corell, R., Hall, J. M., Jaeger, C. C., Lowe, I., McCarthy, J. J., Schellnhuber, H. J., Bolin, B., Dickson, N. M., Faucheux, S., Gallopin, G. C., Grubler, A., Huntley, B., Jäger, J., Jodha, N. S., Kasperson, R. E., Mabogunje, A., Matson, P., Mooney, H., Moore, B., O'Riordan, T. and Svedin, U. 2001. 'Sustainability science', *Science* 292: 641–2.

Kingdon, J. W. 1984. *Agendas, Alternatives, and Public Policies*. Boston, MA: Little, Brown and Company.

Kooiman, J. (ed.) 2003. *Governing as Governance*. London, UK: Sage.

Lindblom, C. E. 1980. *The Policy-Making Process*. Englewood Cliffs, NJ: Prentice-Hall.

Lubchenco. J. 1998. 'Entering the century of the environment: a new social contract for science', *Science* 279: 491–7.

Miller, C. A. 2005. 'The design and management of international scientific assessments: lessons from the climate regime', in Farrell, A. E. and Jäger, J. (eds.) *Assessments of Regional and Global Environmental Risks: Designing Processes for the Effective Use of Science in Decision-Making*. Washington DC: Resources for the Future.

Rhodes, R. A. W. 1997. *Understanding Governance*. Milton Keynes, UK: Open University Press.

Steffen, W., Sanderson, A., Tyson, P. D., Jäger, J., Matson, P. A., Moore III, B., Oldfield, F., Richardson, K., Schellnhuber, H. J., Turner II, B. L. and Wasson, R. J. (eds.) 2004. *Global Change and the Earth System: A Planet under Pressure*. Berlin, Germany: Springer.

Stokes, D. E. 1997. *Pasteur's Quadrant: Basic Science and Technological Innovation*. Washington DC: Brookings Institution Press.

Susskind, L. 1994. *Environmental Diplomacy: Negotiating More Effective Global Agreements*. Oxford, UK: Oxford University Press.

UNDP 2005. *Human Development Report 2005 – International Cooperation at a Crossroads: Aid, Trade and Security in an Unequal World*. New York: UNDP.

# 8 Practitioner evaluations of participatory processes in environmental decision making

JACQUELIN BURGESS AND JUDY CLARK

## Introduction

One striking feature of sustainability debates has been the opening up of decision making to wider ranges of voices and values. Public participation was enshrined in the Rio Declaration of the 1992 Earth Summit and the Johannesburg Declaration of the 2002 World Summit as a vital mechanism to ensure greater equity and legitimacy in the governance of sustainable development. European legislation has actively promoted participation through environmental laws such as the EU Water Framework Directive in 2000, which requires the 'active involvement' of interested parties in developing water resource and environment management plans (Article 14). The UN Economic Commission for Europe (UNECE) led the development of the Aarhus Convention (1998), which has public participation in environmental decision making as one of its three pillars.

In the UK, public and stakeholder participation is, rhetorically at least, a part of the culture of national government, local authorities and regulatory agencies, and an 'essential' part of the sustainable development strategy (DETR 1999, para. 7.87) (see Owens, 2000; Munton, 2003). Strong claims are made for the benefits of participation. Rowe and Frewer (2000: 24), for example, argue that 'public participation in policy making ... is necessary to reflect and acknowledge democratic ideals and enhance trust in regulators and transparency in regulatory systems'. Others, such as Rayner (2003) and Pellizzoni (2003), question whether current participatory practices are achieving the democratic goals claimed for them. One widely recognised weakness that impacts both sides of the argument is the paucity of systematic evaluations of real-world applications of participatory processes (see Chess, 2000; Smith and Beazley, 2000; Petts, 2004; Rowe and Frewer, 2004; Plummer and Armitage, 2007).

This chapter contributes to a more rigorous evaluation of stake-holder participation processes. Its novelty lies in the systematic elicitation of evaluative criteria from a panel of practitioners drawing on their professional experiences, rather than academics working from first principles. The data allow examination of the extent to which there is common ground between these different but potentially overlapping perspectives. The empirical research was supported by the Environment Agency, the primary environmental regulator for England and Wales. The Environment Act (1995) placed a statutory responsibility on the Agency to take account of sustainable development in discharging its regulatory functions. To support this responsibility, the Agency is required 'to develop a close and responsive relationship with the public, local authorities and other representatives of local communities, and regulated organisations' (Environment Agency, 1996).

Between 1997 and 2004, the Agency funded research to better understand how sustainable development should be incorporated into its institutional practices (Burgess *et al.*, 2000), and to determine principles and processes of public participation (Petts and Leach, 2000; Twigger-Ross and Smith, 2000; Petts *et al.*, 2004). In 1999, the Agency commissioned us to evaluate the extent to which participatory activities could contribute to the development of 'close and responsive relationships' with its stakeholders (Clark *et al.*, 2001). In particular, there was concern about how best to undertake these kinds of 'local outreach' activities. Questions included what 'a close and responsive relationship' meant? What kinds of processes would be likely to achieve close and responsive relationships? On what bases should managers decide to invest resources (people, time, money) on relationship building? And how could they evaluate the relative success or failure of such investments?

Working with Andy Stirling, we developed an application of Multi-Criteria Mapping (MCM) to answer these questions. Such mapping methods had been developed in appraisal of energy options (Stirling, 1997) and genetically modified crops (Stirling and Mayer, 1999). In this chapter, we present findings from the empirical study, situating them in the context of debate about participation in environmental decision making. Following a brief review of the literature, we discuss the design of the research and present the quantitative results of the appraisal. This is followed by qualitative analysis of the criteria developed by the interviewees which allows us to consider more generic issues about the development of evaluation criteria for sustainability decision making.

## Evaluating public and stakeholder participation in environmental decision making

The search for theoretically and empirically defensible criteria by which to evaluate participatory processes is a tardy response to the range of innovative governance strategies developing in different public policy arenas (Coenen *et al.*, 1998; Stoker, 1998; Bloomfield *et al.*, 2001; Irwin, 2001; Abelson *et al.*, 2003; Hajer, 2005; Rogers-Hayden and Pidgeon, 2007). Although progress has been made since the early 1990s, when Renn and colleagues asserted that 'confusion about the goals of citizen participation accompanies every practical application' (Renn *et al.*, 1995: 4), the lack of systematic evaluation leaves projects at risk from reduced legitimacy, and the robustness of participation open to challenge. Without effective evaluation mechanisms, participatory decision-making techniques may be inappropriately applied, impact and learning may be reduced, outputs may be ignored or dismissed, and efforts may be duplicated (Goodwin, 1998; Chess and Purcell, 1999; Beierle and Konisky, 2001; Stirling, 2005; Burgess and Chilvers, 2006).

In his seminal paper, Fiorino (1990) argued that evaluative criteria are required to assess the instrumental, substantive and normative dimensions of public participation in decision making. Instrumentally, participation should help improve the quality of decision-making processes and enhance the legitimacy of the outcomes. Substantively, participation should introduce additional knowledge and values into what have characteristically been expert-dominated decisions. Normatively, participation should ensure stronger democratic processes. In a desk-based study, Fiorino developed four 'democratic process' criteria which explored the extent to which different participatory processes allowed for: (i) direct participation of lay people [citizens] in decisions; (ii) citizens to share in collective decision making; (iii) face-to-face discussion over some period of time; and (iv) participation on some basis of equality with administrators and technical specialists. There is, we believe, a need to develop criteria to evaluate substantive and instrumental dimensions. Hence, 'the case for participation should begin with a normative argument' (Fiorino, 1990: 239; see also Dryzek, 2000).

The normative dimension was strengthened through Webler's (1995) translation of aspects of Habermas' (1984) theory of communicative rationality into two meta-criteria suitable for evaluating the discursive aspects of a wide range of participatory processes in different geopolitical contexts (see also O'Hara, 1996). *Fairness*, defined as 'the distribution among participants of opportunities to act meaningfully' (Webler, 1995) asserts that every participant must be free to attend, initiate discussion, discuss (i.e. challenge and defend claims) and decide (influence the collective consensus). Ideally all those whose interests will be affected should have the opportunity to take part, and all citizens should feel that their interests are being properly represented even if they choose not to become involved themselves. *Competence* is 'the construction of the best possible understandings and agreements given what is reasonably knowable to the participants' (Webler, 1995: 65). Participants should be provided with access to information and how it might be interpreted, as well as the procedural tools to resolve disputes about knowledge claims, so as to make the 'best' decision given the specific context. At the time of the research, the majority of participatory process literature was preoccupied with democratic issues associated with fairness and representation. Only recently have questions of competence, often expressed in terms of 'social learning', become more significant as the claims for deliberative democracy are being tested (Bohman, 2000; Pellizzoni, 2001), adaptive co-management strategies are being promoted in response to socio-ecological breakdown (Conley and Moote, 2003; Plummer and Armitage, 2007), and a new generation of analytic-deliberative decision-support tools are being tested in real-world policy contexts (see Stern and Fineberg, 1996; Stirling, 2005; Burgess *et al.*, 2007).

Figure 8.1 schematises stages in a participatory environmental decision-making process. Decision context, inputs, process, outputs and outcomes are represented as separate stages, each offering opportunities for evaluation. The first step in the development of any process involves identifying the dimensions of the problem, accessing resources, and agreeing objectives and baseline indicators. Determining the inputs for a project is highly dependent on problem context and the ability of the process to engage others. Both human and material inputs are vital to

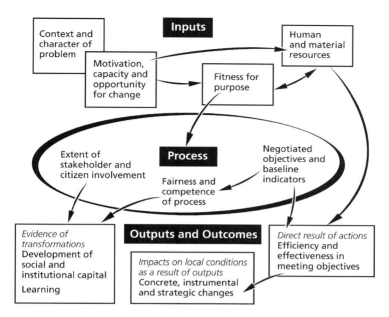

**Figure 8.1** Evaluation issues as input, process and outcome stages of stakeholder participation in environmental decision making

process design. The critical question is whether the process design is fit-for-purpose (Clark *et al.*, 2001).

Process evaluations usually rely on *ex ante* assessments of the extent of participant involvement and the quality of process in terms of its effectiveness, efficiency and equity. Quantitative evaluation measures (see Guba and Lincoln, 1989) attempt to capture some of these qualities by recording numbers of project meetings and their attendance levels; the percentage of different social groups that attend meetings; and numbers of local people actively involved at different stages in the process, for example (see Horlick-Jones *et al.*, 2007a). Based on Webler's (1995) fairness and competence criteria, qualitative process evaluations explore features such as changing levels of involvement of participants, ability of individuals to analyse and explain issues, and the ability of groups to propose and consider different courses of action (Barnes, 1999; Smith and Beazley, 2000; Petts *et al.*, 2004).

*Outputs* are a direct result of the actions taken through the process and depend on the objectives set for the process, such as the development of a management plan, or a better informed and more articulate community (Cowie and O'Toole, 1998; Warburton, 1998). *Outcomes* are the consequences of the outputs and the process. Figure 8.1 distinguishes between project outcomes and process outcomes, the latter being important in situations where project outcomes may be slow to emerge or diffuse. Process outcomes assess the extent and quality of changes in participants, such as acquisition of new social skills, strengthening social networks, developing trust between institutions and the public, and willingness to participate in future processes (Knoepfel and Kissling-Näf, 1998; Rydin and Pennington, 2000; Joss and Bellucci, 2002). The extent to which formal criteria exist to measure or otherwise assess these process outcome claims is limited, however. Institutional learning, along with evidence of real impacts, is hard to demonstrate in a systematic way (Chess and Johnson, 2006; Rogers-Hayden and Pidgeon, 2007).

A small but growing number of studies are attempting to progress the evaluation agenda through the development of generic process-based criteria which are then applied, *ex post*, to a range of applications (for example Renn *et al.*, 1995; Coenen *et al.*, 1998; Rowe and Frewer, 2000; Webler *et al.*, 2001; Petts *et al.*, 2004). Table 8.1 summarises the nine criteria developed in the influential paper on evaluation by Rowe and Frewer (2000).

Rowe and Frewer suggest two meta-criteria: public acceptance, and effectiveness of process. The idea of public acceptance derives from political science principles. Applying these criteria to the stages outlined in Figure 8.1, four of the five address process issues, while 'influence' is an outcome criterion. Of the four effectiveness of process criteria, derived from management and decision analysis, three are relevant to decision context/input phases, while one ('structured decision making') is process-specific. In their review, Rowe and Frewer (2000) use the criteria to evaluate eight standard participatory processes. The appraisal highlights the variety of ways in which any one process can be implemented, the effects of social and environmental factors, and the lack of precision in defining and measuring the criteria. The principal message from the analysis is that every method has its strengths and weaknesses, and that evaluation must, perforce, pay

Table 8.1 *Nine evaluation criteria for the acceptance and effectiveness of participatory processes*

| Criteria | Description |
|---|---|
| **Public Acceptance** | |
| 1. Representativeness | Representative sample of the affected population |
| 2. Independence | Process conducted in an independent, unbiased way |
| 3. Early involvement | The earlier the stage of involvement the greater the sense of ownership of the process, especially at the stage where value judgements are important |
| 4. Influence | Any participatory process should have a visible impact on policy |
| 5. Transparency | The public should be able to see progress and how decisions are being made |
| **Effectiveness of process** | |
| 6. Resource accessibility | Access to appropriate resources (information, experts, time, materials) to enable them to fulfil their brief successfully |
| 7. Task definition | The scope of the exercise, the expected output and the mechanism of the procedure should be defined at the outset |
| 8. Structured decision making | To enable debate over the underlying assumptions of a decision, how the decision was made, the extent to which it was supported |
| 9. Cost effectiveness | Process suitable to the scale and importance of the decision in terms of the investment of time and money |

*Source:* Rowe and Frewer (2000).

very close attention to context. We shall return to this discussion once the results of our empirical study have been presented.

## An evaluation of stakeholder processes

### Methods and data for evaluation

Rather than a routine review of secondary sources and semi-structured, reflective interviews, we undertook a structured and systematic appraisal of a range of participatory processes open to public sector organisations. The Agency supported the research by providing financial resources, technical expertise, professional contacts and five members of the interview panel (see Clark *et al.*, 2001). Multi-Criteria Mapping (MCM) is a novel form of multi-criteria analysis which combines some of the subtlety and openness of qualitative methods with the specificity and transparency of quantitative techniques (Stirling and Mayer, 2001; Davies *et al.*, 2003; Burgess *et al.*, 2007). In a one-to-one interview and following a set protocol, each participant works through the appraisal process in discussion with the researcher, using customised MCM software on a laptop computer to display the emerging outcomes graphically. The interview is audiotaped to ensure a full record of the interviewee's deliberations as they work through the tasks. On average, an MCM appraisal takes two or three hours to complete.

Briefly, to summarise the methodological steps in the study, we first reached agreement with the Agency project team to frame the question as: how well do public participation strategies contribute to a close and responsive relationship between the Agency and its stakeholders (widely defined to include members of the public) at the local level? An interview panel comprising seventeen individuals (five Agency staff and twelve public participation practitioners drawn from private, public and voluntary sectors) was recruited for the study. The second step entailed an extensive review of academic and practitioner literatures to develop a set of core options for the appraisal. Although participatory processes vary widely, reflecting their context dependency, a four-stage classification of participatory processes differentiated by communication strategies and power relations is widely recognised (Wilcox, 1994; Warburton, 1998). These range from general information provision, sometimes with feedback requested, through involvement and consultation at different spatial and temporal scales to more extended involvement in, for example, various forms of multi-sector partnerships. From the perspective of the policy maker, these processes may contribute to different styles of decision making, ranging from informing others about decisions already taken; strategies of listening and learning to allow input of wider views into a decision to be made; and exchanging ideas and views in order to make a decision with others. Drawing on this body of work and our own research experience, we produced a total of seven core options to be

Table 8.2 *Seven options of stakeholder processes for close and responsive relationships*

| | Option | Features and UK examples |
|---|---|---|
| 1 | Take part in processes initiated and run by other organisations | *Face-to-face, Ongoing* Decision makers have little control over who participates in such processes or how they are conducted Examples: Local Agenda 21, Estuary management strategies |
| 2 | Provide-and-respond style consultation | *Remote, Discrete, Open, Individual* Examples: Local Environment Agency plans, catchment abstraction management plans |
| 3 | Face-to-face interaction with individual stakeholders | *Face-to-face, Discrete, Open* or *Closed, Individual* |
| 4 | Remote interaction with individual stakeholders | *Remote, Discrete* or *Ongoing, Open, Individual* |
| 5 | Interaction with citizens in groups | *Face-to-face, Discrete, Open* or *Closed, Group* |
| 6 | Discrete interaction with groups of stakeholders | *Face-to-face, Discrete, Closed, Group* |
| 7 | Ongoing interaction with groups of stakeholders | *Face-to-face, Ongoing, Closed, Group* Examples: statutory committees such as Regional Environment Advisory Committees and non-statutory committees such as Area Environment Groups |

*Notes:*
*Face-to-face:* interaction between two or more physically present individuals
*Remote:* interaction which does not involve physical presence, facilitated by telephone or internet
*Discrete:* interaction is time-limited with explicit start and finish
*Ongoing:* interaction is not time-limited
*Open:* any stakeholder can, in principle, become involved
*Closed:* interaction is limited to those whom the regulator chooses to involve or must involve for statutory reasons
*Individual:* interaction is between regulator and stakeholder on one-to-one basis
*Group:* interaction is between regulator and stakeholders in shared space

appraised (as set out in Table 8.2). This document was sent to participants ahead of their interview to allow for prior reflection.

The third step in the MCM protocol takes place during the early stages of the interview, once discussion and clarification of the core options, plus any additional options the interviewee wishes to add to the set, has been completed. Candidate criteria are elicited through discussion in the interview, and the meaning of each criterion is clarified to allow a consistent definition to be used in assessing the options. A set of criteria will usually represent different dimensions for critical judgements between options, encompassing substantive, normative and utilitarian considerations. Interviewees are also able to identify principles which represent a refusal to 'trade-off' between options. In the study, on average five criteria were used to assess the options, with a range from two to eight across the panel as a whole. The three consultants on the interview panel produced the highest number of criteria (six to eight) whilst the five Agency staff produced the lowest (two to five).

Having developed appropriate criteria, each interviewee then works systematically to assess the performance of core and additional options under each criterion. Scoring is used heuristically in MCM, unlike the rigorous, quantified assessments in most multiple criteria decision analysis processes. It is a means to help individuals think through the bases of their judgements and, to help this process of deliberation, the interviewees are asked for two scores – usually on a ranking of one to ten. One score reflects performance under the most optimistic assumptions while the other represents performance under the most pessimistic assumptions. In this way, interviewees are able to express any uncertainty they feel in assigning scores, and take account of variability in performance from context to context. This provides a systematic framework and allows the interviewer to document, by open-ended questioning, some of the crucial determinants underlying the judgements of the panel members.

To take a specific example, option 2 (Table 8.2) describes provide-and-respond consultations. An optimistic judgement of how that performs under a 'learning' criterion might take account of having a good communications team to write and design the text, staff members trained in public relations, and a dedicated phone-line to deal with enquiries. Under these assumptions, the score may be eight or nine. A pessimistic judgement would assume none of these things and the option would be given a much lower score. The 'units of measurement' in this scoring process are different under each criterion and are, of course, subjective and specific to each interviewee. For this reason, the values for each criterion are normalised using a standard mathematical operation in order to reflect all scores as a function of the difference between the best- and worst-performing options under each criterion. This is done automatically on the computer at the time of the interview. The MCM normalises the results of the judgements under all criteria to produce graphical bars which show the range for each option and, as the software is interactive, they are able to track the impact of their assessments as they proceed.

The final stages of the MCM interview focus on the graphical output, exploring the relative importance of each criterion in terms of a numerical weighting. The weighting process reflects intrinsically subjective judgements about principles and priorities. Interviewees are given the opportunity for further iteration until each is comfortable that all pertinent issues have been taken into account and that the pattern of performance displayed in the option rankings fully reflects their own perspective (but see Burgess *et al.*, 2007, for further discussion). The results of the MCM, shown in graphical form on the laptop as the relative ranking of each option under 'best' and 'worst' assumptions, are reviewed. This provides a concrete basis for the interviewees to deliberate, allowing them to evaluate their rankings for themselves and to consider any surprises in the light of the process that they have worked through.

Each interview produces a range of analytic and discursive outputs. The MCM software records additional options: criteria with brief descriptions of their meaning; scores allocated to each option under each criterion; criteria weightings; and the overall relative perform-ance of the options against the criteria. In addition to these data, audio-taped transcriptions of the interview allow some insights into how the interviewee thought about and justified their judgements. This is not, however, a fully open and transparent process of delib-eration (Yearley, 2001) and subsequent development of MCM to enable citizens and specialists to participate in an analytic-deliberative appraisal process called Deliberative Mapping has sought to address this weakness (Davies *et al.*, 2003; Burgess *et al.*, 2007).

*Results*

In a traditional multi-criteria process, rankings are combined in order to arrive at a single overall picture of the relative performance of the options (Munda *et al.*, 1994). This raises a series of practical and theoretical difficulties concerning the aggregation of subjective perspectives. For instance, what weighting should be placed on each individual viewpoint? How representative is the composition of the group of the full range of different social perspectives? Here, the objective is to understand differences in rankings by 'mapping' the way in which different perspectives on public participation processes yield different pictures of the relative performance of the different options. It is important to stress that the project set out to undertake an *ex ante* assessment of the performance of a range of options – i.e. to assist in the choice of processes that might be considered 'fit-for-purpose' in specific decision contexts. It was not undertaking *ex post* appraisal of the actual performance of options in/after their implementation. At the same time, one substantive goal of the work was to better understand the universe of criteria that a range of practitioners would use, either implicitly or explicitly, to evaluate participatory processes.

Before turning to consideration of the evaluative criteria, we briefly review the results of the appraisal, in part to illustrate the functionality of MCM. Figure 8.2a (upper panel) shows the ranges in the final rankings of the core options, combining the inputs of all seventeen participants, and with equal weighting assigned to each. An enormous degree of variability and uncertainty is demonstrated: for almost all the options, the aggregation shows a range between the extremes of 'worst possible' and the 'best possible' ranking. However, it is also clear from Figure 8.2a that, even under the most favourable viewpoints and assumptions, option 2 (from Table 8.2) (*traditional provide-and-respond style consultation methods*) and option 4 (*remote consultations with citizens*) fail to perform as well as the other options at their best.

Figure 8.2b shows the picture that emerges when the values for the 'pessimistic' and 'optimistic' rankings, respectively, are *averaged* across participants. The extreme values reflected in Figure 8.2a are averaged away and an underlying structure begins to emerge. The relative degree of uncertainty and variability associated with each option, averaged across the different participants, is expressed by the

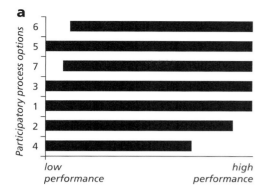

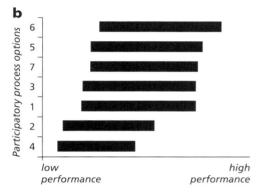

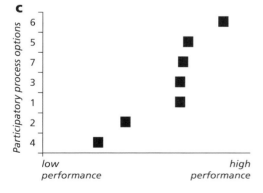

**Figure 8.2** Rank ordering of seven stakeholder processes based on a) inclusion of greatest uncertainty, b) taking average ranking for assumptions and c) excluding concerns of respondents on uncertainty and variability

length of the black bars. The large ranges in the averaged rankings show the high degree of uncertainty and sensitivity to context. Indeed, even taking these average values, it is still the case that the worst-performing option, at its best, performs better than the best-performing option at its worst. However, options 2 and 4 display relatively less uncertainty and variability than the other five.

Figure 8.2c shows the final stage in the aggregation and simplification of results. The uncertainties and variability are stripped away and only the average of the optimistic and pessimistic ends of the ranges in Figure 8.2b is shown. This reveals an underlying ranking order. Option 6 (*discrete interactions with groups of stakeholders*) emerges as the leading option overall in 'achieving a close and responsive relationship' at the local level. Options 2 and 4 are confirmed as performing significantly worse than the other options overall. The remaining four options are effectively indistinguishable in their rankings. The rankings arrived at by each interviewee for the seven core options show a remarkable degree of consistency with the overall picture, suggesting that the overall ranking sequence is not an artefact of the averaging process but reflects a genuine underlying structure in the perspectives of many participants. At the same time, there is evidence that different individuals favour different options and display varying degrees of uncertainty.

A key question thus concerns the main determinants of these differences. Do they reflect individual idiosyncrasies or coherent differences of perspective between different categories of participant? We can explore this question in a variety of ways. For example, it was evident that interviewees approached the appraisal from different professional perspectives and with different goals in relation to the Agency. We found no major differences in performance patterns between the five Agency staff and the twelve interviewees from other professional backgrounds, although Agency staff do appear to be relatively more favourable towards option 3 (*face-to-face interaction with individual stakeholders*) than do other participants. Partitioning the sample by gender also produces relatively little difference between the overall viewpoints of the eleven men and six women involved in the study. Figure 8.3, however, demonstrates more significant differences between professional affiliation (three consultants, seven respondents from the public sector, four from the voluntary sector and two from the private sector).

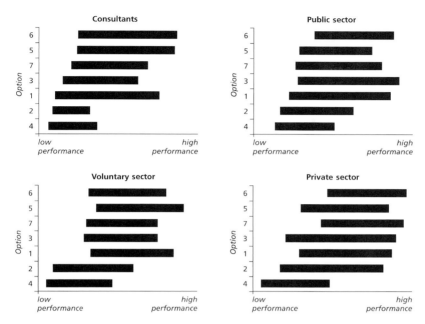

**Figure 8.3** Rank ordering of seven stakeholder processes disaggregated by professional affiliation of respondents

All four groups rank option 6 (*discrete interactions with groups of stakeholders*) very highly. The consultants appear equally favourable towards option 5 (*interactions with groups of citizens*). Those from the public sector rank option 3 equally highly, while the private sector rank option 7 (*ongoing interaction with groups of stakeholders*) equally highly. Those from the voluntary sector rank option 5 even more highly than option 6, with option 1 (*take part in processes initiated and run by other organisations*) performing equally well. Options 2 and 4 are least favoured by all groups. Although caution must be exercised in generalising, the finding does suggest small but discernible differences between the perspectives of some important Agency constituencies.

Differences are also evident when interviewees are grouped according to the perspectives they took in appraising the options. We were able to distinguish the following perspectives: *participatory process, service provision, nature and biodiversity, plan-making, managerial issues,* and *environment protection.* As Figure 8.4 shows again, all

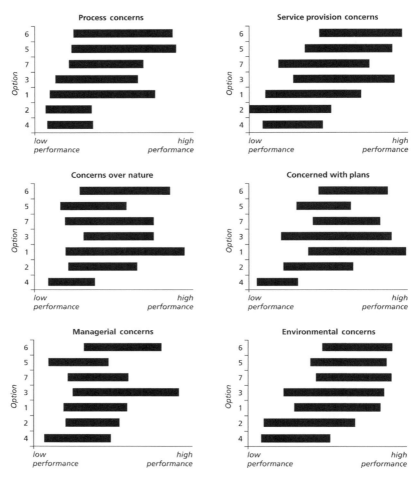

**Figure 8.4** Rank ordering of seven stakeholder processes disaggregated by underlying perspective of respondents

groups were highly favourable towards option 6. The four participants who were more concerned with *process* were equally favourable towards option 5. The two who were more concerned with *nature* and *planning* were more favourable towards option 1. The six who were more concerned about *environmental protection* were equally favourable towards options 5, 6 and 7. The participant with *managerial* concerns was most favourable towards option 3. Interestingly, those more concerned about *nature*, *planning* and *managerial* issues appear relatively less favourable towards option 5 (*interactions with groups of citizens*).

At a broad level of resolution, and suitably qualified in relation to questions of sample size and representativeness, four practical conclusions arise from this performance mapping. First, the performance of each option is highly sensitive to assumptions and context: even the worst-performing option, at its best, performs better than the best-performing option, at its worst. Second, although subject to the above variability, *meetings with groups of stakeholders* for a specific purpose (option 6) performs significantly better overall in potentially helping the Agency secure close and responsive relationships at the local level. Third, *remote consultations with citizens* (option 4) performs worst overall and under the perspectives of most participants and groupings. *Traditional consultation methods* (option 2) also perform remarkably poorly, ranking only just above option 4 overall. Finally, the remaining four options are intermediate and virtually indistinguishable in their overall performance. Option 3 is relatively more favoured by Agency staff and the public sector in general, including those with a particular focus on risk issues. Option 1 is generally more favoured by those from the voluntary sector, those concerned with nature and planning issues, and those with a stakeholder orientation.

## Developing criteria sets to evaluate stakeholder process options

We turn now to an exploration of the criteria developed by each member of the interview panel to appraise the seven options. By representing professional judgements, which may often be implicit in process design and implementation, through its systematic elicitation of criteria, MCM is able to capture the full range of factors considered to be important in participatory processes. For the purposes of analysis, each interviewee's specific meanings and understandings of their criteria were explored, verbally, as they worked through the MCM. There are subtle and nuanced differences which means that, even where the same word or phrase is used, interviewees' criteria do not map simply on to one another. But it is possible, through a discursive analysis, to identify common ground between interviewees in their definition of particular criteria.

Table 8.3 *Categorisation of appraisal criteria by panel member respondents by substantive categories*

| Substantive category | Number of criteria including a concept related to this category[1] | Number of interviewees producing a criterion relevant to category[2] |
|---|---|---|
| 1  Learning | 21 (16) | 14 (3) |
| 2  Productivity | 12 (2) | 10 (2) |
| 3  Transparency | 14 (6) | 9 (1) |
| 4  Supportiveness | 11 (11) | 8 (6) |
| 5  Openness | 9 (12) | 7 (6) |
| 6  Respectfulness | 9 (3) | 8 (2) |
| 7  Efficiency | 8 (8) | 5 (5) |

*Notes:*
[1] Total number of criteria relating primarily to substantive category followed by, in brackets, total number of criteria with a link to substantive category. The number of primary criteria in each category exceeds the number of interviews because interviewees produced two or more criteria falling into the same category.
[2] Number of interviews producing criteria relating primarily to substantive category followed by, in brackets, additional number of interviews producing criteria with a link to substantive category.

Table 8.3 summarises the data upon which this discussion is based. The interview panel produced, in total, seventy-eight criteria. Evidence for the semantic meaning of each criterion was obtained from the working definition given by the interviewee, combined with evidence of its application as they worked through the 'best' and 'worst' thought experiment in the scoring process. The analysis produced seven semantically distinguishable categories – learning, productivity, transparency, supportiveness, openness, respectfulness and efficiency. Some criteria fell primarily into a single category while others touched on more than one. Thus the second column of Table 8.3 shows the number of criteria whose main thrust relates to that category, with the number of criteria with a link to that category shown in brackets. As Table 8.3 shows, learning was the most populated category, with a total of twenty-one criteria including a concept related to it, with a further sixteen that included an element of learning in their construction. The final column of Table 8.3 shows how many members of the interview panel produced criteria that could be mapped under each substantive category. For example, fourteen of the panel produced one or more criteria relevant to the learning category, while the remaining three had a criterion that was linked to it. The substantive categories are ranked by number of respondents deploying criteria within them. But it is also worth noting that almost forty of the criteria are associated with learning; the other categories have far fewer criteria associated with them.

We shall briefly discuss each substantive category in turn, teasing out semantic differences between the different criteria that constitute them. The largest category encompassed criteria concerned with the sponsor listening to, understanding, and responding to what its stakeholders bring to a situation. Learning means coming to understand others' perspectives and positions, as well as a more traditional sense of gaining new knowledge through the acquisition and interpretation of new information. Criteria contributing to learning emphasise the importance of dialogue in promoting understanding and of understanding enabling the negotiation of common ground. Three perspectives were identified through the criteria. Some interviewees focused on communication from stakeholders to the Agency, stressing the need to acknowledge stakeholders' values, fears, knowledge and perceptions but without having to accept unconditionally whatever stakeholders bring to the table. Somewhat fewer interviewees primarily considered the flow of information from the Agency to stakeholders, referring to the need for the Agency to 'get its messages across' to its stakeholders. Finally, a few focused on the importance of dialogue and the need for mutual learning, to facilitate the negotiation of common agendas and consensual solutions to problems.

The second category, labelled productivity, draws together criteria from twelve interview panel members. Criteria here are concerned with the purpose of stakeholder–sponsor interactions. All interviewees who proposed a criterion of this type were agreed that 'close and responsive relationships' should produce concrete outcomes, as expressed in criteria such as *real physical improvements* and *solutions focused*. These outcomes were expressed in a variety of ways including specific environmental improvements as well as enhanced community benefits. There were some tensions between criteria relating to whose goals should be at the forefront – those of the sponsor or its stakeholders.

In many ways, the third category, labelled transparency, is the most complex, since it is concerned with both participatory processes and decision-making procedures. Almost half the interview panel presented a criterion addressing one or both of these concerns. Criteria expressed complementary but distinct meanings, which it is important to clarify. The first concerns making the boundaries of stakeholder involvement clear from the outset. These may address the need to make explicit the relationship between stakeholder involvement and the extent to which stakeholders are able to contribute to framing the questions, setting the agenda, determining procedures and negotiating the boundaries themselves. The second semantic group acknowledges the wider political and social context of engagement, recognising that imbalances of power exist, not only between the sponsor and its stakeholders but also between different stakeholders. Such imbalances relate to the institutions in which interactions are embedded (such as who has powers to take decisions and relative influence in wider political processes), and to the capacity of different stakeholders to engage with the Agency and each other.

A third aspect of transparency relates to having explicit procedures for stakeholder–sponsor interaction, particularly participatory processes. However procedures are agreed, interviewees' criteria suggest that transparency in this context refers to both the 'what' and the 'how' of communication. Procedures for conducting a participatory process should cover how objectives are to be determined; how stakeholders can contribute to framing the issue, question or problem; how debate and deliberation are to be structured; how participants' inputs will be recorded and reported (the audit trail); and, importantly, how their contributions will be dealt with. This last point constitutes a fourth meaning for transparency which is relevant to any type of sponsor–stakeholder interaction, whether a participatory process or a more traditional consultation process. Criteria here expressed the need to be explicit about what decision-making procedures are and how stakeholder contributions will be taken into account, but also to explain a decision once it has been made.

Moving down Table 8.3, the next category captures criteria from eight panellists but also acknowledges that a further six (i.e. virtually the whole panel) had criteria expressing similar sentiments. The supportiveness category is concerned with social interaction. It focuses on building trust through empathetic, helpful and courteous behaviour. Prospects for establishing 'close and responsive relationships' between sponsor and stakeholders, including their ability to reach mutual understanding and willingness to be honest, are likely to be strengthened by a supportive style of behaviour. In proposing criteria relating to this concept, interviewees tended to separate one-to-one, personal relationships from interactions with local communities. The former is particularly concerned with relationships between professionals in organisations, and here interviewees highlighted issues of communication, courtesy and co-operation. These ranged from straightforward matters such as being approachable, being prompt in responding to the other organisation, and being timely in providing information, to more nuanced issues of how to treat and work with others. Good communication, courteous behaviour and empathy are just as important in interactions with local communities, but in this context being supportive was felt to have additional dimensions, including the need to acknowledge potential anxieties in dealing with government bodies, and the need to help people understand technical information and its implications in non-patronising ways.

The openness category groups criteria concerned with whom the sponsor should engage and in what context. Interviewees believed the Agency should be open to all potential stakeholders as a general principle but, in practice, be judicious as to who is involved in what. A common distinction made in this context was between key stakeholders and the public. In other words, stakeholders should be involved as appropriate to the particular local context and decision situation. Thus, the type of engagement process should be tailored to both the decision situation and the stakeholders involved. In particular, it may not always be necessary to involve 'the public'. A final constraint on who can be involved in what kind of process is the availability of resources. Trade-offs are necessary between the requirements of the decision situation, the principle of inclusiveness, process constraints and the availability of resources.

Moving to category 6, twelve criteria expressed concerns about the kind of ethical stance that individual actors adopted towards one another. Respectfulness differs somewhat from the other categories in that it may exist independently of social interaction. Actual experience of interaction between sponsor and stakeholders may affect the level of confidence that one participant has in another, but regarding those with whom one interacts as of equal worth is a prerequisite for attempting an authentic relationship. Feeling stakeholders to be of equal worth implies recognising differences and having regard for their particular circumstances, experience and expertise. In this sense respectfulness links to learning, transparency and supportiveness in that it engenders willingness to listen, to try to understand, to acknowledge the legitimacy of others' concerns, to treat others as you would want to be treated, to be honest, and to enable participation on equal terms. In this sense also, respectfulness can help to build trust.

The final category includes criteria from ten members of the interview panel, and concerns the effective use of both stakeholder and sponsor resources. Under this efficiency grouping, there was concern for economic efficiency in engaging with stakeholders. But more criteria emphasised time as a vital resource. Most obviously, stakeholders' time is limited, while demands for stakeholder and public participation and consultation are increasing, stretching the capacity of many stakeholders to respond. Stakeholder involvement should be appropriate to the scale of the problem or issue, geographically, socially and politically. It should be undertaken when decision makers are still able to take account of stakeholder contributions, and stakeholder concern is evident. But 'close and responsive relationships' also take time for both background and face-to-face activities if they are to be effective. For the sponsor, being efficient implies evaluating the benefits from participatory decision making against the effort devoted to doing so.

Figure 8.5 expresses the relationships between these evaluative categories and identifies where in the model of decision making presented above each would suggest specific criteria be applied to ensure good practice in participation designed to support closer relationships between institutions and their stakeholders. Respect between staff and the stakeholders concerned represents an input necessary, but not sufficient, for interaction to be successful, though it may also be reinforced through the process used. Supportive behaviour, transparent processes of engagement and the associated decision process, efficient use of resources, and an appropriate level of openness contribute to the success of the process adopted and so to the extent to which high-quality relationships are realised through the activity. Finally, productivity and mutual learning represent the output and an outcome of the process. The extent to which they lead to practical action and enhance learning by all parties concerned is

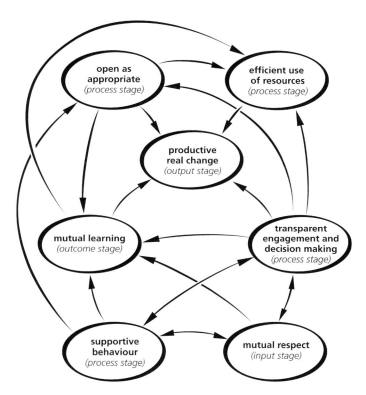

**Figure 8.5** Relationships between the seven evaluative categories and the appropriate stage of decision making for their use

indicative of the quality of relationships developed through the interactions.

These qualities are also linked, as illustrated in Figure 8.5. Respect promotes trust, and hence willingness to behave transparently and supportively in engaging with others, and to learn from that engagement. In turn, they are likely to reinforce mutual respect. As an outcome, mutual learning is also more likely when engagement of stakeholders is appropriate to context and circumstances. Transparency, openness and efficiency help to make interaction meaningful and competent, so contributing to the likelihood of interaction producing real change to the extent that context and circumstances allow. Learning, although an outcome in its own right, occurs during the process and, in enhancing the competence of interaction, also contributes to its productiveness. Similarly, mutual learning, although an outcome, is also an indicator of resource-efficient interaction, while efficiency is likely to be promoted through transparency of process and the appropriate involvement of stakeholders.

## Next steps in the evaluation of stakeholder participation

Although, in this study, options were presented as abstract processes rather than concrete events, the assessors in this study were individuals with a range of professional expertise in the development and application of participatory decision making in a variety of institutional and geographical contexts. All were aware of the constraints and contingencies that influence the outputs and outcomes of specific applications. At the same time, all saw the value of contributing to the development of criteria sets that could promote more rigorous, systematic evaluation of participatory decision making for sustainability. As such, the study is comparable with those by Webler *et al.*, (2001) and Santos and Chess (2003). To what extent is there growing consensus about what, if not necessarily how best, to evaluate?

Some evidence suggests that there are substantive differences between the expectations, values and goals of different participants in participatory processes (Cowie and O'Toole, 1998; Pellizzoni, 2003) which would suggest differences in evaluative criteria as well. For example, Webler and colleagues used Q methodology (McKeown and Thomas, 1988) with a panel of twenty-seven stakeholders who had been actively involved in a forest planning process in northern New England and New York. Each participant sorted forty-five attitude statements, chosen to embody different elements of fairness and competence in participatory processes. Factor analysis produced five competing discourses, suggesting that 'people had different ideas on what is a good process' (Webler *et al.*, 2001: 448). While acknowledging the different methodologies, the tenor of some of the MCM-based substantive categories resemble one of the discourses identified by Webler and colleagues which emphasise the importance of a place-based focus, the need to move from talk to action, an approach which focuses less on widespread citizen participation and more on 'getting the right people in the room'. The participatory process 'should build the relationships necessary for continued dialogue, including respect, trust and greater understanding of different viewpoints on the issues, and strictly enforce the rules for what is acceptable behaviour' (Webler *et al.*, 2001: 443). Interestingly, Webler and colleagues describe this grouping as the most controversial of the five identified and promoted by individuals representing 'translocal' environmental organisations.

In a European context, and specifically in the UK, with its long tradition of negotiation between different perspectives to achieve environmental outcomes (O'Riordan and Weale, 1990; Munton, 2003), these would not be seen as 'controversial'. The different interpretation throws into relief the powerful influence of specific geographical and cultural political contexts in the application of all participatory processes.

Fiorino (1990) identified four normative criteria to assess the extent to which participation might contribute to fundamental demo-cratic goals. Confirmed through theoretical argument (Webler, 1995; Bohman, 2000; Dryzek, 2000), practitioners clearly embrace similar goals while recognising difficulties in achieving them. Political issues, especially those of unequal power relations, present enormous challenges for evaluators (Smith and Beazley, 2000; O'Neill, 2001; Horlick-Jones *et al.*, 2007b). Governance for sustainable development depends on partnership-working between public, private and voluntary sector actors in which boundaries, responsibilities and accountability in dealing with issues become blurred. In such cases, as Stoker comments, 'those in a position to interpret and lead public debate can, often with considerable effectiveness, blame others for failures and difficulties' (Stoker, 1998: 22). More generally, robust evaluation of processes can support the development of more equitable participatory processes and enhance their efficacy for policy makers. But, supporting the conclusions of Rowe and Frewer (2000, 2004), this research confirms the sensitivity of participatory processes to context-specific factors: what works well in one context will not necessarily do so in another.

Recent debate has moved from concern with questions of fairness and representatives to those of competence – specifically the extent to which learning within processes can be evaluated (Tuler and Webler, 2006). In the MCM study reported here, 'learning' was by far the most substantial category, reflecting normative, substantive and utilitarian concerns. Learning acknowledges the importance of exploring knowledge claims between the parties in a process, while also exploring different values and ways of seeing the world. Mutual learning may be possible when there are supportive, ongoing social relationships, both on a personal level and with local communities, which are characterised by mutual respect. These qualities are fundamental to building relationships between actors networked in processes and, under different theoretical assumptions, are vital in building social capital to support governance for sustainability (Rydin and Pennington, 2000; Plummer and Armitage, 2007). The message is reinforced in US studies of small group processes such as that by Santos and Chess (2003: 274): 'interviewees saw the quality of ... meetings as linked to the quality of social interaction and, in particular, norms about the personal behaviour of individuals taking part'.

It is important, as Owens (2000) points out, not to fall into simple 'deficit' models when thinking about the politics of knowledge and information-sharing in participatory processes. Rowe and Frewer's (2000) criteria set did not include a criterion concerned with learning, preferring one of *influence*, since 'participation is not about passive learning of information from the exercise sponsor but is instead about providing information and thereby influencing subsequent policy' (Rowe *et al.*, 2004: 92). However, with moves towards more analytic-deliberative processes, an increasing number of processes are designed to support more critical discussion between sponsors and participants, stakeholders and citizens. Information provision and knowledge acquisition – amongst all parties – are growing more significant. This point is addressed in the Horlick-Jones *et al.* (2007b: 275) reflections on the *GM Nation?* debate, where they propose an additional normative criterion of 'translation quality' to assess the 'effectiveness of information collection and transmission, and knowledge capture'. In principle, it should be possible to undertake evaluative exercises better informed by good practice in other educational contexts (see Guba and Lincoln, 1989; Petts and Brooks, 2006).

In conclusion, sets of criteria for the evaluation of participatory strategies that encompass inputs, process design and conduct, outputs and outcomes are being developed. The majority derive strength from normative theories of democracy and communicative rationality in which personal self-interest and competition are subordinated to the common good and co-operation. There appears to be a significant level of consensus emerging that these are generic criteria that may be adopted to evaluate processes in many different contexts. It will never be possible for all processes to score highly on all criteria. There will always be practical restrictions on numbers who can participate, and the time and resources available for participation.

However, it is also the case that, as our analysis shows, the specific meanings of criteria can vary substantially as a consequence of individual interpretation and institutional context. It is the responsibility of evaluators to ensure maximum clarity in the meanings of criteria sets being used. There is still much to be done in clarifying which criteria are suitable for numerical application and which demand the exercise of qualitative social scientific skills. In these respects, the painstaking, empirical study by Horlick-Jones *et al.* (2007a, 2007b) on the conduct of the *GM Nation?* debate and its aftermath, including some very difficult policy–political relationships, sets the standard for future work on the role of participation in governance for sustainability.

# References

Abelson, J., Forest, P.-G., Eyles, J., Smith, P., Martin, E. and Gauvin, F. 2003. 'Deliberations about deliberative methods: issues in the design and evaluation of public participation processes', *Social Science and Medicine* 57: 239–51.

Barnes, M. 1999. 'Researching public participation', *Local Government Studies* 25(4): 60–75.

Beierle, T. C. and Konisky, D. M. 2001. 'What are we gaining from stakeholder involvement? Observations from environmental planning in the Great Lakes', *Environment and Planning C: Government and Policy* 19: 515–27.

Bloomfield, D., Collins, K., Fry, C. and Munton, R. 2001. 'Deliberation and inclusion: vehicles for increasing trust in UK public governance?' *Environment and Planning C: Government and Policy* 19: 501–13.

Bohman, J. 2000. *Public Deliberation: Pluralism, Complexity, and Democracy*. Cambridge, MA: MIT Press.

Burgess, J. and Chilvers, J. D. 2006. 'Upping the *ante*: a conceptual framework for designing and evaluating participatory technology assessments', *Science and Public Policy* 33: 713–28.

Burgess, J., Collins, K., Harrison, C. M., Munton, R. and Murlis, J. 2000. 'An analytical and descriptive model of sustainable development for the Environment Agency', R & D Report W1–12. (J.). Bristol, UK: Environment Agency.

Burgess, J., Stirling, A. C., Clark, J., Davies, G., Eames, M., Staley, K. and Williamson, S. 2007. 'Deliberative mapping: a novel analytic-deliberative methodology to support contested science-policy decisions', *Public Understanding of Science* 16: 299–322.

Chess, C. 2000. 'Evaluating environmental public participation: methodological questions', *Journal of Environmental Planning and Management* 43: 769–84.

Chess, C. and Johnson, B. B. 2006. 'Organizational learning about public participation: "Tiggers" and "Eeyores"', *Human Ecology Review* 13: 182–92.

Chess, C. and Purcell, K. 1999. 'Public participation and the environment: do we know what works?' *Environmental Science and Technology* 33: 2685–92.

Clark, J., Burgess, J., Stirling, A. and Studd, K. 2001. *Local Outreach: The Development of Criteria for the Evaluation of Close and Responsive Relationships at the Local Level*. Environment Agency R&D Technical Report SWCON 204. Bristol, UK: Environment Agency.

Coenen, F. H. J. M., Huitema, D. and O'Toole, L. (eds.) 1998. *Participation and the Quality of Environmental Decision Making*. Dordrecht, The Netherlands: Kluwer.

Conley, A. and Moote, M. A. 2003. 'Evaluating collaborative natural resource management', *Society and Natural Resources* 16: 371–86.

Cowie, G. M. and O'Toole, L. 1998. 'Linking stakeholder participation and environmental decision making: assessing decision quality for interstate river basin management', in Coenen, F. H. J. M., Huitema, D. and O'Toole, L. (eds.) *Participation and the Quality of Environmental Decision Making*. Dordrecht, The Netherlands: Kluwer, pp. 61–70.

Davies, G., Burgess, J., Eames, M., Mayer, S., Staley, S., Stirling, A. and Williamson, S. 2003. *Deliberative Mapping: Appraising Options for Closing 'The Kidney Gap'*. Final Report to the Wellcome Trust. URL: www.deliberative-mapping.org.uk.

DETR 1999. *Local Evaluation for Regeneration Partnerships: Good Practice Guide*. London: DETR. URL: www.detr.gov.uk/regeneration/info/gp/erp/.

Dryzek, J. 2000. *Deliberative Democracy and Beyond*. Oxford, UK: Oxford University Press.

Environment Agency 1996. *Introductory Guidance on the Agency's Contribution to Sustainable Development*. Sustainable Development Series No. 1. Environmental Strategy Directorate. Bristol, UK: Environment Agency.

Fiorino, D. J. 1990. 'Citizen participation and environmental risk: a survey of institutional mechanisms', *Science, Technology and Human Values* 15: 226–43.

Goodwin, P. 1998. '"Hired hands" or "local voice": understandings and experience of local participation in conservation', *Transactions of the Institute of British Geographers* 23: 481–99.

Guba, E. G. and Lincoln Y. S. 1989. *Fourth Generation Evaluation.* London, UK: Sage.

Habermas, J. 1984. *Theory of Communicative Action – Volume 1: Reason and the Rationalisation of Society.* Boston, MA: Beacon Press.

Hajer, M. A. 2005. 'Setting the stage: a dramaturgy of policy deliberation', *Administration and Society* 36: 624–47.

Horlick-Jones, T., Rowe, G. and Walls, J. 2007a. 'Citizen engagement processes and information systems: the role of knowledge and the concept of translation quality', *Public Understanding of Science* 16: 259–78.

Horlick-Jones, T., Walls, J., Rowe, G., Pidgeon, N., Poortinga, W., Murdoch, G. and O'Riordan, T. 2007b. *The GM Debate: Risk, Politics and Public Engagement.* London, UK: Routledge.

Irwin, A. 2001. 'Constructing the scientific citizen: science and democracy in the biosciences', *Public Understanding of Science* 10: 1–18.

Joss, S. and Bellucci, S. 2002. *Participatory Technology Assessment: European Perspectives.* Centre for the Study of Democracy, University of Westminster, London.

Knoepfel, P. and Kissling-Näf, I. 1998. 'Social learning in policy networks', *Policy and Politics* 26: 343–67.

McKeown, B. and Thomas, D. 1988. *Q Methodology.* London, UK: Sage.

Munda, G., Nijkamp, P. and Rietveld, P. 1994. 'Qualitative multi-criteria evaluation for environmental management', *Ecological Economics* 10: 97–112.

Munton, R. 2003. 'Deliberative democracy and environmental decision making', in Berkhout, F., Leach, M. and Scoones, I. (eds.) *Negotiating Environmental Change: New Perspectives from Social Science.* Cheltenham, UK: Elgar, pp. 109–36.

O'Hara, S. U. 1996. 'Discursive ethics in ecosystem valuation and environmental policy', *Ecological Economics* 16: 95–107.

O'Neill, J. 2001. 'Representing people, representing nature, representing the world', *Environment and Planning C: Government and Policy* 19: 483–500.

O'Riordan, T. and Weale, A. 1990 *Greening the Machinery of Government.* London, UK: Friends of the Earth.

Owens, S. 2000. 'Engaging the public: information and deliberation in environmental policy', *Environment and Planning A* 32: 1141–8.

Pellizzoni, L. 2001. 'The myth of the best argument: power, deliberation and reason', *British Journal of Sociology* 52: 59–86.

Pellizzoni, L. 2003. 'Uncertainty and participatory democracy', *Environmental Values* 12: 195–224.

Petts, J. 2004. 'Barriers to participation and deliberation in risk decisions: evidence from waste management', *Journal of Risk Research* 7: 115–33.

Petts, J. and Brooks, C. 2006. 'Managing public engagement to optimise learning: reflections from urban river restoration', *Human Ecology Review* 13: 172–81.

Petts, J. and Leach, B. 2000. *Evaluating Methods for Public Participation: Literature Review*. Environment Agency R & D Technical Report E135. Bristol, UK: Environment Agency.

Petts, J., Homan, J. and Pollard, S. 2004. *Participatory Risk Assessment: Involving Lay Audiences in Environmental Decisions on Risk*. Environment Agency R & D Technical Report E2–043/TR/01. Bristol, UK: Environment Agency.

Plummer, R. and Armitage, D. 2007. 'A resilience-based framework for evaluating adaptive co-management: linking ecology, economics and society in a complex world', *Ecological Economics* 61: 62–74.

Rayner, S. 2003. 'Democracy in an age of assessment: reflections on the roles of expertise and democracy in public sector decision making', *Science and Public Policy* 30: 163–70.

Renn, O., Webler, T. and Wiedemann, P. (eds.) 1995. *Fairness and Competence in Citizen Participation: Evaluating Models for Environmental Discourse*. Dordrecht, The Netherlands: Kluwer.

Rogers-Hayden, T. and Pidgeon, N. 2007. 'Moving engagement "upstream"? Nanotechnologies and the Royal Society and Royal Academy of Engineering's inquiry', *Public Understanding of Science* 16: 345–65.

Rowe, G. and Frewer, L. 2000. 'Public participation methods: a framework for evaluation', *Science, Technology and Human Values* 25: 3–29.

Rowe, G. and Frewer, L. 2004. 'Evaluating public participation exercises: a research agenda', *Science Technology and Human Values* 29: 512–56.

Rowe, G., Marsh, R. and Frewer, L. 2004. 'Evaluation of a deliberative conference', *Science, Technology and Human Values* 29: 88–121.

Rydin, Y. and Pennington, M. 2000. 'Public participation and local environmental planning: the collective action problem and the potential of social capital', *Local Environment* 5: 153–69.

Santos, S. L. and Chess, C. 2003. 'Evaluating citizen advisory boards: the importance of theory and participant-based criteria and practical implications', *Risk Analysis* 23: 269–79.

Smith, M. and Beazley, M. 2000. 'Progressive regimes, partnerships and the involvement of local communities: a framework for evaluation', *Public Administration* 78: 855–78.

Stern, P. C. and Fineberg, H. V. 1996. *Understanding Risk: Informing Decisions in a Democratic Society*. Washington DC: National Academy Press.

Stirling, A. 1997. 'Multi-criteria mapping: mitigating the problems of environmental valuation', in Foster, J. (ed.) *Valuing Nature*. London, UK: Routledge.

Stirling, A. 2005. 'Opening up or closing down: analysis, participation and power in social appraisals of technology', in Leach, M., Scoones, I. and Wynne, B. (eds.) *Science and Citizens: Globalisation and the Challenge of Engagement*. London, UK: Zed Books.

Stirling, A. and Mayer, S. 1999. *Rethinking Risk: A Pilot Multi-Criteria Mapping of a Genetically Modified Crop in Agricultural Systems in the UK*. Report for the UK Roundtable on Genetic Modification, SPRU, University of Sussex.

Stirling, A. and Mayer, S. 2001. 'A novel approach to the appraisal of technological risk: a multi-criteria mapping study of a genetically modified crop', *Environment and Planning C: Government and Policy* 19: 529–55.

Stoker, G. 1998. 'Governance as theory: five propositions', *International Social Science Journal* 50(1): 17–24.

Tuler, S. and Webler, T. 2006. 'Introduction: recent research in public participation, a focus on learning', *Human Ecology Review* 13: 148–9.

Twigger-Ross, C. and Smith, C. 2000. *Public Involvement in Agency Activities*. Report No. 22. Bristol, UK: Environment Agency.

UNECE 1998. *Convention on Access to Information, Public Participation in Decision Making and Access to Justice in Environmental Matters* (the Aarhus Convention). Geneva: UN Economic Commission for Europe. URL: www.unece.org/env/ppAarhus.

Warburton, D. (ed.) 1998. *Community and Sustainable Development: Participation in the Future*. London, UK: Earthscan.

Webler, T. 1995. ' "Right" discourse in citizen participation: an evaluative yardstick', in Renn, O., Webler, T. and Wiedermann, P. (eds.) *Fairness and Competence in Citizen Participation: Evaluating Models for Environmental Discourse*. Dordrecht, The Netherlands: Kluwer, pp. 35–86.

Webler, T., Tuler, S. and Krueger, R. 2001. 'What is a good participation process? Five perspectives from the public', *Environmental Management* 27: 435–50.

Wilcox, D. 1994. *The Guide to Effective Participation*. Brighton, UK: Partnership Books.

Yearley, S. 2001. 'Mapping and interpreting societal responses to genetically modified crops and food', *Social Studies of Science* 31: 151–60.

# PART IV

# Governance and Decision Making

# 9 | Participation, precaution and reflexive governance for sustainable development

ANDY STIRLING

## Precaution, participation and sustainability

Preoccupations with issues of precaution and participation are two of the most important elements in current discussions of the terms 'governance' and 'sustainable development'. They represent two of the principal forms in which the sustainability agenda might be seen most tangibly to have penetrated the ways in which society at large is governed. Recently, a series of pressing policy challenges surrounding the development of new science and technology have raised difficult questions about the role of precaution and participation in the governance of innovation. Surprisingly, however, there remains relatively little attention to the interlinkages between the issues of sustainability, precaution and participation. Academic and policy discussions alike remain largely segregated. It is in this regard that the work of Tim O'Riordan has – until recently – been rather unusual, in that he has tended to address all three topics in an integrated way and with equal vision and vigour (O'Riordan and Cameron, 1994; O'Riordan *et al.*, 2000; O'Riordan, 2001; O'Riordan and Stoll-Kleemann, 2002).

This chapter seeks to build on his contributions by exploring some of the conceptual and policy implications of the links between these themes, while pointing towards possible future orientations. It begins by exploring some important general characteristics of 'sustainability' as a high-profile concept in contemporary governance discourses. In particular, it will be argued that there exist three quite distinct ways in which the concept of sustainability can be understood: substantively – as a set of publicly deliberated goals; normatively – as a social process; and instrumentally – as a means discursively to support and justify narrow sectional interests. This triad of imperatives forms the basis of an exploration of the relationships between precaution, participation and sustainability. First, precaution is examined in relation to established, so-called sound scientific, approaches to sustainability appraisal. Rather than being seen solely as a normative decision rule, precaution is characterised as a broad-based substantive matter of social learning. Attention then turns to participation, focusing in particular on real-world instrumental pressures in which political and economic power play a dominant role. In seeking to address these pressures, participation can also be seen, not only as a normatively driven feature of democratic governance, but also in substantive terms as a means to enhance the relationship between appraisal and wider processes of governance. If this is to be realised in practice, however, there are a number of practical implications which apply equally to 'sound scientific', precautionary and participatory approaches to sustainability.

This chapter concludes by examining the contribution that can be made to understandings of the practical policy roles of precaution and participation by current conceptual discussions over qualities of reflection and reflexiveness in the governance of sustainability. In particular, it is argued that if we are to avoid some of the more instrumental uses of the concept of sustainability then the properties of reflection and reflexivity warrant much closer attention. A series of further policy conclusions are then drawn concerning the ways in which precaution and participation can be implemented and integrated in order to achieve more robust forms of governance for sustainability.

## Sustainability, legitimisation and process

In seeking to explore the relationships between precaution, participation and sustainability, we encounter a challenge right at the outset with the notion of sustainability itself. The language of sustainability as deployed in governance debates displays a series of significant ambiguities and tensions. These arise from interactions between three specific modes of usage (Stirling, 2005) – all of which differ from the colloquial use of the term 'sustainability'.

The substantive use of this term refers to the sustaining for present and future generations of a particular set of qualities, of a kind that have been publicly deliberated in a high-profile fashion since the publication of the Brundtland Report in 1987 (see Chapter 1). Despite this, the details of this substantive notion of sustainability are variously defined in different contexts (e.g. Murcott, 1997). Yet the essential substance consistently rests on three broad sets of normative aims. The first concerns human wellbeing – including health, education and community as well as economic development (United Nations General Assembly, 2000). The second relates to social equity – both for present and future generations (United Nations, 2002). The third refers to environmental quality – in terms of various forms of ambient pollution, ecological integrity and resource availability (UNEP, 1997).

The broad colloquial usage of the term sustainability, by contrast, refers generally to the maintaining over indefinite periods of unspecified features, qualities or functions (OED, 1989). It is in this vein that we read, for instance in the Treaty Establishing the Constitution for Europe (CEC, 2004), of the need to 'sustain': the internal market (Art. III-130.4); Member State economies (Art. III-179.3); the government financial positions (Art. III-198.1b); and human wellbeing, social equity and environmental quality (Art. III-292d). In order to distinguish these general and colloquial usages from the more specific substantive publicly deliberated meanings, we might refer to the former as sustainability (using a lower case 's') and the latter as Sustainability (using an upper case 'S').

There exists no shortage of careful thinking over the practical attributes of Sustainability in the governance literature (Dobson, 1996; Jordan and O'Riordan, 2003; Meadowcroft *et al.*, 2005). This is also true in policy documentation, for instance where governance institutions have developed explicit sets of Sustainability criteria associated with operational quantitative indicators (DEFRA, 2004). However, it is these very attributes of explicitness, concreteness and applicability that can render substantive notions of Sustainability difficult to relate to parallel policy debates over precaution and participation. As we shall see, the relevance of both precaution and participation arises especially where there is uncertainty, ambiguity or ignorance over the substantive implications of Sustainability (O'Riordan *et al.*, 2000). In particular, questions arise over the rationales both for participation and precaution, if the nature, implications and governance requirements of Sustainability are all entirely clear and uncontroversial. To the extent that substantive usage of the term Sustainability militates against recognition of such uncertainties, then it may appear in some senses to be rather detached from (or even in tension with) rationales for precaution and participation.

Instrumental usage of the language of sustainability, by contrast, exploits the ambiguities which are inherent in the interpretive flexibility of the term Sustainability (Stirling, 2006). The real utility of this ambiguity lies in the role of the language of sustainability as a discursive resource for legitimising certain actions (Wynne, 2001). By exploiting this resource, incumbent interests may hope to sustain particular features of the status quo which are supported for narrow sectional reasons, by tacitly associating them with the more widely supported, publicly deliberated, substantive qualities of Sustainability. This tendency is frequently evident in industry or government documentation, which fails to specify the particular characteristics to which their use of the adjective 'sustainable' actually refers.

Here, the UK government department DEFRA again provides some useful examples. Despite undoubted commitment and effort in pursuit of Sustainability, the current high-level organisational structure of this department nonetheless makes prominent use of the term 'sustainability' in a fashion that is in some tension with its own detailed indicators (DEFRA, 2004). All agricultural activities, for instance, are effectively referred to in an undifferentiated fashion as 'sustainable farming' (Stirling, 2005). Likewise, DEFRA agencies employ the term 'sustainable science' to include areas of research concerned with the use of pesticides in agriculture (DEFRA, 2002), despite the fact that reducing pesticide use features strongly among DEFRA's own Sustainability indicators (DEFRA, 2004). In effect, DEFRA is representing as sustainable, practices that they elsewhere acknowledge to be un-Sustainable.

A similar pattern is evident even more strongly on the part of other official and industry bodies, both in the UK and elsewhere. The term 'sustainable communities', for instance, is deployed in a fashion that reduces the entire environmental agenda to just one of nine mainstream policy aims – on a par with 'good transport services' (DCLG, 2005). And in the commercial world, concepts of 'sustainable business' routinely acquire an emphasis on profitability, competitiveness and market share (SBI, 2005), rather than the social and environmental priorities that are intrinsic to Sustainability in its more substantive sense. Under these kinds of instrumental legitimatory usage of the language of sustainability, the procedural disciplines associated with precaution and participation present even greater mismatches and tensions.

The third – processual – usage of the term 'sustainability' relates not so much to the outcomes but to particular features of the process of governance. Here, it refers to attributes such as agency, accessibility, transparency, representativeness and equity (CEC, 2001) of a kind that are held to be necessary, if not sufficient, in order to achieve more substantively Sustainable outcomes. It is in this vein, for instance, that we encounter the term 'sustainable governance' in certain strands of European Commission policy discussion, to refer to 'the institutional and procedural aspects of sustainability' (ECFESD, 2000). Whether acknowledged or not, it is with this third understanding of the meaning of sustainability that we may recognise the crucial constitutive roles of precaution and participation.

This argument will be examined in detail in the following sections. However, initial support is given simply by the joint presence of precaution and participation in the 1992 Rio Declaration itself (UNCED, 1992). Broad citizen participation is advocated under Principle 10 as a general feature of environmental governance, with injunctions to make particular provision for participation by women and indigenous people further reinforced under Principles 20 and 22, respectively. Likewise, precaution features as a separate consideration under Principle 15, which holds that:

In order to protect the environment, the precautionary approach shall be widely applied by States according to their capabilities. Where there are threats of serious or irreversible damage, lack of full scientific certainty shall not be used as a reason for postponing cost-effective measures to prevent environmental degradation (UNCED, 1992).

What is interesting here, is that both this and subsequent similar juxtapositions of participation, precaution and sustainability say as much about the distinct and separate nature of these themes as they do about their interlinkage. The reason is that when such combined references occur at all, they tend to be quite circumstantial and compartmentalised. In particular, it remains unclear why participation is of specific importance in addressing Sustainability, as distinct from other governance agendas. The argument that those who are affected by the consequences, or have a role in implementation, should be involved in the decision making itself is certainly persuasive. But it applies at least equally in other areas of politics such as employment, security, law-making, education or health. As such, the imperative for participation rests on normative democratic commitments that transcend and subsume the Sustainability discourse, but which appear to hold no unique or exclusive linkage to it.

For its part, precaution appears in the Rio Declaration as a putative decision rule. In effect, it amounts simply to an injunction that uncertainty may not be invoked as a reason for inaction. That the driving motivation is explicitly linked to imperatives for environmental protection does reflect one key focus of the Sustainability agenda. But the particular characteristics of the possible outcomes which provide the trigger for precautionary action (namely seriousness or irreversibility) may also arise under issues other than environment. They apply equally, for instance, to dimensions of Sustainability relating to human wellbeing or social equity. Yet nothing is said about how to respond to contending uncertainties on different dimensions. Likewise, few details are given of the process through which this decision rule should be enacted. Finally, little is said of any particular role for participation in the implementation of precaution. Despite their intimate juxtaposition, then, rationales for participation and precaution remain curiously decoupled, both from each other and from the specific imperatives for Sustainability.

Scope therefore arises for some re-examining of precaution and participation agendas, in order to explore their neglected mutual inter-relationships and their distinctive links with Sustainability as a whole. Before turning to some general implications for governance, each of these issues will be taken in turn: first precaution, and then participation.

## Sound science, framing and precaution

Academic and policy literatures on precaution tend to centre on quite technical legal and methodological issues concerning the appropriate management of risk under what the Rio Declaration refers to in the citation above as 'lack of scientific certainty'. In this vein, debates over the precautionary principle have, for two decades, been a prominent theme in their own right at the heart of global developments in the fields of risk regulation and environment policy (O'Riordan and Cameron, 1994; O'Riordan *et al.*, 2000). The precautionary principle has since become a feature not only of numerous influential EU and national policy instruments (CEC, 2000), but also the draft EU Constitution (CEC, 2004: Art. III-233.2).

Nonetheless, intense political arguments have raged between industry and civil society organisations over the balance to strike between general economic competitiveness and the precautionary regulation of particular industrial strategies and sectors (Johnson *et al.*, 1998; Morris, 2000; Taverne, 2005). Accordingly, it is precaution that repeatedly lies at the crux of some of the most hotly contested international legal disputes, for instance under the auspices of the World Trade Organization (Vogel, 2000; Fisher, 2001). The ferocity of these debates is driven by the scale of the contending political and economic interests. But it is also compounded by the intrinsic ambiguities in formal enunciations of the precautionary principle itself (Fisher, 2002; Sandin *et al.*, 2002). It has already been noted that virtually all official statements of precaution, like that quoted above, take the form of a putative decision rule (Stirling, 2003). But this typically raises a series of intractable questions (see Sand, 2000): What is meant by threat? How serious is serious? What counts as irreversible? Who is to determine scientific certainty? And by what means are we to know when this is 'full'?

It is these kinds of query that form the grounds for unfavourable comparisons with long-established science-based approaches to governance, such as those offered by established techniques of risk assessment (Berlinski, 1976; USDA, 2000). At least these sound scientific methods, so it is argued, are capable of delivering a clear basis for decision making (Byrd and Cothern, 2000; Lloyd, 2000). The UK Prime Minister, Tony Blair, neatly epitomised the influence of this kind of aspiration in statements like this one, made at the height of the debate over genetically modified crops: 'this government's approach is to make decisions on GM crops on the basis of sound science' (Blair, 2003). Adopting this science-based approach, many influential commentators see an acute tension between the imperatives of precaution and of sound science in the governance of Sustainability (Morris, 2000; Taverne, 2005).

In fact, the perception of such a tension involves a fundamentally misconceived understanding of the natures of both scientific and precautionary responses to uncertainty. The reasons for this are summarised schematically in Figure 9.1 (Stirling, 1999). This is structured by the two dimensions of the formal definition of the concept of risk, which underlie the science-based notion of risk assessment (Keynes, 1921; Knight, 1921). For each of a range of outcomes, this comprises two fundamental elements: probabilities and magnitudes. On either dimension, the knowledge informing decision making can be relatively robust or problematic. Under conditions where there exists robust knowledge on both counts, then there exists a state of risk, in the strict 'sound scientific' sense of this term. Examples may be found in areas such as transport safety, the epidemiology of well-known pathogens, and flood risks under conventional weather patterns. Established techniques of probabilistic risk assessment, cost–benefit analysis and decision theory present powerful aids to the appraisal of risk.

The key message summarised in Figure 9.1, however, is that this 'sound scientific' definition of risk also implies a further series of states of incertitude (Stirling, 2003). Under a condition of uncertainty, we can be confident in our characterisation of the different outcomes, but the available empirical information or analytical models simply do not present a definitive basis for assigning probabilities (Luce and Raiffa, 1957; Morgan *et al.*, 1990; Rowe, 1994). Accordingly, it is a matter of sound science that probabilistic techniques like risk assessment are – by definition – not applicable. Examples of such uncertainty abound. They arise, for instance, with many potential carcinogens or eco-logical effects, as well as with prospects of flooding under changed weather conditions due to climate change. Fortunately, there exists a range of other, less ambitious but nonetheless useful, methods. But these are neglected because of a prevailing preoccupation with risk assessment. They include sensitivity (Saltelli, 2001), scenario (Werner, 2004) and interval analysis (Jaulin *et al*, 2001), as well as a variety of different decision heuristics such as the maximin and minimum regret rules (Forster, 1999). Although valuable as appraisal tools, what distinguishes these techniques is that they acknowledge significant latitude for interpretation. They cannot be used to justify a single apparently definitive science-based decision.

The challenge of uncertainty is serious enough for conventional notions of risk assessment. Yet Figure 9.1 shows that the difficulties do not end here. Under the further condition of ambiguity, it is not the probabilities but the definition of the outcomes themselves that is problematic. There are numerous examples where profound disagree-ment exists over the selection, partitioning, bounding, measurement,

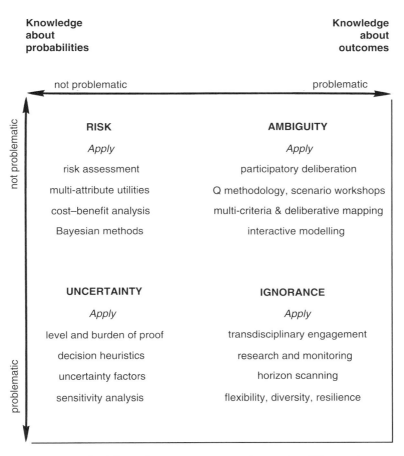

**Figure 9.1** Methodological responses appropriate under different degrees of incertitude. Adapted from Stirling (1999).

prioritisation or interpretation of different possible outcomes (Wynne, 1992, 2002; Stirling, 2003). Examples may be found concerning the appropriate questions to pose in regulation. Is this acceptable? Is this safe? Is this the best option? Likewise, ambiguities arise over the notion of harm from genetic modification technology. Put simply, is this an ecological, agronomic, food safety, economic or social issue (Grove-White *et al.*, 1997; Levidow *et al.*, 1998; Stirling and Mayer, 2001)? When faced with such questions over contradictory certainties (Thompson and Warburton, 1985), Nobel Prize-winning work underlying the 'sound science' of risk assessment itself has shown that analysis alone is unable to guarantee definitive answers (Arrow, 1963; Kelly, 1978; MacKay, 1980; Collingridge, 1982; Bonner, 1986). There now exist a variety of appropriate appraisal tools including Q methodology (McKeown and Thomas, 1988), interactive modelling (De Marchi *et al.*, 1998) and more open forms of multi-criteria appraisal (Stirling, 2005) – as well as participatory deliberation (Fischer, 1990; Irwin, 1995; Sclove, 1995).

Finally, there is the condition of ignorance, under which neither probabilities nor outcomes can be fully characterised (Keynes, 1921; Loasby, 1976; Collingridge, 1980). When 'we don't know what we don't know' (Wynne, 1992, 2001), we face the ever-present prospect of surprise (Brooks, 1986; Rosenberg, 1996). Some of the most important environmental challenges in the governance of Sustainability involve issues that were – at their outset – of just this kind (Funtowicz and Ravetz, 1990; Faber and Proops, 1994). In cases such as stratospheric ozone depletion (Farman, 2001), BSE and endocrine-disrupting chemicals (Thornton, 2000), for instance, the initial problem was not so much divergent social views or mis-estimation of probabilities, but straightforward ignorance over the possibilities themselves. Yet, even here, there are many practical things that can be done and which undue preoccupation with risk assessment can obscure (ESTO, 1999; Gee *et al.*, 2001). Some examples lie in shifting from modelling to monitoring; in undertaking more actively targeted scientific research; in prioritising methods such as horizon scanning; and emphasising the resilience of technology strategies – through highlighting properties such as reversibility, flexibility and diversity (Stirling, 2004, 2007).

The conceptual understanding shown in Figure 9.1 is borne out by the empirical picture illustrated in Figure 9.2 (Sundqvist *et al.*, 2004). It shows that – though rarely declared in the appraisal literature – science-based techniques, such as risk assessment or cost–benefit analysis, actually raise the same kinds of questions under uncertainty, ambiguity or ignorance, that are posed of precaution when it is presented as a decision rule. The individual comparative risk and cost–benefit studies of the impacts of different energy technologies presented here typically express their results with fine precision. This provides an apparently robust 'sound scientific' basis for judgements over the relative merits of nuclear, renewable and fossil fuel options.

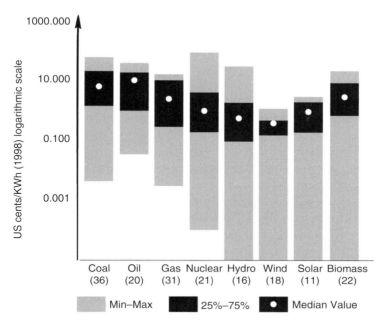

**Figure 9.2** Ambiguity of ranking in sound scientific assessment
*Notes:* Results of 63 detailed risk and cost–benefit studies of the risks of electricity supply options.
*Source:* Sundqvist *et al.*, (2004).

Yet, when results are compared across a range of different studies, such confidence is eroded.

In the case of the sixty-three major studies represented in Figure 9.2, the divergences between the results obtained from different studies extends to several orders of magnitude. More importantly, such is the overlap between the resulting ordinal rankings for these options, that judicious choice of favoured assumptions could support virtually any preference ordering. A similar picture arises repeatedly in sectors other than energy and with sound scientific techniques other than risk assessment of cost–benefit analysis (Amendola *et al.*, 2002).

## Precaution as a broad-based learning process

Despite the rhetoric of science-based decisions, then, reductive aggregative (Stirling, 2003) techniques such as risk assessment are manifestly insufficient to provide a uniquely robust basis for decision making under conditions of uncertainty, ambiguity or ignorance. The results delivered by these procedures depend not only on the available evidence, but on the way this is framed by the choice of questions, methods, priorities and assumptions. This question of framing is a matter on which there can typically be no self-evident or definitively correct answer. Although attempts to uphold the precautionary principle as an unambiguous decision rule certainly present problems, the point is, therefore, that these challenges are not unique to precaution. Questions over precaution such as those raised at the beginning of the last section are intrinsic to the nature of incertitude itself. Conventional 'sound scientific' risk assessment addresses this by effectively denying the more intractable forms of incertitude and the latitude for legitimately divergent framings. By directly confronting uncertainty, ambiguity and ignorance, precaution at least acknowledges the full scope of incertitude and the crucial role for deliberate attention to framing.

The practical value of precaution as a decision rule lies in the explicit normative guidance that it provides in assigning the benefit of the doubt under incertitude: in favour of human health and the environment (Tickner, 1998). Beyond this, the wider pragmatic value of precaution as a feature of the governance of Sustainability lies in the specific implications for the process of social appraisal (Hunt, 1994; Fisher and Harding, 1999). Although not necessarily aspiring to yield firm predictability over outcomes, this processual understanding nonetheless holds quite concrete implications for the ways in which precaution can be implemented (Stirling, 2003; van Zwanenberg and Stirling, 2004). Drawing on work under a series of conceptual (ESTO, 1999), empirical (Gee *et al.*, 2001) and institutional (Renn *et al.*, 2003) studies, Box 9.1 displays a series of seventeen key features of precaution-as-process. Each is accompanied by a brief reference to an example of a case in which this aspect of precautionary process was not applied in past regulation, yielding important lessons for the governance of Sustainability.

One way to think about these diverse features of precautionary appraisal is as elements of social learning (Wynne, 1992, 2001; Stirling, 2006). Some of the more general policy implications will be returned to in the final section of this chapter. But, in their own right, these features of a precautionary approach help to detail the disparate

**Box 9.1** Key features of the precautionary appraisal process with examples

Precaution broadens out the inputs to appraisal beyond the scope that is typical in conventional regulatory risk assessment, in order to provide for:

- independence from vested institutional, disciplinary, economic and political interests (such as long constrained attention to problems due to asbestos)
- examination of a greater range of uncertainties, sensitivities and possible scenarios (addressed early with antimicrobials but later neglected)
- deliberate search for 'blind spots', gaps in knowledge and divergent scientific views (as with assumptions over dispersal in the story of acid rain)
- attention to proxies for possible harm through mobility, bio-accumulation, persistence (as encountered in managing chemicals such as MTBE)
- contemplation of full life cycles and resource chains as they occur in the real world (such as failures in PCB containment during decommissioning)
- consideration of indirect effects, such as additivity, synergy and accumulation (of a kind neglected in occupational exposures to ionising radiation)
- inclusion of industrial trends, institutional behaviour and issues of non-compliance (such as the large-scale misuse of antimicrobials)
- explicit discussion over appropriate burdens of proof, persuasion, evidence, analysis (presently implicated in systematic neglect of Type II errors)
- comparison of a series of technology and policy options and potential substitutes (neglected in the case of the overuse of diagnostic X-rays)
- deliberation over justifications and possible wider benefits as well as risks and costs (insufficiently considered in the licensing of the drug DES)
- drawing on relevant knowledge and experience arising beyond specialist disciplines (such as the knowledge of birdwatchers relating to fisheries management)

**Box 9.1** (cont.)

- engagement with the values and interests of all stakeholders who stand to be affected (such as the experience of local communities in pollution of the Great Lakes)
- general citizen participation in order to provide independent validation of framing (significantly neglected in the management of BSE)
- a shift from theoretical modelling towards systematic monitoring and surveillance (systematically neglected in many cases, including that of PCBs)
- a greater priority on targeted scientific research, to address un-resolved questions (as omitted over the course of the BSE experience)
- initiation at the earliest stages 'upstream' in an innovation, strategy or policy process (fostering cleaner innovation pathways before lock-in occurs)
- emphasis on strategic qualities such as reversibility, flexibility, diversity, resilience (these offer ways to hedge even the most intractable forms of ignorance)

*Sources:* ESTO (1999), Gee *et al.*, (2001).

ways in which such social learning may be useful. Itemised in Box 9.1, they include deliberate efforts to develop more robust understandings of the technical and environmental complexities. Crucially, these include aspects of the social and organisational – as well as physical and biological – context and, in particular, the effects of the exercise of political, economic and institutional power. In all these areas there is deliberate attention to learning about the nature, depth and scope of the different forms of incertitude. Important forms of learning take place also about the potential and dynamic characteristics associated with different possible courses of action. And, throughout the entire process, there is a crucial role for social learning over the implications for appraisal and wider governance of different political, ethical and cultural values.

Taken together, the distinguishing feature of precautionary appraisal as a process of social learning is that it involves a multiple broadening out of the inputs to appraisal, beyond the relatively narrow field of issues typically considered in conventional risk assessment. Precautionary appraisal, as characterised in Box 9.1 extends attention to a wider range of issues, complexities, uncertainties, possibilities, options, benefits, knowledges, strategic qualities, values and perspectives (ESTO, 1999; Stirling, 2003). On this last note, we can begin to appreciate the importance of the neglected link between precaution and participation mentioned above. Before exploring this in more detail, however, attention will first turn to discussing participation in its own right.

## Participation, power and justification

Like precaution, the policy discourses around participation also have a life of their own. Here, concerns on the part of sponsoring organisations often centre on widely perceived general declines in the public credibility and trust enjoyed by policy-making institutions of all kinds – not just those concerned with the governance of Sustainability (Misztal, 1996; Seligman, 1997). In this context, attention has turned to finding new frameworks and methods for fostering engagement by stakeholders and the general public (Joss and Durant, 1995; Renn *et al.*, 1995; Nowotny *et al.*, 2001; Jasanoff, 2003). This drive towards wider social involvement in governance takes the form of what are variously described as more inclusive (Brown, 2002), discursive (Dryzek, 2002), deliberative (Leib, 2004), pluralistic (Bohmann, 1996), reflexive (Voss and Kemp, 2006) and participatory (Pellizzoni, 2003) principles, processes and institutions. The result is a proliferating diversity of specific new frameworks, methods and tools. In the UK alone, over the past decade, these have included initiatives such as stakeholder fora and strategic commissions (AEBC, 2004; CSF, 2004), public dialogues (PDSB, 2003), consensus conferences (BBSRC, 1994; UKCEED, 1999), citizens' panels and juries (Coote and Lenaghan, 1997; UKGF, 1999), focus groups (Grove-White *et al.*, 1997) and deliberative mapping (Burgess *et al.*, 2007). Though the precautionary principle may be addressed in such processes as one among many policy themes, it is rare that precaution is highlighted as displaying a direct, necessary or formative linkage to participation.

While the principle of a move towards greater engagement in governance by otherwise marginalised social constituencies is likely to be welcomed by anyone with democratic values, it is far from automatically clear that this is always achieved in real-world exercises. Just as analytic approaches to appraisal display greater latitude to framing effects than is conventionally acknowledged in practice, so too is this true of participatory approaches (Stirling, 2005). Like sound scientific analysis, the answers obtained in public engagement exercises are sensitive to a host of different contingencies. These include the posing of questions, the bounding of remits, the recruiting of participants, the provision of information, the selection of witnesses, the conduct of facilitators, the constraints of timetables and so on. Such contingencies render participatory exercises no less susceptible, either overtly or tacitly, to the deliberate or unintentional effects of the exercise of political, economic and institutional power (Stirling, 2006).

The practical implications of this depend on the context. As with any aspect of social appraisal – including the concept of Sustainability itself – participation can be addressed in the same three distinct ways noted above (adapted from Fiorino, 1990: 227; NRC, 1996: 23–4; Stirling, 2005, 2006). First there is a process-based view – under which there are many possible normative understandings of good process, without reference to outcomes. The sound science perspective, for instance, invokes criteria such as universalism, disinterest, scepticism, communism, peer review, falsification, experiment, transparency, collegiality and learning (Popper 1963; Merton, 1973). Likewise, under a normative democratic perspective on appraisal, participatory engagement is simply 'the right thing to do' – as an end in itself. Typically based on Habermasian principles of ideal speech (Habermas, 1968, 1984) and Rawlsian notions of public reason (Rawls, 1993, 1997), normative democratic process criteria include various notions of equity, transparency, accessibility, agency and representativeness.

In substantive terms, by contrast, participation is addressed as a means to better ends. This links to the normative democratic perspective, in that the notion of what constitutes a better end is a matter for openly deliberated public reason (Bohmann, 1996). But the crucial difference lies in the fact that a substantive understanding focuses on the outcomes of participation, not on the process. Examples of the kinds of publicly deliberated social aims under which outcomes of participation might be judged positively include, of course, the distinguishing substantive goals of Sustainability: human wellbeing, social equity and environmental quality. The basic idea is that the more participatory the process, the more likely it is that these kinds of outcome will be achieved.

Finally, under an instrumental perspective, participation is also considered in relation to outcomes rather than process. Here, however, participation is addressed as a means to particular ends, without reference to an explicit evaluative frame. Accordingly, an instrumental approach does not relate to general, publicly deliberated values, but to more private, specific but often undeclared sectoral interests. These include the fostering of credibility and trust in the aims or procedures of sponsors, or the provision of social intelligence to help secure consent.

This instrumental perspective is important, because it raises the crucial role of power in appraisal. To help understand this, it is useful to elaborate on Collingridge's notion of decision justification. Weak justification refers to situations in which incumbent interests are quite relaxed about the particular substance of the decision to be justified, but desire a means to ensure blame management, should the decision go awry (Horlick-Jones, 1996; Hood, 2002). In contemporary governance climates, an ability to link such a decision with the conduct of participation can fulfil this demand as readily as invoking sound science. Strong justification, by contrast, involves a situation in which incumbent interests are perfectly clear about the particular substance of the decision which they want to justify. The challenge lies simply in ensuring that appraisal successfully points to this decision as an output.

Recognition of justification need not necessarily imply that participation is somehow corrupt. The volatility of participatory appraisal to framing conditions – just like that of sound scientific analysis discussed earlier – can provide ample latitude for legitimate contingency. This may be exploited, not only by powerful incumbent interests, but also by more marginal political actors. Nor need an instrumental approach necessarily be seen as negative. Evaluation of the merits or otherwise of any particular instrumental intervention will necessarily depend on the extent to which the particular ends involved accord with those framing the evaluation. The point is simply that governance imperatives for weak and strong justification exert powerful instrumental pressures on participation just as on analysis. Within the bounds of acceptable process and undocumented contingency, there exists considerable scope for deliberate or inadvertent conditioning by power.

## Participation as opening up

Just like the remedy to the problems faced by precaution as a decision rule, so the response to this challenge of instrumental justification in participation is also a matter of process. This time, however, it does not relate to the breadth of the inputs to appraisal, but to the openness of the outputs. It has been shown how conventional sound scientific approaches to social appraisal, such as risk assessment, typically attend to a narrower range of issues, options and perspectives than does a broader-based precautionary approach. Together with the other factors addressed in Box 9.1, these represent different types of input to appraisal. The crucial feature of justification, however, is that it concerns the outputs of appraisal to wider governance and decision making. In order to secure either strong or weak justification, it is necessary that the appraisal process – whether analytic, precautionary or participatory – reduces the consequent diversity and presents clear results pointing to particular policy choices. In other words, the distinguishing feature of instrumental pressures for justification is that they act to close down decision making.

Such closing down may as easily be a feature of participatory or precautionary appraisal as of risk assessment or cost–benefit analysis. Indeed, the demanding normative imperatives associated with precaution may sometimes even serve to underscore the pressure for such closure. Likewise, participatory exercises often, in practice, adopt a particular emphasis on the value of closure around consensus. Of course, the modalities by which this is achieved vary from case to case. But the end result is effectively the same: the communication from appraisal to wider policy making takes the form of unitary and prescriptive recommendations (Stirling, 2005). This involves the high-lighting of a single or very small subset of possible courses of action, such as policy or technology choices, which appear to be preferable under the particular framing conditions that happen to have been privileged in appraisal. These conditioning assumptions and sensitivities will typically not be explored in any detail. The outputs will therefore have the instrumental merit of conveying practical implications for policy and clear justification for decision making.

On the other hand, if social appraisal is aimed at opening up the governance possibilities, then this communication is rather different. Here the emphasis lies in revealing to wider policy discourses any inherent open-endedness, contingency and capacity for the exercise of social agency. The aim is then explicitly to examine the degree to which the results obtained in appraisal are sensitive to different framing conditions and assumptions. Instead of using aggregative procedures in analysis, normative rules in precautionary appraisal, or deliberative procedures oriented towards consensus or common ground, appraisal instead conveys its results as a series of plural and conditional recommendations (Stirling, 2003). This involves systematically revealing how alternative courses of action appear preferable under different framing conditions and showing how these dependencies relate to the real world of divergent contexts, public values, disciplinary perspectives and stakeholder interests.

Whether as explicit political decisions or as more implicit and diffuse institutional commitments, *de facto* governance choices will, of course, still occur. Here, an opening up approach may illuminate the potential for accommodating more diverse portfolios of social choices (Stirling, 2007). Attention may usefully be directed at synergies and complementarities between options. Either way, the crucial relevance concerning the exercise of instrumental pressures towards justification is that an opening-up approach makes it much more clear how to apportion responsibility and accountability in decision making and wider governance processes.

Whether in the field of technical analysis, broader-based precautionary appraisal or participatory deliberation, there exist many practical methods by means of which to achieve this kind of opening up. Techniques such as scenario (Werner, 2004) and sensitivity (Saltelli, 2001) analysis or multi-criteria mapping (Stirling, 1997; Stirling and Mayer, 2001) provide quantitative representations of the implications of different assumptions and conditions. Systematic attention to ambiguous findings, contending interpretations and dissenting views can achieve the same thing in specialist deliberation (SRP, 2003, 2004). Likewise, in participatory appraisal, an opening up-approach can employ more pluralistic rather than consensual procedures (Rescher, 1993; Bohmann, 1996; Pellizzoni, 2001; Dryzek and Niemeyer, 2003). Deliberation centres on the sustaining and comparing of a diversity of evaluative frameworks, rather than on forging common ownership of a single framework. Appropriately conducted, processes such as scenario workshops (Ogilvie, 2002), Q methodology (McKeown and Thomas, 1988) and deliberative mapping (Davies *et al.*, 2003) all offer practical approaches.

A distinction between opening up and closing down in social appraisal thus pervades narrow science-based analysis, broad-based precautionary appraisal and inclusive participatory engagement alike.

It is crucially different from notions of breadth of process already discussed in relation to the substantive precautionary rationale for participation. The breadth or narrowness of an appraisal process concerns the range of inputs that are included such as issues, possibilities, perspectives and options. The open or closed orientation of an appraisal process, on the other hand, concerns the range of outputs that are sustained in parallel and conveyed to wider governance as reasonable candidate social choices.

## Reflex, reflection and reflexivity

The above discussion highlights substantive scientific reasons for seeing precaution and participation as a basis for rigorous responses to uncertainty, ambiguity and ignorance. Yet, the mutual dependencies between precaution, participation and Sustainability are under-explored. Table 9.1 addresses this issue. Each row details different possible understandings of the main concepts on which this discussion has focused: sustainability, science, precaution, participation and governance. These are structured in the columns by the distinctions between substantive, instrumental and normative democratic perspectives on the role and function of social appraisal. In order to appreciate the integrated nature of these implications for governance as a whole, it is necessary to introduce one further threefold distinction drawn from the wider social and political science literature. This concerns the differences between reflection, reflexivity and unreflectiveness in the governance of sustainability (as summarised in the bottom row of Table 9.1) (Stirling, 2006).

Discussions of reflexive governance (Voss and Kemp, 2006) build strongly on the work of Giddens (1990) and Beck (1992). Many questions are raised by this literature, not least due to the many proliferating understandings of exactly what it is that is meant by the term reflexivity (Gouldner, 1970; Giddens, 1976; Woolgar, 1988; Steier, 1991; Bourdieu and Wacquant, 1992; Alvesson and Skoldberg, 2000). In particular, specific queries are raised by contemplating the relationships between discussions of reflexivity and discussions of risk and sustainability (Wynne, 2002) and science, technology and innovation (Voss and Kemp, 2006).

Based on a more elaborate treatment elsewhere (Stirling, 2006), the remainder of this chapter will focus on the particular relevance of one

Table 9.1 *Key linkages between sustainability, science, precaution and participation and the implications of power in processes of governance and social appraisal*

| Governance concept | Substantive imperatives driven by outcomes | Emphasis in social appraisal | | |
|---|---|---|---|---|
| | | Normative principles relating to process | Instrumental pressures exerted by power |
| Sustainability | Evaluates outcomes according to publicly reasoned social goals: human wellbeing, social equity and environmental quality | Attention is directed at the institutional and procedural aspects of sustainable governance such as equity, transparency, accessibility, agency and representativeness | A legitimisation discourse substitutes publicly reasoned goals of Sustainability with the aim of simply sustaining privately favoured features of the status quo |
| Science | Strives to maximise theoretical robustness and empirical reliability, thus minimising error and contingency in associated decision outcomes | Aspires to Mertonian and Popperian norms such as universalism, disinterest, scepticism, communism, peer review, falsification, experiment, transparency, collegiality and learning | The language of sound science and evidence-based or science-based decisions denies the crucial roles of subjective interests and values in framing appraisal |
| Precaution | Prompts appropriate consideration (rather than neglect) of more intractable aspects of incertitude over outcomes: uncertainty, ambiguity and ignorance, as well as risk | Broadening out of appraisal addresses a diversity of pros (as well as cons); effects; options (at earliest stages) and perspectives; with an emphasis on monitoring, flexibility and reversibility | Treated simply as a decision rule, conceals latitude for interpretation in appraisal of key concepts such as threat, seriousness, reversibility or scientific certainty |

Table 9.1 (*cont.*)

| Governance concept | Emphasis in social appraisal | | |
|---|---|---|---|
| | Substantive imperatives driven by outcomes | Normative principles relating to process | Instrumental pressures exerted by power |
| Participation | Allows systematic rigour in validating the 'framing' of evidence and analysis and exploring the implications for outcomes (just as science validates the data and methods themselves) | Opening up of appraisal fosters greater accountability in policy making by presenting information and advice in plural and conditional, rather than unitary prescriptive fashion | Provides a means to weak justification aiming at consent, trust, credibility, blame management; and strong justification aiming to secure specific desired outcomes |
| Governance | Aims at reflectiveness in that a broad range of inputs to appraisal build a complete picture of the full range of possible governance interventions and their respective broad consequences | Aspires to reflexivity in that appraisal outputs convey the ways in which results are conditioned by (and co-constructed with) the different governance interventions they supposedly inform | Displays an unreflective stance, in that there is little effective deliberation or 'public reasoning' in appraisal over normative aims or wider substantive consequences associated with governance actions |

strand in this literature for the present understanding of the governance of Sustainability. The crucial issue here lies in the relationship between normative, substantive and instrumental rationales and perspectives on the one hand, and the general distinction that may be made between reflective, reflexive and unreflective governance on the other.

In these terms, a reflective approach to governance involves the deliberate configuring of social appraisal so as to address a complete range of possible policy options and explore exhaustively their respective possible consequences in order to determine the single most acceptable intervention. This approach accords well with substantive perspectives, under which attention is structured exclusively by reference to the fully deliberated evaluation of possible outcomes.

This contrasts with the more subtle and demanding property of reflexivity, under which it is understood that the identification of preferred interventions is not an objective exercise, but one in which governance processes themselves are conditioned by, and themselves help constitute, the problems on which they focus. As such, the reflexive governance of Sustainability involves forms of social appraisal that are not simply broader and deeper in their inputs, but are also more openly reflexive in their outputs – recognising the way in which the relevant issues and their rational responses are to a significant extent conditioned by subjective values and interests – and by the exercise of power. For its part, unreflective governance displays none of these qualities. It confines appraisal to whatever are the most privileged or instrumentally salient ends in question, effectively neglecting any conditioning factors or wider collateral effects.

Thus informed, it is possible to appreciate in more detail some of the key resonances between the roles of science, precaution and participation in the governance of Sustainability. By addressing forms of incertitude under which scientific assessment can give no definitive policy prescriptions, a precautionary process, as outlined earlier, offers a means to enhance the degree of reflection over the inputs to appraisal. However, if precaution is instead viewed as a principle, presented as a definitive decision rule, it can lead to rather unreflexive types of appraisal: opening the door to instrumental interpretations. The real value of precaution as a means to promote greater reflectiveness in governance lies in its role as an appraisal process rather than as a decision rule. In particular, precaution achieves this greater degree of reflection by broadening out the inputs to appraisal.

Participatory processes offer one particular family of ways in which the inputs to appraisal can be broadened out, so as to be considered more precautionary. However, as only one element of this reflective breadth, it need not necessarily be the case that precautionary appraisal is always participatory. Even without participation, the adoption of many of the other features of precautionary process highlighted in Box 9.1 would go a long way towards practical implementation of precaution. Likewise, for their part, if participatory approaches are themselves constrained in breadth in some other fashion that is relevant to precautionary appraisal, then participation may itself be judged to be correspondingly lacking in reflectiveness. Examples here, from the features listed in Table 9.1, might include the exclusion of relevant options, or the neglect of particular possible effects or uncertainties.

## Towards a more reflective and reflexive governance for Sustainability

To conclude, if governance for Sustainable development is not to descend into an instrumental, legitimisation discourse aimed simply at sustaining existing modes of governance, then it must make deliberate efforts to become both more reflective and more reflexive in the multiple senses discussed here. First, this means recognising that, while scientific evidence and analysis are essential, they are not sufficient for the effective governance of Sustainability. To paraphrase Winston Churchill: 'science should be on tap not on top' (Lindsay, 1995). In particular, the rhetoric of sound science and science-based decision making can be dangerously misleading. Overblown claims about the determining role played by science in governance can be very unreflexive about the roles of uncertainty framing and power. Far from supporting the role of science in governance, these claims can themselves be anti-scientific in their effects, by undermining the more modest, but genuinely crucial, value of science.

Second, precaution and participation are more than the sum of their parts. They are not simply bolt-on management measures to be adopted after scientific assessment has delivered its results. They are each in their own right essential elements in appraisal, making more explicit and systematic the particular interests, values and priorities underlying the questions that are posed of science, the assumptions that are adopted, and the interpretations that are placed on results.

Rather than leaving such factors concealed behind the veneer of sound science, they offer a way to validate them and so make the associated process more rigorous, accountable and legitimate.

Third, and more specifically, precaution prompts a concrete checklist of elements in a more reflective governance process. This is reproduced in detail in Table 9.1, but includes provision for the broadening out of inputs to social appraisal, including consideration of wider ranges of effects and associated uncertainties; the pros as well as cons of a variety of different technology and policy options; greater reliance on monitoring and targeted research; more explicit deliberation over burdens of argument and levels of proof; engagement by diverse disciplines, stakeholders and public constituencies; and systematic attention to strategic issues of reversibility, flexibility, diversity and resilience.

Fourth, there is the need to be reflexive about the pressures exercised in the real world by political, institutional and economic power (see also Chapter 5). These can serve to 'close down' the appraisal of sustainability artificially, so as to generate various forms of weak and strong justification. However, it follows from the present analysis that these can be mitigated by deliberately opening up the outputs of appraisal. Results can be conveyed to wider governance processes by means of plural and conditional rather than unitary prescriptive advice. Where this is achieved, it simultaneously reinforces scientific rigour in the treatment of uncertainty and ambiguity as well as democratic accountability in making more transparent the value judgements implied in final decision making.

Finally, there are the wider implications of reflection and reflexivity for achieving more deliberate social choices in the fields of science, technology and innovation. Historically, governance discourses in these fields have been dominated by self-referential notions of progress, under which contending perspectives are reduced to simplistic general pro or anti positions on science, technology and innovation. The advent of explicitly normative discourses on Sustainability offers to change this, presenting a framework for more deliberate public reasoning over the aims and purposes of innovation. Yet, instrumental use of the language of sustainable governance can fatally undermine this, by obscuring the determining role of narrow sectional interests.

Together, these implications of the distinction between reflective and reflexive governance cut across the practice of participation and precaution alike. They point to subtle synergies and to limitations held in common by both. In the end, they help to highlight the several ways in which appropriately conducted precaution and participation are more than the sum of the parts – and crucial to the process of Sustainability.

## References

AEBC (Agriculture and Environment Biotechnology Commission) 2004. *Annual Report 2002–3*. London: Department of Trade and Industry. URL: www.aebc.gov.uk/aebc/reports/2003_report.pdf.

Alvesson, M. and Skoldberg, K. 2000. *Reflexive Methodology*. London: Sage.

Amendola, A., Contini, S. and Ziomas, I. 2002. 'Uncertainties in chemical risk assessment: results of a European benchmark exercise', *Journal of Hazardous Materials* 29: 347–63.

Arrow, K. 1963. *Social Choice and Individual Values*. New Haven, CT: Yale University Press.

BBSRC (Biological and Biotechnology Research Council) 1994. *UK National Consensus Conference on Plant Biotechnology: Final Report*. London: Science Museum.

Beck, U. 1992. *Risk Society: Towards a New Modernity*. London: Sage.

Berlinski, D. 1976 *On Systems Analysis: An Essay Concerning the Limitations of some Mathematical Models in the Social, Political Biological Sciences*. Cambridge, MA: MIT Press.

Blair, T. 2003. 'Response to Questions, 10th November 2003', *House of Commons Hansard*, Column 14 W [cited 15 April 2005]. URL: www.publications.parliament.uk/pa/cm200203/cmhansrd/vo031110/text/31110w04.htm#31110w04.html_spmin1.

Bohmann, J. 1996. *Public Deliberation: Pluralism, Complexity and Democracy*. Cambridge: MIT Press.

Bonner, J. 1986. *Politics, Economics and Welfare: An Elementary Introduction to Social Choice*. Brighton, UK: Harvester.

Bourdieu, P. and Wacquand, L. 1992. *An Invitation to Reflexive Sociology*. Cambridge, UK: Polity.

Brooks, H. 1986. 'The typology of surprises in technology, institutions and development', in Clark, W. C. and Munn, R. E. (eds.) *Sustainable Development of the Biosphere*. Cambridge, UK: Cambridge University Press, pp. 325–48.

Brown, W. 2002. 'The prevalence of inclusive governance practices in nonprofit organizations and implications for practice', *Nonprofit Management and Leadership* 12: 369–85.

Burgess, J., Stirling, A. C., Clark, J., Davies, G., Eames, M., Staley, K. and Williamson, S. 2007. 'Deliberative mapping: a novel analytic-deliberative methodology to support contested science-policy decisions', *Public Understanding of Science* 16: 299–322.

Byrd, D. and Cothern, C. 2000. *Introduction to Risk Analysis: A Systematic Approach to Science-based Decision Making.* Rockville, MD: Government Institutes.

CEC (Commission of the European Communities) 2000. *Communication from the Commission on the Precautionary Principle.* COM (2000) 1 final. Brussels: Commission of the European Communities.

CEC (Commission of the European Communities) 2001. *White Paper on Governance (section II).* Brussels: Commission of the European Communities. URL: http://europa.eu.int/eur-lex/en/com/cnc/2001/com2001_0428en01.pdf.

CEC (Commission of the European Communities) 2004. Brussels: Commission of the European Communities. URL: http://europa.eu.int/eur-lex/lex/LexUriServ/site/en/oj/2004/c_310/c_31020041216en00550185.pdf.

Collingridge, D. 1980. *The Social Control of Technology.* Milton Keynes, UK: Open University Press.

Collingridge, D. 1982. *Critical Decision Making: A New Theory of Social Choice.* London, UK: Pinter.

Coote, A. and Lenaghan, J. 1997. *Citizen's Juries: Theory into Practice.* London: Institute for Public Policy Research.

CSF (Chemicals Stakeholder Forum UK) 2004. *Fifth Annual Report: 2005.* London, UK: Department for Environment, Food and Rural Affairs.

Davies, G., Burgess, J., Eames, M., Mayer, S., Staley, S., Stirling, A. and Williamson, S. 2003. *Deliberative Mapping: Appraising Options for Closing 'The Kidney Gap'.* Final Report to the Wellcome Trust. URL: www.deliberative-mapping.org.uk.

DCLG (Department of Communities and Local Government) 2005. *What is a Sustainable Community?* London: Department of Communities and Local Government. URL: www.communities.gov.uk/index.asp?id=1139866.

De Marchi, B., Funtowicz, S., Gough, C., Guimarães Pereira A. and Rota, E. 1998. *The Ulysses Voyage: The ULYSSES Project at the JRC.* EUR 17760EN. Ispra, Italy: Joint Research Centre. URL: http://zit1.zit.tu-darmstadt.de/ulysses/tutorial.htm.

DEFRA (Department of Environment, Food and Rural Affairs) 2002. *Science for Sustainability: DEFRA Agency Review.* London, UK: Department for Environment and Rural Affairs.

DEFRA (Department of Environment, Food and Rural Affairs) 2004. *Sustainable Development Indicators in Your Pocket.* London: HMSO. URL: www.sustainable-development.gov.uk/indicators/sdiyp/sdiyp04a4.pdf.

Dobson, A. 1996. 'Environmental sustainabilities: an analysis and a typology', *Environmental Politics* 5: 401–28.

Dryzek, J. 2002. *Deliberative Democracy and Beyond: Liberals, Critics, Contestations*. Oxford, UK: Oxford University Press.

Dryzek, J. and Niemeyer, S. 2003. 'Pluralism and consensus in political deliberation', paper presented to the Annual Meeting of the American Political Science Association, Philadelphia, 28–31 August, 2003.

ECFESD (European Consultative Forum on the Environment and Sustainable Development) 2000. *Sustainable Governance: Institutional and Procedural Aspects of Sustainability*. Brussels: European Commission. URL: http://europa.eu.int/comm/environment/forum/governance_en.pdf.

ESTO (European Science and Technology Observatory) 1999. *On Science and Precaution in the Management of Technological Risk. Volume I: Synthesis Study*. EUR19056 EN. Report to the EU Forward Studies Unit. Seville: European Science and Technology Observatory. URL: ftp://ftp.jrc.es/pub/EURdoc/eur19056IIen.pdf.

Faber, M. and Proops, J. 1994. *Evolution, Time, Production and the Environment*. Berlin, Germany: Springer.

Farman, J. 2001. 'Halocarbons, the ozone layer and the precautionary principle', in Gee, D., Harremoës, P., Keys, J., MacGarvin, M., Stirling, A., Vaz, S. and Wynne, B. (eds.) *Late Lesson from Early Warnings: The Precautionary Principle 1898–2000*. Copenhagen: European Environment Agency, pp. 76–82.

Fiorino, D. J. 1990. 'Citizen participation and environmental risk: a survey of institutional mechanisms', *Science, Technology and Human Values* 15: 226–43.

Fischer, F. 1990. *Technocracy and the Politics of Expertise*. London: Sage.

Fisher, E. 2001. 'Is the precautionary principle justiciable?' *Journal of Environmental Law* 13: 317–34.

Fisher, E. 2002. 'Precaution, precaution everywhere: developing a common understanding of the precautionary principle in the European Community', *Maastricht Journal of European and Comparative Law* 9: 7–28.

Fisher, E. and Harding, R. (eds.) 1999. *Perspectives on the Precautionary Principle*. Sydney: Federation Press.

Forster, M. 1999. 'How do simple rules fit to reality in a complex world?' *Minds and Machines* 9: 543–64.

Funtowicz, S. and Ravetz, J. 1990. *Uncertainty and Quality in Science for Policy*. Dordrecht, The Netherlands: Kluwer.

Gee, D., Harremoës, P., Keys, J., MacGarvin, M., Stirling, A., Vaz, S. and Wynne, B. (eds.). 2001. *Late Lesson from Early Warnings: The Precautionary Principle 1898–2000*. Copenhagen: European Environment Agency.

Giddens, A. 1976. *The New Rules of Sociological Method*. London, UK: Hutchinson.

Giddens, A. 1990. *The Consequences of Modernity*. Palo Alto, CA: Stanford University Press.

Gouldner, A. 1970. *The Coming Crisis of Western Sociology*. London, UK: Heineman.

Grove-White, R., Macnaghton, P., Mayer, S. and Wynne, B. 1997. *Uncertain World. Genetically Modified Organisms, Food and Public Attitudes in Britain*. Centre for the Study of Environmental Change, Lancaster University.

Habermas, J. 1968. *Toward a Rational Society: Student Protest, Science and Politics*. London, UK: Heineman.

Habermas, J. 1984. *The Philosophical Discourse of Modernity*. Cambridge, UK: Polity.

Hood, C. 2002. 'Managing risk and managing blame: a political science approach', in Weale, A. (ed.) *Risk, Democratic Citizenship and Public Policy*. Oxford, UK: Oxford University Press, pp. 73–84.

Horlick-Jones, T. 1996. 'The problem of blame', in Hood, C. and Jones. D. (eds.) *Accident and Design: Contemporary Debates in Risk Management*. London, UK: UCL Press, pp. 34–47.

Hunt, J. 1994. 'The social construction of precaution', in O'Riordan, T. and Cameron, J. (eds.) *Interpreting the Precautionary Principle*. London, UK: Earthscan, pp. 117–25.

Irwin, A. 1995. *Citizen Science: a Study of People, Expertise and Sustainable Development*. London, UK: Routledge.

Jasanoff, S. 2003. 'Technologies of humility: citizens' participation in governing science', *Minerva* 41: 223–44.

Jaulin, L., Kieffer, M., Didrit, O. and Walter, É. 2001. *Applied Interval Analysis*. Berlin, Germany: Springer.

Johnson, P., Santillo, D. and Stringer, R. 1998. *Risk Assessment and Reality: Recognizing the Limitations*. Exeter University.

Jordan, A. and O'Riordan, T. 2003. 'An ever more sustainable union? Integrating economy, society and environment in a rapidly enlarging Europe', in Koutrakou, V. (ed.) *Contemporary Issues and Debates in EU Policy: The EU and Internal Relations*. Manchester, UK: Manchester University Press, pp. 149–61.

Joss, S. and Durrant, J. 1995. *Public Participation in Science: the Role of Consensus Conferences in Europe*. London, UK: Science Museum.

Kelly, J. 1978. *Arrow's Impossibility Theorem*. New York: Academic Press.

Keynes, J. M. 1921. *A Treatise on Probability*. London, UK: Macmillan.

Knight, F. 1921. *Risk, Uncertainty and Profit*. Boston, MA: Houghton Mifflin.

Leib, E. 2004. *Deliberative Democracy in America: A Proposal for a Popular Branch of Government*. Philadelphia, PA: Pennsylvania State University Press.

Levidow, L., Carr, S., Schomberg, R. and Wield, D. 1998. 'European biotechnology regulation: framing the risk assessment of a herbicide-
tolerant crop', *Science, Technology and Human Values* 22: 472–505.

Lindsay, R. 1995. 'Galloping Gertie and the precautionary principle: how
is environmental impact assessment assessed?' in Wakeford, T. and
Walters, N. (eds.) *Science for the Earth*. Chichester, UK: Wiley,
pp. 197–236.

Lloyd, L. 2000. 'The tyranny of the L-shape curve', *Science and Public
Affairs* February, 14–15. URL: www.the-ba.net/the-ba/News/
ReportsandPublications/ScienceAndPublicAffairs.

Loasby, B. 1976. *Choice, Complexity and Ignorance: An Inquiry into
Economic Theory and the Practice of Decision Making*. Cambridge,
UK: Cambridge University Press.

Luce, R. D. and Raiffa, H. (1957) 'An axiomatic treatment of utility', in
Luce, R. D. and Raiffa, H. (eds.) *Games and Decisions: Introduction
and Critical Survey*. New York: Wiley, pp. 23–30.

MacKay, A. 1980. *Arrow's Theorem: The Paradox of Social Choice: A
Case Study in the Philosophy of Economics*. New Haven, CT: Yale
University Press.

McKeown, B. and Thomas, D. 1988. *Q Methodology*. London, UK: Sage.

Meadowcroft, J., Farrell, K. N. and Spangenberg, J. 2005. 'Developing a
framework for sustainability governance in the European Union',
*International Journal of Sustainable Development* 8: 3–11.

Merton, R. 1973. *The Sociology of Science: Theoretical and Empirical
Investigations*. Chicago, IL: University of Chicago Press.

Misztal, B. 1996. *Trust in Modern Societies*. Cambridge, UK: Polity.

Morgan, G. M., Henrion, M. and Small, M. 1990. *Uncertainty: A Guide to
Dealing with Uncertainty in Quantitative Risk and Policy Analysis*.
Cambridge, UK: Cambridge University Press.

Morris, J. (ed.) 2000. *Rethinking Risk and the Precautionary Principle*.
London, UK: Butterworth Heinemann.

Murcott, S. 1997. *Sustainable Development: A Meta-Review of Definitions,
Principles, Criteria Indicators, Conceptual Frameworks and Information Systems*. Annual Conference of the American Association for the
Advancement of Science, Seattle, Feb 13–18. URL: www.sustaina-
bleliving.org/appen-b.htm.

Nowotny, H., Scott, P. and Gibbons, M. 2001. *Rethinking Science: Knowledge and the Public in an Age of Uncertainty*. Cambridge, UK: Polity.

NRC (National Research Council) 1996. *Understanding Risk: Informing
Decisions in a Democratic Society*. National Research Council Committee on Risk Characterisation. Washington DC: National Academy Press.

OED (Oxford English Dictionary) 1989. *The Oxford English Dictionary*.
Second Edition. Oxford, UK: Oxford University Press.

Ogilvie, J. 2002. *Creating Better Futures: Scenario Planning as a Tool for a Better Tomorrow*. Oxford, UK: Oxford University Press.

O'Riordan, T. (ed.) 2001. *Globalism, Localism and Identity: Fresh Perspectives on the Transition to Sustainability*. London, UK: Earthscan.

O'Riordan, T. and Cameron, J. (eds.) 1994. *Interpreting the Precautionary Principle*. London, UK: Earthscan.

O'Riordan, T. and Stoll-Kleemann, S. (eds.) 2002. *Biodiversity, Sustainability and Human Communities: Protecting Beyond the Protected*. Cambridge, UK: Cambridge University Press.

O'Riordan, T., Cameron, J. and Jordan, A. (eds.) 2000. *Reinterpreting the Precautionary Principle*. London, UK: Cameron and May.

PDSB (Public Debate Steering Board) 2003. *GM Nation: The Findings of the Public Debate*. London, UK: Department of Food and Rural Affairs.

Pellizzoni, L. 2001. 'The myth of the best argument: power deliberation and reason', *British Journal of Sociology* 52: 59–86.

Pellizzoni, L. 2003. 'Uncertainty and participatory democracy', *Environmental Values* 12: 195–224.

Popper, K. 1963. *Conjectures and Refutations*. London, UK: Routledge.

Rawls, J. 1993. *Political Liberalism*. New York: Columbia University Press.

Rawls, J. 1997. 'The idea of public reason revisited', *University of Chicago Law Review* 64: 767.

Renn, O., Webler, T. and Wiedemann, P. (eds.) 1995. *Fairness and Competence in Citizen Participation: Evaluating Models for Environmental Discourse*. Dordrecht, The Netherlands: Kluwer.

Renn, O., Dreyer, M., Klinke, A., Losert, C., Stirling, A., van Zwanenberg, P., Muller-Herold, U., Morosini, M. and Fisher, E. 2003. *The Application of the Precautionary Principle in the European Union*. Stuttgart, Germany: Centre of Technology Assessment in Baden-Wuerttemberg.

Rescher, N. 1993. *Pluralism: Against the Demand for Consensus*. Oxford, UK: Clarendon.

Rosenberg, N. 1996. 'Uncertainty and technological change', in Landau, R., Taylor, T. and Wright, G. (eds.) *The Mosaic of Economic Growth*. Palo Alto, CA: Stanford University Press.

Rowe, W. 1994. 'Understanding uncertainty', *Risk Analysis* 14: 743–50.

Saltelli, A. 2001. *Sensitivity Analysis for Importance Assessment*. Ispra, Italy: Joint Research Centre. URL: www.ce.ncsu.edu/risk/pdf/saltelli.pdf.

Sand, P.H. 2000. 'The precautionary principle: a European perspective', *Human and Ecological Risk Assessment* 6: 445–58.

Sandin, P., Peterson, M., Ove Hansson, S., Rudén, C. and Juthe, A. 2002. 'Five charges against the precautionary principle', *Journal of Risk Research* 5: 287–99.

SBI (Sustainable Business Initiative) 2005. *Sustainable Business Initiative, Prospectus*. San Jose, CA: Sustainable Business Initiative. URL: www.sustainablebusiness.org/index.html.

Sclove, R. 1995. *Democracy and Technology*. New York: Guilford Press.

Seligman, A. 1997. *The Problem of Trust*. Princeton University Press.

SRP 2003. *GM Science Review Panel First Report*. London: Department for Trade and Industry, July 2003. URL: www.gmsciencedebate.org.uk/report/default.htm#first.

SRP 2004. *GM Science Review Panel Second Report*, London: Department for Trade and Industry, January 2004. URL: www.gmsciencedebate.org.uk/report/default.htm#second.

Steier, F. 1991. *Research and Reflexivity*. London, UK: Sage.

Stirling, A. 1997. 'Multi-criteria mapping: mitigating the problems of environmental valuation?' in Foster, J. (ed) *Valuing Nature: Economics, Ethics and Environment*. London, UK: Routledge, pp. 186–210.

Stirling, A. 1999. 'Risk at a turning point?' *Journal of Environmental Medicine* 1: 119–26.

Stirling, A. 2003. 'Risk, uncertainty and precaution: some instrumental implications from the social sciences', in Berkhout, F., Leach, M. and Scoones, I. (eds.) *Negotiating Environmental Change*. Cheltenham, UK: Elgar, pp. 33–76.

Stirling, A. 2005. 'Opening up or closing down: analysis, participation and power in the social appraisal of technology', in Leach, M., Scoones, I. and Wynne, B. (eds.) *Science and Citizens: Globalization and the Challenge of Engagement*. London, UK: Zed Books, pp. 218–31.

Stirling, A. 2006. 'Uncertainty, precaution and sustainability: towards more reflective governance of technology', in Voss, J. and Kemp, R. (eds.) *Sustainability and Reflexive Governance*. Cheltenham, UK: Elgar, pp. 225–72.

Stirling, A. 2007. 'A general framework for analysing diversity in science, technology and society', *Journal of the Royal Society Interface* 4: 707–19.

Stirling, A. and Mayer, S. 2001. 'A novel approach to the appraisal of technological risk', *Environment and Planning C: Government and Policy* 19: 529–55.

Sundqvist, T., Soderholm, P. and Stirling, A. 2004. 'Electric power generation: valuation of environmental costs', in Cleveland, C. J. (ed.) *Encyclopedia of Energy Volume 2*. San Diego, CA: Academic Press, pp. 229–43.

Taverne, D. 2005. *The March of Unreason: Science, Democracy and the New Fundamentalism*. Oxford, UK: Oxford University Press.

Thompson, M. and Warburton, M. 1985. 'Decision making under contradictory certainties: how to save the Himalayas when you can't find what's wrong with them', *Journal of Applied Systems Analysis* 12, 3–34.

Thornton, J. 2000. *Pandora's Poison: On Chlorine, Health and a New Environmental Strategy*. Cambridge, MA: MIT Press.

Tickner, J. 1998. 'A commonsense framework for operationalizing the precautionary principle', paper presented to Wingspread Conference on Strategies for Implementing the Precautionary Principle, Racine, WI.

UKCEED (United Kingdom Centre for Economy, Environment and Development) 1999. *Final Report of Consensus Conference on Radioactive Waste Management*. Cambridge: UKCEED.

UNCED (United Nations Conference on Environment and Development) 1992. *Final Declaration of the UN Conference on Environment and Development, Rio de Janeiro*. New York: United Nations.

UNEP (United Nations Environment Programme) 1997. *Sustainability Indicators: Report of the Project on Indicators of Sustainable Development*. Chichester, UK: Wiley.

United Nations 2002. *Indicators of Sustainable Development: Guidelines and Methodologies*. United Nations, Division for Sustainable Development, New York. URL: www.un.org/esa/sustdev/natlinfo/indicators/isdms2001/isd-ms2001isd.htm.

United Nations General Assembly (2000) *Millennium Development Declaration*. United Nations General Assembly Resolution A/RES/55/2, 18 September 2000. URL: www.un.org/millennium/declaration/ares552e.pdf.

USDA (US Department of Agriculture) 2000. *The Role of Precaution in Food Safety Decisions: Remarks Prepared for Under Secretary for Food Safety, Food Safety and Inspection Service*. Washington DC: US Department of Agriculture.

van Zwanenberg, P. and Stirling, A. 2004. 'Risk and precaution in the US and Europe', *Yearbook of European Environmental Law* 3: 43–57.

Vogel, D. 2000. 'The WTO vote: the wrong whipping boy', *American Prospect* 11: 14.

Voss, J. and Kemp, R. (eds.) 2006) *Sustainability and Reflexive Governance*. Cheltenham, UK: Elgar.

Werner, R. 2004. *Designing Strategy: Scenario Analysis and the Art of Making Business Strategy*. New York: Praeger.

Woolgar, S. (ed.) 1988. *Knowledge and Reflexivity: New Frontiers in the Sociology of Knowledge*. London, UK: Sage.

Wynne, B. 1992. 'Uncertainty and environmental learning: reconceiving science and policy in the preventive paradigm', *Global Environmental Change* 2: 111–27.

Wynne, B. 2001. 'Creating public alienation: expert cultures of risk and ethics on GMOs', *Science as Culture* 10: 445–81.

Wynne, B. 2002. 'Risk and environment as legitimatory discourses of technology: reflexivity inside out?' *Current Sociology* 50: 459–77.

# 10 | *Precaution and the governance of risk*

ORTWIN RENN

## Introduction

The precautionary principle has been adopted in a variety of forms at international, European Union and national level (Fisher, 2002). It is applied across an increasing number of national jurisdictions, economic sectors and environmental areas (de Sadeleer, 2002). It has moved from the regulation of industry, technology and health risk, to the wider governance of science, innovation and trade (O'Riordan and Cameron, 1994; O'Riordan and Jordan, 1995; Raffensberger and Tickner, 1999; O'Riordan et al., 2001). As it has expanded in scope, so it has grown in profile and authority. In particular, as Article 174(2) in the EC Treaty of 2002 implies, precaution now constitutes a key underlying principle in European Union policy making (European Commission, 2002). In the aftermath of a series of formative public health controversies, economic calamities and political conflicts (such as those involving BSE and GM crops), precaution is of great salience in many fields, including the regulation of chemicals.

Despite the intensity of the policy attention, however, there remain a number of serious ambiguities and queries concerning the nature and appropriate role of the precautionary principle in governance (Cross, 1996; Majone, 2002; Löfstedt, 2004). These are addressed – if not resolved – in a burgeoning academic (Sand, 2000; Fisher, 2001, 2002; Klinke and Renn, 2001; Stirling, 2003; Peterson, 2006) and more policy-oriented (Stirling, 1999; Gee et al., 2001) literature. Although the precautionary approach has been formulated in many different ways in many different places (one root may be the 'foresight principle' in Germany in the 1970s (cf. Sand, 2000)), the formulation in the 1992 Rio Declaration is the most popular:

In order to protect the environment, the precautionary approach shall be widely applied by States according to their capabilities. Where there are threats of serious of irreversible damage, lack of full scientific certainty shall

226

not be used as a reason for postponing cost-effective measures to prevent environmental degradation (Rio Declaration 1992, Principle 15).

The meaning of this principle is hotly debated among analysts and policy makers. It is helpful for understanding the debate to distinguish three positions towards risk analysis (cf. also Resnik, 2003). Within the first frame of scientific risk analysis, risk management relies on the best scientific estimates of probabilities and potential damages and uses expected values as the main input to judge the tolerability of risk as well as to design risk reduction measures that are cost-effective, proportional to the threat, and fair to the affected population. In this frame, precaution may best be interpreted as being conservative in making risk judgements and choosing cautious assumptions when calculating exposure or determining safety factors to cover inter-individual variability.

By contrast, within the frame of precaution, the concept of risk is seen from the perspective of pervasive uncertainty and, in particular, ignorance and non-knowledge. Precautious risk management entails ensuring prudent handling of decision options in situations of high uncertainty about causes and effects and of high vulnerability of the population under risk (Adger, 2004). Instruments of precaution include minimisation requirements, such as the 'as low as reasonably achievable/practicable' (ALARA/ALARP) principles, diversification of risk agents, containment in time and space, and close monitoring.

The third frame (that of deliberation) has been advocated as an alternative or an addition to purely analytical procedures of both assessing and managing risks. The task of risk management here is to organise, in a structured and effective manner, the involvement of stakeholders and interested public in designing risk management strategies based on each stakeholder's knowledge and value system. This strategy can go along with both the risk analysis and the pre-cautionary approach but has been advocated either as an independent path to risk management or, more often, as a policy-oriented imple-mentation of the precautionary approach.

Over the last few years, advocates of the classic risk assessment frame, of the precaution-based frame, and the deliberative frame have launched a fierce debate over the legitimacy of each of their approaches. This debate has been particularly strong between the classic and the precautionary camps. One side argues that precautionary strategies ignore scientific results and lead to arbitrary regulatory decisions (Cross, 1996). The precautionary statement 'one should err on the safe side' could be interpreted as a mandate to ban everything that might result in negative side-effects. Such a rule would logically apply to any substance or human activity, and would lead to total arbitrariness (Stone, 2001; Majone, 2002: 101). The principle has been labelled as ill-defined, absolutist, unscientific, a value judgement or an ideology, and is conceived of as leading to increased risk taking, or as marginalising the role of science (Sandin *et al.*, 2002: 288; Peterson, 2006). Some analysts claim that by using the precautionary principle there is a risk that science might be held 'hostage to interest group politics' (Charnley and Elliott, 2002: 103, 66). In addition, it is feared by some that policy makers could abuse the precautionary principle as a policy strategy to protect their economic interests and to impede world trade (Majone, 2002).

On the other side of the fence, the advocates of the precautionary frame have argued that precaution does not automatically mean banning substances or activities but is a step-by-step diffusion of risky activities or technologies until more knowledge and experience is accumulated (Fisher, 2001, 2002; Stirling, 2003). They have accused their critics of ignoring the complexity and uncertainty of most hazardous situations and relying on data that often turn out to be insufficient for making prudent judgements. Since the application of the precautionary principle has been associated with stricter and more rigid regulations, environmental groups have usually rallied around the precautionary frame, while most industrial and commercial groups have been fighting for the assessment-based frame. Again, the issue is not resolved, and the debate has become even more pronounced with the defeat of the European Union in the recent WTO settlement regarding hormones in beef. The European Union failed to provide sufficient evidence that the precautionary approach could justify the restriction of imported beef treated with hormones.

It is interesting to note that the data-driven frame has been widely adopted by the official US regulatory bodies, while the precautionary frame has been widely advocated by the EU regulatory bodies. There are, however, also numerous elements of precautionary frames interspersed into the actual practices of US regulatory agencies, just as there are judgements about magnitudes of risk in the actual practices of regulators in the EU (Löfstedt, 2004). A strict dichotomy between precautionary in Europe and risk-based in the USA is therefore too simple to describe actual practice (Charnley and Elliott, 2002).

The third frame has found wide acceptance among social scientists and risk analysts from academia but so far has had little impact on the institutional design of risk analysis (Renn, 2004). There are, however, isolated examples of community participation in risk decisions, such as in selecting the remedy under the Superfund clean-up programme or negotiated rule making in the USA (Harter, 1982; Coglianese, 1997). In recent years, however, risk policy makers have acknowledged that participation in risk analysis provides many practical advantages because it transforms difficult issues of resolving epistemic uncertainty into topics of negotiation that can be dealt with at the negotiation table. 'If society participates in the production of policy-relevant scientific knowledge, such "socially robust" knowledge is less likely to be contested than that which is merely reliable' (Funtowicz *et al.*, 2000: 333–4). Accordingly, the EU communication on good governance (European Commission, 2001) highlighted the need for more stakeholder involvement and participation in risk management. How to implement this requirement in day-to-day risk management decisions is still under dispute. Many scholars have also questioned the value of deliberative approaches in some settings, arguing that 'when there is trust in the regulator, a top-down form of risk communication (information transfer) may be better than dialogue' (Löfstedt, 2005: 3; Rose-Ackerman, 1994; Coglianese, 1997).

This chapter aims to provide a common analytic structure for investigating the role and function of precaution within the third frame of precaution as a means of deliberation within a special risk governance framework (IRGC, 2005). The analytic structure suggested here will, it is hoped, facilitate understanding among the advocates of all three concepts of precaution. Rather than relying on substantive rules for precautionary actions, it focuses on procedures and structures of stakeholder and public involvement that promise to promote precautionary approaches without prescribing specific safety or risk reduction criteria.

## Before risk assessment starts

Risks are mental constructions (OECD, 2003: 67). They are not real phenomena but originate in the human mind. In contrast to risk itself, the actual harm and consequence of risk that humans experience is real in the sense that human lives are lost, health impacts can be observed, the environment is damaged, or buildings collapse. The invention of risk as a mental construct is contingent on the belief that human action can prevent harm in advance. Humans have the ability to design different futures, i.e. construct scenarios that serve as tools for the human mind to anticipate consequences in advance and change, within constraints of nature and culture, the course of actions accordingly.

Therefore societies have been selective in what they have chosen to be worth considering and what to ignore (Thompson *et al.*, 1990; Douglas, 1990; Beck, 1994: 9ff.). Specialised organisations have been established to monitor the environment for hints of future problems and to provide early warning of some potential future harm. This selection process is not arbitrary. It is guided by cultural values, such as the shared belief that each individual life is worth protecting; by institutional and financial resources, such as the decision of national governments to spend money or not to spend money on early warning systems against highly improbable but high-consequence events; and by systematic reasoning, such as using probability theory for distinguishing between more likely and less likely events or methods of estimating damage potential or distribution of hazards in time and space.

Based on these preliminary thoughts, a systematic review of risk-related actions needs to start with an analysis of what major societal actors, such as governments, companies, the scientific community and the general public, select as risks, and what types of problems they label as risk problems (rather than opportunities or innovation potentials, etc.). In technical terms, this is called framing. Framing in this context encompasses the selection and interpretation of phenomena as relevant risk topics (Goodwin and Wright, 2004). The process of framing is already part of the governance structure, since official agencies (for example food standard agencies), risk and opportunity producers (such as the food industry), those affected by risks and opportunities (such as consumer organisations) and interested bystanders (such as the media or an intellectual elite) are all involved and often in conflict with each other when framing an issue.

Whether a consensus evolves about what requires consideration as a relevant risk depends on the legitimacy of the selection rule. The acceptance of selection rules rests on two conditions: first, all actors need to agree with the *underlying goal* (often legally prescribed, such as prevention of health detriments or guarantee of an undisturbed environmental quality, for example purity laws for drinking water); second, they need to agree with the implications derived from the *present state of knowledge* (whether and to what degree the identified hazard impacts the desired goal). Even within this preliminary analysis, dissent can result from conflicting values as well as conflicting evidence, and, in particular, from the inadequate blending of the two. Values and evidence can be viewed as two sides of a coin: the values govern the selection of the goal, whereas the evidence governs the selection of cause–effect claims (Jaeger *et al.*, 2001: 16ff.). Both need to be properly investigated when analysing risk governance, but it is of particular importance to understand the values shaping the interests, perceptions and concerns of the different stakeholders as well as to identify methods for capturing how these concerns are likely to influence, or impact on, the debate about a particular risk. The actual measurements of these impacts should then be done in the most professional manner, including the characterisation of uncertainties.

Framing is the first step of a deliberative process towards risk appraisal and management. The term 'deliberation' refers to the style and procedure of decision making without specifying which participants are invited to deliberate (Stern and Fineberg, 1996; Rossi, 1997). For a discussion to be termed deliberative, it is essential that it relies on a mutual exchange of arguments and reflections rather than being based on the status of the participants, subliminal strategies of persuasion, or social-political pressure. Deliberative processes should include a debate about the relative weight of each argument and a transparent procedure for balancing pros and cons (O'Riordan *et al.*, 1999; Tuler and Webler, 1999). In addition, deliberative processes should be governed by the established rules of a rational discourse. The phrase 'discourse' itself has different meanings in the social sciences (Renn, 1998). Discourse is often used to mean either language texts as wholes in their context of use or the world views which inform our understanding. In the theory of communicative action developed by the German philosopher Juergen Habermas, the term 'discourse' denotes a special form of a dialogue, in which all affected parties have equal rights and duties to present claims and test their validity in a context free of social or political domination (Habermas, 1970, 1987). A discourse is called rational if it meets a specific set of requirements (cf. McCarthy, 1975; Habermas, 1991; Kemp, 1985; Renn and Webler, 1998: 48ff.; Webler, 1995; 1999; Renn, 2004).

All participants are obliged first to seek a consensus on the procedure that they want to employ in order to derive the final decision or compromise, such as voting, sorting of positions, consensual decision making, or the involvement of a mediator or arbitrator. Second, there is a need to articulate and critique factual claims on the basis of the state of the art of scientific knowledge and other forms of problem-adequate knowledge; in the case of dissent all relevant camps have the right to be represented. Third, all participants should interpret factual evidence in accordance with the laws of formal logic and analytical reasoning; disclose their relevant values and preferences, thus avoiding hidden agendas and strategic game playing; and, in addition, process data, arguments and evaluations in a structured format (for example a decision-analytic procedure) so that norms of procedural rationality are met and transparency can be created.

The rules of deliberation do not necessarily include the demand for stakeholder or public involvement. Deliberation can be organised in closed circles as well as in public forums. Following our understanding of precaution, however, difficult risk decisions require contributions from scientists, policy makers, stakeholders and affected publics. Therefore, a procedure is needed that guarantees both the inclusion of different constituencies outside the risk management institutions and the assurance of a deliberative style within the process of decision making. I suggest that the term 'deliberative democracy' should be used when one refers to the combination of deliberation and third-party involvement (see also Rossi, 1997).

## Risk assessment

The purpose of risk assessment is the generation of knowledge linking specific risk agents with uncertain but possible consequences (Lave, 1987; Graham and Rhomberg, 1996). The final product of risk assessment is an estimation of the risk in terms of a probability distribution of the modelled consequences, drawing on either discrete events or a continuous loss function.

Risk assessment is confronted with three major challenges that can be best described using the terms complexity, uncertainty and ambiguity. These three challenges are not related to the intrinsic characteristics of the hazards or risks themselves but to the state and quality of knowledge available about both hazards and risks (WBGU, 2000: 195ff.; Klinke and Renn, 2002).

Complexity refers to the difficulty of identifying and quantifying causal links between a multitude of potential causal agents and specific observed effects. The nature of this difficulty may be traced back to interactive effects among these agents (synergisms and antagonisms), long delay periods between cause and effect, inter-individual variation, intervening variables, and others. Risk assessors have to make judgements about the level of complexity that they are able to process and about how to treat intervening variables such as lifestyle, other environmental factors, and psychosomatic impacts. Complexity is particularly pertinent in the phase of estimation with respect to hazards as well as risks.

Uncertainty is different from complexity but often results from an incomplete or inadequate reduction of complexity in modelling cause–effect chains. Whether the world is inherently uncertain is a philosophical question that I will not pursue here. It is essential to acknowledge, in the context of risk assessment, that human knowledge is always incomplete and selective and thus contingent on uncertain assumptions, assertions and predictions (Functowicz and Ravetz, 1992; O'Riordan and Jordan, 1995: 9f.; Laudan, 1996; Bruijn and ten Heuvelhof, 1999). It is obvious that the modelled probability distributions within a numerical relational system can only represent an approximation of the empirical relational system with which to understand and predict uncertain events (Cooke, 1991). It therefore seems prudent to include other, additional, aspects of uncertainty (Morgan *et al.*, 1990; van Asselt, 2000: 93–138).

Although there is no consensus in the literature on the best means of disaggregating uncertainties, the following categories appear to be an appropriate means of distinguishing the key components of uncertainty. These include *target variability* (based on different vulnerability of targets); *systematic and random error in modelling* (based on extrapolations from animals to humans or from large doses to small doses, statistical inferential applications); *indeterminacy or genuine stochastic effects* (variation of effects due to random events, in special cases congruent with statistical handling of random errors); *system boundaries* (uncertainties stemming from restricted models and the need to focus on a limited number of variables and parameters) and *ignorance or non-knowledge* (uncertainties derived from lack or absence of knowledge).

All these different elements have one feature in common: they all reduce the strength of confidence in the estimated cause and effect chain. If uncertainty plays a large role, in particular indeterminacy or lack of knowledge, the estimation of risk becomes fuzzy. The validity of the end results is questionable and, for risk management purposes, additional information is needed, such as a subjective confidence level in the risk estimates, potential alternative pathways of cause–effect relationships, ranges of reasonable estimates, loss scenarios and others.

While uncertainty refers to a lack of clarity over the scientific or technical basis for decision making, ambiguity is a result of divergent or contested perspectives on the justification, severity or wider meanings associated with a given threat (Stirling, 2003). The term 'ambiguity' may be misleading because it has different connotations in everyday English language. In relation to risk governance, it is understood as giving rise to several meaningful and legitimate interpretations of accepted risk assessment results. It can be divided into interpretative ambiguity and normative ambiguity. Interpretative ambiguity refers to different interpretations of an identical assessment result, for example as an adverse or non-adverse effect. Normative ambiguity refers to different concepts of what can be regarded as tolerable, referring, for example, to ethics, quality of life parameters, and the distribution of risks and benefits. A condition of ambiguity emerges where the problem lies in agreeing on the appropriate values, priorities, assumptions or boundaries to be applied to the definition of possible outcomes. What does it mean, for example, if neuronal activities in the human brain are intensified when subjects are exposed to electromagnetic radiation? Can this be interpreted as an adverse effect or is it just a bodily response without any health implication? Many scientific disputes in the fields of risk assessment and management do not refer to differences in methodology, measurements or dose–response functions, but to the question of what all of this means for human health and environmental protection. High complexity and uncertainty favour the emergence of ambiguity, but there are also quite a few simple and highly probable risks that can cause controversy and thus ambiguity.

## Characterising and evaluating risks

The most controversial part of handling risks refers to the process of delineating and justifying a judgement about the tolerability or acceptability of a given risk (HSE, 2001). The term 'tolerable' refers to an activity that is seen as worth pursuing (for the benefit it carries) yet requires additional efforts for risk reduction within reasonable limits. The term 'acceptable' refers to an activity where the remaining risks are so low that additional efforts for risk reduction are not seen as necessary. If tolerability and acceptability are located in a risk diagram (with probabilities on the *y*-axis and extent of consequences on the *x*-axis), the well-known traffic light model emerges (Figure 10.1). In this variant of the model, the lightest-coloured zone signifies intolerable risk, the darker one indicates tolerable risk in need of further management actions in accordance with the 'as low as reasonably practicable' principle, and the darkest zone shows acceptable or even negligible risk.

To draw the line between intolerable and tolerable, as well as tolerable and acceptable, is one of the most difficult tasks of risk governance. The UK Health and Safety Executive has developed a procedure for chemical risks based on risk–risk comparisons (Löfstedt, 1997). Some Swiss cantons, such as Basel county, experimented with roundtables as a means to reach consensus on drawing the two lines, whereby participants of the roundtable represented industry, administrators, county officials, environmentalists and neighbourhood groups (RISKO, 2000). Irrespective of the selected means to support this task, the judgement on acceptability or tolerability is contingent on making use of a variety of different knowledge sources. One needs to include the risk estimates derived from the risk assessment process, data from risk perception studies, and input from stakeholder and public evaluations.

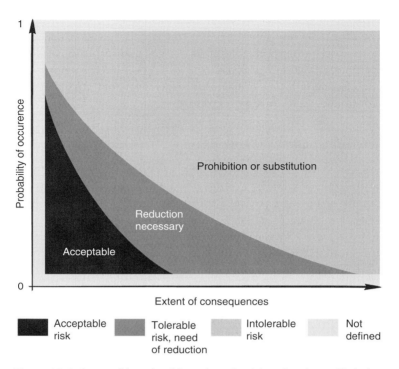

Figure 10.1 Acceptable, tolerable and intolerable risks: the traffic light model

## Risk appraisal

The term *risk appraisal* has sometimes been used in the risk governance literature to include all knowledge elements necessary for risk
characterisation and evaluation as well as risk management (Stirling,
1998, 1999, 2003). For society to make prudent choices about risks, it
is not enough to consider only the results of (scientific) risk assessment. In order to understand the concerns of the various stakeholders
and public groups, information about both risk perceptions and the
further implications of the direct consequences of a risk – including its
social mobilisation potential (i.e. how likely is it that the activity will
give rise to social opposition or protest?) – is needed and should
be collected by risk managers. In addition, other aspects of the risk-
causing activity that seem to be relevant for characterising and
evaluating the risk and selecting risk reduction options should be

pulled together and fed into the analysis. Based on such a wide range of information, risk managers can make more informed judgements and design the appropriate risk management options (Clark, 2001).

Risk appraisal thus includes the scientific assessment of the risks to human health and the environment and an assessment of related concerns as well as social and economic implications. The appraisal process is, and should be, clearly dominated by scientific analyses – but, in contrast to the traditional risk governance model, the scientific process includes both the natural and technical as well as the social sciences, including economics. I envision risk appraisal as having two process stages: first, natural and technical scientists use their skills to produce the best estimate of the physical harm that a risk source may induce; second, social scientists and economists identify and analyse the issues that individuals or society as a whole link with a certain risk. For this purpose the repertoire of the social sciences such as survey methods, focus groups, econometric analysis, macro-economic modelling, or structured hearings with stakeholders may be used.

Risk appraisal intends to produce the best possible scientific estimate of the physical, economic and social consequences of a risk source. It should not be confused with direct stakeholder involvement, which will be covered later. Involvement by stakeholders and the population is only desirable at this stage if knowledge from these sources is needed to improve the quality of the assessments.

## Risk management

Risk management starts with a review of all relevant information, including the results of risk assessments, the results of the risk appraisal, including studies of social concerns and other important information about context. This information, together with the judgements made in the phase of risk characterisation and evaluation, forms the input material, based on which risk management options are assessed, evaluated and selected. Based on the distinction between complexity, uncertainty and ambiguity, it is possible to design generic strategies of risk management to be applied to classes of risks, thus simplifying the risk management process as outlined above. One can distinguish four such classes: simple risk problems; complex risk problems; risk problems due to high unresolved uncertainty; and risk problems due to interpretative and normative ambiguity.

Simple risk problems require hardly any deviation from traditional decision making. Data are provided by statistical analysis, goals are determined by law or statutory requirements, and the role of risk management is to ensure that all risk reduction measures are implemented and enforced. Traditional risk–risk comparisons or risk–risk trade-offs, risk–benefit analysis and cost-effectiveness studies are the instruments of choice for finding the most appropriate risk reduction measures. Additionally, risk managers can rely on best practice and, in cases of low impact, on trial and error. It should be noted, however, that simple risks should not be equated with small or negligible risks. The major issues here are that the potential negative consequences are obvious, the values that are applied are non-controversial, and the remaining uncertainties low. Examples are car accidents, known food and health risks, regularly occurring natural disasters, or safety devices for high buildings.

For complex risk problems, major input for risk management is provided by the scientific characterisation of the risk. Complex risk problems are often associated with major scientific dissent about complex dose–effect relationships or the alleged effectiveness of measures to decrease vulnerabilities. Complexity in this context refers to both the risk agent and its causal connections, and the risk absorbing system and its vulnerabilities. Complex risk problems are in strong contrast to risk managers' expectations to receive a complete and balanced set of risk assessment results that fall within the legitimate range of plural truth claims.

In a situation where there are no complete data, the major challenge is to define the factual base for making risk-management or risk-regulatory decisions. Once these input variables are defined and affirmed, evaluation is done on the basis of risk–benefit balancing and normative standard setting in risk-based and risk-informed regulation. When it comes to balancing pros and cons, traditional methods such as risk–risk comparison, cost-effectiveness and cost–benefit analysis are well suited to facilitate the overall judgement of risk evaluation. These instruments, if properly used, provide effective, efficient and fair solutions with respect to finding the best trade-off between opportunities and risks.

If there is a high degree of unresolved uncertainties, risk management needs to incorporate hazard criteria which are comparatively easy to determine, including aspects such as reversibility, persistence, and ubiquity, and select management options empowering society to deal even with worst-case scenarios such as containment of hazardous activities. Risks characterised by multiple and high uncertainties are the domain where precaution is specifically warranted. Since high unresolved uncertainty implies that the true dimensions of the risks are not yet known, one should pursue a cautious strategy that allows learning by restricted errors. The main management philosophy for this risk class is to allow small steps in implementation (containment approach) that enable risk managers to stop, or even reverse, the process as new knowledge is produced or the negative side-effects become visible. The primary thrust of precaution is to avoid irreversibility (Klinke and Renn, 2001).

The final class of problems relates to risk problems due to inter- pretative and normative ambiguity. If risk information is interpreted differently by different stakeholders in society, and if the values of what should be protected or reduced are subject to intense contro- versy, risk management needs to address the causes for these con- flicting views (von Winterfeldt and Edwards, 1984). Very often they are not fuelled by differences about factual explanations or predictions but, instead, are based on different viewpoints about the relevance, meaning and implications of these findings for risk evaluation and risk management actions, and about which values and priorities should bear on a decision. Since, in this risk class, the intended as well as non-intended consequences of an activity are highly controversial, risk management should initiate a broader societal discourse to enable participative decision making. Here, methods of deliberative demo- cracy are of utmost importance. These deliberative procedures are aimed at finding appropriate conflict resolution mechanisms capable of reducing the ambiguity to a manageable number of options that can be further assessed and evaluated. The main effort of risk management is hence the organisation of a suitable discourse combined with the assurance that all stakeholders and public groups can question and critique the framing of the issue as well as each element of the entire risk chain.

## Stakeholder involvement and participation

Each decision-making process has two major aspects: what and whom to include on the one hand, and what and how to select on the other hand (Hajer and Wagenaar, 2003; Stirling, 2005). Inclusion and selection are therefore the two essential parts of any decision- or policy-making activity. Classic decision analysis offers formal methods for generating options and evaluating these options against a set of predefined criteria. With the advent of new participatory methods, however, the two issues of inclusion and selection have become more complex and sophisticated than is assumed in these conventional methods.

The concept of deliberative democracy advocates the notion of inclusive governance, in particular with respect to environmental risks. First and foremost, this means that the four major actors in risk decision making, i.e. political, business, scientific and civil society players, should jointly engage in the process of framing the problem, generating options, evaluating options and coming to a joint conclusion. It is obvious that, in doing so, these actors are guided by particular interests which derive not only from the fact that some of them are risk producers whereas others are exposed to it but, equally, from their individual institutional rationale and perspective. Such vested interests require specific consideration and measures so that they are made transparent and, if possible, can be reconciled. Tim O'Riordan and colleagues have characterised inclusive governance as follows:

Deliberative and inclusionary processes (DIPs) cover a wide range of procedures and practices. These are all designed to widen the basis of direct participation in environmental decision making, and to deepen the level of discussion so that underlying meanings and values are more fully explored. The purpose of DIPs is, in essence, profoundly democratic. DIPs are aimed not just at creating more richly informed decisions that are owned by and have the broad consent of those participating. DIPs also seek to build and to engender a creative sense of citizenship in participants. This is why the objective inclusionary is incorporated: it applies to a process of defining and redefining interests that stakeholders introduce as the collective experience of participation evolves. As participants become more empowered, i.e. more respected and more self-confident, so it is assumed they may become more ready to adjust, to listen, to learn, and to accommodate to a greater consensus. For this outcome to happen it depends on a co-operative formal governance that is willing to incorporate and to respond to such procedures, as well as a citizenry with the capacity to carry through the arduous processes of co-governing for a better society and environment (O'Riordan *et al.*, 1999: 3).

Inclusive governance, as it relates to the inclusion part of decision making, requires a number of necessary conditions (Webler, 1999; Wynne, 2002). First, there needs to have been a major attempt to involve representatives of all major actor groups, and a major attempt to empower all actors to participate actively and constructively in the discourse. Next, there needs to have been a major attempt to co-design the framing of the risk problem or the issue in a dialogue with these different groups. There needs to have been a major attempt to generate a common understanding of the magnitude of the risk based on the expertise of all participants as well as the potential risk management options, and to include a plurality of options that represent the different interests and values of all parties involved. Finally, there needs to have been a major effort to conduct a forum for decision making that provides equal and fair opportunities for all parties to voice their opinion and to express their preferences; and to provide a clear connection between the participatory bodies of decision making and the political implementation level.

If these conditions are met, evidence shows that actors, along with developing faith in their own competence, use the opportunity and start to place trust in each other and have confidence in the process of risk management (Kasperson *et al.*, 1999; Viklund, 2002). This is particularly true at the local level, where the participants are familiar with each other and have more immediate access to the issue (Petts, 1997). Reaching consensus and building trust on highly complex, uncertain and ambiguous subjects such as global change is, however, much more difficult. Being inclusive and open to social groups does not guarantee, therefore, constructive co-operation by those who are invited to participate. Some actors may reject the framing of the issue and choose to withdraw. Others may benefit from the collapse of an inclusive governance process. It is essential to monitor these processes and make sure that particular interests do not dominate the deliberations and that rules can be established and jointly approved to prevent destructive strategising.

Inclusive governance needs to address the second part of the decision-making process as well, i.e. reaching closure on a set of options that are selected for further consideration, while others are rejected. *Closure* does not mean to have the final word on a development, a risk reduction plan or a regulation. Rather, it represents the product of a deliberation, i.e. the agreement that the participants reached. The problem is that the more actors, viewpoints, interests and values that are included and thus represented in an arena, the more difficult it is to reach either a consensus or some other kind of joint agreement. A second set of criteria is thus needed, to evaluate the process by which the closure of debates (be they final or temporary) is achieved, as well as the quality of the decision or recommendation that is generated through the closure procedure.

The quality of the closure process itself is dependent on a number of dimensions. Have all arguments been properly treated? Have all truth claims been fairly and accurately tested against commonly agreed standards of validation? Has all the relevant evidence, in accordance with the actual state-of-the-art knowledge, been collected and processed? Was systematic, experiential and practical knowledge and expertise adequately included and processed? Were all interests and values considered and was there a major effort to come up with fair and balanced solutions? Were all normative judgements made explicit and thoroughly explained? Were normative statements derived from accepted ethical principles or legally prescribed norms? Were all efforts undertaken to preserve plurality of lifestyles and individual freedom and to restrict the realm of collectively binding decisions to those areas in which binding rules and norms are essential and necessary to produce the desired outcome?

Turning to the issues of outcome, additional criteria need to be addressed. These have been discussed in the political science and governance literature for a long time (Dryzek, 1994; Rhodes, 1997). They are usually stated as comprising effectiveness, efficiency, accountability, legitimacy, fairness, transparency, acceptance by the public, and ethical acceptability. They coincide with those that have been postulated earlier for the evaluation of risk management options.

When contemplating the requirements for inclusion, closure process and outcome quality, it is assumed that more inclusive procedures enrich the generation of options and perspectives, and are therefore more responsive to the complexity, uncertainty and ambiguity of the risk phenomena which are being assessed; and more rational closure processes provide fairer and socially and culturally more adaptive and balanced judgements (Stern and Fineberg, 1996; Beierle and Cayford, 2002; Mitchell *et al.*, 2006). It is further assumed that the interaction of voluntary and regulatory actions in the form of public–private partnerships can be improved through early and constructive involvement procedures; and that the outcomes derived from these procedures are of higher quality in terms of effectiveness, efficiency, legitimacy, fairness, transparency, public acceptance, and ethical acceptability than the outcomes of conventional decision-making procedures.

The potential benefits resulting from stakeholder and public involvement depend, however, on the quality of the participation process. It is not sufficient to gather all interested parties around a table and merely hope for the catharsis effect to show up. In particular, it is essential to treat the time and effort of the participating actors as scarce resources that need to be handled with care and respect (Chess *et al.*, 1998; Mitchell *et al.*, 2006: 320ff.). The participation process should be designed so that the various actors are encouraged to contribute to the process in which they feel they are competent and can offer something to improve the quality of the final product.

## Stakeholder involvement in risk governance

The four risk classes discussed earlier, i.e. simple, complex, high uncertainty and high ambiguity risk problems, support generic suggestions for participation in risk appraisal and management (Renn, 1999, 2004). For making judgements about simple risk problems, a sophisticated approach to involve all potentially affected parties is not necessary. Most actors would not even seek to participate, since the expected results are more or less obvious. In terms of co-operative strategies, an instrumental discourse among agency staff, directly affected groups, such as product or activity providers, and immediately exposed individuals, as well as enforcement personnel, is advisable. One should be aware, however, that often risks that appear simple turn out to be more complex, uncertain or ambiguous than originally assessed. It is therefore essential to revisit these risks regularly and monitor the outcomes carefully.

The proper handling of complexity in risk assessment and risk management requires transparency over the subjective judgements and the inclusion of knowledge elements that have shaped the parameters on both sides of the cost–benefit equation. These inputs could be provided by an epistemological discourse aimed at finding the best estimates for characterising the risks under consideration.

This discourse should be inspired by different science camps and the participation of experts and knowledge carriers. They may come from academia, government, industry or civil society, but their legitimacy to participate is their claim to bring new or additional knowledge to the negotiating table. The goal is to resolve cognitive conflicts. Exercises such as Delphi, Group Delphi and consensus workshops would be most advisable to serve the goals of an epistemological discourse (Gregory *et al.*, 2001).

Characterising risks, evaluating risks and designing options for risk reduction pose special challenges in situations of high uncertainty about the risk estimates. How can one judge the severity of a situation when the potential damage and its probability are unknown or highly uncertain? In this dilemma, risk managers are well advised to include the main stakeholders in the evaluation process and ask them to find a consensus on the extra margin of safety that they would be willing to invest in exchange for avoiding potentially catastrophic consequences. This type of deliberation, called reflective discourse, relies on a collective reflection about balancing the possibilities for over- and under-protection. If too much protection is sought, innovations may be prevented or stalled; if we go for too little protection, society may experience unpleasant surprises. The classic question of 'how safe is safe enough?' is replaced by the question of 'how much uncertainty and ignorance are the main actors willing to accept in exchange for some given benefit?' It is recommended that policy makers, representatives of major stakeholder groups, and scientists take part in this type of discourse. The reflective discourse can take different forms: roundtables, open space forums, negotiated rule-making exercises, mediation, or mixed advisory committees including scientists and stakeholders (Amy, 1983; Perrit, 1986; Rowe and Frewer, 2000).

If major ambiguities are associated with a risk problem, it is not enough to demonstrate that risk regulators are open to public concerns and address the issues that many people wish them to take care of. In these cases the process of risk evaluation needs to be open to public input and new forms of deliberation. This starts with revisiting the question of proper framing. Is the issue really a risk problem or is it in fact an issue of lifestyle and future vision? The aim is to find consensus on the dimensions of ambiguity that need to be addressed in comparing risks and benefits and balancing the pros and cons. High ambiguities require the most inclusive strategy for participation, since

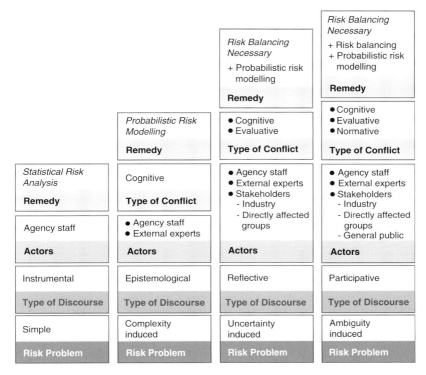

**Figure 10.2** The risk management escalator and stakeholder involvement from simple via complex and uncertain to ambiguous phenomena

not only directly affected groups but also those indirectly affected have something to contribute to this debate. Resolving ambiguities in risk debates requires a participatory discourse. Available sets of deliberative processes include citizen panels, citizen juries, consensus conferences, ombudspersons, citizen advisory commissions, and similar participatory instruments (Dienel, 1989; Fiorino, 1990; Durant and Joss, 1995; Armour, 1995; Applegate, 1998).

Figure 10.2 provides an overview of the different requirements for participation and stakeholder involvement for the four classes of risk problems. As is the case with all classifications, this scheme shows an extremely simplified picture of the involvement process. In addition to the distinctions made in the figure, it may, for instance, be wise to distinguish participatory processes based on risk agent or risk

absorbing issues. Also, categorising risks according to the quality and
nature of available information on risk may, of course, be contested
among the stakeholders: it is possible that no consensus may be
reached as to where to locate a specific risk. In those cases, a detailed
(worst-case) analysis of possibilities of monitoring and surveillance
may constitute the only achievable compromise (reversible removal of
risk sources, etc.; timely detection of adverse effects; strength of surveillance systems, etc.). Such a situation may also require a design
discourse to reach some closure on the characterisation process. In this
sense, the figure provides only a general orientation for analysing and
designing stakeholder involvement processes.

## Risk communication

Effective communication is a necessary complement to (but not substitute for) deliberative risk governance. Since all decision-making
processes involve a limited amount of people when relying on a face-
to-face interaction (rather than internet exchange), the outside world
needs to be properly informed and the process of deliberation needs
to be conveyed to all affected parties in a transparent and easy-
to-understand manner. Risk communication is needed throughout
the whole risk handling chain, from the framing of the issue to the
monitoring of risk management impacts. The precise form of communication needs to reflect the nature of the risks under consideration,
their context and whether they arouse, or could arouse, societal
concern. The ultimate goal of risk communication is to assist stakeholders in understanding the rationale of risk assessment results and
risk management decisions, and to help them arrive at a balanced
judgement that reflects the factual evidence about the matter at hand in
relation to their own interests and values (OECD, 2002). Good practices in risk communication help stakeholders make informed choices
about matters of concern to them and to create mutual trust (Hance
*et al.*, 1988; Lundgren, 1994). Communication has to be a means to
ensure both that those who are central to risk framing, risk assessment
or risk management understand what is happening, how they are to be
involved, and, where appropriate, what their responsibilities are; and
that others outside the immediate risk assessment or risk management
process are informed and engaged.

Risk communication requires professional performance by both risk and communication experts. Scientists, communication specialists and regulators are encouraged to take a much more prominent role in risk communication, because effective risk communication can make a strong contribution to the success of a comprehensive and responsible risk management programme.

## Conclusions

This chapter first discussed a comprehensive risk handling chain, breaking down its various components into three main phases: framing, appraisal and management. Risk evaluation has been placed between the appraisal and management phases and can be assigned to either of them, depending on the circumstances: if the interpretation of evidence is the guiding principle for characterising risks, then risk assessors are probably the most appropriate people to handle this task; if the interpretation of underlying values and the selection of yardsticks for judging acceptability are the key problems, then risk managers should be responsible. In an ideal setting, however, this task of determining a risk's acceptability should be performed in a joint effort by a deliberative body including risk assessors, managers, and representatives of industry and civil society. A prototype version of this framework is summarised in Figure 10.3.

This chapter, secondly, has addressed the issue of precaution. Risk managers face the problem of how to make regulatory decisions under conditions of complexity, uncertainty and ambiguity. What lessons can be drawn when linking these challenges to the application of the precautionary principle? I conclude that precaution is a necessary and prudent strategy when risk assessors cannot resolve the uncertainties in their cause–effect modelling. If uncertainty (and, in particular, ignorance) plays a large role, the traditional risk-based frame becomes counter-productive. Judging the relative severity of risks on the basis of uncertain parameters does not make much sense. Under these circumstances, management strategies belonging to the precautionary frame are required. In addition to risk reduction, there is a need to meet additional objectives that promise to enhance resilience and decrease vulnerability. These goals may conflict with the aim of efficiency based on optimising trade-offs between costs and

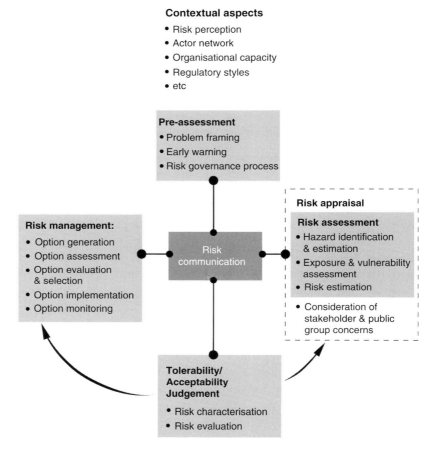

**Figure 10.3** Risk governance framework incorporating classical components and contextual aspects

opportunities. Yet the possibility of irreversible harm necessitates protective measures beyond the point of optimal resource allocation. Strategies based on resilience include specific measures of precaution, such as ALARA or Best Available Control Technology, or the strategy of containing risks in time and space (Klinke and Renn, 2001).

It may be helpful in this respect to resort to a differentiation that Resnik (2003: 332) has proposed: decisions under certainty where the outcomes of different choices are known; decisions under risk where probabilities can be assigned to the outcomes of different choices; and decisions under ignorance where it is not possible to assign probabilities to the outcomes of different choices. A similar distinction has been made by O'Riordan and Jordan (1995: 9) and Stirling (2003). Using a precautionary approach for the first two cases is neither necessary nor prudent, given that regulation needs to both protect public health and the environment and secure economic welfare. The legitimate realm of using precaution is in the case of unresolved uncertainty, ignorance or high ambiguity. In order to avoid misunderstanding, some analysts have proposed that the term 'precaution' be avoided and replaced with the more adequate term 'the principle of insufficient reason' (see Peterson, 2003: 71). This is the place where precaution is required. The main purpose of precaution in this respect is to avoid irreversible decisions. Although highly critical about the use of the precautionary principle, Majone concedes that it does have a role, namely where 'losses (or utilities) are unbounded' and where it is 'clearly impossible to calculate expected values', for example, where there is a threat of 'serious and irreversible damage' (Majone, 2002: 104). In this chapter, I make a strong plea for screening risks according to the degree of complexity, which can be modelled by scientific means, leaving uncertainties and ambiguities. The screening is instrumental for identifying those risks that need a precautionary treatment.

This substantive suggestion does, however, entail a major problem. Looking only to the uncertainties does not provide risk managers with a clue as to where to set priorities for risk reduction. How can one judge the severity of a situation when the potential damage and its probability are unknown or highly uncertain? In this dilemma, risk managers are well advised to resort to deliberative methods throughout the entire risk governance process. I have termed this type of deliberation 'reflective discourse', since it rests on a collective reflection about balancing the possibilities for over- and under-protection based on uncertain data and ignorance (Renn, 2004).

The first question for which deliberation is necessary relates to the task of screening in the framing phase of risk governance. Who decides whether a risk is complex, uncertain or ambiguous? Further questions arise in later processes of the risk governance framework. How should one exercise precaution if indeed there is a consensus that a risk is characterised by high uncertainty and ambiguity? What management options are best suited to avoid irreversibilities, and what discursive methods are advisable in situations of high ambiguity?

There are no substantive solutions to these questions. The class-ification suggested here may help to assign risks to different classes of concern but they do not offer any foolproof recipes or automatic rules. These questions demand deliberative methods or procedures that act as catalysts in the debate about what society regards as acceptable and intolerable. Such deliberative procedures are specifically required in the phases of framing, evaluation and selection of intervention methods. They are also suited for risk appraisal and risk assessment as long as they are based on knowledge, and respected rules of knowledge acquisition and interpretation are adequately taken into account.

Deliberation implies inclusion and selection. It is important to include representatives of politics, industry and civil society. The new angle is on integration not specialisation. This is also true for selecting the proper frame for subject areas. Often the debate is not about risks but about the desirability of the envisioned benefits. Equally often the debate is about the choice of technology not the acceptability of risks. This needs to be clarified in the framing phase using discursive methods of deliberation. With respect to selection, it is crucial to find transparent and consensual means of generating, evaluating and choosing options for risk prevention, reduction or mitigation. Methods for conducting meaningful and effective deliberation are available and have been tested all around the world (Stern and Fineberg, 1996; Beierle and Cayford, 2002; Mitchell *et al.*, 2006). It is up to the risk management agencies to put them into practice.

A deliberative approach to risk regulation does not only meet the requirements of the precautionary principle, it also fits the concept of sustainability as Tim O'Riordan and Andrew Jordan emphasised in a 1995 paper on this subject:

Civic science aims to reposition society's relationship to nature by giving its role and its potential vulnerability fuller appreciation. This is the basis on which precaution can become more reliably implanted in the sustainable transition (O'Riordan and Jordan, 1995: 21f.).

Sustainability in this understanding can be seen as a substantive eth-ical norm to ensure that future generations will not be worse off than the present generation (O'Riordan, 1991a). It can also be framed as an environmental or ecological imperative to live from the interest of natural capital rather than from the assets. The term 'sustainable development' is a prophetic combination of two words which unites both aspects – economic progress and environmental quality – in one vision. This vision of an economic structure that meets all the needs of this generation without restricting the needs of future generations is highly attractive, because it reconciles the terms 'economy' and 'ecology' – terms seen so often as opposites – and postulates a generally acceptable distribution rule among generations. As attractive as the concept may be, of course, few concern themselves with the question as to how the magic formula can be transformed into reality.

The problem with a concept that so many people share as a common goal, and that has become a political catchword showing up in many discussions without anyone considering what it really means, is that it can be defined and operationalised in many different way. When environmental activists and conservative executives use the same term for their very different purposes, they are sure to be using it with different meanings. Sustainability is used all too often as a convenient buzzword to legitimise one's own interests and to hide concealed conflicts. Then the concept loses its normative effect, which could otherwise ultimately be an integrating one.

Should we then do without the term 'sustainability'? That would be throwing the baby out with the bathwater. On the one hand, the concept has to be understood correctly; only then can it serve as a realistic and ethical guide for the future development of both industrialised and developing countries. On the other hand, getting the many players in politics and society to agree on any common ground at all offers a great chance to begin making common strategies to implement a concept. There is already a change under way in society towards thinking and acting in a more sustainable spirit. The type of structural change called for by the concept of sustainable development always requires that a change be under way in one's own behaviour and goals. And reflection on those personal aspects involves a vision of the future that is considered worth living for. Sustainable development has become a common vision for many groups and can serve as an integrative engine to keep parties with diverse interests heading for the same goal (O'Riordan, 1991b).

This vision is useless unless it can unfold itself in a broader societal discourse. Deliberative methods are well suited to becoming the main focus of such a discourse. Much of what Tim O'Riordan has written and initiated was directed towards deliberative actions for triggering structural changes (O'Riordan, 1976, 1991a). These changes can neither be prescribed nor logically deduced and implemented by decree. They rely on communicative and participative procedures that help all participants to define their known vision, discuss common strategies, and find closure about what needs to be done. This is the case for sustainability as well as prudent risk management.

At the end of the day, precautionary risk governance means nothing else but ensuring that those who are likely to suffer the most and those who are likely to benefit the most should sit around a table and find an agreement about how to make an appropriate trade-off between opportunities and risks. It is one of Tim O'Riordan's most cherished quotes that in the Chinese language the word for risk also means opportunity. This does not imply that there is harmony between opportunities and risks. Conflicts will prevail and there are no easy ways out of risk dilemmas. Yet, looking holistically at opportunities and risks together and deliberating about the best way to harvest one without imposing unacceptable burdens onto others is the only viable opportunity for progressing on the stony path towards sustainability. In *Environment* magazine Tim O'Riordan summarised this thought in the following way:

Overall, we seem to be failing at the strategic level to link sustainability, democracy, and justice. The sustainability movement genuinely tries to marry these approaches ... Building on such initiatives, it is vital too that schools the world over enable awareness and training skills to be fostered so that all future generations learn to establish the kinds of sustainable livelihoods that will result in a better citizenry for a healthier planet. (O'Riordan, 2005)

## References

Adger, W. N. 2004. 'Vulnerability', in Forsyth, T. (ed.) *Encyclopaedia of International Development*. London, UK: Routledge, pp. 742–3.

Amy, D. J. 1983. 'Environmental mediation: an alternative approach to policy stalemates', *Policy Sciences* 15: 345–65.

Applegate, J. 1998. 'Beyond the usual suspects: the use of citizens advisory boards in environmental decision making', *Indiana Law Journal* 73: 903.

Armour, A. 1995. 'The citizens' jury model of public participation', in Renn, O., Webler, T. and Wiedemann, P. (eds.) *Fairness and Competence in*

*Citizen Participation: Evaluating New Models for Environmental Discourse.* Dordrecht, The Netherlands: Kluwer, pp. 175–88.

Beck, U. 1994. 'The reinvention of politics: towards a theory of reflexive modernization', in Beck, U., Giddens, A. and Lash, S. (eds.) *Reflexive Modernization: Politics, Tradition and Aesthetics in the Modern Social Order.* Palo Alto, CA: Stanford University Press, pp. 1–55.

Beierle, T. C. and Cayford, J. 2002. *Democracy in Practice: Public Participation in Environmental Decisions.* Washington DC: Resources for the Future.

Bruijn, J. A. and ten Heuvelhof, E. F. 1999. 'Scientific expertise in complex decision-making processes', *Science and Public Policy* 26: 151–61.

Charnley, G. and Elliott, D. E. 2002. 'Risk versus precaution: environmental law and public health protection', *Environmental Law Reporter* 32: 10363–6.

Chess, C., Dietz, T. and Shannon, M. 1998. 'Who should deliberate when?' *Human Ecology Review* 5: 60–8.

Clark, W. C. 2001. 'Research systems for a transition toward sustainability', *Gaia* 10: 264–6.

Coglianese, C. 1997. 'Assessing consensus: the promise and performance of negotiated rulemaking', *Duke Law Journal* 46: 1255.

Cooke, R. M. 1991. *Experts in Uncertainty: Opinion and Subjective Probability in Science.* Oxford, UK: Oxford University Press.

Cross, F. B. 1996. 'Paradoxical perils of the precautionary principle', *Washington and Lee Law Review* 53: 851.

de Sadeleer, N. 2002. *Environmental Principles: From Political Slogans to Legal Rules.* Oxford, UK: Oxford University Press.

Dienel, P. C. 1989. 'Contributing to social decision methodology: citizen reports on technological projects', in Vlek, C. and Cvetkovich, G. (eds.) *Social Decision Methodology for Technological Projects.* Dordrecht, The Netherlands: Kluwer, pp. 133–51.

Douglas, M. 1990. 'Risk as a forensic resource', *Daedalus* 119(4): 1–16.

Dryzek, J. S. 1994. *Discursive Democracy: Politics, Policy, and Political Science*, Second edition. Cambridge, UK: Cambridge University Press.

Durant, J. and Joss, S. 1995. *Public Participation in Science.* London, UK: Science Museum.

Environment Agency 1998. *Strategic Risk Assessment. Further Developments and Trials. R&D Report E70.* Bristol, UK: Environment Agency.

European Commission 2001. *European Governance: A White Paper* COM (2001) 428 final. URL: http://europa.eu.int/eurlex/en/com/cnc/2001/com20010428 en01.pdf.

European Commission 2002. *Treaty Establishing the European Community: Official Journal of the European Commission*, C 325, pp. 33–184,

24 December 2002. URL: http://europa.eu.int/eur-lex/en/treaties/dat/
EC_consol.pdf.

Fiorino, D. J. 1990. 'Citizen participation and environmental risk: a survey
of institutional mechanisms', *Science, Technology and Human Values*
15: 226–43.

Fisher, E. 2001. 'Is the precautionary principle justiciable?' *Journal of
Environmental Law* 13: 317.

Fisher, E. 2002. 'Precaution, precaution everywhere: developing a common
understanding of the precautionary principle in the European Community', *Maastricht Journal of European and Comparative Law* 9: 7–28.

Functowicz, S. O. and Ravetz, J. R. 1992. 'Three types of risk assessment
and the emergence of post-normal science', in Krimsky, S. and Golding,
D. (eds.) *Social Theories of Risk*. Westport, CT: Praeger, pp. 251–73.

Funtowicz, S. O., Shepherd, I., Wilkinson, D. and Ravetz, J. 2000. 'Science
and governance in the European Union: a contribution to the debate',
*Science and Public Policy* 27: 327–36.

Gee, D., Harremoes, P., Keys, J., MacGarvin, M., Stirling, A., Vaz, S. and
Wynne, B. 2001. *Late Lesson from Early Warnings: The Precautionary
Principle 1898–2000*. Copenhagen: European Environment Agency.

Goodwin, P. and Wright, G. 2004. *Decision Analysis for Management
Judgment*. Chichester, UK: Wiley.

Graham, J. D. and Rhomberg, L. 1996. 'How risks are identified and
assessed', in Kunreuther, H. and Slovic, P. (eds.) *Challenges in Risk
Assessment and Risk Management*. London, UK: Sage, pp. 15–24.

Gregory, R. S. 2004. 'Valuing risk management choices', in McDaniels, T. and
Small, M. J. (eds.) *Risk Analysis and Society: An Interdisciplinary Characterization of the Field*. Cambridge, UK: Cambridge University Press, pp. 213–50.

Gregory, R. S., McDaniels, T. and Fields, D. 2001. 'Decision aiding, not
dispute resolution: a new perspective for environmental negotiation',
*Journal of Policy Analysis and Management* 20: 415–32.

Habermas, J. 1970. 'Towards a theory of communicative competence',
*Inquiry* 13: 363–72.

Habermas, J. 1987. *The Philosophical Discourse of Modernity*. Cambridge,
UK: Polity.

Habermas, J. 1991. *Moral Consciousness and Communicative Action*.
Second edition translated by C. Lenhardt and S. Weber Nicholson.
Cambridge, MA: MIT Press.

Hajer, M. and Wagenaar, H. 2003. *Deliberative Policy Analysis: Understanding Governance in the Network Society*. Cambridge UK:
Cambridge University Press.

Hance, B. J., Chess, C. and Sandman, P. M. 1988. *Improving Dialogue with
Communities: A Risk Communication Manual for Government*.

Environmental Communication Research Programme, Rutgers University, New Brunswick, NJ.

Harter, P.J. 1982. 'Negotiating regulations: a cure for malaise', *Georgetown University Law Journal* 71: 1.

HSE (Health and Safety Executive) 2001. *Reducing Risk – Protecting People*. London, UK: Health and Safety Executive.

IRGC (International Risk Governance Council) 2005. *Risk Governance: Towards an Integrative Approach*. Geneva: International Risk Governance Council.

Jaeger, C., Renn, O., Rosa, E. and Webler, T. 2001. *Risk, Uncertainty and Rational Action*. London, UK: Earthscan.

Kasperson, R.E., Golding, D. and Kasperson, J.X. 1999. 'Risk, trust and democratic theory', in Cvetkovich, G. and Löfstedt, R. (eds.) *Social Trust and the Management of Risk*. London, UK: Earthscan, pp. 22–41.

Kemp, R. 1985. 'Planning, political hearings, and the politics of discourse', in Forester, J. (ed.) *Critical Theory and Public Life*. Cambridge, MA: MIT Press, pp. 177–201.

Klinke, A. and Renn, O. 2001. 'Precautionary principle and discursive strategies: classifying and managing risks', *Journal of Risk Research* 4: 159–73.

Klinke, A. and Renn, O. 2002. 'A new approach to risk evaluation and management: risk-based, precaution-based and discourse-based management', *Risk Analysis* 22: 1071–94.

Laudan, L. 1996. 'The pseudo-science of science? The demise of the demarcation problem', in Laudan, L. (ed.) *Beyond Positivism and Relativism: Theory, Method and Evidence*. Boulder, CO: Westview, pp. 166–92.

Lave, L. 1987. 'Health and safety risk analyses: information for better decisions', *Science* 236: 291–5.

Löfstedt, R.E. 1997. *Risk Evaluation in the United Kingdom: Legal Requirements, Conceptual Foundations, and Practical Experiences with Special Emphasis on Energy Systems*. Working Paper No. 92. Akademie für Technikfolgenabschätzung: Stuttgart, Germany.

Löfstedt, R.E. 2004. *The Swing of the Pendulum in Europe: From Precautionary Principle to (Regulatory) Impact Assessment*. Working Paper 04–07. New York: AEI-Brookings Joint Center for Regulatory Studies.

Löfstedt, R.E. 2005. *Risk Management in Post-Trust Societies*. New York: Palgrave.

Lundgren, R.E. 1994. *Risk Communication: A Handbook for Communicating Environmental, Safety, and Health Risks*. Columbus, OH: Battelle Press.

Majone, G. 2002. 'What price safety? The precautionary principle and its policy implications', *Journal of Common Market Studies* 40: 89–109.

McCarthy, T. 1975. 'Translator's introduction', in Habermas, J. *Legitimation Crisis*. Boston, MA: Beacon Press.

Mitchell, R. B., Clark, W. C., Cash, D. W. and Dickson, N. M. 2006. *Global Environmental Assessments: Information and Influence*. Cambridge, MA: MIT Press.

Morgan, G. M., Henrion, M. and Small, M. 1990. *Uncertainty: A Guide to Dealing with Uncertainty in Quantitative Risk and Policy Analysis*. Cambridge, UK: Cambridge University Press.

OECD 2002. *Guidance Document on Risk Communication for Chemical Risk Management*. Paris, France: OECD.

OECD 2003. *Emerging Systemic Risks: Final Report to the OECD Futures Project*. Paris, France: OECD.

O'Riordan, T. 1976. *Environmentalism*. London, UK: Pion.

O'Riordan, T. 1991a. 'Stability and transformation in environmental government', *Political Quarterly* 62: 167–85.

O'Riordan, T. 1991b. 'The new environmentalism and sustainable development', *Science of the Total Environment* 108: 5–15.

O'Riordan, T. 2005. 'On justice, sustainability, and democracy', *Environment* 47(6), 2.

O'Riordan, T. and Cameron, J. (eds.) 1994. *Interpreting the Precautionary Principle*. London, UK: Earthscan.

O'Riordan, T. and Jordan, A. 1995. *The Precautionary Principle: Science, Politics and Ethics*. Working Paper PA-95-02. Centre for Social and Economic Research on the Global Environment, University of East Anglia, Norwich.

O'Riordan, T., Burgess, J. and Szerszynski, B. (eds.) 1999. *Deliberative and Inclusionary Processes: A Report from Two Seminars*. Working Paper PA-99-06. Centre for Social and Economic Research on the Global Environment, University of East Anglia, Norwich.

O'Riordan, T., Cameron, J. and Jordan, A. (eds.) 2001. *Reinterpreting the Precautionary Principle*. London, UK: Cameron and May.

Perritt, H. H. 1986. 'Negotiated rulemaking in practice', *Journal of Policy Analysis and Management* 5: 482–95.

Peterson, M. 2003. 'Transformative decision rules', *Erkenntnis* 58: 71–85.

Peterson, M. 2006. 'The precautionary principle is incoherent', *Risk Analysis* 26: 595–601.

Petts, J. 1997. 'The public–expert interface in local waste management decisions: expertise, credibility, and process', *Public Understanding of Science* 6: 359–81.

Raffensberger, C. and Tickner, J. 1999. *Protecting Public Health and the Environment: Implementing the Precautionary Principle*. Washington DC: Island Press.

Renn, O. 1998. 'The role of risk communication and public dialogue for improving risk management', *Risk Decision and Policy* 3: 5–30.

Renn, O. 1999. 'Participative technology assessment: meeting the challenges of uncertainty and ambivalence', *Futures Research Quarterly* 15(3): 81–97.

Renn, O. 2004. 'The challenge of integrating deliberation and expertise: participation and discourse in risk management', in MacDaniels, T. L. and Small, M. J. (eds.) *Risk Analysis and Society: An Interdisciplinary Characterization of the Field*. Cambridge, UK: Cambridge University Press, pp. 289–366.

Renn, O. and Webler, T. 1998. 'Der kooperative Diskurs – theoretische Grundlagen, Anforderungen, Möglichkeiten', in Renn, O., Kastenholz, H., Schild, P. and Wilhelm, U. (eds.) *Abfallpolitik im kooperativen Diskurs: Bürgerbeteiligung bei der Standortsuche für eine Deponie im Kanton Aargau*. Zürich: Hochschulverlag, pp. 3–103.

Resnik, D. 2003. 'Is the precautionary principle unscientific?' *Studies in History and Philosophy of Biological and Biomedical Sciences* 34: 329–44.

Rhodes, R. A. W. 1997. *Understanding Governance: Policy Networks, Governance, Reflexivity and Accountability*. Milton Keynes, UK: Open University Press.

RISKO 2000. 'Mitteilungen für Kommission für Risikobewertung des Kantons Basel-Stadt: Seit 10 Jahren beurteilt die RISKO die Tragbarkeit von Risiken', *Bulletin* 3 (June), 2–3.

Rose-Ackerman, S. 1994. 'Consensus versus incentives: a skeptical look at regulatory negotiation', *Duke Law Journal* 1: 1206.

Rossi, J. 1997. 'Participation run amok: the costs of mass participation for deliberative agency decision making', *Northwestern University Law Review* 92: 173–249.

Rowe, G. and Frewer, L. 2000. 'Public participation methods: an evaluative review of the literature', *Science, Technology and Human Values* 25: 3–29.

Sand, P. H. 2000. 'The precautionary principle: a European perspective', *Human and Ecological Risk Assessment* 6: 445–58.

Sandin, P., Peterson, M., Hansson, S. O., Rudén, Ch. and Juthé, A. 2002. 'Five charges against the precautionary principle', *Journal of Risk Research* 5: 287–99.

Stern, P. C. and Fineberg, H. V. 1996. *Understanding Risk: Informing Decisions in a Democratic Society*. National Research Council, Committee on Risk Characterization. Washington DC: National Academy Press.

Stirling, A. 1998. 'Risk at a turning point?' *Journal of Risk Research* 1: 97–109.

Stirling, A. 1999. *On Science and Precaution in the Management of Technological Risk, Volume I: Synthesis Study.* EUR19056 EN Report to the EU Forward Studies Unit. Seville: European Science and Technology Observatory. URL: ftp://ftp.jrc.es/pub/EURdoc/eur19056IIen.pdf.

Stirling, A. 2003. 'Risk, uncertainty and precaution: some instrumental implications from the social sciences', in Berkhout, F., Leach, M. and Scoones, I. (eds.) *Negotiating Environmental Change.* Cheltenham, UK: Elgar.

Stirling, A. 2005. 'Opening up or closing down: analysis, participation and power in the social appraisal of technology', in Leach, M., Scoones, I. and Wynne, B. (eds.) *Science and Citizens: Globalization and the Challenge of Engagement.* London, UK: Zed Books, pp. 218–31.

Stone, C. 2001. 'Is there a precautionary principle?' *Environmental Law Reporter* 31: 10790.

Thompson, M., Ellis, W. and Wildavsky, A. 1990. *Cultural Theory.* Boulder, CO: Westview.

Tuler, S. and Webler, T. 1999. 'Designing an analytic deliberative process for environmental health policy making in the US nuclear weapons complex', *Risk: Health, Safety and Environment* 10(65): 65–87.

van Asselt, M. B. A. 2000. *Perspectives on Uncertainty and Risk.* Dordrecht, The Netherlands: Kluwer.

Viklund, M. 2002. *Risk Policy: Trust, Risk Perception, and Attitudes.* Stockholm School of Economics.

Von Winterfeldt, D. and Edwards, W. 1984. 'Patterns of conflict about risk debates', *Risk Analysis* 4: 55–68.

WBGU (Wissenschaftlicher Beirat der Bundesregierung Globale Umweltveränderungen) 2000. *World in Transition: Strategies for Managing Global Environmental Risks.* Berlin, Germany: Springer.

Webler, T. 1995. 'Right discourse in citizen participation: an evaluative yardstick', in Renn, O., Webler, T. and Wiedemann, P. (eds.) *Fairness and Competence in Citizen Participation: Evaluating New Models for Environmental Discourse.* Dordrecht, The Netherlands: Kluwer, pp. 35–86.

Webler, T. 1999. 'The craft and theory of public participation: a dialectical process', *Risk Research* 2: 55–71.

Wynne, B. 2002. 'Risk and environment as legitimatory discourses of technology: reflexivity inside out?' *Current Sociology* 50: 459–77.

# 11 | *Economics and the governance of sustainable development*

### SIMON DIETZ AND ERIC NEUMAYER

## Introduction

In this chapter we assess the role of economics in the governance of sustainable development. First, we investigate how well the mainstream environmental and resource economics paradigm has helped us understand the nature of sustainable development. We explain the context in which this paradigm developed and the main propositions made during its formative years. These help us to understand the paradigm's approach to sustainable development (or sustainability – we do not distinguish between these two terms, although some do). Taken to the limits of formalism, it culminates in the social planner's desire to optimise human welfare over time and the drive to place monetary values on, and aggregate, all forms of wealth, including natural assets. This chapter then outlines the strengths and weaknesses of this paradigm by comparing it with an alternative set of approaches that have come to be known as ecological economics.

Our second question is, how can economics inform governance systems for sustainable development? Thus the final section of this chapter reflects on the contributions that economics can make to the policy process, using two high-profile examples: the Copenhagen Consensus devised by Bjørn Lomborg (Lomborg, 2001) and the Stern Review of the Economics of Climate Change (Stern, 2007). Although economic analysis has much to offer (for example in the design of policy instruments for delivering sustainable development), we caution firmly against a reliance on formal modelling to prescribe a single, optimal path of policy. Instead we should draw upon a broader range of evidence, in which such formal approaches are nevertheless useful. We emphasise the need for economic research on sustainable development to take serious and explicit account of its ethical implications, of uncertainty about the consequences of depleting the natural

environment, and of the possibly essential and non-substitutable role
of the natural environment in sustainable development.

Before proceeding, we should define what we mean by sustainable
development and governance. Across many disciplines and perspectives, most would agree that a theory of sustainable development
should, first, engage with equity, both across and within human
generations (if not further between humans and non-humans); and,
second, comprise three pillars – economic, environmental and social.
In this context, the approach to sustainable development that we
follow is strongest in its focus on intergenerational (human) equity
and on environmental sustainability. In particular, we focus on sustaining the world's capacity to meet human needs and provide for
human welfare. A much trickier task is defining what constitutes this
capacity, as we discuss later in the chapter.

We define governance for sustainable development as the sum of
decision-making structures and principal guidelines for shaping the
process of policy making in ways that support sustainable development. In this chapter, we ask what input economics should make to
the design of these governing arrangements.

## Economic approaches to the sustainability challenge: an introduction

When, in the 1960s, a new wave of environmental concerns emerged
in popular, political and social-scientific consciousness, economics
responded by opening its existing analytical toolbox. This toolbox
exemplified so-called neoclassical or marginalist economics, and its
application to contemporary problems of natural resource depletion
and environmental degradation gave birth to environmental and
resource economics as we recognise it today.

Neoclassical economics is a remarkably self-contained – some
would say introspective – theory of the economy involving a high
degree of abstraction and mathematical formalism. Neoclassical
economics is largely based on the idea of optimisation, whereby
producers and consumers behave as if they optimise a function, thus
comparing their private benefits at the margin (that is, incentives
resulting from incremental changes) with their private costs at the
margin. It attempts to explain the value of goods, services and factors

of production in terms of an exchange between supply and demand. That is, the value of something is reflective not just, as classical economists such as Smith, Ricardo and Marx postulated, of how much it costs to make, but moreover of how much consumers are willing to pay for it.

In particular, in assuming that both producers and consumers are driven by the rational desire to maximise their own lot, neoclassical economics shows that, given other key assumptions, an equilibrium price exists where supply and demand intersect. This arises because, to both parties, the cost of producing and consuming one more or less unit of something is greater than the benefit. In any given market, this equilibrium represents the most efficient allocation of scarce economic resources. The notion of an efficient (thereby optimal) equilibrium naturally attained via the independent, self-interested behaviour of economic agents is the *leitmotif* of neoclassical economics. In fact, it goes right back to Adam Smith's 'invisible hand' of the market.

Modern neoclassical economics focuses almost exclusively on microeconomic issues. This has two important consequences. Firstly, it emphasises the structure of economic activity and its allocative efficiency rather than its overall scale. Secondly, it is fundamentally a theory of resource scarcity in a static economy, lacking the long-run focus of classical economics. Although plenty of dynamic equilibrium models exist that do project decades into the future, the transition of the economy is represented in a very basic way.

A further important feature of the economic mainstream is that welfare economics – the dominant normative theory – is usually grounded in a variant of utilitarianism that emphasises sovereign consumer preferences as the moral yardstick against which to make judgements about whether the allocation of resources to one purpose is better than another. Although the theoretical limits to this approach have been intensively debated even within the discipline (for example, the difficulty of making (cardinal) inter-personal comparisons of utility), the practical result is that such judgements are ultimately reduced to the question of which configuration of the economy produces the most utility or welfare on aggregate terms, possibly after allowing for some weighting within and between generations.

By seeking – as far as is possible – to transfer neoclassical economic axioms to environmental problems, environmental economics has developed a set of fairly restrictive assumptions, of which the following are the most salient (Weintraub, 1985):

1. economic agents exist;
2. they have invariant, complete preferences over outcomes;
3. they optimise independently of each other in relation to constraints such as the availability of production factors, technological possibilities and disposable income;
4. they have full, relevant knowledge of their decision problems;
5. their choices are made in fully integrated markets;
6. observable outcomes are fully co-ordinated and must therefore be discussed with respect to a general equilibrium.

Clearly, not all of these will hold when the economy–environment interface is brought into the equation. Indeed, it was precisely by focusing on the circumstances in which one or two of these assumptions might break down (primarily number 5) that environmental economics was best able to make a unique contribution. The point, however, is that environmental economics:

concentrated on the development of auxiliary conditions in partial equilibrium settings which allow at least some features (for example, invariant preferences) of the standard paradigm to fit observed phenomena (Crocker, 1999: 36).

Hence, the key outputs of the environmental economics research programme from the 1960s to the 1980s included, most notably, the theory of missing markets, the attempt to place monetary values on the surpluses foregone when markets are missing (via environmental valuation), the design of allocation systems capable of realising foregone surpluses (e.g. Pigovian taxes, tradeable permits, the Coase theorem, etc.), and rules on the optimal depletion of renewable and non-renewable resources.

## Environmental and resource economics approaches to sustainable development

### *Origins and key assumptions*

The emergence of the sustainable-development agenda toward the end of the 1980s was bound up with the growing prominence of pervasive, global environmental problems such as climate change. Evidently the tripartite objective of long-term economic, environmental and social sustainability could not be realised without countering such problems. Yet as Siniscalco (1999), among others, has pointed out, up to this point environmental and resource economics had largely, though not exclusively, focused on environmental problems that were relatively limited in time and space (i.e. ones which were presumed to arise in a closed, competitive, full-information economy). The same could less confidently be said of sustainable development. It places several important demands on environmental economics that are covered later on in this chapter.

In fact, environmental economics resisted the temptation to break with orthodoxy, and applied the neoclassical theory of economic growth and its various models to understand sustainable development. These consider the optimal division of economic output, which is produced using labour and capital, between consumption and saving. The rule they seek to establish is how much to consume now and how much to invest in capital to increase consumption later. The typical model is highly aggregated, and assumes there is one representative economic agent or social planner making an economy-wide decision, where production, consumption, saving and investment are summed over all the economy's sectors. Suspending, for the time being, a particular concern for future generations, this type of model is traditionally solved by estimating the highest possible discounted consumption path over time: the optimal growth path or so-called 'golden rule' of human development.

In early versions of such analysis, production was specified as a function of produced or man-made capital (e.g. machinery and infrastructure) and labour. As the role of the environment and natural resources was embraced, natural resources – both non-renewable (fossil fuels and minerals) and renewable (e.g. timber) – were included as a factor of production (Dasgupta and Heal, 1974; Solow, 1974). These are considered to be forms of natural capital. This analysis can also be extended to include human capital (i.e. the knowledge and skills embodied in people) and, conceptually if not empirically, social capital (networks of shared norms and values that facilitate productive co-operation between people and groups). Crucially, early studies using such analysis assumed that natural capital was similar to produced capital and labour, and so could easily be substituted for them. This is the essence of what came to be known as 'weak sustainability' (Pearce *et al.*, 1989).

The key question posed in these pioneering studies was whether optimal growth, as defined above, was sustainable in the sense of allowing non-declining welfare in perpetuity. This was shown to be unlikely in a model including an essential, non-renewable natural resource as a factor of production. The basic result was that, save for great optimism about how little the economy is constrained by the natural resource, consumption falls to zero in the long run (Solow, 1974). Therefore it became necessary to establish specific rules allowing non-declining welfare over all time based on some maintenance of the capital stock, including natural capital. This was addressed by Hartwick (1977), who derived the rule that the rents from non-renewable resource depletion should be reinvested in other forms of capital.

Later, Pearce and Atkinson (1993) and Hamilton (1994) built on the so-called Hartwick rule, by setting out a theoretical and empirical measure of net investment in produced and natural capital (and later human capital – Hamilton, 1994) that has become known as genuine savings. Genuine savings measures net changes in produced, natural and human capital stocks, valued in monetary terms, in principle at their shadow prices. The aim of governance therefore should be to keep genuine savings above or equal to zero. Hence it is closely associated with another of environmental economics' great research endeavours: the construction of environmental, or green, accounts, which attempt to add natural assets to the decades-old practice of compiling national economic accounts (see United Nations *et al.*, 2003). The World Bank now regularly publishes a comparatively comprehensive set of genuine savings estimates for over 150 countries, which it calls net adjusted savings.

## Stylistic policy prescriptions

Before we can assess the contribution that environmental economics has made to the understanding and governance of sustainable development, we set out its main policy recommendations. At the outset, it must be stressed that environmental and resource economics does not advocate a neoliberal, laissez-faire approach in which the free market is left to its own devices. A basic premise of environmental economics is that many environmental resources lack an appropriate price because of missing markets. Hence the environmental economics doctrine is entirely compatible with state intervention. We must impute a price for environmental resources where the scarcity signal is absent and find the most efficient policy design that will re-allocate the economy's other resources around this price. Typically, economists prefer flexible and efficient instruments of governing, such as environmental taxes and tradable resource or emission permits, to inflexible and inefficient 'command-and-control' type instruments. Often, policy makers fail to heed the economists' advice: command-and-control regulation remains the instrument of choice in most national environmental policy systems (see Chapter 1). This has prompted some economists to wonder why the patient (i.e. the policy maker) does not follow the doctor's (i.e. the economist's) preferred cure (Kirchgässner and Schneider, 2003).

Not even the correct shadow-pricing of environmental resources would be sufficient to ensure intergenerational equity (defined as non-declining utility), because optimal growth may well still be unsustainable. This is the extra condition (or 'rider') required by sustainable development. Instead, a policy maker following the prescriptions of environmental economics could set a macroeconomic constraint on investment, in which total net investment in all forms of capital (including natural capital) is forbidden from becoming negative. Following this rule would, without doubt, be of tremendous benefit in resource-rich developing countries, many of whom have an imprudent track record of resource management (see World Bank, 2006). Perhaps surprisingly then, environmental economics privileges an explicit ethical standpoint in favour of future generations above the efficient allocation of resources in the present.

## Environmental and resource economics: strengths and weaknesses

### *The positive contributions*

Simply put, the key claim made in environmental economics research is that the environment can, and indeed should, be given what Frank Convery terms a 'parity of esteem' in managing the macro and the micro economy. Thus from the economic side of the sustainability problem, the greatest contribution made by environmental economics is that of demonstrating, through flexible and powerful concepts such as externality, that environmental degradation has an economic cost. Equally, environmental economics has sought to point out that there are opportunity costs to environmental protection. Although one can legitimately object on ethical grounds to placing monetary values on natural assets (see below), it is difficult to escape the point that environmental sustainability has to compete with other sustainability objectives, and with 'extra-sustainability' objectives, in securing scarce economic resources. One of the greatest strengths of environmental economics is that it calls for these dilemmas to be addressed head-on.

In some respects, the rigorous and (internally) consistent theoretical framework of environmental economics is a great strength, provided we suspend for now any lingering doubts about the validity of its assumptions. One can think of it as an analytical corset into which sustainability concerns are squeezed. To understand why this is a benefit, it is important to realise that the objective and even the science of sustainability has become deeply politicised (O'Riordan, 2004), due in large part to the flexibility of interpretation enjoyed by those wishing to wear the badge of sustainability. There can be little disagreement with the ultimate aim of development that lasts, but in trying to arrive at a more workable definition, it would not be an exaggeration to suggest that there are almost as many definitions as there are stakeholders. This is amply reflected in the measures of sustainability chosen by many governmental institutions. For instance, the UK government has set out no less than sixty-eight indicators of sustainable development (twenty framework indicators and forty-eight others) in its latest strategy (DEFRA, 2005).

If the purpose of such indicators is managerial rather than communicative (MacGillivray and Zadek, 1995), then the problems are twofold. Firstly, for any given indicator, there is rarely an obvious, direct interpretation of a unit change vis-à-vis sustainability. For example, indicator 4 in the UK's set is the amount of renewable energy generated as a percentage of total electricity. But how much renewable energy do we need to generate in order to move onto a sustainable path? Environmental economics argues that this puzzle cannot be solved without considering many other indicators on a common numeraire. Secondly, what are we to make of a positive change in one indicator at the same time as a negative change in another? We are, for example, accustomed to seeing increases in greenhouse gas emissions (indicator 1) accompany increases in gross domestic product (indicator 32). The meaning of this dichotomy is a question of their contribution to human welfare and the degree of substitutability permitted between them. Even if the objective of shadow-pricing these very disparate changes in the total capital stock is thought unrealistic, environmental economics has, at the very least, contributed a theory that forces us to confront and possibly resolve such trade-offs.

A similar argument, put forward by Dubourg and Pearce (1996), is the question of what is the appropriate scale at which to target sustainable development policy? Increasingly, policy discourses focus on meso- or even micro-units such as the sustainable business sector, the sustainable city or the sustainable household. But ensuring that every one of these units is potentially sustainable is unlikely to be efficient. Instead, such policies could restrict welfare to a level below that actually possible on a sustainable path. For environmental economics, the appropriate point of policy intervention is rather the macro level, supported by environmental accounts that lead to economy-wide sustainable investment decisions.

On a more practical level, the toolbox of environmental governance is certainly richer as a result of several decades of research into economic policy instruments, such as environmental taxes, tradable permits, incentives for innovation and so on. These may not always be suited in a simple and unfettered manner to the policy issue in question, but they are likely to be a key component in the eventual mix of governing instruments.

## The weaknesses

Unsurprisingly, the unbending cost–benefit logic of welfarist approaches to sustainable development, in which policies to preserve the environment are only justified if the monetary benefits of environmental degradation are smaller than the monetary costs, is as much a weakness as a strength. First, the preference-satisfaction brand of utilitarianism on which welfare economics is founded precludes incompatible systems of ethics and conceptions of equity. In other words, as much as we can praise environmental economics for what it includes, we must recognise what it excludes. Second, in order to ensure tractability, complex and unpredictable natural and social phenomena are usually forced to take on a relatively simplistic form that may be a poor and, even more critically, misleading representation of reality. Of course, science often proceeds on the basis of theories and models that simplify reality. The key is to accept this in a transparent fashion and place caveats on any policy recommendations that are made. Sadly, this point is not always embraced, as we show in a later section.

As a consequence of the first point, environmental economics relies upon a narrow theory of ethics and equity. In some sense this is a facile critique, since favouring one particular theory of moral philosophy usually results in the exclusion of others (the efforts of Amartya Sen being a notable exception – see Sen, 1999). Yet the extensive demands of the sustainable development agenda compel environmental economics to address much greater inequities than it is familiar with, including those between human generations and between human beings and non-human beings. On the one hand, environmental economics is wary of any conception of environmental preservation that is not directly based on economic values. For example, the bioethical principle that humans should preserve other species because they possess an intrinsic value and hence moral standing – even if they create a net economic benefit when they are pushed to extinction – is anathema to the mode of utilitarianism that focuses on the satisfaction of human preferences. On the other hand, this comparison reveals a further limitation to environmental economics, because it reflects elements of both consequential and procedural equity. Utilitarianism is a consequentialist theory of moral philosophy, whereby the moral worth of a policy is determined solely by its consequences. This differs from procedural or deontological theories, according to which the policy process itself makes the resulting action right or wrong. Hence, environmental economics is also difficult to reconcile with a procedural approach to sustainability (see, for example, Chapters 2, 7, 8 and 9), in which the primary objective is equitable participation in the decision-making process. According to the terminology developed in Chapter 1, a fair process that results in a below-par outcome may still be judged a success.

On the other hand, it is also true that environmental economics has done much to invigorate the debate on intergenerational fairness to human beings through debates about discounting future benefits and costs (see Pearce *et al.*, 2003). What is implicit in the environmental-economic analysis of sustainable development in particular is a commitment not to diminish the opportunities of future generations. The early work on optimal growth and sustainable development found that a welfarist approach does not guarantee sustainable development. Thus the interest in sustainable development from an environmental and resource economics perspective is ultimately rooted in some explicit ethical commitment to future generations that comes from beyond its traditional normative basis. Nevertheless, in other respects it has a limited amount to say on the role of equity in sustainable development. Where intra-generational concerns are addressed, they tend to be reduced to the objective of increasing total consumption (more for everyone) or weighting the overall social welfare function in such a way that extra consumption is worth more to low-income groups.

Turning to its representation of natural and social phenomena, we focus on the treatment of the natural world in environmental economics, especially the 'weak sustainability' assumption that natural capital is infinitely substitutable. It is often claimed (most famously by Daly, 1977) that natural capital has no easy substitutes, which is the basis of the 'strong sustainability' paradigm (Pearce *et al.*, 1989). It is highly unlikely, for instance, that there are substitutes for basic life-support systems (Barbier *et al.*, 1994). Most generally, this means the global environmental and ecological system that provides us with the basic functions of food, water, breathable air and a stable climate. The prescription that follows is precautionary: preserve critical natural capital in physical terms so that its functions remain intact. Although the capital approach to sustainability may thus continue to be valid, the overall cost–benefit calculus of environmental economics must be scaled back, because the shadow price of critical natural capital is, by definition, infinite.

Even if natural capital were in principle substitutable, it can have two further complicating features that environmental economics is fundamentally ill-equipped to deal with: (1) the uncertainty attached to the way in which natural processes such as the global carbon and biogeochemical cycles work; and (2) the threat of large-scale, discontinuous and irreversible losses of natural capital.

Environmental economics regards risk as a situation in which the set of all possible states of the world, the probability distribution over this set, and the resulting welfare effects can be objectively known.

Uncertainty differs from risk in that no objective knowledge exists (see Chapters 9 and 10), merely subjective beliefs. The standard response of economics has been to use option and quasi-option values. Option value is the expected value of refraining from an action that leads with some objective or subjective probability to irreversible environmental damage, in order to keep the option open of using the environmental resource in the future. Quasi-option value is the value of delaying irreversible environmental damage in order to acquire the improved knowledge that would facilitate a better-informed decision in the future. The problem with this approach is that in cases of severe uncertainty, we cannot rely on estimates of option and quasi-option value.

This would not matter so much if all environmental damage were local and reversible. However, the sustainability problem emphasises that humankind has initiated many processes that lead to large-scale, often global, potentially discontinuous and often irreversible environmental change. Global climate change and biodiversity extinction are the most prominent examples. What are the option and quasi-option values connected with keeping greenhouse gas emissions within the limits of the absorptive capacity of the atmosphere? What are the option and quasi-option values connected with preventing large-scale biodiversity extinction? To these questions we cannot give an acceptably precise answer, not even a 'ball park' figure.

## Ecological economics: a brief summary

Starting in the late 1980s – but with roots going much further back – a new paradigm coalesced known as ecological economics. It aspires to build on some of the strengths of environmental economics, while at the same time overcoming some of its major limitations. For example, it dismisses neither the idea of allocative efficiency nor the policy prescription to internalise environmental externalities. However, it superimposes on efficiency considerations the idea that the overall scale of the economy matters (Daly, 1977). It also affords much more prominence to issues of equity and fairness.

Contrary to the environmental and resource economics paradigm, the ecological economics paradigm is more diffuse. In large part, this reflects the challenge of bringing together diverse perspectives in developing an ecological economic identity, including elements of economics, ecology, thermodynamics and ethics, etc. At its heart lies a recognition that ecosystems and ecological processes are of the utmost importance to humankind, are highly complex and sometimes vulnerable to perturbations and, as a result (and most importantly of all), are difficult to monetise. It is premised on a precautionary approach (see Chapter 9) towards the idea of substituting natural capital for other forms of capital. Indeed, most ecological economists would subscribe to the idea of strong sustainability, which has two main schools of thought (Neumayer, 2003). One requires that the value of natural capital be preserved. The second requires that a subset of total natural capital be preserved in physical terms so that its core functions remain intact. This is so-called critical natural capital. In dealing with risk and uncertainty, ecological economics rejects option and quasi-option values, instead calling for the application of a less formalised precautionary principle. This requires the preservation of critical natural capital, unless the costs of preservation are demonstrated to be unacceptably high. Whatever the interpretation of strong sustainability, the size of the economy relative to the ecosystem becomes relevant, which partly explains why scale has reasserted itself as a legitimate economic concern.

The application of a less formalised precautionary principle, balanced against a criterion of excessive cost, has been rather obviously criticised by environmental and resource economists, because it represents an arbitrary substitution of natural capital for other forms of capital. In essence, they argue that unless one uses a formal cost–benefit framework, the outcome is likely to be inefficient and therefore undesirable. Yet this tends to ignore the difficulties that we have already highlighted in pinning down what is an efficient level of environmental protection. Therefore economics cannot give society a definitive answer, a point which we return to below. Some have rightly argued that the precautionary principle is vague (Turner and Hartzell, 2004). Yet this feature could also be regarded as a strength: the principle has to be applied flexibly, its meaning depending on the context and process in which it is used (see Chapters 9 and 10).

Hanley *et al.* (2001) doubt that environmental and ecological economics are really so different, 'merely stressing different aspects of the same problems' (Hanley and Atkinson, 2003: 102). Hence this (false) distinction is neither useful nor productive. It reminds us that many of the same people who founded environmental economics went on to found ecological economics, although this seems to deny the

possibility that minds (and with them allegiances) can change. They
also recall that some ambitious valuation exercises in ecological
economics have sought to monetise ecosystem functions (e.g. Costanza
*et al.*, 1997), although we would argue that the true thrust of
ecological economics remains the idea of limited substitutability of
natural capital. They go on to point out that few environmental and
resource economists would unequivocally endorse weak sustainability
and that recent advances in the monetary valuation of environmental
assets have emphasised qualitative inputs (e.g. Kenyon *et al.*, 2001)
and competing, non-economic criteria (as incorporated in multi-
criteria analysis). We commend this move, but point out that it is
often because of, rather than in spite of, work in complementary
disciplines that horizons are broadening. The development of a more
pluralistic environmental economics in certain key areas is thus
something to be welcomed.

## How should economics engage in governing for sustainable development?

Having discussed the strengths and weaknesses of environmental and
ecological economics, we would like to explore the role of economic
analysis in governance for sustainable development. We focus on the
overarching analytical questions, rather than detailed questions about
which policy instruments to apply in which circumstances. To this
end, we consider two recent, high-profile examples. The first was the
so-called Copenhagen Consensus (www.copenhagencon
sensus.com), which in our view offered a salutary lesson in the role it
should *not* play. The second was the Stern Review on the Economics
of Climate Change (Stern, 2007). Much has been written in support
and in opposition to the Stern Review. Even these two authors have
aired their differences (compare Dietz *et al.*, 2007, with Neumayer,
2007). Nonetheless, together we argue that the Stern Review takes a
broader and more suitable approach than the Copenhagen Consensus,
but leaves some unresolved questions about the relationship between
formal economic modelling and other methods of assessing the worth
of policy intervention.

The Copenhagen Consensus event was organised by the self-
proclaimed 'sceptical environmentalist', Bjørn Lomborg. He invited a
panel of eminent economists to set priorities among a very broad

range of global public-policy problems, from hunger and malnutrition through to trade reform and climate change. For each problem, the panel was asked to consider a 'challenge' paper, which was commissioned to estimate the net benefits of various policy proposals within a welfarist, cost–benefit framework. In addition, two further economists were commissioned to review each challenge paper. By monetising the net benefits of each proposal, it was in principle possible to compare policies across the entire list of global problems drawn up. The overall question was: how can the world best spend its scarce financial resources to maximise human wellbeing? The answer was summarised in a ranking of seventeen policies, based on their net present benefits. Table 11.1 reproduces the ranking from Lomborg (2004).

We focus on the ranking of climate-change policy. The three climate change policies considered in the exercise – an optimal carbon tax, the Kyoto Protocol and a value-at-risk tax designed to protect against low-probability and high-damage risks – were ranked lowest of all public policy options and branded 'bad' in absolute terms. The challenge paper for climate change was written by William Cline (2004) and adapted the formal cost–benefit model of Nordhaus and Boyer (2000). Cline attempted to monetise the global costs of reducing greenhouse gas emissions and the global damage costs of climate change over a period of several centuries, with the ultimate aim of prescribing the optimal path of emissions reductions that maximised utility. Although he argued that there were large net benefits to emissions reductions in each of the policies he considered, the review papers (Manne, 2004; Mendelsohn, 2004) and later the Consensus panel doubted his claims. Strong action on climate change was thus considered to be a bad idea.

By contrast, the Stern Review on the Economics of Climate Change (Stern, 2007) was commissioned by the UK Prime Minister and his Chancellor of the Exchequer to provide a wide-ranging economic assessment of climate change. It was led by Nicholas Stern, their chief advisor on the economics of climate change and development, and head of the UK Government Economic Service. This Review had a narrower focus than the Copenhagen Consensus, in that it only considered climate change. But it took a broader methodological approach, comparing the costs of reducing greenhouse gas emissions with the risks thereby avoided using a mixture of physical/natural scientific and economic studies. Notably no attempt was made to

**Table 11.1.** *The ranking of environmental and development problems in the Copenhagen Consensus*

| Project rating | Rank | Policy problem | Policy remedy |
|---|---|---|---|
| Very good | 1 | Diseases | Control of HIV/AIDS |
| | 2 | Malnutrition | Providing micronutrients |
| | 3 | Subsidies and trade | Trade liberalisation |
| | 4 | Diseases | Control of malaria |
| Good | 5 | Malnutrition | Development of new agricultural technologies |
| | 6 | Sanitation and water | Small-scale water technology for livelihoods |
| | 7 | Sanitation and water | Community-managed water supply and sanitation |
| | 8 | Sanitation and water | Research on water productivity in food production |
| | 9 | Government | Lowering the cost of starting a new business |
| Fair | 10 | Migration | Lowering barriers to migration for skilled workers |
| | 11 | Malnutrition | Improving infant and child nutrition |
| | 12 | Malnutrition | Reducing the prevalence of low birth weight |
| | 13 | Diseases | Scaled-up basic health services |
| Bad | 14 | Migration | Guest-worker programmes for the unskilled |
| | 15 | Climate change | 'Optimal' carbon tax |
| | 16 | Climate change | The Kyoto Protocol |
| | 17 | Climate change | Value-at-risk carbon tax |

*Source:* Lomborg (2004).

calculate the optimal climate policy within a single cost–benefit model, although such models were considered in various parts of the review. It arrived at a radically different conclusion to the Consensus panel (but similar of course to Cline, 2004) that strong and urgent reductions in greenhouse gas emissions should be a global policy priority.

What explains the different conclusions reached by these two apparently similar economic analyses? One important explanation centres on their treatment of intergenerational equity, which is at the heart of sustainable development. In formal economic analysis, this debate revolves around the discount rate, which is clearly of tremendous significance when the costs of reducing greenhouse gas emissions are relatively immediate yet the benefits occur with a lag of several decades.

In standard cost–benefit analysis of climate change, it is conventional to use a discount rate approximately equal to the opportunity cost of investment i.e. to market interest rates. This is known as a 'descriptive' approach to discounting and would typically lead to a discount rate of, say, 5 per cent per year. The discount rate used should not diverge from the opportunity cost of investment, since using a lower rate would channel scarce resources away from investments that provide the future with a higher real rate of return. However, in the Copenhagen Consensus exercise, Cline (2004) set a lower discount rate of around 2 per cent per year (variable) on the grounds of intergenerational fairness. This is known as a 'prescriptive' approach. Stern (2007) similarly set his rate to around 1.5 per cent per year. Cline was strongly rebuked for this by the Consensus reviewers and panel on the grounds that it leads to inconsistent conclusions and inefficient choices. Largely for this reason, climate change was ranked so low. Stern was similarly criticised (Nordhaus, 2007, is the best example).

This debate represents a revealing example of the problems that can be created by the narrow ethical basis of environmental and resource economics, especially when that ethical basis is largely implicit. Opponents of Cline and Stern insist that economists should look to existing market data in order to set a discount rate for climate-change policy. Anything else would in fact be 'unfair', they would argue, because applying a lower discount rate to climate-change policy than to other policies will be contrary to people's revealed preferences (recall the doctrine of consumer sovereignty) and divert scarce resources away from their most socially productive uses. This was the basic *modus operandi* of the Copenhagen Consensus. But Cline and Stern would presumably object that ethical decisions across many generations cannot simply be made by recourse to market interest rates, which are the result of a complex interaction of private decisions by consumers. With a discount rate of, say, 5 per cent per

year, even fairly catastrophic consequences of today's emissions of
greenhouse gases would be essentially worthless in one or two hun-
dred years. This provides a neat illustration of why optimisation from
the perspective of the market behaviour of the current generation
might not be sufficient to guarantee sustainable development.

To put this another way, there is at least one sense in which the
outcome of the Copenhagen Consensus – where short-term policies
win – was pre-ordained. In this case, an additional rider would be
required to try to secure the endowment of a stable climate system for
future generations. It so happens that Cline and Stern sought to do this
through the discount rate, although elsewhere it has been suggested
that sustainable climate policy could be brought about with a market
discount rate, subject to some safe maximum stock of greenhouse
gases in the atmosphere (see Weyant, 2008). In the end, there may not
be much difference between the outcomes of these approaches. Which
is more tractable will depend to a large extent on what sort of
evidence is available to answer their key questions.

But Neumayer has argued that discounting may be beside the point
(1999, 2003, 2007). The assumption that the costs and benefits of
climate policy can be discounted in respect of the real rate of return
elsewhere in the economy is only justified if all forms of capital are
truly substitutable, i.e. if one subscribes to a weak sustainability
paradigm. Drastic action can only be justified if climate change causes
damage that cannot be compensated by building up manufactured and
human capital. Sterner and Persson (2007) similarly show that strong
action on climate change can be justified even with conventionally
high discount rates by assuming sufficiently large future increases in
the relative prices of environmental goods and services, which would
dramatically raise the non-market damages from climate change and
counteract the effect of discounting the future.

This points us towards a second important pivot on which the cost–
benefit modelling of climate policy balances: how can we sensibly
represent the full set of complex relationships that link the growing
world economy with rising greenhouse gas emissions, increases in
temperature, climate change, environmental impacts and eventually
socio-economic responses? Formal economic models comprise a very
small number of simple equations to capture these processes. This
would not in itself be a problem, provided these were a good representation of reality. However, tremendous uncertainty characterises

every link in this chain. As a result, estimates of the marginal damage cost or social cost of greenhouse gas emissions, which are an alternative expression of the modelling problem to the optimal path, are hugely uncertain. A recent analysis of the uncertainty behind such estimates, in relation to carbon dioxide in particular, shows a range spanning at least three orders of magnitude (Downing *et al.*, 2005).

In making bold and ambitious comparisons between 'chalk and cheese' policy problems, the Copenhagen Consensus panel believed that narrow economic formalisms could give a fairly definitive indication of how systems of governance should prioritise their resources. But uncertainty of the kind bedevilling climate change policy makers renders their conclusions hugely unstable. To begin with, Cline (2004) conducted most of his modelling using best guesses; so he did not even presume to assess climate change from the perspective of risk. Moreover, we know that it is very restrictive to model climate change as a risk in the sense of a complete set of outcomes with associated probabilities. Hence the benefit–cost ratio underpinning the Copenhagen Consensus ranking could have been orders of magnitude higher, propelling climate change policy to the top of the table. By contrast, the Stern Review presented the larger part of its analysis on multiple metrics such as the consequences of climate change for food security and water availability. This required fewer assumptions and presented decision makers with a more transparent picture. However, its approach to formal modelling dominated the popular and academic debate. While it made some improvements to the previous literature, notably in extensive modelling of risks, this formal component was nevertheless subject to most of the same limitations, normative and positive, as any other studies. Thus the intention was to draw on the wider set of evidence presented in the Stern Review, particularly where the formal economics was weakest. The problem was, however, that it left the role of formal economic analysis (of other modes of analysis) open to interpretation.

To summarise, economic research has much to offer the sustainability debate. However, we need to avoid relying on catch-all answers that purport to tell us what sustainable development is and what should be done to achieve it. This reminds us of the chronically overworked super-computer Deep Thought, which appeared in Douglas Adams' *The Hitchhiker's Guide to the Galaxy*. Deep Thought had been commissioned to provide the ultimate answer to life, the universe and everything. After 7.5 million years of deliberation, it arrived at the eminently useless number of 42! When challenged to provide a better answer, Deep Thought responded: 'I think the problem, to be quite honest with you, is that you've never actually known what the question is.'

In looking for better questions (and answers), we need to draw upon diverse economic perspectives that seek to provide a richer understanding of the process of formulating sustainable development policy, as well as the detailed directions, if not the precise distances, in which such policies may take us.

## Conclusions

Environmental and resource economics offers important insights into the governance of sustainable development. At the practical level, it has given us a set of policy instruments, including taxation and tradable permit systems, that seek to harness the efficient forces of markets. At the theoretical level, it has given us the notion of opportunity cost and the consequent imperative of valuing natural assets based on their multifunctional contribution to human welfare. Although one can legitimately object on ethical grounds to placing monetary values on natural assets, it is difficult to escape the reality that environmental sustainability will have to compete with other sustainability objectives (as well as many other 'extra-sustainability' objectives) to secure scarce economic resources. Because sustainability has become a political concept – used by many organisations as a legitimating tool for essentially business-as-usual policy – as much as a rigorous scientific one, the consistent theoretical basis on which environmental and resource economics depends can only be considered a strength if the set of assumptions that underpin it hold true. But this is a very big 'if'.

We would argue that the nature of the sustainability problem stretches the credibility of narrow economic formalism, mandating a wider variety of approaches and a less ambitious overall objective. Large-scale environmental problems such as climate change and biodiversity loss are characterised by complex and novel ethical quandaries, by significant risk and uncertainty, by the threat of major, discontinuous and irreversible changes and often by the fundamental irreplaceability of many assets. None of these elements has been adequately or fully addressed by environmental and resource economics thus far. In many cases, relevant research has been undertaken from alternative economic standpoints, including ecological economics.

We have argued strongly that the Copenhagen Consensus provided a salutary lesson in how *not* to use economics to govern for sustainable development. It involved a select group of economists, including several Nobel laureates, being asked to prioritise on cost–benefit grounds tremendously disparate global public-policy problems, including climate change, education and migration. The suggestion, for instance, that trade reform is 'very good' but the Kyoto Protocol is 'bad', received the backing of a number of very reputable commentators, including *The Economist* magazine (although not any longer). This conclusion betrayed the fact that even if many environmental and resource economists recognise the limitations of economic models of climate change, other interested parties do not. This form of hubris is not supported by the theoretical and empirical state-of-the-art. The Stern Review approached its task with more humility. Indeed the task set for it was considerably less ambitious. But in pursuing a multi-track analysis, with formal economic modelling alongside physical and natural scientific analysis, it did raise some important questions about the significance of the different sources of evidence, even if it did not definitively answer them.

To conclude, we argue that economics has much to offer those seeking to govern for sustainable development, but it is not, and never will be, able to give a definitive answer to the ultimate question of what is the optimal path to sustainable development. Boundaries need to be set and a more pluralistic form of economics encouraged. Pulling back from the ideal of maximising global utility will allow economists to engage better with the true needs of national and international policy making, which include debating the merits and demerits of specific policies that govern for sustainable development.

# References

Barbier, E. B., Burgess, J. C. and Folke, C. 1994. *Paradise Lost? The Ecological Economics of Biodiversity*. London, UK: Earthscan.
Cline, W. R. 2004. *Meeting the Challenge of Global Warming*. Copenhagen Consensus, Copenhagen. URL: www.copenhagenconsensus.com.

Costanza, R., D'Arge, R., de Groot, S., Farber, S., Grasso, M., Hannon, B., Limburg, K., Naeem, S., O'Neill, R., Paruelo, J., Raskin, R., Sutton, P. and van Belt, M. 1997. 'The value of the world's ecosystem services and natural capital', *Nature* 387: 253–60.

Crocker, T. D. 1999. 'A short history of environmental and resource economics', in van den Bergh, J. C. J. M. (ed.) *Handbook of Environmental and Resource Economics*. Cheltenham, UK: Elgar.

Daly, H. E. (1977). *Steady-State Economics: The Economics of Biophysical Equilibrium and Moral Growth*. San Francisco, CA: Freeman.

Dasgupta, P. and Heal, M. G. 1974. 'The optimal depletion of exhaustible resources', *Review of Economic Studies* 41 (Supplement): 3–28.

DEFRA 2005. *The UK Government Sustainable Development Strategy*. London, UK: The Stationery Office.

Dietz, S., Hope, C. and Patmore, N. 2007. 'Some economics of "dangerous" climate change: reflections on the Stern Review', *Global Environmental Change* 17: 311–25.

Downing, T. E., Anthoff, D., Butterfield, R., Ceronsky, M., Grubb, M., Guo, J., Hepburn, C., Hope, C., Hunt, A., Li, A., Markandya, A., Moss, S., Nyong, A., Tol, R. S. J. and Watkiss, P. 2005. *Social Cost of Carbon: A Closer Look at Uncertainty*. Oxford, UK: Stockholm Environment Institute.

Dubourg, R. and Pearce, D. 1996. 'Paradigms for environmental choice: sustainability versus optimality', in Faucheux, S., Pearce, D. and Proops, J. (eds.) *Models of Sustainable Development*. Cheltenham, UK: Elgar.

Hamilton, K. 1994. 'Green adjustments to GDP', *Resources Policy* 20: 155–68.

Hanley, N. and Atkinson, G. 2003. 'Economics and sustainable development: what have we learnt and what do we still have to learn?' in Berkhout, F., Leach, M. and Scoones, I. (eds.) *Negotiating Environmental Change: New Perspectives from the Social Sciences*. Cheltenham, UK: Elgar, pp. 77–108.

Hanley, N., White, B. and Shogren, J. F. 2001. *Introduction to Environmental Economics*. Oxford, UK: Oxford University Press.

Hartwick, J. M. 1977. 'Intergenerational equity and the investing of rents of exhaustible resources', *American Economic Review* 67: 972–4.

Kenyon, W., Hanley, N. and Nevin, C. 2001 'Citizens' juries: an aid to environmental valuation?' *Environment and Planning C: Government and Policy* 19: 557–66.

Kirchgässner, G. and Schneider, F. 2003. 'On the political economy of environmental policy', *Public Choice* 115: 369–96.

Lomborg, B. 2001. *The Skeptical Environmentalist: Measuring the Real State of the World*. Cambridge, UK: Cambridge University Press.

Lomborg, B. (ed.) 2004. *Global Crises, Global Solutions*. Cambridge, UK: Cambridge University Press.

MacGillivray, A. and Zadek, S. 1995. *Accounting for Change: Indicators of Sustainable Development*. London, UK: New Economics Foundation.

Manne, A. S. 2004. *Global Climate Change: An Opponent's Notes*. Copenhagen Consensus. URL: www.copenhagenconsensus.com.

Mendelsohn, R. 2004. *Opponent Paper on Climate Change*. Copenhagen Consensus. URL: www.copenhagenconsensus.com.

Neumayer, E. 1999. 'Global warming: discounting is not the issue, but substitutability is', *Energy Policy* 27: 33–43.

Neumayer, E. 2003. *Weak versus Strong Sustainability: Exploring the Limits of Two Opposing Paradigms*, Second edition. Cheltenham, UK: Elgar.

Neumayer, E. 2007. 'A missed opportunity: the Stern Review on climate change fails to tackle the issue of non-substitutable loss of natural capital', *Global Environmental Change* 17: 297–301.

Nordhaus, W. D. 2007. 'A review of the Stern Review on the economics of climate change', *Journal of Economic Literature* 45: 686–702.

Nordhaus, W. D. and Boyer, J. 2000. *Warming the World: Economic Models of Global Warming*. Cambridge, MA: MIT Press.

O'Riordan, T. 2004. 'Environmental science, sustainability and politics', *Transactions of the Institute of British Geographers* 29: 234–47.

Pearce, D. W. and Atkinson, G. 1993. 'Capital theory and the measurement of sustainable development: an indicator of "weak" sustainability', *Ecological Economics* 8: 103–8.

Pearce, D. W., Markandya, A. and Barbier, E. B. 1989. *Blueprint for a Green Economy*. London, UK: Earthscan.

Pearce, D. W., Groom, B., Hepburn, C. and Koundouri, P. 2003. 'Valuing the future: recent advances in social discounting', *World Economics* 4: 121–41.

Sen, A. K. 1999. *Development as Freedom*. New York: Knopf.

Siniscalco, D. 1999. 'Impacts of economic theories on environmental economics', in van den Bergh, J. C. J. M. (ed.) *Handbook of Environmental and Resource Economics*. Cheltenham, UK: Elgar, pp. 1209–29.

Solow, R. M. 1974. 'Intergenerational equity and exhaustible resources', *Review of Economic Studies* 41(Supplement): 29–46.

Stern, N. H. 2007. *The Economics of Climate Change: The Stern Review*. Cambridge, UK: Cambridge University Press.

Sterner, T. and Persson, U. M. 2007. *An Even Sterner Review: Introducing Relative Prices into the Discounting Debate*. Discussion Paper 07–37. Washington, DC: Resources for the Future.

Turner, D. and Hartzell, L. 2004. 'The lack of clarity in the precautionary principle', *Environmental Values* 13: 449–60.

United Nations, European Commission, International Monetary Fund, Organisation for Economic Co-operation and Development and World Bank 2003. *Integrated Environmental and Economic Accounting 2003: Handbook of National Accounting, Studies in Methods*. New York: United Nations.

Weintraub, E. R. 1985. *General Equilibrium Analysis*. Cambridge, UK: Cambridge University Press.

Weyant, J. P. 2008. 'A critique of the Stern Review's mitigation cost analyses and integrated assessment', *Review of Environmental Economics and Policy* 2(1): 77–93.

World Bank 2006. *Where is the Wealth of Nations?* Washington DC: World Bank.

# 12 Sustainability, welfare and value over time

JOHN O'NEILL

## Addressing the paradox of sustainability

Sustainability and sustainable development have become key phrases in the unfolding politics of the environment. These terms are widely institutionalised in policy documents and governance systems. However, as Tim O'Riordan himself has remarked, at the same time the transition to a sustainable society looks, at best, difficult (O'Riordan, 1996). It is not my purpose in this chapter to offer a complete diagnosis as to why this is the case or to offer a solution. What I do want to do, is to look at one set of conflicting intuitions and experiences that in part underpin that difficulty and to explore the problems in some of the standard responses found in economic theory.

It is a now a commonplace assertion that the concept of sustainability appears to be used in a wide variety of different ways (see, for example, Chapter 1). The sheer variety of uses raises questions about what it is supposed to mean: the sustainability of what, for whom, and why? There are two different kinds of answer to these questions, often associated with different disciplines. One set of answers appeals to specific goods. What is to be sustained is a particular fishing stock, particular woodlands, particular agricultural systems, or habitats. For whom will often refer to some particular community – for example a fishing community, an agricultural community or indeed an association of non-human beings. The why will refer to particular goods, interests and values of those groups. These are the kinds of appeal one will find in geographically local discussions of sustainability. They are also the kind of answer that is typical of the natural sciences.

Another set of answers appeals, however, to much more general goods than this. In the economic literature the answer to the what, for whom and why runs roughly as follows. What is to be sustained is a certain level of human welfare, which, in standard welfare economics, is understood in terms of preference satisfaction. The whom for which it is to be sustained are present and future generations of humans. There are two standard answers to why it should be sustained – either to maximise welfare over time, or to meet the demands of distributional justice between generations. In its basic sense, sustainable development is defined as economic and social development that at least maintains a certain minimum level of human welfare. The maintenance of a certain minimum level of human welfare over generations requires each generation to leave its successor a stock of capital assets no less than it receives. It requires that capital should be constant, or at any rate should not decline, over time. The term sustainable here is being applied to an entire set of economic arrangements to describe tendencies in what has traditionally been called the wealth of nations.

These two sets of answers, the specific and the general, need not be in conflict. Indeed the two uses of the concept can clearly come apart without inconsistency. Islands of unsustainable uses of specific resources can exist within what an economist might describe as globally sustainable economies. And, vice versa, globally unsustainable economies can contain islands of local sustainability. However, there is a paradox in these two uses of the concept, in that they appear to come apart not just occasionally but systematically. If one examines the descriptions by natural scientists of the sustainability of specific resources, then we appear to be looking at a series of unsustainable practices. When we turn to the more global story of economic development, the impact of those local failures of sustainability seems to disappear from view. Dasgupta captures this paradox well when he refers to:

a puzzle created by conflicting intuitions that have been derived from two different empirical perspectives concerning the question of whether the character of contemporary economic development is sustainable. On the one hand, if we look at specific resources and services (e.g. fresh water, ecosystem services, and the atmosphere as a carbon sink), there is convincing evidence that the current rates of utilization are unsustainable. On the other hand, if we look at historical trends in the prices of marketed resources or the recorded growth in GNP per capita in countries that are currently rich, resource scarcities would not appear yet to have bitten (Dasgupta, 2001: 87–8).

These conflicting intuitions receive a number of different expressions in different fields. On the one hand there are those, such as

Beckerman, who claim that, looking at both historical and current rates of growth, there are no good reasons for supposing that future generations will not be better off than ourselves, just as our generation is better off than those that went before. The very concept of sustainability is a distraction from the more pressing issue of ensuring justice within current generations and passing on to future generations a decent society (Beckerman, 1999). On the other hand, if one looks at pictures such as those recently produced by the United Nations Environment Programme (UNEP) in their atlas *One Planet, Many People*, the situation appears very different. Lakes and forests shrink, glaciers disappear, topsoil is eroded. The prospects for sustainability look very poor.

The conflict here is not just a conflict at a theoretical level between different perspectives. It is also one that is experienced by people at an everyday level and in part explains some of the difficulty in mobilising individuals and groups to move towards a more sustainable future. At an everyday level, most individuals will look at their family histories and find each new generation living longer and, on the whole, with higher real incomes, better health, and with wider opportunities for education and travel. However, at the same time, individuals look at particular places and environments that matter to them and lament the losses they experience. And while, when they look at their family histories and see a growth in a standard of living, there is no great evidence that life in all aspects is better. Life satisfaction rates have remained remarkably static while income has risen.[1]

How should one respond to these conflicting perspectives? The answer depends at which level one is talking. In this chapter, I will only touch in passing on the problem of how one responds to the conflict at the everyday level, although this is, I think, pressing for understanding what is required for a transition to a more sustainable future. Instead I will consider one popular set of responses to the conflict within the economic literature. Here, at least part of the response of proponents of the second, more sceptical, view of economic growth has been to charge their opponents with having mischaracterised sustainability or sustainable development. Changes in the monetary prices of market goods are not good indicators of sustainability over time. There is more to sustainability than continuing growth in GNP per capita. There are a variety of versions of that response. However, perhaps the most influential has been to insist on the distinction between weak and strong versions of sustainability, which tends to permeate much of the debate on sustainability (see, for example, Chapter 11).

The disagreement between weak and strong conceptions of sustainability has been a central focus of debates on the governance of sustainability. Both sides agree that sustainability should be understood in terms of passing on a level of capital required to maintain or improve human wellbeing over time. The disagreement is taken to be around whether the injunction to pass on capital should be understood as passing on a total stock of capital, human and natural, or whether it should be understood in terms of passing on a particular level of natural capital. The debate over weak and strong sustainability is presented as turning on the degree to which natural capital and human-made capital can be substituted for each other, as shown by Simon Dietz and Eric Neumayer in Chapter 11. Proponents of weak sustainability are often taken by critics to affirm that natural capital and human-made capital are indefinitely or even infinitely substitutable. Proponents of strong sustainability, on the other hand, hold that because there are limits to what natural capital can be replaced or substituted by human-made capital, sustainability requires that we maintain the level of natural capital, or at any rate that we maintain natural capital at or above the level which is judged to be critical.

This debate, however, has been a problematic one. As in many academic debates, the discussion has been marked by both concealed agreement and exaggerated conflict (Holland, 1997). Weak sustainability is rarely as weak and strong sustainability is rarely as strong as each of its critics maintain. For instance, it is difficult to find a defender of weak sustainability who affirms unequivocally that natural capital and human-made capital are infinitely substitutable. Thus, even Solow, who is often taken to be the most notable proponent of weak sustainability, asserts: 'the world can, in effect, get along without natural resources, if it is very easy to substitute other factors for natural resources' (Solow, 1974: 11). He certainly does not assert unconditionally that natural and man-made capital are infinitely substitutable. Indeed, it is hard to find any economist who makes this claim.

The response of the neoclassical economist is to claim that substitution between natural and human capital at the margins is at issue, not total substitutability of one for the other (Beckerman, 2000). On the other hand, critics of strong sustainability like Beckerman often set up something of an easy target. Beckerman ascribes to defenders of strong sustainability the view that no species should be allowed to go extinct, nor any non-renewable resource exploited, no matter what the cost in poverty for current generations, which allows him to criticise the concepts as both morally repugnant and impractical (Beckerman, 1994). Defenders of strong sustainability properly reject that version of their position (Daly, 1995; Jacobs, 1995).

Given that neither side actually holds the position which their opponents ascribe to them, what is at stake in this debate? It looks as if it might come down to an empirical question over which parts of natural and human capital can be substituted for each other, which can only be addressed case by case. If it did turn out that this was all the debate was about, then maybe so much the better. However, that characterisation is, I think, unsatisfactory. Prior to the empirical question are some important conceptual and normative questions to be addressed. For example, what is it to say that one thing is a substitute for another? What are the criteria for saying that something is an acceptable substitute for something else? What I want to suggest in this chapter is that there are conceptual and normative assumptions built into standard economic analysis that encourage the view that, when seeking to make sound decisions about the governance of society, goods are ubiquitously substitutable. In particular, I want to look at two assumptions of standard economic analysis of environmental goods: (a) a preference-satisfaction theory of wellbeing; (b) additive separability of value over time. Those assumptions, I will suggest, are false. Their rejection indicates a much less promiscuous substitutability than the standard account suggests. At the same time, it points to the limits of the metaphor of capital that is shared by proponents of both sides in this debate about governing sustainability.

## Human wellbeing and substitutability

What is it for one thing to be a substitute for another? There are two distinct conceptions of substitutability in the economic literature which I will call the technical and the economic. The concept of a technical substitute involves reference to some specific end or purpose. One good is said to be a substitute for another if it achieves the same end, if it does the same job. For example, we say that margarine can be used as a substitute for lard in a recipe, or a plastic stopper can substitute for a cork in wine bottles. The particular object serves a similar function in achieving some end – cooking a meal or keeping wine from going sour. A feature of the concept of technical substitution is that only very specific goods can substitute for others – a lump of lard won't substitute for a cork stopper. The criterion for the acceptability of a substitute on this account is a matter of how well it performs the same function as the original. In deciding whether something is a good substitute, we need to specify the end for which substitution is defined. Plastic bottle stoppers are good substitutes for corks if one is simply concerned with keeping wine from going sour. If one has other aims – the aesthetics of the stopper or the maintenance of the biological systems in which cork is produced – then one may arrive at a different appraisal.

The concept of technical substitutability needs to be distinguished from the concept of economic substitutability employed in welfare analysis in neoclassical economics. According to this concept, for any particular person a good $x$ is said to be a substitute for another good $y$ if replacing $y$ by $x$ does not change the overall level of welfare of that person. A loss in one good $y$ can be compensated by a gain in a good $x$ in the sense that the person's level of welfare remains unchanged. Economic substitutes are much more promiscuous than technical substitutes. One good can be a substitute for another, not if it functions to achieve the same end, but if the end that it achieves is as good for a person's wellbeing as the end that would have been achieved by the other good. Two goods are substitutes for another not in the sense that they do the same job, but rather in the sense that, as Steiner puts it 'although they each do a different job, those two jobs are just as good as one another' (Steiner, 1994: 171). On this account, a cork and a lump of lard could be substitutes for each other, for example, if the wine preserved by one and the meal created by the other are each as good for the person as the other. Substitutability in this sense raises the question of what is it for one alternative to be as good for a person as another. The answer to that question depends on the account of wellbeing one assumes.

Standard neoclassical economics assumes a preference-satisfaction account of wellbeing. Wellbeing or welfare consists in the satisfaction of preferences – the stronger the preference satisfied, the greater the improvement in wellbeing. According to this view, two alternatives, *x* and *y*, are as good as each other for a particular person if they are equally preferred: *x* is at least as preferred as *y* and *y* is at least as preferred as *x*. The person is, in this sense, indifferent between them. Standard economic theory makes a set of assumptions about the formal structure of those preferences of rational economic agents which have the consequence that different goods are widely substitutable for each other. Preferences are transitive, complete, reflexive and continuous. These assumptions allow the economist to construct the smooth continuous indifference curves that are to be found in any basic welfare economics textbook, which join equally preferred bundles of goods. The slope of the curve indicates the marginal rate of substitution between goods; that is, how much of one good a person is willing to give up in order to gain an improvement in the other.

Should we accept this analysis? Consider an implication of the assumption of continuity:

[G]iven any two goods in a bundle it will always be possible – by reducing the amount of one fractionally and increasing the amount of the other fractionally – to define another bundle which is indifferent to the first. This means that there is no good in a bundle which is absolutely necessary in some amount and which cannot be traded-off at the margin for some other good (Hargreaves-Heap *et al.*, 1992: 6).

Here is a putative counter-example to the assumption, offered by Vivian Walsh.

[T]here are some important choice situations in which the object of choice must be available in exactly one form to be any good at all – where the idea of slightly more or less just does not apply. This can be so even when the thing chosen happens to be a physical thing which is highly divisible, like a chemical. Most of the drugs prescribed by physicians are highly divisible. Yet it is a matter of common practice that what he prescribes is some exact dose; quantities less than the right one may be useless and greater ones may be fatal (Walsh, 1970: 27, cf. 142).

Walsh's example is not immediately a counter-example to the axiom of continuity. After all, it is possible that an agent might be willing to trade off the loss in health with a marginal gain elsewhere, say for a holiday they always wanted. They can ignore the doctor's advice and trade their drug for another good. However, nothing in rationality forces that trade and, indeed, if the drug is for a serious condition the opposite would be true. A reasonable person would follow the doctor's advice and refuse any further shift in the bundle of goods. No gain of welfare in other dimensions compensates for the loss of health. The drug satisfies a need that must be satisfied if a person is to have a minimally flourishing life at all. However, to shift from the language of preferences to that of needs is to change the account of welfare one is assuming. Welfare is being used to refer not to a person's preferences, but to what makes for a flourishing life on some more objective account of a good life.

If one moves from a preference-satisfaction to an objective-state account of wellbeing, goods begin to look a lot less substitutable for each other. Compare, for example, a preference-satisfaction model of wellbeing with one that is founded upon the concept of need. There are two clear differences between the concepts of preference and of need. First, the logic of the concepts differs. A sentence of the form '*a* needs *x*' is extensional, i.e. if *a* needs *x*, and *x* is *y*, then it follows that *a* needs *y*; a sentence of the form '*a* prefers *x* to *z*' is intensional, i.e. it is not the case that if *a* prefers *x* to *z*, and *x* is *y*, that it follows that *a* prefers *y* to *z*'. For example, from 'Joseph needs glucose' and 'glucose is $C_6H_{12}O_6$' we can infer 'Joseph needs $C_6H_{12}O_6$'. However, from 'Oedipus prefers to marry Jocasta to any other woman in Thebes' and 'Jocasta is Oedipus's mother', one cannot infer 'Oedipus prefers to marry his mother to any other woman in Thebes'. Whether or not a person needs something depends on the objective condition of the person and the nature of the object and its capacities to contribute to the flourishing of that person. Whether a person prefers one object to another depends rather upon the nature of the person's beliefs about the objects. The differences in the logic of the concepts point to one sense in which one conception of welfare is objective, the other subjective.

A second difference between the concept of preference, at least as it is formalised in mainstream economic theory, and the concept of need, is that the concept of non-instrumental need is a threshold concept in a way that the concept of preference is not. Need claims are of different kinds. Some needs are relative to specific projects. If I am to get to Chicago by tomorrow, then I need to take a plane. However, one might respond to that need claim by asking if I really need to be in Chicago tomorrow. However, some needs claims are not like that.

There are some needs that must be satisfied if a person is to have a flourishing life at all. Non-instrumental needs are those conditions that are necessary for a flourishing life, the absence of which would be said to harm the person (Wiggins, 1998). For example, a person needs a certain amount of water, food and shelter, and also certain social relations, if they are to flourish at all. A feature of such non-instrumental needs is that there are thresholds such that if a person goes below or above them their wellbeing will suffer. One can have too much or too little of a particular good. Consider Walsh's counter-example to the axiom of continuity. From the perspective of the doctor making recommendations about what the patient needs to recover their health, there is a precise amount of a particular drug that the individual requires. Neither more nor less will do. The fact that the patient has a preference for a holiday and is willing to trade the good is not relevant to the appraisal of need. As far as a person's needs are concerned, the holiday and the drugs are not substitutes.

However, couldn't it be the case that we can still substitute over different dimensions to maintain some total level of need? It is not clear to me that we could. Given an objective account of welfare, for example, one based on needs understood as the necessary conditions for a person to live a flourishing human life, or to realise basic functional capabilities (Sen, 1987, 1992) there is no reason to assume that goods are ubiquitously substitutable in the way that standard welfare economics assumes. Human capabilities to function are plural, and the goods that satisfy one of them are not substitutable for by goods that satisfy others.

Consider, for example, Nussbaum's version of the central human functional capabilities, where these are broadly categorised under different headings: life; bodily health; bodily integrity; senses, imagination and thought; emotions; practical reason; affiliation; other species; play; control over one's political and material environment (Nussbaum, 2000). Each heading defines a space of capabilities to achieve basic human functionings. Each space can itself be internally plural, including an irreducible variety of capabilities. Each might also be open to being realised in different ways – thus there are a variety of different forms that affiliation might take. Clearly this approach does allow for the substitutability of different goods. Consider, for example, the capacity for mobility: there are different goods that might realise that capacity. However, there are limits to substitutability on this account which are not apparent on the preference-satisfaction account of welfare.

One cannot expect substitutability to be promiscuous across different dimensions of need. It is not the case that, for a loss of good under one heading, say bodily health, there is a gain in another, say practical reason, that leaves the person's wellbeing unchanged. There is, as people say in everyday parlance, no substitute for good health, for good friends, for particular places and environments. The drug that the doctor offers does not have a substitute in an increase in entertainment. A loss in one dimension can only be properly addressed by the provision of goods in that dimension.[2]

Welfare, on this account, is an inclusive good that incorporates a variety of different dimensions, and there is no reason to assume that a loss in one dimension can be compensated for by a gain in another. This point underpins quite rational refusals of monetary compensation. Consider, for example, the refusal to consider monetary compensation for eviction to make way for the development of the Narmada dam (e.g. Bava Mahalia, 1994). Here, the response is rational. A person facing eviction from the place in which the life of their community has been lived for generations, facing the disintegration of that community as their homes are flooded for a dam, can properly respond by saying that there is no good that can compensate for that loss. The loss of basic goods in the dimension of human affiliation and community cannot be compensated for by a gain in other dimensions. This is not to say that it would not be better that those who leave should receive something in compensation. However, the idea that there is a sum of money that can be offered that would maintain their level of welfare in the manner assumed by the standard economic theory is a myth founded upon a mistaken theory of welfare.

What implications do these limits have for debates around the governance of sustainability? In so far as sustainability is about sustaining or improving human welfare over generations similar points apply. What sustainability requires us to pass onto future generations is a bundle of goods that can maintain welfare across the different dimensions of human functioning – we need to be able to pass down the conditions for life and good health, for social affiliation, for the development of capacities for practical reason, for engaging with the wider natural world. To do that requires that we pass on goods that are disaggregated and which cannot be substituted for each other.

Practical reason requires formal and informal institutions for education. Sustaining affiliation requires sustaining the cultural and physical
conditions for community, including particular environments that are
constitutive of communities. Maintaining the capacity to appreciate
the natural world and to care for other species requires us to sustain
particular environments. In none of these cases will an increase
in entertainment or the quality of consumer goods be adequate
substitutes.

There are a variety of different human functional capabilities that
require distinct and non-substitutable goods to realise them. It is not
simply that natural and human capital are not substitutable for each
other. It is rather that environmental goods are not substitutable by
other goods because they answer to quite distinct dimensions of
human wellbeing.[3] Once wellbeing is understood in this way there is
much less of a distance between the particular and general uses of
the concept of sustainability we noted in the first section of this
chapter. A more pluralist understanding of wellbeing highlights the
need for a disaggregated account of the objects that are required to
sustain a certain level of human wellbeing.

## Narrative, human wellbeing and sustainability

One source of the promiscuous substitutability of goods in welfare
economics is a particular preference-satisfaction theory of wellbeing.
A second source is the assumption of additive separability. Consider
the standard formula used in cost–benefit analysis to arrive at the
value of the project (PV) over a time period $t = 0$ and $t = n$:

$$\text{PV} = \sum_{t=0}^{t=n} \{\text{B}t - \text{C}t\}(1+r)^{-t},$$

where B$t$ is the benefit at time $t$, C$t$ is the cost at time $t$, and $r$ is the
discount rate.

Most critical discussion of this approach has focused on the
assumption that future benefits should be discounted. They do so for
good reason. The assumption appears to sanction intergenerational
inequity. Hence Ramsey's remark that the practice of discounting is
'ethically indefensible and arises merely from the weakness of the

imagination' (Ramsey, 1928: 543). However, the formula also relies on another assumption that Ramsey accepts. It assumes that the values of different events at different moments of time are additively separable. Informally, to say they are separable is to say that the value of what happens at some point in time, $t_i$, is independent of the value of what happens at another point, $t_j$; and to say that they are additively separable is to say that the total value of a project over a period of time is the sum of these independent values. As Ramsey puts it: 'enjoyments and sacrifices at different times can be calculated independently and added' (Ramsey, 1928: 543).[4]

How might one reject the assumption of additive separability? One reason is that it doesn't seem to capture the narrative dimension to our judgements of how well people's lives go. Consider the following example, which I have employed before:

**A.** A newly married couple, couple A, go on a two-week honeymoon. The holiday begins disastrously: they each discover much in the other which they had not noticed before, and they dislike what they find. The first two days are spent in an almighty row. However, while they argue continuously over the next seven days, they begin to resolve their differences and come to a deeper appreciation of each other. Over the last five days of the holiday they are much happier and both feel that they have realised a relationship that is better than that which they had before their argument. The holiday ends happily. Sadly, on their return journey, the plane that carries them explodes and they die.

**B.** A newly married couple, couple B, go on honeymoon. The first twelve days proceed wonderfully. On the thirteenth day their relationship deteriorates badly as each begins to notice and dislike in the other a character trait which they had not noticed before, at the same time realising that the other had a quite mistaken view of themselves. On the last day of the holiday they have a terrible row, and sit at opposite ends of the plane on the return journey. They both die in an explosion on the plane (O'Neill, 1993: 53–4).

Which holiday goes better? Which would one choose? From a simple maximising perspective the answer is holiday B: on any simple summing of goods over bads over time, holiday B contains more of the good, less of the bad. However, a few hedonistically inclined students and colleagues aside, most individuals claim that holiday A is better. They characterise the story of holiday A as a happier one than that of holiday B. What counts in favour of holiday A is the narrative order of events. People's lives have a narrative structure, and the ending of a narrative is crucial to the genre to which a person's life, or an episode of that life, belongs – tragic, comic, pathetic and so on. Our evaluation of how well a person's life goes depends on the narrative we can truly tell of it. The temporal structure of a life matters. Moreover it matters to the evaluation we place on the different moments. Thus the way we characterise the moments in my honeymoon stories depends on their place in a larger narrative frame. For example, in holiday A, the argument at the start of the holiday is not simply a moment of pain. Rather, taken in context, it might be a turning point in the relationship, one which clarifies the relationship and lays the foundation for the ensuing happiness. Within the context of the individuals' entire lives, it has another significance. For that reason, one can also talk of the earlier event having been redeemed by the later reconciliation to which it gave rise.

A similar point applies to public choices. For communities with their particular traditions and histories, what is taken to improve their lives from a maximising atemporal perspective may not be the most worthy path to follow. Consider again the rejection of compensation by members of the community faced with being displaced to make way for the dam in the Narmada. Even given a generous package of compensation, to shift a community in this way can involve the loss of the context that makes sense of its members' lives. This is not inevitable – people can prove remarkably resilient, and the very process of resistance can sustain a community through a loss. But what is potentially at stake in such cases is the temporal as well as physical dislocation of a community, the loss of a context of what went before and what follows that is a condition of a meaningful life. Part of what makes for a flourishing human life is the narrative structure that gives it coherence.

The role of narrative is of particular significance in the environmental domain. A feature of deliberation about environmental value is that history matters and constrains our decisions as to what kind of future is appropriate. This is true of the conservation of natural objects. We value natural objects, forests, lakes, mountains and ecosystems specifically for the particular history they embody. The very ascription of 'naturalness' to them depends upon the specific history we can tell of them. It is the source of the block on faking nature (Elliot, 1982, 1997; Goodin, 1992). The significance of history is still more evident in the problems that are typical of nature conservation in the European context. Most nature conservation problems are concerned with flora and fauna that flourish in particular sites that are the result of a specific history of human pastoral and agricultural activity, not with sites that existed prior to human intervention.[5] The relevance of the past is evident also in the conservation of the embodiments of the work of past generations. The value of specific locations is often a consequence of the way that the life of a community is embodied within it. Historical ties of community have a material dimension in both the human and the natural landscapes within which a community dwells. The city is an environment that has suffered its own dislocations. In all these cases, the past is relevant to our current evaluations.

Because the value of environmental goods is, in part, to do with their embodying a particular past, they cannot be substituted for by new artificial replacements. History matters. We aim to preserve an ancient meadowland or an ancient stone wall in virtue of their history. A reproduction will not do. As such, the past does constrain our current decisions. The constraint that the past places upon us is best understood as one founded in the significance of the narrative order for the values that objects and places have for us. Our environments are embodiments of past histories, the narratives of lives and communities from which our own lives take significance. Part of the problem of environmental choices is how best to continue the narrative: what would make the most appropriate trajectory from what has gone before that sustains this significance (Holland and Rawles, 1994: 37)?

This historical dimension of environmental valuation has implications for the technical substitutability of goods for each other. Those limits have implications for sustainable governance. Consider one of English Nature's position statements on sustainable development. It defines environmental sustainability thus: 'environmental sustainability ... means maintaining the environment's natural qualities and characteristics and its capacity to fulfil its full range of activities, including the maintenance of biodiversity' (English Nature, 1993). Having thus defined the concept, the position statement continues thus:

Those aspects of native biodiversity which cannot be readily replaced, such as ancient woodlands, we call critical natural capital. Others, which should not be allowed, in total, to fall below minimum levels, but which could be created elsewhere within the same Natural Area, such as other types of woodland, we refer to as constant natural assets (English Nature, 1993).

Sustainability, on this account, is a matter of protecting critical natural capital – that part of the natural environment which cannot be readily replaced – and a set of constant natural assets that do have possible substitutes through re-creation and translocation. What are the criteria of adequate substitutability or replaceability? Capital, both natural and man-made, is conceived of as a bundle of assets. On the natural capital side we have a list of valued items: habitat types, woodlands, heathlands, lowland grasslands, etc. We maintain natural capital if, for any loss of these, we can re-create another of the same type. Time appears as a technical constraint on re-creation. Landscapes that are the result of long periods of evolution are treated as critical natural capital for this reason: 'the environmental conditions that moulded them cannot be technically or financially re-created within acceptable time scales' (Gillespie and Shepherd, 1995: 14). The more ephemeral habitats – the pond, secondary woodland and heathland, etc. – which are more easily reproduced, become parts of constant natural assets. We can lose one so long as another is re-created from it.

Is this approach to sustainability satisfactory? It is not, because it gets the role of narrative and history wrong. Time and history do not matter simply as technical constraints on the possibility of re-creating certain landscapes with certain physical properties. Rather they matter because habitats are valued precisely in virtue of embodying a certain history. The history and processes of their creation matter, not just the physical attributes they display. We value an ancient woodland in virtue of the history of human and natural processes that together went into making it: it embodies the work of human generations and the chance colonisation of species and has value because of the processes that made it what it is. No reproduction could have the same value, because its history is wrong. Correspondingly, some relatively ordinary places that are technically easily reproducible are less open to substitution than is usually supposed. Particular habitats matter for the history they contain even if they are reproducible at the level of physical and functional attributes.

A problem in a great deal of discussion of sustainability, and environmental policy more generally, is that it defines the environment only in functional terms. To use the metaphor of natural capital is to conceive of the natural world as a stock of assets which give a stream of benefits for humans. The assets are understood as capacities to 'provide humankind with the services of resource provision, waste assimilation, amenity and life support' (Jacobs, 1995: 582). The question of the acceptability of substitution turns, therefore, on whether one stock of assets can be replaced by another, while still maintaining the same capacities. This dimension of the relations of humans to the natural world is clearly an important one. We have argued in the last section that there are limits to the substitutability of goods that meet distinct human functional capacities. However, we do not value environmental goods only as resources in this sense. We also value places, landscapes and goods as spatio-temporal particulars. This value they have places further limits on the substitutability of certain environmental goods. They do not lend themselves to technical substitution for the reasons we have just outlined.

Many goods and beings that are valued as spatio-temporal particulars, although not all, are also non-substitutable in the economic sense. This is most clearly true of relations to particular others. The loss of a particular family member, for example, will affect our wellbeing in ways that cannot be compensated for in any other dimension. However, it is true also of environmental goods. Consider, for example, those goods that embody particular ties of social affiliation that make for part of a good human life. For such goods there are no substitutes on other dimensions of human wellbeing that can compensate for their loss. Thus to return to the Narmada case discussed above; faced with the flooding of a place that has been the home of some community, it is a quite proper response to say that there is nothing that could compensate for that loss. The loss is of a different kind to that involved in the loss of functional goods that might have replacements. It is irreplaceable in a person's life and will remain a loss, for all that life might continue in its absence.

## Sustainability, governance and natural capital

What implications do these arguments have for the conflicting intuitions with which we began this discussion? One central implication is that standard economic analysis is premised on assumptions about human wellbeing and about valuation over time, which lead it to exaggerate the degree to which different goods can be substituted for each other and miss the way in which particular goods matter to human wellbeing. Even if we stay within a perspective that is concerned with human wellbeing, it misses the way that environmental goods matter to the lives of individuals. If we move to a pluralist and more objectivist understanding of welfare, we need to have a much more disaggregated account of sustainability.

Sustainability is not a matter of simply maintaining some aggregate level of human and natural capital. It requires the maintenance of specific resources and goods that meet different human needs and capacities. It also requires the recognition of particular environments and places that matter to the lives of individuals and communities as they develop over time. This disaggregated view also has the advantage of overcoming some of the distance noted at the start of this chapter between the particular and general uses of the concept of sustainability. A proper understanding of wellbeing points to the importance of sustaining particular specific goods, to particular woodlands, particular agricultural systems, places or habitats that are central to the wellbeing of particular communities.

This approach to wellbeing also accounts for at least part of the dissonance between the image of continuously improving welfare as measured by income, and the realities of felt loss and decline that are experienced in people's lives. Over a range of the central dimensions of human welfare, such as life expectancy, health, educational opportunities and mobility, in at least the wealthier parts of the globe, life over the generations has improved. However, there are significant dimensions in which the story is much less clear, for example in work, affiliation and relations to the non-human world.[6] They form the source of everyday conversation. The length of the working day and conditions and security of work have not improved. The conditions for sociality in the modern urban environment – in particular for children and the old – have significantly worsened. The absence of familiar sights, sounds and scents in the natural world have been an understandable source of loss. Physical spaces for quiet contemplation of the natural world have been eroded. Some of these losses are talked about in quite general terms. However, they often find their natural expression in more specific concerns about the loss of particular places that are constitutive of communities, from major losses of the kind experienced in Narmada to the loss of ordinary places that matter – a local copse, pond, neighbourhood or urban park.

The account of the limits of substitution developed here also has implications for questions of governance that are central to other chapters in this volume. One implication concerns the limits of particular decision tools in environmental choices, in particular of cost–benefit analysis. The standard underlying rationale for the use of cost–benefit analysis is the Kaldor-Hicks compensation test. Situation A is an improvement over situation B if the gains are greater than the losses, so that the gainers could compensate the losers and still be better off. There are a variety of technical objections to the test and some major moral objections that arise from the fact that it appeals only to hypothetical compensation: 'it is no consolation to losers, who might include the worst off members of society, to be told that it would be possible to compensate them even though there is no actual intention to do so' (Sen, 1987: 33).

However, even if one appeals to actual rather than hypothetical compensation, there is a prior question here as to whether compensation is possible at all. The possibility of compensation in the particular sense it is used in the compensation test turns on the possibility of substitution that maintains a particular level of welfare. The loss of goods in one dimension of human welfare can be compensated for by a gain in another which leaves total wellbeing unchanged. For the reasons we have developed in the last two sections of this chapter, no such compensation might be possible in the sense of the provision of goods that leave welfare levels unchanged. Hence, for example, the rationality of the refusal of compensate in the case of the Narmada dam – there is no benefit in other dimensions that could compensate for the possible loss of affiliation that the loss threatens.

A final implication is about the limits of accounts of sustainability that are couched in terms of capital. For reasons just noted, there are good reasons to question the purely functional view of the natural and cultural worlds that the metaphor of capital suggests. We do not aim to sustain places simply in virtue of their providing certain services, centrally important as this is. We also value places, landscapes and objects as historical particulars that have a wider significance in human lives and to which we have a wider set of relations. We do not live in capital or stocks or bundles of assets. We live in places that have a variety of different significances for different communities and individuals. The natural world itself can be understood as a spatio-temporal entity with its own history; it is not just capital. Environments are not mere bundles of resources. They are where human lives go on, places to which humans have a relation of struggle, wonder and dwelling.

The failure of the metaphor of natural capital to capture the significance of the temporal and historical dimensions of environmental values is symptomatic of a failure to capture the different dimensions of the relations of humans to their environments. Sustainability raises political and ethical debates about the kinds of communities over time to which we understand ourselves to belong. Those debates cannot be captured simply in economic terms or indeed by any purely technical decision-making procedures.[7] It requires governance procedures through which judgements are formed by public deliberation. As Tim O'Riordan has reminded us, we need to understand valuation as an 'educational, revelatory and democratising process' (O'Riordan, 1997: 181).

## Acknowledgements

This chapter draws on material that appears in O'Neill, J. *Markets, Deliberation and Environment* (London: Routledge, 2007) and O'Neill, J., Holland, A. and Light, A. *Environmental Values* (London: Routledge, 2008). I would like to thank the publishers for their permission to use the material here.

## Notes

1 Claims about 'life-satisfaction' do, however, need to be treated with care. For a critical discussion, see O'Neill (2006a, 2006b).

2 To say that different goods are not substitutable across different dimensions of welfare is not to say that there are no causal relations between goods in different dimensions: clearly there are relations, for example, the quality of social relations and the capacity to control one's life have major effects on a person's physical health (Marmot, 2004). However, they do not substitute for, say, the nutritional conditions of health.

3 In this respect the original Brundtland formulation of sustainability has more to be said for it than its more recent economic relatives. Brundtland's formulation is written in the language of needs, not the language of preferences: 'Sustainable development is development that meets the *needs* of the present without compromising the ability of future generations to meet their own *needs*' (WCED, 1987) (emphasis added) (see

also Chapter 1). Needs, for the reasons we have just emphasised, allow much less room for substitutability than do preferences. Hence the shift from a preference-satisfaction account of wellbeing to a more objectivist account places clear limits on the substitutability of goods.

4  For a detailed and more technical discussion of the concept of separability and different dimensions over which separability can be considered, see Broome (1991).

5  Nor is this a typically Old World phenomenon. Many of the conservation issues in the New World have the same form: indeed their presentation as problems of wilderness preservation is misleading if one means by a wilderness a landscape or habitat that is undisturbed by human activity. Rather, many so-called wildernesses in Africa, Australia and America are the Old World pastoral landscapes shaped by those who had previously lived in those places, and whose activities are rendered invisible and their memory lost. That this is so has been a source of many of the practical problems in managing wilderness, for the wilderness as discovered by Europeans was a landscape that depended upon pastoral activities such as burning (O'Neill, 2002).

6  This observation is borne out by recent empirical surveys on what is called subjective welfare (Lane, 2001; Frey and Stutzer, 2002; Layard, 2005), although the results of those surveys need to be treated with some caution. For a critical discussion, see O'Neill (2006a, 2006b).

7  To make these points is not to deny the value of formal decision-making tools. For example, non-compensatory forms of multi-criteria decision analysis within a suitably deliberative context, as discussed by Andy Stirling in Chapter 9 and Jacquie Burgess and Judy Clark in Chapter 8, could conceivably capture the different dimensions of human welfare involved (Martinez-Alier *et al.*, 1998). However, any such tools need to recognise the limits to substitutability of goods across different dimensions of human welfare (see also Simon Dietz and Eric Neumayer in Chapter 11).

## References

Bava Mahalia 1994. 'Letter from a tribal village', *Lokayan Bulletin* 11(2/3): Sept–Dec.

Beckerman, W. 1994. 'Sustainable development: is it a useful concept?' *Environmental Values* 3: 191–209.

Beckerman, W. 1999. 'Sustainable development and our obligations to future generations', in Dobson, A. (ed.) *Fairness and Futurity: Essays on Environmental Sustainability and Social Justice*. Oxford University Press, pp. 71–92.

Beckerman W. 2000. 'Review of J. Foster ed. *Valuing Nature? Ethics, Economics and the Environment*', *Environmental Values* 9: 122–4.

Broome, J. 1991. *Weighing Goods*. Oxford: Blackwell.

Daly, H. E. 1995. 'On Wilfred Beckerman's critique of sustainable development', *Environmental Values* 4: 49–55.

Dasgupta, P. 2001. *Human Well-Being and the Natural Environment*. Oxford, UK: Oxford University Press.

Elliot, R. 1982. 'Faking nature', *Inquiry* 25: 81–93.

Elliot, R. 1997. *Faking Nature*. London, UK: Routledge.

English Nature 1993. *Position Statement on Sustainable Development*. Peterborough, UK: English Nature.

Frey, B. and Stutzer, A. 2002. 'What can economists learn from happiness research?' *Journal of Economic Literature* 40: 402–35.

Gillespie, J. and Shepherd, P. 1995. *Establishing Criteria for Identifying Critical Natural Capital in the Terrestrial Environment*. Peterborough, UK: English Nature.

Goodin, R. 1992. *Green Political Theory*. Cambridge, UK: Polity.

Hargreaves-Heap, S., Hollis, M., Lyons, B., Sugden, R. and Weale, A. 1992. *The Theory of Choice*. Oxford, UK: Blackwell.

Holland, A. 1997. 'Substitutability: or, why strong sustainability is weak and absurdly strong sustainability is not absurd', in Foster, J. (ed.) *Valuing Nature*. London, UK: Routledge, pp. 119–34.

Holland, A. and Rawles, K. 1994. *The Ethics of Conservation*. Report presented to The Countryside Council for Wales. Thingmount Series No.1. Department of Philosophy, Lancaster University.

Jacobs, M. 1995. 'Sustainable development, capital substitution and economic humility: a response to Beckerman', *Environmental Values* 4: 57–68.

Lane, R. 2001. *The Loss of Happiness in Market Democracies*. New Haven, CT: Yale University Press.

Layard, R. 2005. *Happiness: Lessons for a New Science*. London, UK: Allen Lane.

Marmot, M. 2004. *The Status Syndrome*. London: Bloomsbury.

Martinez-Alier, J., Munda, G. and O'Neill, J. 1998. 'Weak comparability of values as a foundation for Ecological Economics', *Ecological Economics* 26: 277–86.

Nussbaum, M. 2000. *Women and Human Development: The Capabilities Approach*. Cambridge, UK: Cambridge University Press.

O'Neill, J. 1993. *Ecology, Policy and Politics: Human Well-Being and the Natural World*. London, UK: Routledge.

O'Neill, J. 2006a. 'Feature review: *Happiness: Lessons for a New Science* by Richard Layard', *New Political Economy* 11: 447–50.

O'Neill, J. 2006b. 'Citizenship, well-being and sustainability: Epicurus or Aristotle?' *Analyse & Kritik* 28: 158–72.

O'Riordan, T. 1996. 'Democracy and the sustainability transition', in Lafferty, W. and Meadowcroft, J. (eds.) *Democracy and the Environment*. Cheltenham, UK: Elgar, pp. 140–56.

O'Riordan, T. 1997. 'Valuation as revelation and reconciliation', *Environmental Values* 6: 169–83.

Ramsey, F. 1928. 'A mathematical theory of saving', *Economic Journal* 38: 543–59.

Sen, A. 1987. *On Ethics and Economics*. Oxford, UK: Blackwell.

Sen, A. 1992. 'Well-being and capability', in Nussbaum, M. and Sen, A. (eds.) *The Quality of Life*. Oxford, UK: Clarendon, pp. 30–53.

Solow, R. M. 1974. 'The economics of resources or the resources of economics', *American Economic Review* 64: 1–14.

Steiner, H. 1994. *An Essay on Rights*. Oxford, UK: Blackwell.

Walsh, V. 1970. *Introduction to Contemporary Microeconomics*. New York: McGraw-Hill.

Wiggins, D. 1998. 'The claims of need', in Wiggins, D. (ed.) *Needs, Values, Truth*, 3rd edition. Oxford, UK: Blackwell.

WCED (World Commission on Environment and Development) 1987. *Our Common Future*. Oxford, UK: Oxford University Press.

# PART V

# Conclusions

# 13 | Reflections on the pathways to sustainability

TIM O'RIORDAN

We are now at an exciting stage in the awkward, but vital, transition to sustainability. In international government, in national strategies, in business, in community action, and in individual behaviour and outlook, we are beginning to witness a dawning realisation that global humanity has to shift if future generations are to survive with any meaningful sense of prosperity and wellbeing. We have no excuse about not knowing what may happen; modern science, the power of modelling and scenario building, together with the democratising effect of the internet, make any further denial impossible. We also know we have the global wealth and the technological wherewithal to change course if we have the will.

In this chapter, I start by summarising the major themes of this book. Then I look again at the morphology of the shift from the environmentalism of the 1970s to the rhetoric and politics of sustainability in the 2000s and beyond. My intent here is to show that we have not yet seriously completed this adjustment in paradigms, and that the environmental labelling of sustainability continues to plague its political acceptability and public empathy. In this section I also analyse why sustainability is such a slippery concept for governance. In part, this is because of its intensely ambiguous qualities. But I also claim that we have not yet devised governance arrangements that can resonate, promote and champion sustainability. The irony is that sustainability is supposed to be transformational. Yet efforts at transforming governance frequently build in reforms that resist, not promote, any meaningful transition to effective sustainability. Or to put it slightly differently, modern governance is proving to be too dependent on non-sustainable models of human values and developmental goals to be suitable for sustainability.

Then, in the fourth section I turn my attention briefly to the notion of tipping points. These are of two kinds. Abrupt changes may occur to the planetary functions so that step-shifts take place in the working of the life-support processes of the globe. This is the earth scientists' approach. But tipping points also refer to culture shifts in citizen outlook and behaviour, in consumer habits and choices, and in shifting political perceptions of what has to be done, even if not all are politically acceptable. The so-called cultural tipping point towards sustainability may prove to be the force for change that proceeds and reshapes governance which is genuinely for sustainability. In the following section, I link these tipping points to the notion of human wellbeing as a measure of prosperity and being better off.

In the sixth section, I draw together all this material into three big questions about the governance of sustainable development, which I then make an attempt to answer. Finally, in the concluding section, I reconsider the existing governing structures and processes in the world today, in the hope that this book may inform how we govern and share the journey to sustainability.

## Major themes in this book: a personal summary

The chapters in this book represent the first truly serious attempt to assess governance arrangements, as they currently operate, for the promotion and pursuit of sustainability. In their different ways, all of the authors are justifiably sceptical that society is producing political structures and governors who really can guide it towards a more sustainable future. But, then, no-one really knows just what such a future would look like. No-one is ready to shoulder the responsibility of taking decisions and changing behaviour to create more sustainable outcomes a century hence. Moreover, as we are only just beginning to grapple with the immensity and complexity of sustainability as a concept, the task of defining the processes of governing to support it is terribly complex.

In Chapter 1, Neil Adger and Andrew Jordan conclude that sustainability is both a set of outcomes (long-term viability of ecosystems, social relations and prosperity) and processes (governing, guiding, participating and collective decision making). The outcome is a greater awareness and collective correction of current outlooks and practices (reflexivity), rather than a transformation. Yet they also point out that if a successful shift to sustainability is ever to meet the needs of poverty alleviation and societal justice, such a move may prove all too tricky in a limits-driven world.

They regard governance as more a set of networks than hierarchies or markets. But they also believe that all three modes of governing must be involved. I also share their view that we need more well-monitored experiments, more design of genuinely new institutional arrangements and ways of re-defining problems as opportunities.

In her chapter, Katrina Brown is healthily sceptical of any successful move towards ecological resilience and the maintenance of social justice in a world of ecological safeguards. She sees the synergies between livelihoods, wellbeing and sustainability, but does not observe any evidence that governance is addressing this in a reliable or convincing manner. She makes a plea for more adaptive living and more adaptive governance, along the lines suggested by Adger and Jordan at the end of their analysis. She rightly points out that the trade-offs between losers and gainers are not taking place in a coherent or fair manner, and that the language of interdependency may be better than the language of losers and gainers.

Albert Weale enjoys his frown over my idealism. He is quite right in proclaiming that governments matter, and that sectoral politics will first have to be upgraded in order to achieve fair outcomes amongst competing demands. He urges us not to forget that the competition for power is still a virtue of democracy. The key issue is to ensure that the competition is fair and that the values to be traded are fully represent-ative of ecological and social resilience and robustness.

Philip Lowe and Katy Wilkinson remind us that powerful business and third sector lobbies are at their best when they are adaptable. To some extent, the farming lobby in the UK has begun to transform in the context of environmental pressures. It now realises that environ-mental improvement is an income earner. But look carefully. Farming in the UK and Europe, as elsewhere, is still by no means sustainable – environmental payments offer shallow and often self-promoting investing practices, rather than the creation of new outlooks or management. Moreover, meeting the current global food insecurity may well add to overall unsustainability, not promote sustainability. In short, the European farming lobby of the 1970s is alive, well and kicking, and unsustainable. Adaptive change by the environmental and producer lobbies to new realities does not, by any means, lead to sustainability.

Matthew Paterson also develops this theme by suggesting, rightly in my view, that international agreements cannot promote sustainability

in a world of non-sustainable social values and international capitalism. There is no synergy between the legal agreement, the underlying
incongruous values, and the delivery of a multinational sustainability
scheme. Even in the frame of competing scientific evidence about
climate change and rising public concern, the levers of capital and
politics grind slow, and often in perverse directions. The larger the
governance scale, the less sustainable the process and outcome.

Andy Stirling and Ortwin Renn both emphasise the role of better
risk framing and participatory procedures in the governance of
sustainable development. Stirling sees the manner of reflection more as
a means to rectify imperfect governance, than as a route to genuine
awareness and corrective action. Yet the sustainability imperative is
opening up in science, as Jill Jäger outlines. This is the exciting part.
The modern scientist is more explicitly interdisciplinary, more attuned
to social science perspectives and more ready to engage with civil and
political structures and outlooks than ever before. Yet there is still a
fundamental unwillingness to let go of the notion that science is still
searching for better, peer-reviewed and more rationalistic knowledge
than is appropriate for sustainability. Social scientists do not always
help themselves to gain credence by their constant squabbling over key
terms and theories. Yet, even today, science is still rarely regarded
as explicitly incorporating social science. The call by both Renn and
Stirling for a more interactive and learning style of participation is
widely shared in the chapters by Jäger and by Burgess and Clark.

I have grouped together the economics Chapter 11 (Simon Dietz
and Eric Neumayer), the John O'Neill piece on philosophy and values
(Chapter 12) and Andy Dobson's Chapter 6 on ecological citizenship
into a single final comment. These offer more hope than some of the
equally thoughtful earlier commentaries on governance as a struggle.
The economists recognise that economic paradigms are shifting in
favour of much greater interest in how natural resources are seen
as social as well as ecological phenomena, not just mimicking
monetary values. They also touch on the manner in which wider
sustainability accounts are being pursued to favour work on better
ecological economics and social resilience. There is movement here.
Dietz and Neumayer argue that the Stern Review on climate change,
for example, shows the power of economic arguments in public policy
in pointing to the material risks of unsustainability. Admittedly
progress is slow, but at least it is discernible.

John O'Neill touches on the more fundamental role that nature still plays in many people's lives. The spiritual quality of the natural world mimics the emerging spiritual qualities of a citizenry that is beginning to care for its future and that of its neighbours. Here is where Andy Dobson does us a service. Good citizenship does not just come from behaviour. It must be spurred by profound values of compassion and justice, and by a form of government that resonates, promotes and emphasises such virtue. Virtuous citizenship is integral with virtuous politics. One cannot possibly expect to fashion a form of governance for sustainability that does not create a form of governing that is deeply virtuous. This is the ultimate test. We are not yet virtuous as citizens, and we have not crafted styles of governance that promote and champion virtue. Until we do, there can be no lasting transition from environmentalism to sustainability.

## The transition from environmentalism to sustainability

The political transition of the late 1960s environmental movement was explained by Anthony Downs in 1972 and his model still has some resonance today (see Figure 13.1). I realise that this model is dated. I also recognise that the environmental movement has swept through science, government, economics and social behaviour since Downs produced his political analysis. But his perspective offers a sense of the ultimate failures of environmentalism to get to so-called one-planet living, even when the evidence for Earth system transformation is overwhelming.

Downs postulated that any environmental revolution begins with new scientific and observational evidence which is alarming, compelling and will, if proven actually to happen, carry unknown numbers of innocent bystanders into unjust pain and grief. In the late 1960s and 1970s, the concern was for environmental pollution, destruction of biodiversity, toxicity, and possible natural resource scarcity. All of this placed environmental wellbeing on the international agenda. It instigated the first UN Conference on the Human Environment in Stockholm in 1972. And it introduced an era of international environmental agreements along with a plethora of new regulatory and legal institutions, such as environmental protection agencies and international protocols. Many of those organisations are still with us, and some, such as the Law of the Sea and the Convention

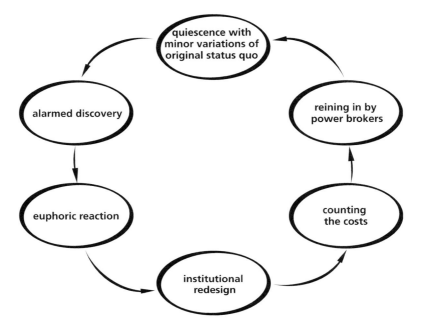

**Figure 13.1** The Downs issue attention model reset for the sustainability transition

*Note:* Downs recognised that this was only a general model, and that the detail would vary by issues and over time. Nevertheless, if one looks at sustainability in transition, much of his original analysis holds.

*Source:* based on Downs (1972).

on the International Trade of Endangered Species (CITES), though flawed, are vitally important for managing the global environmental heritage. These are by no means perfect, but the world would be a much poorer and endangered place if such international agreements did not exist at all.

An enduring legacy of Stockholm is the resentment amongst poor countries that the environmental agenda is a purposeful strategy by the rich to ensure that there is sufficient ecological space for them to continue to create wealth, whilst seeking to reduce pollution and waste. The sustainability agenda is still not clear of this stigma.

Downs placed his finger on the political pulse when he noted that reactionary forces would look critically at the mounting political and economic consequences of all of these measures, and would lobby to rein in the emerging but hesitant political enthusiasm. This, of course, did happen in the early 1970s and still occurs every day, even in the modern era. The analysis in chapters by Albert Weale, Matthew Paterson and Andy Dobson all attest to this. Lobby groups abound in all the nations' capitals, but especially in Washington and Brussels, and exist primarily to ensure that environmental excitement of the kind described by Downs (1972) does not get too out of hand.

Downs, therefore, argued that environmental movements would inevitably wax and wane, pushed along by catastrophic events such as Bhopal, Chernobyl and Hurricane Katrina, yet jolted to a halt by those supporting the political and economic status quo. In general, then, environmentalism has been characterised as a powerful, but ultimately marginal, political movement that stirred the social conscience, created a fresh tranche of aware and concerned citizens in all walks of life, galvanised a mass of extremely determined pressure groups, scrutiny organisations and consumer bodies, and generally redefined the science of environmental assessment and of integrated environmental regulation. I remain struck by the arguments of influential journalists such as George Monbiot (2007) and Naomi Klein (2007), who claim that neoliberalism remains in the ascendant, and that even environmental calamity carries in its wake more corporate investment for corporate profit in reconstruction. Environmental transformation, it seems, can reinforce the neoliberal economic order. I do not believe these arguments can easily be dismissed.

Even so, nowadays we are witnessing exciting changes to the Downs model. Here is my take on the present arrangements, as outlined in Figure 13.2. I admit it is slightly flaky but it helps to portray the points I would like to make at the end, that a more profound sustainability tipping point is in the offing. I begin with the global tipping points as environmental science writing on the wall. Then I move to the shift to experiments and innovations at all scales of governing that do give some hope for sustainability. It is the very ambiguity of sustainability that encourages experimentation to flourish, even when not labelled as such. The new economics of sustainability follows, and I complete the transition with the emergence of civic virtue and a more earth-focused fundamentalism in a future citizenry and sustainable consumerism.

Environmentalism is morphing into sustainability. Neil Adger and Andrew Jordan correctly emphasise in Chapter 1 that sustainability is

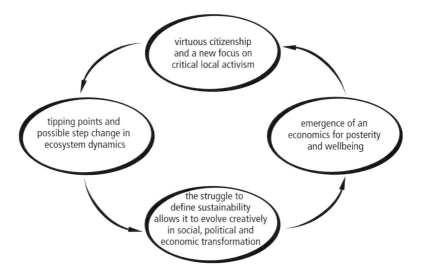

**Figure 13.2** The sustainability transition tipping point

still vague, messy, easily manipulated and redefined, and therefore ultimately fruitless for a political soundbite or a ministerial mission. It is essentially revolutionary and radicalising, demanding a huge step change in culture, behaviour and outlook for which almost all citizens are still unprepared and mostly unwilling. It demands a form of multi-agency governmental and public involvement at a host of levels of political scale that simply cannot be delivered by present-day bureaucracies, nationalistic political endeavours and inadequate participatory approaches.

Yet Figure 13.2 does suggest some very important shifts in economics, social transformation and politics are occurring that are truly revolutionary. No longer is environmentalism seen as a threat to the economy; the economy itself is increasingly seen as the main threat to our environment, and particularly our climate. And no longer is environmentalism marginal to politics. At every level of government, and not least the G8 group of leading industrial nations, as well as the World Economic Forum, climate change, biodiversity, ill-health and inadequate safeguards for local secure livelihoods are seen as deeply troubling political, commercial and moral issues. The possibility of a growing link between terrorism, violence generally, and the mass movement of desperate peoples into unprepared lands and cultures, raises the scope for prolonged conflict, with all that this entails for the politics and economics of destabilisation, resentment and social breakdown.

Environmental issues have become fully integrated into an economic, social, moral and political transformation. In his review of the economics of climate change, Sir Nicholas Stern (2007) showed that the possible costs of change offer a genuinely serious economic challenge to development trajectories with business-as-usual carbon intensity and emissions – the very activities that Downs claimed would defeat the earlier environmental movements.

What Figure 13.2 suggests is that global tipping points are becoming more and more visible. It also emphasises that to solve sustainability issues, the character of the sustainability problem has to be redefined. Verweij and Thompson (2007) refer to wicked problems, uncomfortable knowledge and clumsy solutions. *Wicked problems* are interpretations of challenges that so narrowly base their analysis for defining a solution that new variations of problems spring up to create endless suites of continuing unsolved outcomes. The biofuels debate is one such case. Producing biofuels in an attempt to reduce carbon emissions from automobiles creates a series of discomforting repercussions on land use, loss of biodiversity, price rises for basic foodstuffs for the poor, and mischievous accounting of carbon savings, much of which is quite deliberately manipulated (Naylor *et al.*, 2007). Wicked problems are unsolvable if conventional patterns of institutional design and decision tactics are followed. Only step changes in problem analysis and institutional attention will overcome the inevitable tendency to generate more difficulties as well-meaning solutions are offered.

*Uncomfortable knowledge* is the confounding evidence that wicked solutions throw up. It is also the contradictory data and interpretation of long-established cultural norms of behaviour that lie out of step with any effective transformation to sustainability. Above all, uncomfortable knowledge is the basis of a genuine recognition that present-day patterns of institutional thought and scope for action are inadequate for what the evidence suggests really has to be done.

In my own work on coastal change (Milligan and O'Riordan, 2007), uncomfortable knowledge appears in many guises. Planning bodies seek to address what to do about future roads, pipelines, telecommunications, as well as the economic and social networks for viable settlements for a future soft coastline facing inundation and hazard from a rising sea and a diminishing coastal nourishment of sediment and saltmarsh. Coastal agencies vie with each other over whether to continue to protect an eroding coastline, and gain public support, or let coasts evolve more naturally and face the hostility of aggrieved residents and businesses. No democracy exists in coastal areas that can plan 100 years ahead for a coastline that could vary in so many ways, depending on climate change and many other policy interventions (Urwin and Jordan, 2008). One way forward is to visualise the possible benefits of a wholly new coastline designed and implemented over a period of fifty years. This is not easy. There are no convenient institutional arrangements for delivering such a vision, nor are existing residents necessarily the best guardians of the long-term interests of communities.

Another example of uncomfortable knowledge lies in the UK debate on genetically modified (GM) organisms which took place between 2003 and 2005. An analysis in which I was involved (Horlick-Jones *et al.*, 2007) came to the conclusion that the many social interpretations of GM food could not be contained by the science of GM or biotechnology. Indeed, many of the social interpretations of GM crops in general, and GM food in particular, were inflamed by the manner in which scientists were closing off public disquiet so that it became impossible to run a rational and scientifically informed public debate. Also, because of the open-ended nature of the various procedures, the anti-GM lobbies tended to dominate public meetings. In addition, the more formal evidence offered by science reviews and cost–benefit analysis turned out to be ambiguous and confusing. The upshot of this major exercise in participation was that the process was suffused with politics, notably by the government in deliberately not being clear as to what decisional status was to be given to the debate in its final politically motivated decisions. Nevertheless, the overall purpose of the introductory focus group work, and the final reflective evidence for committed bystanders, did suggest that meaningful interpretations of GM issues could be richly garnered for well-judged and managed participatory events.

The final decision was a classic political fudge: one GM crop could be licensed, but there would be penalties of continuous surveillance and an ambiguous liability clause. In the final outcome, it is unlikely that GM crops will be grown in the UK in the foreseeable future, as the companies do not want to get involved and the supermarkets do not wish to sell the products. Yet, on a global basis, GM is being advocated for the much-needed food revolution. So we may have learnt a new process, but not yet delivered the sustainable outcome.

*Clumsy solutions* remind me of the ox-cart in Ravel's orchestration of Mussorgsky's *Pictures at an Exhibition*. The cart is characterised by trombones and tubas lurching from one muddy rut to another, while there is no stable or orderly track for sure progress. The combination of wicked problems and uncomfortable knowledge usually produce clumsy and ill-fitting solutions that still do a job, however inadequately. Many examples spring to mind. We will see it in carbon capture and storage and in voluntary carbon offsets; and we will witness it in the renewables saga, especially where large construction projects are concerned, such as major offshore wind farms, geothermal stations and tidal energy projects such as the proposed Severn barrage in the UK renewable energy arena.

Clumsy solutions set a challenge for us to visualise the minimal governance conditions (e.g. market and regulatory arrangements, public participatory arrangements) required to facilitate sustainable solutions. This may involve visualising a more sustainable world of fifty years hence that would be far less clumsy and far more adaptable. This is an enormous governance challenge. We do not yet have the thinking or the visionary capability to imagine unimaginable future states where so many variables hinge on each other. Lying at the heart of all of this is the notion of the virtuous and responsible citizen. Admittedly such individuals do not yet exist in any meaningful numbers. But the notion of such a citizen is one who seeks joyfully to live for a sustainable future, and who adapts their behaviour into a mould of shared responsibility for the transition to come. This is the essence of the difference between the two models depicted in Figures 13.1 and 13.2. Downs could not foresee a genuine transformation of politics, though to be fair to him, he did hint that this might be necessary in the aftermath of major environmental crises.

## Global tipping points

At this point I turn to the earth science interpretation of tipping points. I see this important work as a vital trigger for the transformation to virtue citizenship. I am struck by the revealing work of John

Schellnhuber and his colleagues (2004). Earth systems are notorious because they do not follow predictable paths, so cannot be synthetically modelled. The very act of modelling to dissect highly integrated and unexpectedly random relationships deprives us of the essence of complexity and unpredictability. In any case, we have no external models of the planet to compare one treatment or cure with another. In addition, it is evident that any outcome of a given set of human activities may only reveal itself in both planetary systems and human outlooks once the act is under way. Any outcome is emergent, and rooted mysteriously in its initiating conditions. For example, if we try to issue carbon tradable quotas to every citizen on the planet, we can have absolutely no idea ahead of time as to how such a policy would affect national economies, social relations, consumer behaviour and popular interpretations of climate change science. Even well-meaning pilot schemes in the UK cannot seriously give us an idea of what would ultimately happen on a global scale.

Of course the tipping points agenda has yet to emerge centre stage. When it does, I suspect three outcomes are likely. First, public alarm will be heightened. This process needs to be handled very carefully by scientists, who are still regarded as trustworthy. Fear and denial can make any adaptive cultural shift very difficult and contentious. These two unhappy bedfellows are magnified when governments are not regarded as accountable and reliable. Leadership cannot come from flawed institutions. The process in science would be especially acute if the scientific prognosis seems unsupported or too dramatic, and if the case for human behaviour change is too strident there could be a backlash against the integrity of science. Downing and Ballantyne (2007: 4) find evidence that some 56 per cent of the UK public is not convinced about the scale of climate change threat; uncertainty in the science, they remark, is matched by widespread confusion about what actions to take and what products to buy. This remains a particularly awkward issue, and hence may have repercussions for any deep and profound transition to civic virtue discussed earlier.

Second, the role of the business community, coupled to consumer pressure, could be critical. Indeed, this is yet another arena for a tipping point. In his wide-ranging assessment of the future of so-called sustainable capitalism Jonathon Porritt (2007: 264–90) admits to his ambivalence about how far the current models of capitalism and business culture can handle sustainable development. A number of

**Table 13.1** *How businesses perceive the benefits of sustainable development*

| Issue | Perception of opportunity and threat |
|---|---|
| Efficiency of minimising materials flows and wastages | Reduced costs; new inventions; commercial potential of selling technology and management systems |
| All-encompassing management | Better risk sensing and avoidance; improved communications and strategic guidance in the company; corporate upgrade of the company culture and employee–community–customer relations |
| Licence to operate forever | Better relations with regulators; adaptive potential of local communities to provide a public interest service, not just a private interest profit |
| Market advantage | Better brand recognition and customer loyalty; improved employee recruitment and retention; stronger influence on favourable regulation and competition; new business opportunities |
| Reliable profits | Creative partnerships with public, private and civil sectors; in-built commercial adaptive capacity in a changing world |

*Source:* based on Porritt (2007: 241).

prominent and profitable businesses have opened up their thinking in favour of the commercial and reputational advantages of moving towards sustainability (see Porritt, 2007, and also Table 13.1). We are nowhere near a business model for sustainability. But if the notion of tipping points is to be believed, then capitalism will have to recognise and adjust to them.

Third, one likely outcome of the transition to more sustainable businesses could be the blurring of the distinction between the public, private and non-profit sectors. The concept of governance draws attention to and, in so doing, problematises this. For example, in a more sustainable age, businesses might be participating with governments and civic society to help incorporate local sustainable societies and economies so that business is conducted fairly and co-operatively with local people. Such arrangements are just beginning to appear in the supply chain of cocoa and coffee, and in the scope for a living wage supported by a few retailers. There is a long way to go, but the signs are there for the optimistic to see.

The science of Earth and human systems connections and adaptation has a huge and vital task ahead of it. Jill Jäger shows that this cannot be achieved by scientists alone. We are entering a new era of participatory science and public understanding, the likes of which are still untried, even though at more modest scales, much has been done in this arena. I like what Katrina Brown says in her contribution. Unless science is more sensitive to the many resilience facets of ecosystems, and we can work on the trade-offs with the support of people and their governors, then we cannot possibly move forward. The final section of the Dahlem Conference (Schellnhuber *et al.*, 2004: 404–31) addresses this experience. Better conceptions of story telling, artistic interpretation, visualisation and simulation of possible future states and conditions need to take place with care and calm to allow grounded civic dialogue.

In sum, the emergence of the science and popular understanding of tipping points is an alarming but necessary trigger for government, business and civil society to march onto the path to sustainability. We seem to need the drivers of calamity for the human race (*not* for the planet) to focus our attention. But every calamity should be seen as an opportunity, not a crisis. This is the next challenge in the sustainability transition.

## On wellbeing

The idea of wellbeing for many years has captured the attention of economists, politicians and social theorists. While governments seek to do much to meet happiness criteria, wellbeing is altogether a more profound notion, linked to civic virtue and good governance, not just security, satisfaction and esteem. Wellbeing is not the same as happiness, the source of economic reassessment, and political interest by a number of leading UK politicians. Wellbeing is much more fundamental, as Figure 13.3 indicates. I concocted this with Jonathon Porritt and it appears in his book *Capitalism: As If the World Matters* (Porritt, 2007).

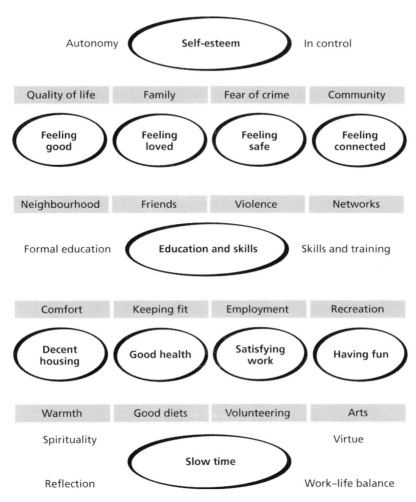

**Figure 13.3** Components of wellbeing
*Source:* Porritt (2007, 254).

The international notions of sustainable consumption, social capital, civic virtue, schools of sustainability and a fresh look at measuring prosperity all connect with Figure 13.3. Porritt (2007: 255) admits that this is a heady brew to place in one metric. I do not believe this is necessary. The two framing themes at the top and foot of the diagram are deliberately selected. *Self esteem* and *slow time* are the designated frames of the notion of wellbeing. We need to believe in ourselves and our self worth, via our civic virtue. We can visualise the closure of wellbeing as a central framework for a sustainable society and economy. Equally, government as well as governance more broadly has to win the trust and support of citizens. Here we find the essence of good governance as outlined by Adger and Jordan in Chapter 1, namely governing that aims to create the conditions and the incentives for virtue and wellbeing amongst all citizens. Maybe this is the ultimate goal of governance for sustainability.

## Some fundamental questions

Having summarised the previous chapters and drawn out a number of additional themes from the wider literature, I would now like to identify three fundamental questions that I attempt to answer, as part of my overall conclusions for this book.

*Is sustainability just too big to handle by any form of government or governance?* I fear the answer is yes. All of the contributions here look at various aspects of sustainability, laid out in bite-sized chunks. Even the widening of perspective in recent years leaves government far short, as Albert Weale and Matthew Paterson indicate in their complementary, but contrasting, contributions. Weale notes the difficulties for the process and scope of government arising from the pervasiveness and amorphousness of sustainability, while Paterson sees the failure of genuine transformation of non-sustainable governing structures as an Achilles heel of sustainability governance. Getting close to sustainability challenges the credibility and effectiveness of both national and transnational government. Jill Jäger concludes the same for science. I therefore conclude that unless we somehow manage to establish new creative institutional arrangements, fully integrating the public, private and civil sectors, along with new forms of regulation and assessment, participation and scenario-building, I cannot see even the most imaginative of contemporary governance meeting the challenge of sustainability.

Innovative approaches to participatory science in the form of precaution and sensitive civic and political engagement cannot yet meet the credibility and legitimacy challenges for a sustainability science offered by Jill Jäger. Ortwin Renn believes that genuine participation is not fully feasible, while Stirling sees a need for a more reflexive governance that is not yet in the bloodstream and nervous system of current patterns of societal steering. My ultimate conclusion here is that all forms of government and governance will have to develop new formulations to deliver sustainability. I see these conclusions in the material of Weale (keep it tight and focused); Stirling (open up but be aware); Burgess and Clark (evaluate more fully then make accountable); and O'Neill (develop more ecological and social empathy).

*Can we ever get to a universally accepted notion of sustainability and its strategic significance for the future of humanity without having to define it?* My answer here is no. We cannot properly get to a universal meaning through the circumstances of many initiatives aimed at governing economic change and experimenting with shifts in social values. I do not see any realistic scope for a sustainability enlightenment of the kind that transformed science, technology, the arts, and political institutions in the eighteenth century. Maybe this is just as well. Previous cultural shifts were essentially promoted by elites. We some-how need to get this transformation to sustainability into the masses, many of whom are as yet unborn. A sustainability culture is, however, elusive, unless it occurs primarily at the local level, fitting in well with more multi-levelled patterns of governance.

*Even with current shifts in business practice, governmental activities, local government and civil society, can we still not move forward constructively to sustainability?* Here I am more optimistic. I turn to Andy Dobson for guidance. Behaviour shift may come from a new sense of civic virtue, and this could be born with the changes occurring in consumer and civic behaviour. The consumer analysts see in Western society the emergence of a new consumer culture. This is mainly in young people, and especially women. It covers personal health, good quality of product, ethical sourcing in the retail sector, where good corporate behaviour needs to be demonstrated, and a genuine concern that consumption is designed to make a future planet more habitable. Such feelings seem to be attractive for around a quarter of this group. But this cultural cohort is growing and its demands are becoming more vociferous. What cannot be answered is whether all of these shifts will reduce consumption, or simply make increasing levels of consumption more sustainable. This remains a deeply contested arena. I admire the hard core of low-impact lifestyles that are becoming popular, particularly amongst the young. This is heartening, but it is by no means widely shared.

## Conclusions

I have already touched on my key observations arising from this volume of essays in the first part of this chapter. We are indeed at a turning point, and the next decade will chart how well we can adjust to the huge transformations that lie before us. Whatever, the rest of this century will be the testing ground. Sustainability may prove elusive to define, but it will not go away. I am not convinced we can do this, so we will be confronted with a troubling mix of environmental crises, violence, terrorism, local conflict and huge injustice. But we will also witness heroes, local survival and adjustment, innovation and heartening acts of charity and humanity. These will give us the hope and energy to continue the transition.

We are slowly grasping that wellbeing and posterity matter. These will increasingly become the guiding lights of new economic and social analysis where we finally fully promote the requirement to integrate environmental considerations into all areas of policy making, with new approaches to measuring and establishing social resilience and sustainable economic livelihoods. All of these phenomena will require new participatory measures and many experiments of trial and error. Finding the right mix between government and governance at a variety of spatial scales is the key to all of this. I see much more focus on subnational activity, possibly a new form of co-operative federalism of the kind that Frey and Eichenberger (1999) chart for Europe, and which may result in new configurations of governance. There is much to be done in terms of identifying and experimenting with new forms of federal co-operation (Benson and Jordan, 2008).

As for possible research topics, I suggest the following.

- *At the civic level, there is a need for much better interpretations of wellbeing for many different groups in modern society, locally, regionally and across the globe.* Wellbeing therefore needs to be grounded in culture, in social class and social justice, across all manner of localities. It needs a local and regional framing, as this perspective is desperately missing in current research. And we need to discover that if we invest in sustainability incentives, maybe we can create a wellbeing community where none existed before. For example, if immigrants became the basis of building insulation and low-carbon transformation, and converted used electrical products and used bicycles into reconstructed, valuable items, would they be better assimilated and recognised in a sustainability culture? This is certainly a research objective worth pursuing.

- *Civic virtue has, in part, to be learnt.* Schools as 'sustainability laboratories' offer exciting new approaches to sustainability education the world over. We need to establish and monitor the achievements of schools for sustainability as test beds for ecological citizenship. Investing in sustainability may lead to greater peace and security, more settled populations, and improved means for creating the mix of ecological and social resilience we all seek. Again, this should be the basis of a network of experiments shared culture by culture, the world over. I confess I am not yet convinced that even serious and comprehensive commitments to sustainability will change the existing order and outlook. To test that such sustainability investments will actually work to effect a genuine transition will require fundamental and carefully evaluated research. Doing such evaluative work will be no mean achievement. We also need to take seriously the critique of Matthew Paterson, namely that the ascendant economic and political order will always strive to retain power and control over any transformation, particularly following crises and calamities.

- *New forms of federalism deserve special analysis.* These may embrace various configurations of space, policy integration, long-term thinking and the capacity to design novel measures for future sustainability states to chart development in science, technology and infrastructure through the present time. Setting decision making for policy and projects in fresh frameworks and then testing them would be a good start (Benson and Jordan, 2008). Charting the private sector as amalgams of public and civic responsibility is very much in need of careful assessment. New approaches to co-operative research, grounded at local levels of activity would, as Katrina Brown argues, be highly beneficial.

- *Boundary organisations need to be tied down.* They are, as Jill Jäger suggests, potentially creative and innovative centres of actions, thinking, experience and co-operation involving people, agencies, governmental levels and behaviour. The more these are formed and are created, the more their success or failure needs to be charted and guided. This is a vital arena for sustainability science partnerships. Research is needed to define them, evaluate them and encourage them.

- *We need to know far more about how China and India and other rapidly developing societies will develop their economies.* We need to follow the advice of Katrina Brown and test various forms of development against the Millennium Development Goals. We need to see how new forms of sustainable livelihoods could be generated by transfers under carbon credits or other sustainable investments by the new private–public and civil sectors. Dealing with the emerging issue of allocating embedded carbon in trade will rank high in future climate change negotiations.

- *Localism may well become the vogue for governance for sustainability in the decades to come.* We still have no idea how networks of sustainable experimentation can play out locally yet not be thwarted by a failure at higher levels of government to deliver the appropriate conditions for sustainable development to flourish. A combination of serious thinking plus carefully monitored experiments would be most valuable here. I see this as a central plank in what Jill Jäger refers to as sustainability science. Somehow we need to examine forms of governance that are respected by, and which encourage, virtue in civic outlooks and behaviour. Yet the paradox is that real virtue may be anarchic. It may lie in the hearts, minds and spirits of citizens, beyond government and maybe even governance.

- *There has to be a link between Earth system tipping points and some more profound societal transformation to sustainability.* In all important positive tipping points, there also has to be experimentation in new forms of governance, new patterns of participation and new ways of learning about wellbeing and virtue. I do not know if society can achieve this: at present it is not evident in the international climate change discussions or the endless struggle for survival for at least half the world's peoples. But the human is a reflexive creature: it can understand that its survival requires full-blooded governance for sustainability. This is why this book is important, why there is a vital need to experiment, evaluate and explore the transformation that will create governance that is genuinely *for* sustainability. I remain optimistic that this will indeed happen. I will not be alive when the outcome is evident, but I hope my grandchildren will be able to judge its success.

## Acknowledgements

I owe a huge debt of gratitude to Neil Adger and Andrew Jordan for organising the conference in 2005 and editing this publication to mark my 'retirement' from academia. Equally, all of the contributors are also highly valued friends, whose ideas and support have hugely encouraged me to be the person I am in the academic world. To conclude this enormously valuable collection of essays is a massive honour. I cannot do justice to all of the ideas in the previous chapters, but I have done my best.

## References

Benson, D. and Jordan, A. 2008. 'Understanding task allocation in the European Union: exploring the value of federal theory', *Journal of European Public Policy* 15: 1–20.

Downing, P. and Ballantyne, J. 2007. *Tipping Point or Turning Point? Social Marketing and Climate Change*. London, UK: IPSOS Mori Social Research Institute.

Downs, A. 1972. 'Up and down with ecology – the issue-attention cycle', *Public Interest* 28: 38–50.

Frey, B. and Eichenberger, R. 1999. *The New Democratic Federalism for Europe: Functional, Overlapping, and Competing Jurisdictions*. Cheltenham, UK: Elgar.

Horlick-Jones, T., Walls, J., Rowe, G., Pidgeon, N., Poortinga, W., Murdoch, G. and O'Riordan, T. 2007. *The GM Debate: Risk, Politics and Public Engagement*. London, UK: Routledge.

Klein, N. 2007. *The Shock Doctrine: The Rise of Disaster Capitalism*. London, UK: Allen Lane.

Milligan, J. and O'Riordan, T. 2007. 'Governance for sustainable coastal futures', *Coastal Management* 35: 499–509.

Monbiot, G. 2007. *Heat: The Politics of Climate Change*. London, UK: Allen Lane.

Naylor, R. L., Liska, A. J., Burke, M. B., Canmany, L., Falcon, W. P., Gaskell, J. and Rozelle, S. D. 2007. 'Ripple effects of crop-based biofuels on global security and the environment', *Environment* 49(9): 30–43.

Porritt, J. 2007. *Capitalism: As If the World Matters* (revised edition). London, UK: Earthscan.
Schellnhuber, H. J., Crutzen, P. J., Clark, W. C., Claussen, M. and Held, H. (eds.) 2004. *Earth System Science for Sustainability*. Cambridge, MA: MIT Press.
Stern, N. H. 2007. *The Economics of Climate Change: The Stern Review*. Cambridge, UK: Cambridge University Press.
Urwin, K. and Jordan, A. 2008. 'Does public policy support or undermine climate change adaptation? Exploring policy interplay across different scales of governance', *Global Environmental Change* 18: 180–91.
Verweij, M. and Thompson, M. (eds.) 2007. *Clumsy Solutions for a Complex World: Governance, Politics and Plural Perceptions*. Basingstoke, UK: Palgrave.

# Index

public dialogues, 207
public goods, 100
public participation, 38, 41, 55, 56, 62,
   133, 322
   and competence, 162
   and deliberative and inclusionary
      processes, 41
   and fairness, 162
   and political representation, 62
   and the precautionary principle, 25,
      229
   as a defining feature of governance,
      25
   as a means of opening up, 209
   as a principle of sustainable
      development, 25
   as a sub-principle of sustainable
      development, 25
   closing down of, 211
   cost-effectiveness of, 165
   evaluation of, 64, 161, 163,
      175, 182
   ex ante assessments of, 163
   ex post evaluations of, 164
   goals of, 161
   importance of its context, 165
   in decision making, 9
   in developing countries, 37
   instrumental perspective on, 208
   involvement of participants in,
      163
   key lessons in, 42
   legitimacy of, 161
   meta-criteria of, 164
   moves upstream in policy making, 25
   need to move beyond, 42
   normative assessment criteria and,
      183
   normative democratic perspective
      on, 208
   opening up approach to, 211
   outcomes of, 161, 164
   outputs of, 164
   political commitments to enhancing,
      159
   process-based view of, 208
   processes of, 161
   quality of, 243
   representativeness of, 165
   role of context in, 208

transparency of, 165
public trust in policy making, 207

Q methodology, 182, 202, 211

radical politics, 83
recycling, 134, 140
reflexive governance, 212, 323
   for sustainable development, 193
reflexivity, 308
   in policy appraisal, 212
regulation, 19
renewable resources, 262
resilience, 34
Resilience Alliance, 36, 39
Rio Declaration, 9, 17, 159, 197, 198,
   226
Rio Summit. *See* United Nations
   Conference on Environment and
   Development
risk, 235
   and deliberative methods and
      procedures, 250
   as a mental construct, 230
   classical approach to understanding,
      26
   deliberative approach to
      understanding, 26
   different frames of, 227
   evaluation of, 235, 247
   screening of, 249
   and the traffic light model, 236
risk appraisal, 200, 236, 247
   purpose of, 237
   role of science in, 237
   role of social science in, 237
risk assessment, 199, 200, 210,
   232
   challenges to, 233
   conventional forms of, 206
   handling of complexity, 233,
      243
   handling of uncertainty, 233
   role of modelling in, 202
   role of monitoring in, 202
risk communication, 229, 246
   goal of, 246
   mechanisms of, 246
risk governance, 249
   stakeholder involvement in, 243